AFTER INDEPENDENCE

AFTER INDEPENDENCE

MAKING AND PROTECTING THE NATION IN POSTCOLONIAL & POSTCOMMUNIST STATES

EDITED BY
Lowell W. Barrington

THE UNIVERSITY OF MICHIGAN PRESS Ann Arbor

Published in the United States of America by
The University of Michigan Press
Manufactured in the United States of America
∞ Printed on acid-free paper

2009 2008 2007 2006 4 3 2 1

A CIP catalog record for this book is available from the British Library.

Library of Congress Cataloging-in-Publication Data

After independence : making and protecting the nation in postcolonial and postcommunist states / edited by Lowell W. Barrington.
p. cm.
Includes index.
ISBN-13: 978-0-472-09898-9 (cloth : alk. paper)
ISBN-10: 0-472-09898-5 (cloth : alk. paper)
ISBN-13: 978-0-472-06898-2 (pbk. : alk. paper)
ISBN-10: 0-472-06898-9 (pbk. : alk. paper)
1. Nationalism—Case studies. 2. Newly independent states—Politics and government. 3. Postcolonialism—Case studies. 4. Post-communism—Case studies. I. Barrington, Lowell W., 1968–

JC311.A3548 2006
320.54—dc22 2005024419

ISBN-13 978-0-472-02508-4 (electronic)

Contents

IV. CONCLUSION

Preface & Acknowledgments

An independent state is often thought of as the ultimate goal of nationalists. As a result, much of the existing work on nationalism has centered on its role in the creation of new states. While acknowledging the importance of that aspect of nationalism, this volume instead seeks answers to two less obvious questions: What happens to nationalism and nationalists when they have achieved their ultimate goal? What happens to nationalism after independence?

These are the central questions that the chapters in this book answer by examining several different cases of postindependence nationalism. Following my introductory chapter, Joshua Forrest provides an overview of the development of nationalism in states that gained their independence during the wave of decolonization in the 1950s and 1960s. Modifying the discussion of causal factors presented in my introduction, he proposes numerous factors to consider when seeking to understand nationalism in the postcolonial cases. His discussion also highlights some of the arguments presented in the subsequent postcolonial case studies, as he points to two general tracks of postindependence nationalism—those states that have pursued (at least marginally successfully) civic nation-building and those that have fractured along ethnic lines.

The first of these tracks is discussed in Diane Mauzy's overview of the development of national identity and nationalism in Malaya and Malaysia. She outlines the development of a more civic approach to national identity (the "Vision 2020" policy), following the initial heavy emphasis on ethnic identity in the years immediately preceding and following independence. Her chapter highlights the ebbs and flows of postindependence nationalist ideas and movements. While civic national identity may be the stated goal, the journey toward its development has been neither quick nor consistent.

In the first of two chapters on Africa, John Clark examines the case of

Rwanda. In his chapter he proposes a "dual-nationalism" framework for understanding Rwanda, challenging the conventional thinking by many scholars of the country. While arguing that Rwanda is far from representative of the African postcolonial experience, Clark does point to lessons from the case for our understanding of the importance of elite action (instrumentalist triggering) in the emergence of ethnonationalist conflict.

The final postcolonial case covered in the book,[1] and the focus of Peter Schraeder's chapter, is Somalia. Schraeder tracks the decline of Somali nationalism, explaining the attempts at an overarching pan-Somali identity and why they were ultimately unsuccessful. He argues that scholars failed to realize that the relative ethnic homogeneity of Somali was no guarantee of successful postindependence nation-building. Among the lessons he discusses from the Somali case is the importance of "turning points," moments at which elites can no longer continue to pursue an inclusive nationalist project, as well as the enduring nature, and importance, of clan-based identities in seemingly homogeneous states.

The next section of the book focuses on postcommunist nationalisms, specifically those of the Eurasian region of the former Soviet Union. In addition to providing an overview of the arguments of the postcommunist case study chapters, Ian Bremmer's chapter focuses on a factor not at the center of the chapters that follow: Russia. Rather than providing an overview of Russian nationalism, as many others have done, Bremmer highlights the way in which nationalist approaches in the postcommunist states shaped relations with Russia as well as how the need for close relations with Russia limited the nationalist options of the post-Soviet ruling elites.

In Terry Clark's chapter on Lithuania, he demonstrates how the development of Lithuanian national identity—and its view of the nation as one of "innocent sufferers"—led both to an emphasis on ethnic identity as well as a tolerance for the "ethnic other." It also made possible, encouraged by the defeat of nationalist parties in the 1992 elections and the desire "to rejoin Europe," the transformation of Lithuanian nationalism into a multifaceted movement with a heavy emphasis on civic nation-building. Among the lessons from Lithuania that Clark highlights is the importance of external factors in shaping postindependence nationalism. Similar to its neighbors of Estonia and Latvia to the north, the pursuit of European integration (EU, NATO membership) has constrained nationalist elites in Lithuania and pushed them in a more inclusive direction.

Taras Kuzio's chapter on Ukraine challenges the way in which scholars have traditionally used the term *nationalism* (especially with the modifiers *civic* and *ethnic*). He pushes scholars not to equate nationalism with "ethnic nationalism," even in Eastern Europe, where scholars have generally emphasized ethnic answers to the national membership question. In addition, he highlights the way in which the nationalist movement in pursuit of independence must not be confused with postindependence nationalism.

In the first of two chapters on the volatile region of the Transcaucasus, Razmik Panossian tracks the decline of nationalism in postindependence Armenia, arguing that the country has entered a period of "postnationalist" and "normal" politics. According to Panossian, while nationalist symbols continue to be used in political campaigns, nationalist politics (policy-making based on national identity concerns) has taken a backseat to more pragmatic policy concerns.

In the final case study chapter, Stephen Jones discusses the case of Georgia. While providing a detailed overview of the violence of the postindependence period, Jones is careful to separate the issues of violence and nationalism. He even cautions scholars not to assume that violence between ethnic groups can automatically be labeled *ethnic violence.* Jones believes that a civic nationalist approach is unlikely in Georgia, but he argues that this is largely due to the structural issues and conditions that contribute to the conflicts and subsequent incompatibilities.

In the conclusion to this volume, Ronald Suny revisits the concepts of nation and nationalism, arguing for a "radical middle" position between primordialism and constructivism, and between views that the nation is situational and that it is persistent. He also proposes a refined typology of postindependence nationalism, overlapping heavily, but not completely, with that proposed in my introductory chapter. He then walks through the arguments of all the case study chapters, emphasizing certain points and challenging others. He is, for example, not completely convinced of Armenia's transition to a period of "postnationalist politics." He concludes his chapter, and the book, with a call for scholars not to ignore the past when looking ahead to the future of nationalism in particular cases.

Indeed, the nationalist past of a given state can take its "revenge" on the present and future.[2] But, as the authors of this book point out in numerous ways, nationalism after independence is influenced by many causal factors, not the least of which is the role of intellectual, social, and political elites. The form that it will take is not predetermined—either prior to or at the time of independence. There are many possible roads that newly independent states can take: ethnic nationalist, civic nationalist, or barely nationalist at all. The authors of this book have taken us a long way toward understanding these various roads, though more work clearly remains to be done.

The work on this book would not have been possible without the support and effort of many people. The authors not only provided me with excellent material but also were more than accommodating to my tinkerings with their chapters. The reviewers of the manuscript gave the authors helpful advice about ways in which to improve the text; the book is better for their thoughtful comments. At Marquette University, I received a great deal of support from department chairs Chris Wolfe, Rich Friman, and Duane Swank, assistance from Leah Manney and Josephine Morstatter, and especially crucial service from several research assistants who helped with this project: William Muck, Brandon Wilkening, John Lyle, and Anne Mozena.

Finally, and most important, my wife, Therese, and children, Alex, Colin, Tristan, and Quinn, put up with my many extra hours in the office, late or missed dinners, and play times put off until later. To them, I am especially grateful.

L.B., December 2005

NOTES

1. Ronald Suny's provocative labeling of the post-Soviet states as *postcolonial* in his concluding chapter notwithstanding.

2. See the concluding sentence of Suny's chapter in this volume, the idea borrowed from the title of his 1993 book. See Ronald G. Suny, *The Revenge of the Past: Nationalism, Revolution, and the Collapse of the Soviet Union* (Stanford, CA: Stanford University Press, 1993).

I. Introduction

1. Nationalism & Independence

LOWELL W. BARRINGTON

NATIONALISM WAS ARGUABLY the most powerful force in international politics in the twentieth century.[1] Its ideas revolutionized international politics, affecting everything from trade to the number of states in the international system itself. It aided in the collapse of the central, eastern, and southeastern European empires; it contributed significantly to the events of World War II and its horror; it led to the end of colonialism; and it played a crucial role in the breakup of three federal Communist states: the Soviet Union, Yugoslavia, and Czechoslovakia. Many politicians in the successor countries to these three states quickly abandoned their Communist Party roots for nationalist movements. Even in the liberal democratic West, nationalists pushing for protection of the homeland and national culture against outsiders had electoral success in the latter part of the century.

Scholars have linked nationalism to everything from the French and American revolutions to the worst atrocities committed against ethnic minorities. The large number of phenomena that have been attached to the label *nationalism* indicates that it is a complex, multifaceted concept. Yet it is possible to define nationalism to allow one to include different events under its heading, while at the same time not defining it in such a broad way as to be meaningless.[2] The definition proposed in this chapter, based in part on a survey of definitions in the nationalism literature, indicates that no matter what variant of nationalism one is discussing, nationalism is about two things: the nation and control over territory—specifically, the perceived national "homeland."

Because of its emphasis on territorial control, nationalism's power as a maker (and destroyer) of states is well recognized.[3] And no one can deny the mobilizing power of nationalist ideas over the last two centuries. Although nationalism is elite driven, the masses have often enthusiastically followed nationalist leaders. But what happens to these nationalists and their ideas after they have achieved their ultimate goal of the creation of a new state? What happens to nationalism after independence? This is the central question of this book, a work that brings together analyses of a variety of postcolonial and postcommunist cases to help us understand how independence affects the ideas of nationalism and the fate of its movements and political parties.

Nations and Nationalism: What They Are & Are Not

Nation

The starting point for any discussion of nationalism is an understanding of the concept of nation. This is especially true of the definition of nationalism in this chapter, since nation is included within it.[4] As discussed in this section, there are a number of different ways that scholars of nationalism have discussed the nation. Yet there is some overlap, and in the case of both nation and nationalism, it is possible to bring together many of these ideas into a single working definition.

There are two particular things that nations are not, which are, unfortunately, associated with the term in everyday language and even by some scholars: states and ethnic groups. The misuse of nation by equating it with "state" or "country" appears in a large number of political science works, including many textbooks, though it is not generally a problem for those who specialize in the study of nationalism.[5] A state is the principal political unit in the international political system corresponding to a territory, a relatively permanent population, and a set of ruling institutions. A country is the territorial component of the state. Nigeria is a state (and a country); it is not a nation.[6]

The second misuse of nation, and one that some nationalism scholars are guilty of, is the intermixing of the term nation with "ethnic group" or "ethnicity." Nations can evolve from ethnic groups, but a nation is more than an ethnic group. In an era where the effects of ethnic nationalism receive international attention, it is perhaps not surprising that many people would think of ethnic groups and nations in similar ways. This is certainly the case for many journalists, though some nationalism scholars have also fallen into the trap of defining nations in such a way as to make them indistinguishable from ethnic groups. For Tamir, for example, a nation is a "community whose members share feelings of fraternity, substantial distinctiveness, and exclusivity, as well as beliefs in a common ancestry and continuous genealogy."[7] While this would be a good definition of an ethnic group, the definition lacks a way to differentiate between nations and ethnic groups. Likewise, Connor's definition of nation would be better suited as a definition of ethnic group. He uses the two terms almost interchangeably, stating that the only real difference is that a nation must be self-defined, while an ethnic group can be "other defined."[8] Chinn and Kaiser's definition, while adding important criteria to distinguish ethnic groups from nations, still indicates that nations only come from ethnic groups.[9] Most scholars, however, understand that, while nations *can* come from ethnic groups, they often do not; they are something more than, and can be something quite different from, such groups.

Even assuming that nationalism scholars generally agree on what nations are not, the nationalism literature indicates that agreeing on what they are is no simple task. As Hutchinson and Smith put it, "Perhaps the central difficulty in the study of nations and nationalism has been the problem of finding adequate and agreed definitions of the key concepts, nation and nationalism."[10] While the various definitions of nation differ in many ways, arguably the most significant division among nationalism scholars is between "subjective" and "objective" ideas of national identity. The subjective concept of the nation is based on the notion that nations are constructed around ideas, and the key to national identity is that the people have come to believe that they are a nation. Emerson, for example, claims that the most basic thing that can be said about a nation "is that it is a body of people who feel that they are a nation."[11] Hobsbawm adds, "As an initial working assumption, any sufficiently large body of people whose members regard themselves as members of a 'nation,' will be treated as such."[12] Perhaps the best example of the subjective view of the nation is the statement of Renan that a nation

> is a grand solidarity constituted by the sentiment of sacrifices which one has made and those that one is disposed to make again. It supposes a past, it renews itself especially in the present by a tangible deed: the approval, the desire, clearly expressed, to continue the communal life. The existence of a nation (pardon this metaphor!) is an everyday

> plebiscite; it is, like the very existence of the individual, a perpetual affirmation of life.[13]

Objective definitions of the nation focus on a list of observable, concrete characteristics, some or all of which all nations share. One such list is contained in Joseph Stalin's definition: "A nation is a historically constituted, stable community of people, formed on the basis of a common language, territory, economic life, and psychological make-up manifested in a common culture."[14] For Stalin, all of these characteristics had to be present in order for a nation to exist.[15] Of course, at least some of the traits that Stalin mentions are far from objective, a criticism that those who favor the subjective approach level against all objective definitions.[16]

Yet this valid criticism by subjectivists should not be taken to mean that one should ignore which characteristics tend to be emphasized by nationalist elites. Is it important that nations consider themselves nations? Of course. Is it possible to find a list of easily measurable characteristics that apply to every group considered by scholars to be a nation? No. But it is also important that there are certain characteristics that have a tendency to be used to link members of the nation together.[17] It is inconceivable to think that a nation could exist without shared cultural features, such as common myths, values, and customs,[18] and a prevailing single language is something found in most nations. In other words, to say that nations are groups that consider themselves nations, without considering the kinds of things that make people feel that they are nations, is not a fruitful approach to defining the term. No other concept in the social sciences is defined by saying that it exists when people think it exists.[19]

While shared cultural features are a necessary part of national identity, there is more to being a nation than having such mutual features. Members of a nation are also linked by a belief in the right of the group to territorial self-determination. The importance of this belief for the group is a central part of many definitions of nation in the nationalism literature, and it provides an important criterion for differentiating between nations and other social categories.[20] Nodia, for example, states that "a nation is a community of people organized around the idea of *self-determination*."[21] Some take this idea of self-determination to mean control of an independent state, though not all feel that the nation must pursue its own state. Haas is one who does, defining the nation as "a socially mobilized body of individuals, believing themselves to be united by some set of characteristics that differentiate them (in their own minds) from outsiders, striving to create or maintain their own state."[22]

How can one bring together these various ideas about the nation to form a working definition? First, a nation is a collective of people. This is a necessary part of the definition, but obviously one that does not differentiate between nations and other groups in society. What makes nations different from other groups is that they are *collectives united by shared cultural features (such as language, myths, and values) and the belief in the right to territorial self-determination.*[23] Put another way, they are groups of people linked by unifying cultural characteristics and the desire to control a territory that is thought of as the group's rightful homeland.[24] "Culture" here includes a range of traits and beliefs, and the particular ones stressed by one nation may differ from those stressed by another. Likewise, while the belief in the right to territorial control is common to all nations, the particular type of territory and even the degree of control will vary from case to case.

Both of these elements—culture and the belief in territorial control—play powerful unifying roles in national identity. But the belief in territorial self-determination is the key to understanding the difference between nations and other social collectives. Many groups have shared myths, values, and symbols (e.g., religious groups, ethnic groups, or even professional associations). But nations are not just unified by culture; they are also unified by a particular—and particularly powerful—sense of purpose: controlling the territory that the members of the group believe belongs to them.[25]

It should now be clear why the term nation cannot be used interchangeably with ethnic group. Nations differ from ethnic groups because of a nation's belief in its right to territorial control, or what Richmond calls its "territorial referent."[26] Also, nations need not even be based on a certain ethnic identity. The cultural features used to unite the nation may privilege one ethnic group over another, even in civic nations (English-speaking ethnic groups that immigrated to the United States and became Americans, for example). But ethnicity does not necessarily determine national identity. Thus, the words "shared cultural features" in the preceding definition of nation should not be read as "shared ethnic identity." What are called "civic" or "political" nations in the nationalism literature[27] have shared cultural features but are multiethnic in their makeup.[28]

Nationalism

As with the term nation, there are differences and divisions in the nationalism literature over the meaning of nationalism itself. But, also like nation, it is possible to bring together certain parts of the definitions of nationalism scholars into a broadly acceptable working definition. Before introducing that definition, it is useful to consider what most nationalism scholars believe nationalism is not.

Just as nations are related to, yet distinct from, states and ethnic groups, there are three things that nationalism is not, yet which some think it to be: patriotism, ethnic politics, and ethnic conflict. The most basic misapplication of nationalism is to equate it with patriotism. Just as a nation is a group of people and not a state, nationalism is first and foremost about the nation, and not necessarily about an existing state. Because nationalism includes the pursuit of territorial control, and because the idea of the nation-state still dominates the international state system, it is easy to fall into the trap of associating nationalism with loyalty to an existing state.[29] While pride in or loyalty to one's state is not a bad definition of patriotism, it is a bad definition of nationalism. Likewise, pride in or loyalty to one's nation is not patriotism and for that matter is, at best, only a part of nationalism.[30]

A second misuse of the term nationalism is to equate it with "ethnic politics." Rutland, for example, defines nationalism as a "statement of claims on behalf of an ethnic group."[31] Ethnic politics—the political mobilization of people based on ethnicity—can be a *starting point* for something that becomes nationalism, but it alone is not nationalism. Richmond makes clear the difference between nationalism and the political mobilization of ethnic groups:

> An ethnic group when politically mobilized can have different goals. These may include the right to franchise, the use of the ethnic vote to swing results in marginal constituencies, the achievement of special status for particular languages or religions (especially in education), the removal of injustices and the enforcement of human rights codes, affirmative action programs, compensation for past deprivation, the restitution of property, or the recognition of special treatment such as exemption from military service. "Nationalist" movements may also establish such claims but go further in seeking to achieve self-govern-

> ment within a given geographic area. . . . The politicization of ethnicity is not the same thing as ethnic nationalism although it may lead to it where a historical claim to a particular territory can be established.[32]

In addition, the problem with labeling nationalism as something better labeled ethnic politics is the same as the problem with mixing up nations and ethnic groups: it assumes that the nation is ethnic. A definition of nationalism from Gellner, "a theory of political legitimacy, which requires that ethnic boundaries should not cut across political ones," is representative of this problem.[33] Such a definition leaves no room for "civic" nations or nationalism.

What is true of the difference between ethnic politics and nationalism is also true of ethnic conflict and nationalism. Ethnic conflicts, including those that turn quite violent, may emerge over many things (affirmative action policies, language laws, etc.). *National* conflicts, on the other hand, must involve disputes over territory to be truly "national." While territorial control often emerges as an issue in ethnic disputes, such disputes need not be national at the start, and some do not evolve into territorial-control conflicts at all.[34]

All this does not mean that finding a broadly acceptable definition is an easy task; there may be as many definitions of nationalism as there are nationalism scholars. The main "definitional divide" in the literature is whether nationalism is a belief or a movement. One set of approaches to the definition of nationalism considers it to be a belief, idea, concept, or principle. Ignatieff, for example, sees nationalism as a notion that combines the political idea of territorial self-determination, the cultural idea of the nation as one's primary identity, and a moral idea of justification of action to protect the rights of the nation against the "other."[35] Gellner's definition, "a principle which holds that the political and national unit should be congruent,"[36] is a standard for many people who study the topic. Haas's definition is even more basic: "a belief held by a group of people that they ought to constitute a nation, or that they already are one."[37] Armstrong has labeled nationalism a "political doctrine,"[38] while Kohn sees it as an "idea" and "state of mind."[39]

The other approach to defining nationalism takes it to be a process or movement. It is thought of as the *creation* of the unifying features of the nation or as the *actions that result from* the beliefs of the group. Nationalism defined as an organized endeavor to control the national homeland is common in the nationalism literature.[40] Brass, for example, states that nationalism "is a political movement by definition."[41] Dan Smith claims that the nation "is a political idea and nationalism is a political movement."[42] Mellor's definition of nationalism—"the *political expression* of the nation's aspirations," including control over territory that members of the nation "perceive as their homeland by right"[43]—is an improvement over definitions of nationalism as simply an idea; his definition combines the ideas and activities of nationalists. While the ideas of nationalism are important, ideas of national rights alone should not be thought of as nationalism without at least the open articulation of these ideas to the general population.

Just as it is possible to bridge other definitional divides in the nationalism literature, one is able to reconcile the movement versus ideas debate. One way to overcome the division is to consider nationalism both an ideology and a movement. Hutchinson and Smith take such an approach, claiming, "As an *ideology and movement,* nationalism exerted a strong influence in the American and French Revolutions."[44] Another way to bring the two ideas together is also found in Hutchinson and Smith: label nationalism an "ideological movement."[45] Van Evera takes a similar approach, defining nationalism as a movement but with two belief-centered features at its core:

> I define nationalism as a political movement having two characteristics: (1) individual members give their primary loyalty to their own ethnic or national community; this loyalty supercedes their loyalty to other groups, for example, those based on common kinship or political ideology; and (2) these ethnic or national communities desire their own independent state.[46]

While the combination of the terms ethnic and national in the definition is awkward, Van Evera's consideration of nationalism as an idea-based movement is beneficial in bridging the movement/idea divide.

Bringing these visions of nationalism together, *nationalism* is defined here as *the pursuit—through argument or other activity—of a set of rights and privileges for the self-defined members of the nation, including, at a minimum, territorial autonomy or independence.* All nationalisms, therefore, share two important ideas about boundaries of the nation: (1) they define, at least roughly, the *territorial boundaries* that the nation has a right to control, and

(2) they define the *membership boundaries* of the population that makes up the nation—the group that deserves this territorial control and that is entitled to the supreme loyalty of other members of the collective.[47] Put another way, the ideas of nationalism answer two questions: Who is the nation? And what territory does the nation have a right to control?

The membership boundaries are set by members of the nation themselves, generally by an intellectual or political elite,[48] though they may be based on ideas of surrounding groups as well. They establish the *we* that possesses the right to control the homeland (and as a result the *they* that does not share this right). This does not mean, however, that the boundaries are set easily. The development of successful claims over boundaries may involve struggles with another group, serious struggles *within* the nation over competing definitions of the territorial and membership boundaries, and difficulty in transmitting the ideas of national membership boundaries to the masses. One set of answers to the two questions of nationalism often "wins," and at the time of independence one set of ideas about the nation and its homeland is likely to be dominant. But because of the controversial nature of the nationalism questions, rival ideas of the nation and national homeland (and the movements and parties that espouse them) may exist long after independence.

Ethnic versus Civic Nationalism & Primordialist, Constructivist, & Instrumentalist Views of National Identity

The Problems, and Usefulness, of the Ethnic/Civic Nationalism Typology

For a long time, it was commonplace in the nationalism literature to discuss two types of nationalism, ethnic (where the nation is defined in ethnic terms) and civic (where it is defined in political-territorial terms).[49] Recently, the use of this framework has fallen out of fashion for two reasons. First, scholars have begun to emphasize the ethnic characteristics of purportedly civic states and the apparent civic nation-building policies in what had been considered "ethnic-nation-states." In other words, they have realized that the world is not so neat and tidy as the ethnic/civic dichotomy implies. Second, scholars have criticized the tendency to associate ethnic nationalism with the negatives of national identity (ethnic conflict, etc.), especially in developing countries and Eastern Europe, while civic nationalism is seen as a kinder, gentler nationalism associated with tolerance and the overcoming of ethnic divisions, especially in Western Europe and North America.[50]

To an extent, I take exception with both of these criticisms of the ethnic/civic divide. There are many cases in social science where a given typology does not match neatly with reality. This is something of which scholars must be aware, but it is not something that is fatal to the endeavor of creating typologies. Typologies, in particular what are known as "ideal types," are not only a useful but arguably a necessary step in the development of broader social science theories. Such is the case, I argue, with civic and ethnic nationalism. While the pure ethnic and pure civic types may not be easy to find, thinking of the ideal civic or ethnic national identity is valuable as a way to measure the national identity choices, and their consequences, in real cases. As discussed in the next section, the factors that influence nationalism after independence work very differently in cases of more civic or more ethnic national identity.

In addition, while it is fair to question how tolerant and unifying civic nationalism was in cases like the American nation-building project, it is also fair to acknowledge that reprehensible practices in civic nation-building projects have appeared precisely when the usually civic nationalism has most emphasized ethnic features of the nation.[51] An important part of the power of ethnic nationalism is the concept of the (ethnic) nation as an extended family, linked by blood ties. The result is that the development of a perception of threat to the survival of the nation—and its transmission to the masses—is easier in a more ethnic nationalism than in a more civic nationalism.

Finally, it is important to consider the ethnic versus civic divide because of its implications for democracy. Often, the existence of liberal democratic institutions will not limit the persecution of ethnic minorities. In democratic theory, one of the ways that minorities are protected in majority rule systems is that they will often be more "intense" about an issue than the majority. They will participate more and break apart the apathetic majority. But, when a perception exists that the survival of the ethnic nation is at stake, there is no apathetic majority. Either the minority will be excluded from participating in politics, or it will continually be on the losing end of majority rule decisions. At best, such a system becomes an "ethnic democracy." At worst, it leads to secessionism and violence.

Primordialist, Constructivist, and Instrumentalist Views of National Identity

Reflecting a debate in the cultural anthropology literature on ethnic identity, a major divide in the study of nationalism relates to where national identity comes from. The different positions can generally be grouped into three rival theoretical perspectives. As hinted at earlier in the discussion of subjective versus objective definitions of nation, the first two views provide opposing answers to the question of whether nations are natural and objective or constructed and subjective. The other idea relates to the role of nationalist elites in *triggering* national identity—inducing, for example, political mobilization in the name of a particular nationalist "cause" or against a particular "other" that threatens the nation.

The first approach, labeled by most as the *primordial* approach, holds that national identity is natural, based on deep-rooted features such as race, language, religion, and other cultural features. Such features lead us/them national boundaries to form naturally. The primordial view of nationalism has been popular with the media and government officials. While the primordial approach is widely criticized by many scholars today, it has had its supporters within the scholarly community. It is often associated with Anthony Smith, who has argued that nations have "ethnic cores" and that "ethnies" share several common components.[52]

The second major theoretical perspective, and counter to primordialism, is usually given the label of *constructivism.* The constructivist approach argues that national identity—like other group identities, including those that primordialists point to as markers of national identity—is a social construction. Comaroff points to several strands of constructivism (cultural, political, etc.), but argues they are all based on the same idea: that social identities "are products of human agency."[53]

While not all the authors in this volume would agree with my viewpoint, I take a middle-ground position between the primordial and constructivist positions. In the earlier discussion of definitions of a nation, I mention that both cultural features and a sense of right to control territory are necessary components of national identity. Certainly, both of these elements are "constructed"; elites both shape the cultural features that unify the nation and develop the arguments about territorial control. But while these features of national identity are constructed, they are not constructed out of thin air.[54] Things such as language, religion, and historical events provide the tools to create nations. While no one element is emphasized in all cases of national identities, many of these elements show up over and over.

The final theoretical approach to understanding national identity formation is labeled *instrumentalism.* As this label implies, national identity is seen as instrumental and manipulated by elites. Some scholars see instrumentalism and primordialism as connected. For Young, primordialism "completed instrumentalism by explaining the power of the 'affective tie' through which interest is pursued."[55] Comaroff agrees that primordialism and instrumentalism can be linked and labels such a hybrid *neoprimordialism.*[56] Most scholars, however, argue that instrumentalism is more related to constructivism, and some even use the terms interchangeably.[57]

Again, while emphasizing the importance of elites in the development and triggering of national identity, one must not overlook the importance of existing features of the population, historical events, and current happenings in shaping the actions of elites. Thus, when considering causal factors related to nationalism after independence, one must consider these conditions that limit the choices that elites have in how membership in the nation is defined and, especially, how national identity can be used instrumentally. The opportunities for, and constraints on, elites are an important part of the story about postindependence nationalism.

Territorial & Membership Boundaries, Causal Factors, & Five Possible Variants of Nationalism after Independence

Nationalist elites, as with all elites, tend both to believe in their cause and to have a desire to obtain and maintain power. They are, in other words, both "true believers" as well as self-interested "rational actors." Too often, social scientists fail to understand either the true believer side of nationalist elites or their rational calculations and pursuit of power, leaving these scholars unable to explain apparently contradictory acts of nationalist leaders.

One such paradoxical act, at least on the surface, is the effort to maintain the nationalist movement after its ultimate goal—independence—has been achieved. While nationalist elites will be exhausted, ecstatic, or just pleasantly surprised when independence comes, they will also generally seek to continue the momentum of the nationalist movement. As not only something that they believe in but also their ticket to power, nationalists will search for ways to keep nationalism alive.[58] But since the nationalism can no longer be about achieving independence, it must be transformed. This transformation can take one or more of several different routes presented in this section.

The various routes that nationalism after independence can take depend, just as independence-seeking nationalism does, on the two central concerns of nationalism: the nation and the territory the nation seeks to control. If the national membership boundaries are well established and accepted, and if the national homeland's territorial boundaries are also well established and accepted *and* correspond to the borders of the new state, and if there is no perceived threat to the national culture or independence of the state, nationalism after independence would be difficult to sustain. While elites play a crucial role in developing and triggering nationalism, nationalist appeals by them will fail to mobilize the general population if the masses do not believe that membership, territorial, and/or threat concerns exist. In such a situation, nationalism and its respective parties and movements may disappear quickly if not quietly.

But one of the fascinating things about nationalism is its resiliency. It has survived long after other ideologies and movements have passed into history. Thus, one should be able to identify causal factors that tend to be associated with the survival of nationalism after independence. The following sections provide an overview of several such causal factors and the resulting forms of postindependence nationalism.

Controlling the "Homeland" and Nationalism after Independence

By now it should be obvious to the reader that one cannot understand nationalism without understanding the role of territory, in particular the role of the perceived national homeland.[59] While national identity may or may not be based on ethnicity, it always contains a territorial component. An ethnic group becomes "national" when it recognizes a particular territory that it feels it belongs to and has a right to control politically. The development of a "sense of homeland" and an emotional attachment to that homeland coincides with the development of national self-consciousness, and it is claimed that "for a nation to exist, it must have some place that it can claim as its own"[60] and "nations cannot be conceived without a specific territory or homeland."[61] Thus, understanding a particular group's idea (or ideas) of homeland is necessary for understanding its political and social conduct and its relations with a national "other." As Kaiser puts it, "the national homeland is a powerful geographic mediator of sociopolitical behavior."[62]

The reason that territorial boundaries do not go away as an issue after independence has to do with the failure of state boundaries and national homeland boundaries to coincide. Put simply, these two types of territorial boundaries rarely line up. Either the nation sees its homeland as something more than the existing state, or it sees its new territorial control as threatened by homeland claims of minority groups in the state, claims on its homeland by other nations outside the state, or both. Few nations in the world in control of their own state do not face one of these homeland problems. That perceived homelands of different national groups often overlap helps explain much of the violence frequently associated with nationalist struggles, as well as the persistence of nationalism after independence.[63] This situation of overlapping homelands is common in the former Soviet Union, especially where regions within the existing successor states are named for a particular ethnic minority (Chechnya, Abkhazia, etc.).[64] Thus, when new states are created, border issues are not magically resolved. As the post-Soviet states, Ethiopia and Eritrea, India and Pakistan, and numerous other cases demonstrate, in the minds of nationalists the territory of the state in its present form may not be *the* homeland but a part of a larger homeland still to be pursued.[65]

For nations with their own states, there are two possible relationships between the state of residence and the national homeland. The first is when the state and homeland boundaries correspond. This happens occasionally, especially in the cases of civic nations whose membership boundaries and homeland boundaries developed over time to coincide with the population of the state and the territorial boundaries of the state respectively. The second, found especially in cases of ethnic nations with their own states, is when the perceived national homeland extends beyond the boundaries of the state.[66]

THE FAILURE TO CAPTURE CONTROL OF ALL OF THE PERCEIVED HOMELAND AND POSTINDEPENDENCE VARIANT 1: NATIONALISM AS "EXTERNAL-TERRITORY-CLAIMING"

This perception that the homeland extends beyond the state leads to the first variant of postindependence nationalism. Here, nationalists look beyond the new state to territory abroad and pursue control over such territory. Since homelands are nearly always geographically contiguous, this desired territory is likely to be in neighboring countries.

The claiming of further territory is most likely to occur in the "core" state of a former empire. In this case, nationalists see the independence of the new state as a defeat more than a victory, as the symbol of a surrender by, or a general weakness of, the nation. Thus, they pursue nationalism in the form of rebuilding the former state or empire and reclaiming land that the nation is "entitled to."[67] Again, elites cannot make up the existence of such a past empire. Rather, that such an empire did exist provides them ammunition with which to make further territorial claims.

But this expansive form of territorial postindependence nationalism may not only be about rebuilding a lost empire. It could also develop in the case of nations that possess a strong belief that an emotionally important part of the homeland remains outside the borders of the new state. In such a case, nationalists may pursue control over the missing territory by manipulating history to their benefit. As in the case of Nagorno-Karabakh (in Azerbaijan), they will emphasize arguments and points in time that validate their claims to the territory. In other words, they cannot completely make up that history; the period they choose must be one in which the nation in question had a significant presence. To say historical events are like malleable clay is one thing; to say that one can completely imagine the clay is another.

THE PRESENCE OF INTERNAL AND EXTERNAL THREATS TO TERRITORIAL CONTROL AND POSTINDEPENDENCE VARIANT 2: NATIONALISM AS "SOVEREIGNTY-PROTECTING"

When minority groups are present in the new state, they may provoke nationalist responses from the majority. One reason that minorities are so potentially provocative is that they may perceive their homeland to be part or all of their state of residence. There are at least three types of homelands for minorities in relation to the state of residence—labeled here *internal, external,* and *mixed.* The first type of homeland, the internal, occurs when part of the minority's state of residence is perceived to be a homeland. This is a common occurrence, in particular where a given state contains a sizable and concentrated ethnic minority. In such a case, the minority is not just ethnic but national, desiring political control over the territory in the state of residence. Such a situation fuels secessionist drives and is at the heart of various ethnonational conflicts around the world.[68]

The second homeland possibility is the external variant. In this case, members of a minority do not consider any part of their state of residence to be their homeland, viewing some region (or most likely independent state) outside their state of residence as the true homeland for the group. Such a situation would not fuel secessionist claims, though it certainly could lead the government of the external homeland to intervene on behalf of the minority group. Especially if there is a legitimate basis for claims of discrimination, the external homeland may put diplomatic, economic, or military pressure on the minority's state of residence in an effort to protect the minority from further discrimination.

In postcommunist studies, the idea of an "external national homeland" for national minorities has been presented most forcefully by Brubaker. His "triadic nexus" framework includes the external national homeland as a key component of postcommunist ethnic relations.[69] The external national homeland is part of a "relational nexus" containing three fields, the other two being nationalizing states and national minorities. The triadic nexus concept has been criticized for its assumption of a central role for the external national homeland, its assumption that the minorities are truly national rather than just ethnic, its assumption that minorities actually perceive of the putative external homeland as their homeland, and its failure to incorporate international organizations into the framework.[70] But Brubaker's consideration of an external actor (or "field") in his examination of ethnic relations in the postcommunist states is a valuable contribution. It is certainly the case that some ethnic minorities in central Europe and Eurasia are truly national and that some of these are also attached to an "external national homeland."

The third type of homeland for minorities is best called the "mixed" (or "internal-external") homeland. In this situation, members of a minority in one state see their homeland as made up of both a part of their state of residence and of an external region or state. An oft-mentioned example in the case of the former Soviet Union is the idea of Russians living in Kazakhstan seeing both the northern part of the country and Russia (or Russia, Ukraine, and Belarus) as their homeland.[71] In such situations, nationalist claims would take the form of a desire to break part of the state of residence away from the rest and join with the rest of the homeland group.

Of the three homeland options for minorities, the internal and mixed are the most threatening to the majority national group. In the internal case, the majority national group, having just won territorial control for itself, faces secessionist threats in its new state, and the problem of overlapping homelands moves to the fore.[72] In such a case, the majority group nationalism is *reactive*. It becomes a movement to maintain territorial control for the nation in the face of a perceived threat to state independence, to the hard-fought territorial control that the nation so recently achieved.[73]

In the mixed case of minority group homeland claims, the perceived threat to the independence of state A may come both from the minority and from an external enemy, if, for example, the government of state B accepts the ideas of the minority that its homeland is composed of both state B and all or part of state A. Again, overlapping homelands are at issue, and it is sometimes hard to separate the threat from the external state from the threat posed by the ethnic minority. During the first decade of independence in many of the post-Soviet states, for example, nationalists perceived Russia as posing such a threat to their still-recent independence, and nationalists in Azerbaijan have certainly felt similarly about Armenia.[74] As a result, nationalists also suspect the intentions of ethnic Russians (or ethnic Armenians, or some other ethnonational group with a "mixed homeland") living within the given state.

"Who Is the Nation?" and Nationalism after Independence

The other part of the story of nationalism's survival after independence has to do with the question of national membership. If the "Who is the nation?" question has been answered in a relatively civic way, leaders of the newly independent state may work to build such an overarching national identity. Nationalism becomes a nation-building project. However, if the ethnic answer to the "Who is the nation?" question has won, nationalism may turn to using the new territorial control to protect and enhance the national culture, in this case at the expense of national minorities in the state, or to protect co-nationals abroad.

THE NEED TO FORGE A NEW NATIONAL IDENTITY AND POSTINDEPENDENCE VARIANT 3: NATIONALISM AS CIVIC "NATION-BUILDING"

Thus, a third potential route for nationalism after independence is that nationalists turn to civic "nation-building." Nation-building concerns the development of a national identity among the population of a state. A collective of people in a given state becomes self-aware and united, accepts this group identity as its overarching political identity, and develops a feeling of the right of the collective to control politically a given territory. Islam points out that nation-building involves imbuing "discrete communities or groups within a political framework with an understanding and a sense of national consensus or identity."[75] That *nation-building* and *national integration* are often used interchangeably in the political development literature is a sign that nation-building usually requires the bringing together of groups with various cultural, economic, or regional identities.[76] Nationalists pursue the further development of national identity among the masses, with the goal of developing an overarching national identity among the entire population of the new state.

While civic nationalism is often portrayed as "good" nationalism, it is not necessarily an easy nationalist project. Myths and symbols that emphasize common experiences and backgrounds are useful to help create unity in a population that may otherwise be quite diverse.[77] But there is likely to be a sense by many groups that not enough of *our* symbols are being emphasized while too many of *theirs* are. This is especially true of ethnic minorities, who often see civic nation-building as more of an assimilation process than a melting pot.

If the membership boundary question ("Who is the nation?") was answered in a civic way during the struggle for independence, this is the most likely outcome of nationalism after independence. But it is also possible, as a couple of the cases in this book make clear, for a nationalism that began as more ethnic than civic to transform itself into the converse. In ethnically divided states, this may be the only way to hold the new state together and/or to avoid ethnic conflict.

This is especially likely when nation-building is required at the same time as state-building, something that was common in both the postcolonial and postcommunist states. In this situation, leaders are not free only to worry about (ethno-) national identity issues. They must also worry about state-building.[78] This dual role leads to what I have called the "nation-builder's dilemma" in newly independent states.[79] The dilemma is that while the emphasis on an ethnic approach to national identity makes nation-building easier,[80] it makes state-building more difficult.[81] This dilemma can lead nationalist movements to transform from ethnic to civic when the state-building concerns take precedence over ethnonational ones.

REACTION TO PERCEIVED CULTURAL THREATS AND POSTINDEPENDENCE NATIONALISM VARIANT 4: NATIONALISM AS ETHNIC "NATION-PROTECTING"

For many in the ethnic majority group in control of a new state, the independence of the state may not immediately bring the *cultural* security for which they had hoped. As a result, a fourth possible route is for nationalists to reject the civic nation-building approach and continue their struggle against the (ethnic) "other" in the name of protecting the culture of the ethnic group. Here, nationalists emphasize the idea of a threat not to the state but to the very existence of the group itself. This is a likely approach for those who stressed the ethnic answer to the national membership question in the struggle for independence, especially in the case of small nations such as Estonia and Latvia, even when the state-building concerns discussed in the preceding section exist.[82] This concept of threat to the nation can be a very powerful mobilizing tool for nationalist elites. If leaders can get the masses to believe that the survival of the nation is at stake, ordinary people will suddenly consent to extraordinary actions by their leaders and even themselves.

One obvious arena for this form of nationalism is state policy in the newly independent state. In the minds of nationalists, the state, as a nation-state, exists for the benefit of the nation. As such, if the nation's cultural identity is threatened, state policy must be adopted to protect the culture from the threatening "other." Policy issue areas that nationalists may see as "nation-protecting" include citizenship and naturalization, education, religion, and language.[83] In the case of "ethnic nations," such policies would privilege the majority group at the expense of ethnic minorities. The ideas of the nation as an ethnic nation and the state as a nation-state combine to produce an "ethnic-nation-state." In such a state, there is little place for the protection of ethnic minorities, and in the case of a perceived threat posed by the minority group, discriminatory state policies will likely result.[84]

THE EXISTENCE OF THREATENED MEMBERS OF THE NATION ABROAD AND POSTINDEPENDENCE VARIANT 5: NATIONALISM AS "CO-NATIONAL-PROTECTING"

The ethnic answer to the "Who is the nation?" question also opens the door to concern for members of the ethnic nation not living in the new state. Thus, a final possible variant of nationalism after independence would focus on "coethnics" (or, better, "co-nationals") abroad. Nationalists may claim that these co-nationals are in physical danger, that they are being discriminated against, or just that they have been unfairly cut off from their "brothers and sisters" in the new state. Resolving the co-national abroad problem could involve easing restrictions on immigration for the co-nationals, pressuring the neighboring state(s) in question, and even making claims over the territory where these co-nationals live.[85] Again, Russia and the ethnic Russians outside its borders provide an on-going current example. While less volatile to date than some had predicted, the issue of Russians outside the Russian Federation remains one of the most potentially explosive issues in post-Soviet international relations.

Nationalism as the Combination of the Possible Variants, and the Evolution of Nationalism from One Type to Another

Because several of the causal factors discussed in the preceding sections may exist at the same time, there is no reason why postindependence nationalists would pursue only one of the possible routes mentioned. Different nationalist elites may support different nationalist variants. Even the same elite could support more than one of the previously mentioned routes at the same time. In fact, many of the five routes fit together quite well. The "external-territory-claiming" and the "co-national-protecting" forms, for example, are a natural fit. The claim over territory beyond the new state may be based in part on a desire to protect the co-nationals, especially if there is a sense that pressuring neighbors on their behalf is not working. The "independence-protecting" form of nationalism can exist with nearly any of the variants where nationalism has survived. Even bringing together civic nation-building and ethnic nation-protecting is not impossible. Hutchinson and Smith point out that in India and Africa the anticolonial nationalism was civic, while at the same time ethnic and pancultural movements were common.[86]

Thus, there are numerous possible patterns, given the number of possible variants, their compatibility, and the amount of time one examines a case in question. But this does not mean that comparison is fruitless. Understanding the particular route or routes for nationalism after independence in various cases can tell us not only about those cases but also a great deal about nationalism itself and about how nationalism is likely to evolve, survive, or die out in other newly independent states in the future.

Conclusion: The Ideas & Movements of Postindependence Nationalism

No matter how much elites believe in their views of the nation, its homeland, and claims to its independence, nationalism will die without the support of the masses.[87] Thus, nationalist elites must transmit their ideas to the masses and make certain that the masses are inspired and willing to act on these ideas. But, as mentioned earlier, while a nationalist elite must mobilize the masses for nationalism to be successful, it is misleading to treat nationalists within a state (or within an ethnic group) as a unitary actor. Nationalists may disagree about the "Who is the nation?" and "What territory does the nation have a right to control?" questions.

Complete independence of an internationally recognized state is generally considered the ultimate nationalist goal. Yet some nationalists may be content to settle for something short of independence, such as territorial "autonomy." After independence, nationalist elites may disagree about whether the new state is indeed the national homeland or whether there is more territory to pursue, and they certainly may fight over the appropriateness of surrendering control over some of the territory of the new state to an ethnic minority.

Even if contentions over territory are somehow resolved, nationalists may argue over the membership boundaries of the nation. Some may want a national identity based on ethnicity and strict rules for justifying ethnic descent. Others may want to pitch the nation more broadly, with the entire population of a former colony, for example, belonging to the nation and deserving to control the new state as its own homeland.

Thus, the transmission of nationalism to the masses can involve a battle between competing nationalist elites with competing visions of the nation and of territorial control.[88] In this book, the authors focus primarily on these battles and on the transformation of nationalism after those favoring independence have won. How do the ideas and movements of nationalism change? How do nationalists maintain mass support when they have achieved their ultimate goal? We know a great deal about the emergence of nationalism in general and in particular cases. While there is a vast literature on the development of nationalism, this literature has not addressed with the same vigor the question that is the topic of this book: what happens to nationalism after independence? We now turn to the answers to that question in several postcolonial and postcommunist states. The chapters that follow examine the development of nationalist ideas and movements, the factors shaping these ideas and movements in the postindependence period, and the lessons of each particular case for our understanding of nationalism after independence.

NOTES

1. Portions of the text of this chapter are similar to text in the following two articles: Lowell Barrington, "'Nation' and 'Nationalism': The Misuse of Key Concepts in Political Science," *PS: Political Science and Politics* 30, no. 4 (December 1997): 712–16; and Lowell Barrington, "Examining Rival Theories of Demographic Influences on Political Support: The Power of Regional, Ethnic, and Linguistic Divisions in Ukraine," *European Journal of Political Research* 41, no. 4 (June 2002): 455–91.

2. Chinn and Kaiser point out that discussions of nation and nationalism portray wider (dichotomized) splits in understanding of the concepts than is actually the case. See Jeff Chinn and Robert Kaiser, *Russians as the New Minority: Ethnicity and Nationalism in the Soviet Successor States* (Boulder: Westview Press, 1996), chapter 2. I would take this further, arguing that there is an emerging convergence among nationalism scholars over meanings of the two terms.

3. See Shu-Yun Ma, "Nationalism: State-Building or State-Destroying?" *Social Science Journal* 29, no. 3 (July 1992): 293–306.

4. This is not unusual. Smith, for example, also uses the word *nation* in his definition of nationalism. See Anthony Smith, *National Identity* (London: Penguin Books, 1991), 73.

5. For a more detailed discussion of the misuse of both *nation* and *nationalism* by political scientists, see Barrington, "'Nation' and 'Nationalism.'" International relations scholars do better than most political scientists in keeping nation and state separate, possibly because of the importance placed on the nature of states in the study of international politics.

6. Ibid., 713. Nigerians, on the other hand, may comprise a nation, though one could certainly question the degree to which a Nigerian national identity has taken hold at the mass level.

7. Yael Tamir, "The Enigma of Nationalism," *World Politics* 47, no. 3 (1995): 425.

8. See Walker Connor, "A Nation Is a Nation, Is a State, Is an Ethnic Group, Is a . . . ," *Ethnic and Racial Studies* 1, no. 4 (1978): 377–400. This emphasis on ethnic characteristics leads Connor, in this same work (p. 381), to claim that Americans are "not a nation in the pristine sense of the word." Even Kaiser, whose book focuses on the essential role of territory in the development of national identity, leaves out the reference to territory in his definition of *nation* and, as a result, provides a definition that, again, only distinguishes itself from *ethnic group* by the reference to being "self-defining." For Kaiser, a nation is "a self-defining community of belonging and interest whose members share a sense of common origins and a belief in a common destiny or future together." See Robert J. Kaiser, *The Geography of Nationalism in Russia and the USSR* (Princeton: Princeton University Press, 1994), 6.

9. Chinn and Kaiser, *Russians as the New Minority,* 19: "Nations thus may be viewed as future-oriented, politicized, and territorialized ethnic groups whose members seek to gain control over their destinies."

10. John Hutchinson and Anthony Smith, "Introduction," in *Nationalism,* ed. John Hutchinson and Anthony Smith (Oxford: Oxford University Press, 1994), 3–4.

11. Rupert Emerson, quoted in Walker Connor, *Ethnonationalism: The Quest for Understanding* (Princeton, NJ: Princeton University Press, 1994), 112. Seton-Watson similarly claims that a nation exists "when a significant number of people in a community consider themselves to form a nation, or behave as if they formed one." See Hugh Seton-Watson, *Nations and States* (London: Methuen, 1977), 5.

12. E. J. Hobsbawm, *Nations and Nationalism since 1780* (Cambridge: Cambridge University Press, 1990), 8.

13. Ernest Renan, "Qu'est-ce qu'une nation?" in *Nationalism,* ed. John Hutchinson and Anthony Smith (Oxford: Oxford University Press, 1994), 17.

14. Joseph Stalin, "The Nation," in *Nationalism,* ed. John Hutchinson and Anthony Smith (Oxford: Oxford University Press, 1994), 20.

15. Anthony Smith's definition is very close to that of Stalin. For Smith, the nation

is a "named human population sharing an historic territory, common myths, and historical memories, a mass public culture, a common economy and common legal rights and duties for all members." See Smith, *National Identity,* 14.

16. Hobsbawm, for example, mentions Stalin's definition and states that "all such objective definitions have failed." See Hobsbawm, *Nations and Nationalism since 1780,* 5–6. Dan Smith has gone so far as to say that every element in Stalin's definition is "contestable." See Dan Smith, "Reconciling Identities in Conflict," in *Europe's New Nationalism,* ed. Richard Caplan and John Feffer (Oxford: Oxford University Press, 1996), 200.

17. Geoff Eley and Ronald Suny, while taking a strongly subjectivist position, admit that features such as territory, language, and culture provide the "raw materials" for national identity, though they add that these characteristics themselves are contested: "Culture is more often not what people share, but what they choose to fight over." See Geoff Eley and Ronald Grigor Suny, "Introduction: From the Moment of Social History to the Work of Cultural Representation," in *Becoming National,* ed. Geoff Eley and Ronald Grigor Suny (Oxford: Oxford University Press, 1996).

18. Kupchan proposes the idea that members of nations share an "imagery that gives definition to a unique and distinctive national grouping." See Charles Kupchan, "Introduction: Nationalism Resurgent," in *Nationalism and Nationalities in the New Europe,* ed. Charles Kupchan (Ithaca, NY: Cornell University Press, 1995), 4.

19. *Democracy,* for example, is one of the most contested terms in political science. Yet no serious scholar would propose that democracy exists any time people think their political system is democratic.

20. See Kaiser, *The Geography of Nationalism in Russia and the USSR,* 10–11, however, for a discussion of the way that the national territory itself is also a subjective, constructed concept.

21. Ghia Nodia, "Nationalism and Democracy," in *Nationalism, Ethnic Conflict, and Democracy,* ed. Larry Diamond and Marc F. Plattner (Baltimore: Johns Hopkins University Press, 1994), 11, italics in original.

22. Ernst Haas, "What Is Nationalism and Why Should We Study It?" *International Organization* 40, no. 3 (1986): 726.

23. Barrington, "'Nation' and 'Nationalism,'" 713.

24. As Schopflin puts it, "Nations may be defined by various characteristics, but crucial among them is their relationship to a particular territory and their claim to exercise political control over that territory in the name of the nation." See George Schopflin, "Nationalism and Ethnicity in Europe, East and West," in *Nationalism and Nationalities in the New Europe,* ed. Charles Kupchan (Ithaca, NY: Cornell University Press, 1995), 38.

25. Barrington, "'Nation' and 'Nationalism,'" 713.

26. See Anthony Richmond, "Ethnic Nationalism: Social Science Paradigms," *International Social Science Journal* 111 (1987): 3–18.

27. See the later discussion on ethnic versus civic nationalism.

28. The idea of political versus ethnic nations is not accepted by all nationalism scholars. Clearly, these are ideal types, with most nations failing to meet either ideal. But as ideal types they are useful ways to distinguish how one nation sees itself and how its nationalism differs from another nation's.

29. Ignatieff provides an example of the blurred lines, stating that "one person's patriotism is another person's nationalism"; he goes on, however, to discuss how the two terms are, in fact, different. See Michael Ignatieff, "Nationalism and Toleration," in

Europe's New Nationalism, ed. Richard Kaplan and John Feffer (Oxford: Oxford University Press, 1996), 218.

30. Some include this idea of loyalty in their definitions of nations and nationalism. Emerson, for example, states that a nation is the "largest community that, when the chips are down, effectively commands men's loyalty, overriding the claims both of lesser communities within it and those that cut across it." See Rupert Emerson, *From Empire to Nation: The Rise and Self-Assertion of Asian and African Peoples* (Boston: Beacon Press, 1960), 95–96.

31. Peter Rutland, "State Failure and State Building in Post-Socialist Europe: Implications for Theories of Nationalism" (presented at the annual meeting of the American Political Science Association, New York, 1994), 4.

32. Richmond, "Ethnic Nationalism," 4–5.

33. Ernest Gellner, *Nations and Nationalism* (Ithaca, NY: Cornell University Press, 1983), 1. It should be pointed out that this definition from Gellner is far less cited than the one presented in the next section, though both come from the same page of Gellner's classic book.

34. See Kaiser, *The Geography of Nationalism in Russia and the USSR*, for a discussion of various "ethnoterritorial conflicts" on the territory of the former Soviet Union. For an excellent overview of the topic of ethnic conflict, see Donald L. Horowitz, *Ethnic Groups in Conflict* (Berkeley: University of California Press, 1985).

35. Michael Ignatieff, *Blood and Belonging: Journeys into the New Nationalism* (New York: Farrar, Straus and Giroux, 1993).

36. Gellner, *Nations and Nationalism*, 1.

37. Haas, "What Is Nationalism and Why Should We Study It?" 727.

38. John Armstrong, *Nations before Nationalism* (Chapel Hill: University of North Carolina Press, 1982), 4.

39. Hans Kohn, *The Idea of Nationalism* (New York: Macmillan, 1945), 18.

40. One interesting definition along these lines is Kaiser's labeling of nationalism as "activated national territoriality." See Kaiser, *The Geography of Nationalism in Russia and the USSR*, 22.

41. Paul Brass, *Ethnicity and Nationalism* (London: Sage, 1991), 48.

42. Smith, "Reconciling Identities in Conflict," 200. On the next page, however, Smith states that nationalism is both a doctrine and a movement.

43. Roy Mellor, *Nation, State, and Territory: A Political Geography* (London: Routledge, 1989), 4–5, my italics.

44. Hutchinson and Smith, "Introduction," 3, my italics. See also their comment on p. 4 of their work: "Once again, there are important differences in ways of defining the concept, some equating it with 'national sentiment,' others with nationalist ideology and language, others again with nationalist movements."

45. Ibid., 5.

46. Stephen Van Evera, "Hypotheses on Nationalism and the Causes of War," in *Nationalism and Nationalities in the New Europe*, ed. Charles Kupchan (Ithaca, NY: Cornell University Press, 1995), 136.

47. One might be concerned about the similarity between the proposed definitions of *nation* and *nationalism*. They are closely related (as we would expect them to be), but they are not the same thing. The fact that a nation has a sense of homeland is not the same thing as its pursuit of control over that territory. In addition, by setting the mem-

bership boundaries, nationalism lays out the characteristics of the people considered a nation. It also sets the territorial boundaries of the homeland that, as a nation, the group should control. But unless the people themselves accept these ideas—unless they believe they are a nation—nationalism is doomed to fail. Thus, I would argue that nationalisms (or, better, nationalists) try to produce nations, but they are in no way guaranteed success.

48. Weber believed that intellectuals play the major role in forming nationalist ideas, while political leaders develop the ideas of the state. See Max Weber, "The Nation," in *Nationalism,* ed. John Hutchinson and Anthony Smith (Oxford: Oxford University Press, 1994), 25. But see the discussion in this chapter about constraints on the ability of elites to formulate national membership boundaries.

49. See, for example, Kohn, *The Idea of Nationalism;* and Liah Greenfeld, *Nationalism: Five Roads to Modernity* (Cambridge, MA: Harvard University Press, 1992).

50. See, for example, the discussion by Stephen Jones in the chapter on Georgia in this volume.

51. The practice of slavery, the treatment of Japanese Americans during World War II, and the persecution and killing of American Indians throughout the nineteenth and twentieth centuries, for example.

52. See the discussion in Soren Rinder Bollerup and Christian Dons Christensen, *Nationalism in Eastern Europe* (New York: St. Martin's Press, 1997), 36–38.

53. John L. Comaroff, "Ethnicity, Nationalism, and the Politics of Difference in an Age of Revolution," in *The Politics of Difference: Ethnic Premises in a World of Power,* ed. Edwin N. Wilmsen and Patrick McAllister (Chicago: University of Chicago Press, 1996), 165.

54. Likewise, while they pursue territorial control for the nation, nationalist elites cannot pursue any territory.

55. Crawford Young, "Evolving Modes of Consciousness and Ideology: Nationalism and Ethnicity," in *Political Development and the New Realism in Sub-Saharan Africa,* ed. David E. Aptar and Carl G. Rosberg (Charlottesville: University Press of Virginia, 1994), 79.

56. Comaroff, "Ethnicity, Nationalism, and the Politics of Difference in an Age of Revolution."

57. See Hans Vermeulen and Cora Govers, "From Political Mobilization to the Politics of Consciousness," in *The Politics of Ethnic Consciousness,* ed. Hans Vermeulen and Cora Govers (New York: St. Martin's Press, 1997), 22 n. 2. Yeros claims that "a form of instrumentalism" can be labeled as *constructivism.* See Paris Yeros, "Introduction: On the Uses and Implications of Constructivism," in *Ethnicity and Nationalism in Africa: Constructivist Reflections and Contemporary Politics,* ed. Paris Yeros (New York: St. Martin's Press, 1999), 2.

58. Again, some elites will be more successful at this than others.

59. See Anthony Smith, *The Ethnic Origins of Nations* (Oxford: Basil Blackwell, 1986), 163, who states that the necessity of a "'homeland,' a national space of one's own, is a central tenet of nationalism." Homelands are generally thought of by nationalism scholars as sizable areas, such as a large region within an existing state, an entire existing state, or part or all of more than one state. Yet, historically, most people had a more localized perception of homeland. Typically, homeland meant the village or small region around where someone was born. See Hobsbawm, *Nations and Nationalism since*

1780, 15. But nationalists must make the homeland more than one's village for nationalism to succeed. Nationalists have tended to characterize the group homeland in one of three ways, labeled here *internal, external,* and *mixed homelands.*

60. Kaiser, *The Geography of Nationalism in Russia and the USSR,* 5, 8.

61. Guntram Herb, "National Identity and Territory," in *Nested Identities: Nationalism, Territory, and Scale,* ed. Guntram Herb and David H. Kaplan (Lanham, MD: Rowman and Littlefield, 1999), 17. For another discussion of the interaction between territory and national identity, in this case on the Armenian-Azerbaijan conflict, see Nora Dudwick, "The Cultural Construction of Political Violence in Armenia and Azerbaijan," *Problems of Post-Communism* 42 (1995): 4.

62. Kaiser, *The Geography of Nationalism in Russia and the USSR,* 5.

63. The existence of overlapping homelands means two things. First, dividing up existing states cannot be done neatly along "homeland" lines. While the international community increasingly favored the partitioning of existing states to solve ethnonational conflicts at the end of the twentieth century, the failures of this approach (in the former Yugoslavia, for example) seemed to outweigh the successes (such as the "velvet divorce" of Czechoslovakia). Second, it means that governments of all new states are likely to perceive threats to their territorial integrity well after independence is established.

64. But, even if the minority succeeds in gaining independence for the (now former) "internal homeland," the overlapping homelands problem does not go away. The creation of a new state, especially one that can be characterized as an "ethnic-nation-state," will likely create a new minority (or minorities) as well as its new majority group. This minority may see part of the new state as its homeland (creating a new internal homeland), or—especially if it was part of the old majority group—it may see the new state and an external area as its homeland, creating a new "mixed" homeland.

65. For a discussion of postindependence Eritrean nationalism, see Fouad Makki, "Nationalism, State Formation and the Public Sphere: Eritrea 1991–96," *Review of African Political Economy* 23, no. 70 (December 1996): 475–97.

66. In principle, a third possibility exists: that the state is larger than the perceived national homeland. This is extremely unlikely in practice, however, since it would imply that the nation does not have a right to control all of the territory of its state. While elites will generally agree that the homeland is *at least* the new state, they may not agree on much else. Because homeland boundaries are open to dispute, nationalist elites in the same national group may, again, argue over the state-homeland relationship. Some may accept the boundaries of the national state as equivalent to the boundaries of the homeland. Others may not only dispute this but argue with each other about how much more than the existing state the homeland comprises.

67. Kaiser mentions this possibility as well for Russia. He discusses the claims over Belarus, Ukraine, and northern Kazakhstan by Russian nationalists. See Kaiser, *The Geography of Nationalism in Russia and the USSR,* 371.

68. Ignatieff makes an amusing comparison between patriotism and nationalism, which is relevant to the discussion of internal homelands here. He states, "Patriotism is love of a country one can take for granted as one's own. . . . Nationalism, by contrast, is love of a country that happens to belong to someone else." See Ignatieff, "Nationalism and Toleration," 218.

69. See Rogers Brubaker, *Nationalism Reframed: Nationhood and the National Question in the New Europe* (Cambridge: Cambridge University Press, 1996); and Rogers

Brubaker, "National Minorities, Nationalizing States, and External National Homelands in the New Europe," *Daedalus* 124, no. 2 (winter–spring 1995): 107–32.

70. See, for example, Lowell Barrington, "Rethinking the Triadic Nexus: External National Homelands, International Organizations, and Ethnic Relations in the Former Soviet Union" (presented at the annual meeting of the Association for the Study of Nationalities, New York, April 15–17, 1999).

71. While this is a common view among those writing on Russians outside Russia, there is almost no empirical support for the idea that ethnic Russians in Kazakhstan would think of their homeland in this way. See Lowell W. Barrington and Brian D. Silver, "The External Homeland among Russians in the Near Abroad" (presented at the annual meeting of the Midwest Political Science Association, Chicago, April 14–17, 1999).

72. Kaiser mentions this possibility for nationalism in Russia following the collapse of the Soviet Union. See Kaiser, *The Geography of Nationalism in Russia and the USSR*, 367.

73. Admittedly, despite the earlier discussion of the need to separate the two concepts, the lines between nationalism and patriotism are blurred when one is discussing this variant of nationalism after independence. But it is still possible to distinguish actions that are about the nation and its territorial control of the state from a general sense of loyalty to the state by all its inhabitants.

74. See Chinn and Kaiser, *Russians as the New Minority*, 29.

75. M. Nazrul Islam, *Problems of Nation-Building in Developing Countries: The Case of Malaysia* (Dhaka, Bangladesh: University of Dhaka, 1988), 64.

76. Ibid., 1.

77. While the United States had an advantage in the nation-building process because of its relatively homogeneous population, Zelinsky points out the importance of national symbols in the development of American identity: "But, if the presence or manipulation of symbols is not always among the first causes for the creation of nations, and if they may be missing during earliest infancy, one may still argue forcefully for their indispensability during the formative adolescent years, and for their utility during the nation-state phase. All the factual material leads to that emphatic conclusion for the United States." See Wilbur Zelinsky, *Nation into State: The Shifting Symbolic Foundations of American Nationalism* (Chapel Hill: University of North Carolina Press, 1988), 230.

78. State-building can be defined as the development (or redevelopment) of the capacity of the state in the areas of security and of state penetration into society to extract and distribute economic, social, and political goods. For more on the idea of state-building as security and penetration, see Lowell Barrington, "Citizenship and the 'Nation-Builder's Dilemma': Ethnicity, Nation-Building, and State-Building in Newly Independent States" (presented at the annual meeting of the American Political Science Association, Chicago, September 1995).

79. Ibid.

80. Because all national identities need shared cultural features, the question of which features to emphasize is more difficult in the civic case than in the ethnic case. The existing similar cultural features of the ethnic group, on the other hand, make it generally easier to unify the group and put in place identity-related policies. Specifically, there are fewer disagreements about policies related to language.

81. Performing state functions when minorities have been excluded from the

definition of the nation usually requires coercion or "buying off" these groups by giving them already scarce resources. The exclusion also has obvious implications for the security component of the state-building project.

82. Chinn and Kaiser, *Russians as the New Minority,* 30. Chinn and Kaiser (borrowing from Shantha Hennayake) discuss how many variants of nationalism are "interactive," responding to the nationalism of others. In the cases of Estonia and Latvia, however, the nationalism of ethnic Russians in the two countries was quite weak, but demographic changes during the Soviet period fed Estonian and Latvian fears that Russians would come to culturally dominate the Baltic nations.

83. As Kaiser points out, language is an especially potent issue for nationalists: "Having one's native language declared the lingua franca of the entire state or a region therein clearly provides strategic advantages to the 'native' speakers." See Kaiser, *The Geography of Nationalism in Russia and the USSR,* 9.

84. For a discussion of the ways in which the ethnic nation idea and the perception of threat came together in Latvia and Estonia, see Lowell Barrington, "The Making of Citizenship Policy in the Baltic States," *Georgetown Immigration Law Journal* 13, no. 2 (winter 1999): 159–99. Also see Robert M. Hayden, "Constitutional Nationalism in the Formerly Yugoslav Republics," *Slavic Review* 51, no. 4 (winter 1992): 654–73, for a discussion of such policies in the Balkans.

85. In such a case, this variant of postindependence nationalism would merge with the previously mentioned external-territory-claiming variant. Many such combinations of the variants are possible.

86. Hutchinson and Smith, "Introduction," 9.

87. See Walker Connor, "When Is a Nation?" *Ethnic and Racial Studies* 13, no. 1 (1990): 92–103.

88. What is involved in making the masses "national" in a particular case is an interesting question, but one that has been discussed elsewhere. See, for example, Eugen Weber, *Peasants into Frenchmen: The Modernization of Rural France, 1870–1914* (Stanford: Stanford University Press, 1976).

II. Postcolonial Nationalism

2. Nationalism in Postcolonial States

JOSHUA B. FORREST

IN MOST COUNTRIES that experienced some form of direct colonial rule, nationalism emerged as a political and intellectual movement embraced by a broad spectrum of social elites. Nationalist leaders of varying backgrounds shared a common interest in extricating the nation from colonial rule and in establishing an independent nation-state with a distinct, unified national identity. In most cases, however, the common bond that had been crafted during the course of the independence movement was subsequently challenged by divisive tendencies—some new, some historically entrenched—after national independence had been achieved. This, in turn, made the erstwhile unifying bond of nationalism difficult to sustain. An increasingly common type of divisive force has been the rise of multiple *internal* nationalisms, often within a common ethnic frame, calling for special rights or secession.

Indeed, consistent with the analysis presented by Lowell Barrington in the volume's introduction, we may suggest a broad analytical division between those postcolonial nations that have been able to continue to forge nationalist unity and those nations marked by internal ethnic nationalist challenges. In the first case, political systems continue to be characterized by the consolidation (however uneven) of a strong civic nationalist spirit, which, as Barrington indicates, generally reflects ties among political elites from divergent political and ethnic backgrounds who share a commitment to common political rules and institutions. Here we may suggest that in the cases of Botswana, Namibia, Mauritius, and possibly South Africa, such elites have created inclusivistic polyarchical regimes, nearly consociational in structure, based on accommodation, negotiation, and the fundamental acceptability of autonomous social interests.[1]

The second pattern in postcolonial nations has been marked by the degeneration of civic nationalist unity in the wake of parochial, "ethnic nation-protecting"[2] political claimants, while narrowly based patrimonial regimes cling to power by relying on a praetorian, centralist, and exclusivist pattern of rule.[3] In the worst cases, including Rwanda, Somalia, Sudan, and the Democratic Republic of the Congo,[4] the nation-state breaks apart (formally or de facto) into either separate communal movements with ethnonationalist aggrandizing goals or mixed interethnic movements with separatist goals, in both cases with sufficient social support and military resources to ensure the perpetuation of relatively circumscribed ethnopolitical, territorial goals.[5]

The three countries examined in detail in part 2 of the book—Malaysia, Somalia, and Rwanda—provide particularly dramatic examples of each of these two development lines. Malaysia exemplifies a torturous road toward a relatively successful polyarchical regime construction (in recent years), while Somalia and Rwanda are cases in which nationalism became diffused into a multitude of highly parochial interests that assumed a zero-sum, nonnegotiable political stance. In Somalia, this led to the eventual breakup of the nation-state, and in Rwanda it led to genocide.[6]

The Malaysian case has been paralleled by the postcolonial polities of Suriname, Singapore, and Mauritius, where long-term policies of inclusion in ethnically plural social contexts eventually produced cross-segmentary ties and political cooperation among ethnic elites.[7] In the eyes of some observers, the South African case suggests the recent emergence of sufficient cross-ethnic accommodation to generate a similar type of polyarchical, cooperative nationalism.[8] However, it should be noted that this effort at interelite accommodation in South Africa has not proven entirely successful, as some leaders have used their entry into national politics to play an ethnic political card, leading one analyst to claim that instrumentalist ethnic mobilization and intercommunal strife intensified in the mid-to-late 1990s.[9] Still, it does appear that a relatively substantial segment of political leaders from most of the key social groups remains strongly committed to building civic nationalism in South Africa, and no serious effort at ethnic secession has as yet been initiated (Zulu nationalism brokered by some instrumentalist leaders remains a serious problem, but secession has not emerged as a realistic proposition). Malaysian nationalist evolution provides a possible role model for South Africa, as ethnic accommodation, following an early postcolonial history of exclusion, has thus far succeeded in keeping extreme interethnic strife at bay.

This contrasts starkly with the cases of postcolonial Somalia and Rwanda. There, the social fabric of the nation-state has been shattered in the past decade by intensive internal warfare, the secession of Somaliland engineered by the northern Isaaq people, and genocidal massacres of Tutsi followed by massive migrations of Hutu out of Rwanda and into the Democratic Republic of the Congo (which in turn helped to stimulate secessionist warfare in that troubled state). In regard to these events, one can argue that the mismatch between the national/territorial and ethnic community during colonial rule in many parts of Africa and Asia—also including Sudan, Chad, Ethiopia-Oromo, Eritrea, Pakistan-Bangladesh, and Sri Lanka—helped generate an extended period of unresolved communal and irredentist strife after independence. This dramatized the ill-advised placement of national borders across ethnically shared zones, a problem that has yet to be addressed by government leaders and that helps to preclude the emergence of civic nationalism. Barrington's observation that the territorial division of ethnic groups can profoundly affect the course of nationalist evolution, and help to generate serious secessionist or irredentist claims,[10] is verified in the cases of Somalia, Sudan, Eritrea, and much of South Asia.

Additional Factors Affecting Postcolonial Nationalist Elites

The causal factors discussed in the introduction—including the failure to capture all of the perceived national homeland, the presence of internal and external threats to territorial integrity and cultural survival, and the existence of threatened co-nationals abroad—are all clearly important elements of the dynamic evolution of postcolonial nationalism. At the same time, I would suggest that three additional factors may be identified that affect the ability of elites to pursue nationalist policies and to mobilize the mass populace to support nationalist parties in postindependence contexts. These three additional factors are (1) the colonial legacy of ethnoregional policy preferences (equitable or discriminatory), (2) the social bases of support for civic versus ethnic nationalists, and (3) the density of social structures and nature of traditional belief systems. A brief discussion of these factors provides a contextual framework for understanding the particular cases of Somalia, Malaysia, and Rwanda.

In the first place, we may point out that the postcolonial state's reaction to the ethnic and ethnoregional inequities engineered by colonial boundary makers has proven significant in setting the stage for the subsequent resolution of colonially created ethnic cleavages. The case of India is especially noteworthy here, as its postcolonial leaders immediately decided to annul the 580 princely states that existed at independence, replacing them with new provincial boundaries that did not coincide with the older states. Although this initially precipitated a number of new insurgencies and subregional political movements, in the long run this boundary restructuring also appeared to forestall more serious ethnopolitical strife and lay the social foundations for a relatively unifying civic nationalism.[11]

In contrast, the consolidation of civic nationalism has proven particularly challenging in Africa, where state leaders have often elected to provide preferential treatment to ethnic allies despite analytic claims regarding pluralistic tolerance. The case of Rwanda, as chapter 4 makes clear, presents a particularly compelling example of such preferential treatment as having been initiated by colonial decision making, although ethnic favoritism did not assume a prominent regional character. Instead, the colonialists ensured the consolidation of Tutsi leadership and the social, political, and economic exclusion of Hutu throughout the national territory. This favoritism set the stage for the genesis of Tutsi and Hutu political consciousness and activism in the postcolonial period. As conflict between the two communities began to occur, the country did not become divided into ethnoregions; Hutu and Tutsi political mobilization each increasingly assumed a nationwide territorial claim.

In Somalia, as Peter Schraeder makes clear in a particularly insightful analysis in chapter 5, the tripartite colonialist division among British, French, and Italian Somaliland was never adequately addressed after independence. It subsequently proved a major fault line in the disintegration of the Somali nation-state—beginning in Mogadishu itself and initially manifested by a general split between northern-based and southern-based political groupings. This further degenerated into multiple intraclan divisions in the south, but in the north Somaliland reemerged as a coherent political entity. Schraeder indicates that, although this likely spells the end of any potential for pan-Somali nationalism, it does suggest the regionally specific basis on which a new political stability can be reached, presuming (he argues) that the international community provides support for a negotiated, territorially based compromise.

In view of the civil disarray and dissipation of civic nationalist nationalism occurring in much of Africa, not only in Somalia and Rwanda, one may note that the decision to avoid challenging the colonial-state-engineered internal boundaries after independence ended up perpetuating state-ethnic mismatches and helped set the stage for internal strife and the dissipation of early-stage postcolonial civic nationalist movements. However, we may also observe that, in some African cases, after a generation of internal conflict, the installment of new regimes was intended to create the basis for new regional restructurings that leaders hoped would diminish past grievances and begin the process of creating a civic nationalist spirit.

Thus, in the 1990s, leaders in Ethiopia, Ghana, Zambia, Namibia, and South Africa redrew their respective internal boundaries in part in order to reduce the perception of exclusion and to move toward a more balanced allocation of benefits to long-ignored regions.[12] To be sure, the building of civic nationalist feeling remains tenuous in all these cases, as the incentive of the new national elites appears to reflect instrumentalist manipulation to ensure that ethnoregions support the new central governments rather than simply the elites' desire to achieve nation-state unification. Nonetheless, in the long run these new redistrictings could facilitate the emergence of more stable, if somewhat smaller-scale, nation-states that are more contiguous with ethnically coherent, regionally based political support structures. In some cases, a redistricting that provides more (or full) autonomy to regions historically marked by internal *interethnic* cooperation and unified mobilization against a hegemonic state—such as occurred in the case of Eritrea—could also prove favorable to improved stability and to the eventual reconstruction of civic nationalism.[13]

Social Bases of Support: Civic or Ethnic Nationalist? Dual Identity or Dual Nationalism?

In the introduction, Barrington portrays civic nation-building as reflecting a shared perception among political elites in newly independent states that unifying political motifs are central to the achievement of stablity and national political development. In regard to mass behavior in particular, it is important to investigate the extent to which civic nationalism in postcolonial states displaces a more narrow value framework that emphasizes ethnic nationalism. In the relatively successful case of Malaysia (and elsewhere in South Asia), it is telling to note that a form of what Diane Mauzy refers to in chapter 3 as *dual identity* has emerged that reflects not so much the convergence but rather the coexistence of a civic and an ethnic identity. In Malaysia—as in other (but not all) parts of South Asia—this dual identity has reflected the predominance of the civic aspect in recent years, in turn bearing positively on national unity.[14]

In contrast to South Asia, the spread of autonomy-seeking movements in parts of Africa makes clear the limited citizen engagement with the nation-state.[15] The Rwandan and Somali cases, as described in chapters 4 and 5, provide additional evidence of the difficulty, in Africa, of generating a civic culture. John Clark offers an unorthodox analysis of ethnic politics in Rwanda by suggesting the emergence of a "dual nationalism," in which Hutu leaders instrumentally engineered a particularly violent form of ethnic politicization. Tutsi ethnic politics was more reactive in character, with political parties forming in response to Hutu aggression. Clark argues in chapter 4 that this led to the crystallization of two national identities and ethnonational movements within the same country—that is, within what he refers to as "overlapping territorial spaces." This form of ethnic nationalism precluded the evolution of civic nationalism, as it was conceived through efforts to create a Hutu national state and a Tutsi national state on the same territory, generating a zero-sum politics of violence.

Clark's interpretation of the Rwandan conflict as struggles between national communities is important conceptually because—in responding to the query posed in the introduction, "Who is the nation?"—the Rwandan analysis resurrects the older view of nationalism as reflecting a singular people sharing a myth of common descent searching for a state or for political autonomy. This conceptualization of nationalism has been emphasized in the work of Connor for the past four decades,[16] and it is especially helpful in understanding the emergence of repeated episodes of mass violence.

In the case of postindependence Somalia, as Schraeder shows, inter- and intraclan warfare among members of the same ethnic group makes clear that ethnic and state confluence do not necessarily make for postnationalist unity. Still, Rwanda, Somalia, and other cases marked by inter- or intracommunal warfare may be viewed as extreme ends of a more typically ambiguous range of civic attachments. In regard to Kenya, for example, Ndegwa argues that despite the instrumentalist tendencies of many Kenyan political elites, civic nationalism pervades ordinary people's consciousness to the point that it is possible to speak of "dual citizenship."[17] By this Ndegwa refers to loyalties flowing to either the nation or the ethnic group depending upon circumstance and issue. This somewhat mirrors the "dual identity" described by Mauzy with regard to Malaysia; in Kenya the civic component of nationalism remained relatively latent until the changed circumstances of the 2002 electoral campaign, when pan-Kenyan political integration supplanted the previously communal and instrumentalist character of political mobilization.

Thus, a distinct aspect of postcolonial nationalism in most cases has been the formation of dual civic and ethnic identities, with the outcome of the nationalist movement in part determined by whether civic or ethnic leaders are able to mobilize ordinary citizens in their preferred political direction. Even in Somalia, now considered an extreme case marked by intrastate violence, ethnic mobilizers during the initial postcolonial decades had vied unsuccessfully with civic activists for popular support, and the civic politicians had appeared to generate a degree of attachment to the nation-state to the point that dual civic and ethnic identities pertained. It is important not to fully lose sight of this mixed-identity aspect of the Somali postcolonial trajectory, even though it did not prove durable, for it is more representative of most third-world postcolonial contexts than the preeminence of the factional and communalistic mobilization that has characterized Somalia in recent years.

Density of Social Structures and Traditional Belief Systems

By the density of social structures I refer to the solid, "thick," enduring nature of old, community-based social networks, whose origins are found in precolonial times and which have not been structurally disarticulated by modernizing forces. Dense social structures are marked by strong, locally based sources of authority, economic exchange, and personal ties and provide community refuge from what is so often the unforgiving competitiveness of state-(mis)managed capitalism that pervades the formal economies of many postcolonial nations. Precisely because of the perpetuation of dense social structures in all three cases discussed in this section of the book, as elsewhere in postcolonial contexts, *ordinary communities have been able to make choices about which political elites to support* so that—at least in part and in certain time periods—peasants and other "mass" groups have helped to determine whether nationalism assumes a broad civic or narrow ethnic form.

Also, in many postcolonial nations, belief systems that originated in ancient times continue to wield a significant impact on the political choices made by the mass populace. The most dramatic example of this is Malaysia. As demonstrated by Mauzy, a traditional, deeply held proclivity to respect central state leadership, along with a historically entrenched reluctance to associate ethnic power with territory, helped represent sociohistorically reinforced values favorable to the production of civic nationalism after independence.

In Somalia, clan societies were historically characterized by segmented political systems without adherence to centralized state structure, and this tradition of social segmentation clearly wielded a more enduring and profound impact in society than did the state-building experience of colonialism or the (brief and superficial) nation-building efforts of the Siad Barre regime. In Rwanda, Clark demonstrates that first Hutu nationalists and then Tutsi nationalists rose to power precisely because they were able to obtain the intensive support of the vast majority of their respective nationalist communities, despite the social reality of intermarriage and interpersonal cooperation that had characterized the recent histories of these two peoples.

This match between social structures, belief systems, and nationalist movements (whether civic or ethnic) highlights the psychological factor in communal mobilization, as suggested in the introduction to this volume. Connor has previously made clear that nationalist movements become meaningful only when elite-level nationalist goals become shared more fully within mass society.[18] If and when nationalist ideologies and strategies coincide with the basic values and belief systems that hold fast at the mass level, they then have the potential to provide the psychological "glue" that helps make the rise of nationalist movements (whether civic or ethnic) possible. It is this psychological factor, reflecting, in part, the particular nature of the density of indigenous social structures, which helps to create the conditions necessary for nationalist ideologies to take root in a popular base and to elicit a mobilizational response from ordinary people. In this respect, it is important to examine already-existing social bases of support for nation-building and to identify the ways in which they may contribute elements of the sociohistorical glue that are essential to the success of a given civic nation-building project.

From Underlying Factors to Instrumentalist Capacity

In the introduction to this volume, Barrington emphasizes that factors consistent with primordial, instrumentalist, and constructivist visions of national identity development each play a role in determining the various courses of action taken by nationalist elites. As the following chapters make clear, the postcolonial cases of Malaysia, Rwanda, and Somalia support such a balanced approach. At the same time, the discussion of causal factors in this chapter highlights ways in which elites are constrained by older, and more recent, contextual political and social influences. In this section, we underline the role of instrumentalist analysis in explaining how nationalist elites are able to successfully craft nationalist movements. This, in turn, requires appreciation of the political skill of nationalist elites in addressing postcolonial problems in ways that appear convincing to substantial segments of the mass public.

This skill is directly related to what this volume refers to as *instrumentalist capacity*—the success or failure of ethnic or civic elites—which we regard as crucial to determining the trajectory of postnationalist politics. To be sure, it is also important to take into account blood-tie bonds and emotional impulses (primoridalism) as well as the social shaping of ethnic perspectives through historical circumstances or state-led manipulations (constructivism). However, instrumentalist ability—the extent to which leaders of ethnic versus civic nationalist movements are able to convince the local populace to support their aims and the determination of political elites to pursue an ethnic or civic course of action—is especially central in explaining postcolonial political outcomes.

Thus, in Somalia, argues Schraeder, an elite pact agreed upon by political leaders helped to shape the early effort at nation-building, while the later devotion of political elites to clan-based militarism and their instrumentalist success in raising popular armies to back their differing claims were central to Somalia's nation-state undoing. We may also mention here the role of (ethnic) "external-territory claiming,"[19] referring to President Siad Barre's invasion of Ethiopia's Ogaadeen region, which is predominantly inhabited by ethnic Somalis. Schraeder makes clear that this wielded a devastating impact on internal pan-Somali nationalist solidarity.

Similarly, for the Rwandan case, Clark indicates the Tutsi-led political regime in Rwanda sent troops into Congo to protect co-Tutsi nationalists—*co-national protecting* in Barrington's terminology—as well as to ensure the defeat of Hutu armies and to assert sovereignty claims over Congolese regions in which ethnic Tutsis reside. Clark also makes clear the instrumentalist skill of Hutu nationalists in the 1960s through the early 1990s and of Tutsi nationalists as of 1994 in gaining state power, consolidating it, and using it to bolster the interests of the respective nationalist elites. This instrumentalist success was, in part, predicated on the conscious support of the majority of members of each of the two communities, after Hutu and Tutsi identities had been "constructed" by Belgian colonialists and after ethnic violence had been organized and perpetrated by political elites.

In Malaysia, by contrast, Mauzy describes a postcolonial progression from a narrowly constructed, quasi-primordial nationalism during the early stages of mass politics to a more instrumental concern with specific elite interests. However, Mauzy also insightfully indicates points at which instrumental efforts "to construct" or maneuver certain identities did not succeed. She furthermore emphasizes the extent to which a historically grounded perspective can often prove complementary to a full appreciation of the ebb and flow of instrumentalist politics, one of the important contributions of her study to the broader understanding of nationalism after independence.

In all of these cases, the combination of primordial mass motivation with historically generated constructivist identities proved to be important aspects of postcolonial nationalism, but those motivations and identities were only fully mobilized once political elites assumed an effective instrumentalist capacity. Thus, the cases in chapters 3–5 make clear that elite behavior is central to civic nationalist versus ethnic nationalist outcomes; however, it is also evident that instrumentalist success—whether ethnic or civic in orientation—is unlikely to prove effective without deeply rooted consciousness and self-definition (ethnic or civic) at the mass level.

Ongoing Battles between Ethnic and Civic Nationalisms

In conclusion, the success or failure of nationalism in most postcolonial states is in large part determined by varying combinations of the underlying factors discussed in this chapter, including particular strategies and decisions by nationalist elites who assume power after independence. In each postcolonial context, whether nationalism develops in a more civic or more ethnic form has reflected particular precolonial historical experiences, colonial inheritances, and the dynamics of unique social structures, along with leadership capacity and mass-level choice making. This makes it crucial to examine the particular combination of historical, psychological, political, social, and external elements that determine the direction of nationalism after independence in a given postcolonial setting.

Moreover, it can be observed from the cases in chapters 3–5 that each decade typically brings significant shifts in the struggle between civic and ethnic nationalism. Contrary to conventional wisdom (and primordialist expectations), ethnic nationalism can prove relatively fleeting, while polyarchical regimes by no means guarantee the enduring perpetuation of civic nationalism. The need to analyze the changing dynamics of these movements rather than presuming nationalism to occur as a fait accompli is emphasized in the volume's introduction and resonates in both the European and postcolonial contexts. As Connor has stressed, nationalist movements are continuing processes without a teleological endpoint, instead reflecting ebbs and flows.[20] At the same time, it is advisable not to overly generalize on the basis of the experience of South Asia or sub-Saharan Africa precisely because of the extent of changing patterns of success and failure of both civic nationalist and ethnic nationalist movements.

While Connor underlines the difficulty in pinpointing the time period of the rise or decline of nationalism,[21] Schraeder shows in his chapter that it is indeed possible to determine moments that spell the end of civic nationalism in postcolonial cases. He begins by identifying the ten-year period during which a pan-Somali nationalist ideology was consolidated among political elites (1970s) and then argues that Somali nationalism was marked by a key event—what Schraeder refers to as a "turning point"—in the decay of nationalist integrity, after which the cycle of violence spun out of control. He insightfully suggests that the study of such turning points represents one important way in which current research into the study of postcolonial nationalism may profitably lend new insight not only to contemporary cases but also more generally to our ability to understand when, why, and how nationalist movements succeed, become paralyzed, or recede from political life.

NOTES

1. Donald Rothchild, *Managing Ethnic Conflict in Africa: Pressures and Incentives for Cooperation* (Washington, DC: Brookings Institution Press, 1997), 42–43, 72–73;

and Arend Lijphart, *Democracy in Plural Societies: A Comparative Exploration* (New Haven: Yale University Press, 1977).

2. See chapter 1 of this volume.

3. See also Rothchild, *Managing Ethnic Conflict in Africa,* 40–42.

4. Formerly Zaire.

5. Rothchild, *Managing Ethnic Conflict in Africa,* 31–36.

6. Ibid., and see chapters 4 and 5 of this volume.

7. J. R. Clammer, *The Cultural Politics of Pluralism in a Multiethnic Society* (Brookfield, VT: Ashgate, 1998); Edward M. Dew, *The Difficult Flowering of Surinam: Ethnicity and Politics in a Plural Society* (The Hague: Martinus Nijhoff, 1978); and Thomas Hylland Eriksen, *Common Denominators: Ethnicity, Nation-Building and Compromise in Mauritius* (New York: Berg, 1998).

8. Timothy D. Sisk, "Electoral System Choice in South Africa: Implications for Intergroup Moderation," *Nationalism and Ethnic Politics* 1, no. 2 (summer 1995): 178–204.

9. Cheryl Hendricks, "The National Question, Ethnicity, and the State: Some Insights on South Africa," in *The State and Democracy in Africa,* ed. Margaret C. Less and Georges Nzongola-Ntalaja (Trenton, NJ: Africa World Press, 1998).

10. See chapter 1 of this volume.

11. Raju G. C. Thomas, "Nations, States, and Secession," *Mediterranean Quarterly* 5, no. 4 (fall 1994): 55.

12. Rothchild, *Managing Ethnic Conflict in Africa,* 75–82.

13. Joshua B. Forrest, *Subnationalism in Africa: Ethnicity, Alliances, and Politics* (Boulder: Lynne Rienner, 2004).

14. See also Raju G. C. Thomas, "Nations, Nationalism and the State in South Asia: A Comparative Analysis" (paper presented at the annual meeting of the American Political Science Association, Atlanta, September 2–5, 1999).

15. Forrest, *Subnationalism in Africa.*

16. See Walker Connor's collection of essays, *Ethnonationalism: The Quest for Understanding* (Princeton: Princeton University Press, 1994).

17. Stephen Ndegwa, "Citizenship and Ethnicity: An Examination of Two Transition Movements in Kenyan Politics," *American Political Science Review* 91, no. 3 (1997): 599–616.

18. Walker Connor, "When Is a Nation?" *Ethnic and Racial Studies* 12, no. 1 (January 1990): 92–103.

19. See chapter 1 of this volume.

20. Connor, "When Is a Nation?"

21. Ibid.

3. From Malay Nationalism to a Malaysian Nation?

DIANE K. MAUZY

THE FEDERATION OF MALAYA gained its independence in 1957. Singapore and the Borneo states of Sabah and Sarawak joined with Malaya in 1963 to make the new country of Malaysia.[1] But the creation of an enlarged Malaysian federation never diluted Malay nationalism or confused the Malays as to "who belongs to the nation." The cleavages dividing the Malays from the non-Malays—the latter a residual category comprising mostly Chinese and Indians—coincide closely for race, religion, and culture[2] and have been the most salient political problem in Malaysia. Nationalism in Malaysia has always been associated with the Malays, as the indigenous race, while the group aspirations of the "immigrant races" have been marginalized as expressions of ethnic chauvinism.

This chapter seeks to explore the evolution of Malay nationalism from its fiery inception to the proposed goal of an ethnically inclusive civic nationalism.[3] Today, after three decades of elaborate economic preferences and with demographic changes making them a safe majority,[4] Malays are more sociopolitically and economically secure. This has allowed the government to articulate an ambitious goal of transforming, in thirty years, the basis of national identity in Malaysia from an ethnic-based form to a civic one it calls *Bangsa Malaysia*,[5] that is, from the fourth variant of Lowell Barrington's typology ("ethnic nation-protecting") to his third variant of "civic nation-building." However, because the Malay elites can and do periodically manipulate Malay fears and raise nationalist feelings for immediate political advantage, it is doubtful that the goal of achieving a civic nationalism can be achieved in the short term.

This chapter considers nationalism, with its great mobilizing power, to be largely, but not entirely, an elite-driven or constructed process. Still, as Barrington notes in his introductory chapter to this volume, nations and nationalisms are "not constructed out of thin air." In order for elites to be able to manipulate nationalist support, there must be some characteristics that seem to define the membership and territorial boundaries of the nation and make it somewhat cohesive and receptive to elite nationalist ideas. Elites and ideas cannot do everything—there must be some building blocks. These blocks are often described as "primordial" or "objective" characteristics by the cultural theorists, and they include such traits as language, religion, cultural values, and shared myths, especially concerning collective origins, as well as traditions fashioned by circumstances.[6]

While cultural distinctions and common objective characteristics help explain the identities of groups and nations, they cannot adequately explain the differences in political saliency and intensity of ethnic issues between different groups and nations at particular times, nor the actions taken or not taken. This has led some theorists to the conclusion that nations are subjective—the "largest community which, when the chips are down, effectively commands men's loyalty."[7] These theorists believe that nations are malleable to elite manipulation and that nationalism is constructed by elites, their ideas, and their control of the media, language, and education.[8] Hobsbawm and Ranger have shown how many "traditional" practices are quite recent inventions, and how an "existing customary traditional practice" is modified, ritualized and institutionalized to promote new national purposes.[9] Thus, when conflict arises, it generally comes from elite initiation as a result of political, economic, or status competition, or rational responses to incentives, rather than from the existence of cultural differences.[10]

Fortunately, there is a middle ground between the cultural theorists and the social constructionists. Some writers, often institutionalists such as Horowitz and Lijphart, when looking at ethnic conflict and nationalism, consider the interaction of a number of variables—cultural characteristics, beliefs and passions, elite manipulation, competition, the use of ideas, and prevailing institutional arrangements—to evaluate how identity, status, and power can all be reshaped and changed by elites, circumstances, and events.[11] This is the approach taken in this chapter.

National Identity & Nationalism Development

Before British colonial rule was established in the late nineteenth century, the Malay peninsula was an underpopulated and relatively ethnically homogeneous area controlled by a number of Malay rulers and powerful chiefs residing in reasonably well-defined territorial units. Malay was the common language, and Islam the predominant religion.

The British "forward movement" led to two indirectly ruled and decentralized segments—the four Federated Malay States (FMS) and the five less-regulated Unfederated Malay States (UMS)—as well as the directly ruled Straits Settlements (Singapore, Penang, and Malacca). Collectively this was known as British Malaya. Both the FMS and UMS were governed with the collaboration of the Malay rulers and chiefs and members of the traditional elite, many of whom served in the civil service. For its labor supply and commerce, the British opened the doors to Chinese immigration and later encouraged the immigration of Indians to work on the rubber plantations. The Malays were told to follow the guidance of their state rulers and were given certain legal "protections" to ensure the survival of their traditional culture and agricultural economy, separate from the modern export economy rapidly developing in the non-Malay- and European-populated urban areas.

The Impact of British Indirect Rule

Malay nationalism was conditioned by the nature of colonial rule as well as the prevailing feudal traditions. It was slow in developing, primarily because the Malays were loyal to their feudal rulers. These leaders showed little interest in political change, particularly after the British raised their incomes and status and thus enhanced feudalism. Early Malay nationalism was inspired by pan-Islamic activism in the Middle East, leading to a growth of religious schools and the spread of Islamic literature on the peninsula.[12] This was contained by Britain's promotion of a professional rural religious hierarchy, which struck an alliance with the rulers, who were in charge of state religious matters, and the traditional establishment.[13] There was also a small pan-Indonesian left-wing nationalist movement led by a group of Malay intelligentsia that resulted in the formation of some pen clubs and later some radical political organizations. However, the movement remained small and on the fringe until it died out. There were no peasant revolts in Malaya to stimulate left-wing support.

These three major Malay nationalist factions—the traditional elite, the Malay left, and the Islamic group—all believed in the idea of a Malay nation (*Bangsa Melayu*), and all were engaged in the task of resolving what constituted a Malay. According to Shamsul, all the factions agreed on the Malay language as a marker of Malayness but disagreed over the role of Islam and the state rulers.[14] The traditional elite supported language, religion, and royalty as constituting the key pillars of Malayness, but within a secular state that restricted the political role of Islam. The leftists concurred with the secular state but wanted to end feudalism, whereas the Islamic group favored ending royalty but sought a much larger role for Islam.[15] The British favored the traditional aristocratic faction, whose nationalism was only faintly anticolonial. It was clear also that when exposed to prospects of change or perceived threats, the Malays on the whole "instinctively turned towards their traditional leaders."[16]

During the war between Japan and China, the Chinese in British Malaya remitted large sums of money to China. The Malay elites, already fearful of Chinese numbers and startled by evidence of Chinese wealth, began expressing concern that they might end up like the "Red Indians" of North America, with their culture relegated to a museum. Nonetheless, as British historian Hall notes, "before the Japanese invasion [of Malaya] the Malays were the most unpolitically-minded people in South-East Asia. That blissful state of mind, however, was not to survive the occupation period."[17]

The Impact of the Japanese Interregnum

The Japanese occupation (1941–45) contributed to the growth of Malay nationalism by destroying the myth of European superiority and by promoting the anticolonial theme of "Asia for the Asians," which found a receptive chord among Malays. It also had the effect of greatly worsening ethnic relations. Most Malays passively collaborated, whereas in the jungles the almost entirely Chinese Malayan People's Anti-Japanese Army, later the Malayan Communist Party, worked with the Allies to oppose the Japanese. "The rigors of war and occupation . . . generated tensions that produced escalating political mobilization based on ethnicity."[18] At the end of the war, in the absence of authority before the Allies returned, widespread ethnic "score settling" and random violence left a legacy of ethnic fear and distrust. Still, it could be said in 1945 that "the development of nationalism in Malaya seemed twenty-five years behind the rest of Southeast Asia."[19]

Nationalism Leading to Independence

But it was the British decision in 1946, without consultation, to implement a new and strikingly altered political system in Malaya that galvanized Malay nationalism. The Malayan Union, as it was called, represented a total departure from prewar policy. It called for liberal citizenship terms for the non-Malays, the end of Malay "special rights," and the elimination of the powers and status of the rulers. One possible reason for this "about face" was that Britain wanted to get the tin and rubber industries stabilized quickly in order to help pay for reconstruction.[20]

Malay popular reaction against the Malayan Union, to the surprise of the British, was swift, bitter, and intense. It was the key causal factor that provided the catalyst to Malay nationalism that prewar colonialism, pan-Islamic reform, pan-Indonesianism, and a world war could not stimulate. The Malay elites believed that a political system that offered a common citizenship and equal political rights for all would destroy the Malay race and unjustly strip Malays of their inherent rights as the historical community.[21] The Malay congresses held in 1946, to ward off the prospect of "racial extinction," led to the creation of a central organization, the United Malays National Organization (UMNO), which became the primary organization for protecting and promoting Malay interests. The conservative, English-speaking traditional leaders, formerly supportive of British rule, now led the struggle against the Malayan Union. "They constituted the leadership core of UMNO . . . [and they] emerged as the undisputed leaders of Malay society as a whole."[22]

The British, occupied with fighting a communist guerrilla insurrection, agreed to abrogate the Malayan Union. They invited UMNO to draft a plan for a more suitable constitutional arrangement. UMNO then pushed through a plan for a federation with centralized powers, Malay special rights were restored, many of the powers of the rulers were reinstated, and citizenship regulations were made complex and strict. The Federation of Malaya came into force in February 1948. As Shamsul notes, the English translation of the federation does not capture the full meaning or emotive symbolism of the Malay words *Persekutuan Tanah Melayu,* which really mean "federation of the land of the Malays."[23] With the federation, the Malays prevailed over competing visions of nation, state, and citizenship.

The non-Malays had been basically apathetic about the Malayan Union. Although supporting it seemed to be in their interest, most attention was focused on important events taking place in China and India, respectively.[24] After the British announced they were abandoning the Malayan Union, there was a belated attempt to organize a nationwide protest, but it failed, and the non-Malays acquiesced to a federation with safeguards for the Malays.

The Membership Boundaries

The struggle to defeat the Malayan Union brought together Malays—elites and followers—from all the states under an umbrella organization, UMNO, and this served to set the membership boundaries and, at least informally, to define "who belongs to the nation." In terms of "objective" characteristics, race itself was not a criterion, and the boundaries were to some considerable extent malleable.[25] Many Malays have ancestry derived from other groups—Thais, Burmese, Bugis, Acehnese, Menangkabau, as well as Chinese and Indian.

Thus, the issue of "who was a Malay" was worked out on the bases of culture, religion, and language. A Malay was a Muslim who habitually followed Malay customs and habits and spoke the Malay language. Additionally, to be a Malay, one needed to be the subject of a state ruler, since the state monarchical system was an integral part of Malay culture and helped make Malays distinctive from some of the groups in Sumatra that share certain racial, religious, and language similarities. While there was a growing identification with the federal state, state allegiances and identities gave way only slowly and incompletely. For the non-Malays, self-perceptions of identity, coinciding with those of the Malays, appeared to be more racial: a "Baba Chinese" who spoke Malay but not Chinese, and who dressed and ate like a Malay, was still a Chinese. In fact, religion was a stronger distinguishing marker than race.

With the membership boundaries relatively established, the emphasis of nationalism in the country turned to the threat the "other" posed to the essential survival of the nation. To the Malays, the "others" were the "non-Malays," primarily the Chinese. A key feature of Malay nationalism was its highly developed sense of "us versus them" and its keen sense of purpose in defending everything considered Malay. For the non-Malays, on the defensive and belatedly recognizing that Malaya was in fact their home, the "other" meant the Malays and Malay demands that seemed to relegate them to second-class status.

After 1946, the British realized they could not cultivate a civic nationalism in Malaya as the country progressed toward independence. The vast majority of Malays would not countenance the idea that there should be political equality or common citizenship. But the colonial authorities insisted that they would consider a transfer of power only when the major communities demonstrated that they could coexist peacefully. To this end, the British attempted to promote a multiethnic political party. However, the communities were already mobilized on the basis of ethnic political organizations: UMNO, PAS (Partai Islam), and the Malay Nationalist Party (MNP) for the Malays—the Malayan Chinese Association (MCA) and the Malayan Indian Congress (MIC) for the "others." Few Malays were attracted to the idea of a multiethnic party.

Among the Malay elites and followers there was a high degree of agreement on the content and organization of Malay nationalism: UMNO, as the dominant Malay organization in the country, would protect the interests of the Malays while charting the course toward independence. "Protection" was the most important factor driving Malay nationalism. Any perceived weakening of protection generated an emotional outpouring of nationalist fervor designed to reinvigorate this protection. The case of the first president of UMNO, Dato Onn bin Ja'afar, provides an example. Influenced by strong British support for a multiethnic party, Onn tried to get UMNO to open its membership to all communities in 1950.[26] So strong was the Malay fear of the "other" that despite the fact that Onn was perceived as the preeminent Malay leader, the effect was that the membership rejected both him and his proposal. As Muzaffar concludes, Onn was viewed as "no longer capable of performing the role of a protector. . . . Unquestioning loyalty then had a condition: the leader had to guarantee the security of the Malay position in relation to the non-Malay situation."[27] Because Onn's new views were grasped out of "thin air," it is a prime example of elite manipulation or social construction *not* working. UMNO elected a new president, Tunku Abdul Rahman, who vowed to keep UMNO exclusively as the vanguard of the Malays.

Onn went on to inaugurate a multiethnic party in 1951. The Independence of Malaya Party (IMP), however, was decisively beaten in municipal elections in 1952 because the Malays would not support it, and it was disbanded two years later. Ethnic issues were paramount, boundaries were becoming less malleable, and political support gravitated to the ethnic-based parties.[28]

The Territorial Boundaries

Unlike many other postcolonial cases, the territorial boundaries of the Malay nation were largely established before colonial rule. The British contributed to the historical integrity of the peninsula by reclaiming the four northern states from Siamese (Thai) control in 1909. The post–World War II British proposal to unite the nine Malay states and add the enclaves of Malacca and Penang made sense demographically and politically. The Malayan Union and its successor, the Federation of Malaya, unified the peninsula. The only geographic aberration was the exclusion of the heavily Chinese-populated island of Singapore at the southern tip of the peninsula. The territorial boundaries proposed by the British were adopted by UMNO as the appropriate ones. Although some Malay nationalists coveted Singapore—for its riches and its historical connections—all agreed that demographically it was impossible to incorporate Singapore because it would make the Malays a minority in their own country.

While Malays' allegiance to their states remained strong, the idea of the larger federal state as the historic "homeland" of the nation took hold. The concept of territory became a highly emotional feature of Malay nationalism vis-à-vis the other communities as the country progressed toward independence. The Malays were constantly told by their elites that, unlike the Chinese or Indians, they had no other homeland and that the Malays were the rightful "sons of the soil" of the Federation of Malaya. The "others" were always immigrants, no matter how long they had been there, because they could always "go home," whereas the Malays had no where else to go. This argument complemented the perception of threat posed by the "other." Integrated into Malay nationalism was a deeply ingrained fear that if the Malays somehow lost control of their territory, they would become racially extinct.

Nationalist Movements/Parties in Malaya

UMNO, the Malay mass movement that was set up "to save" the Malays from the constitutional changes proposed by the British in 1946, transformed itself into an independence movement and then the leading nationalist party competing for political power. When the Tunku was elected president of UMNO in 1951, one of his first actions was to amend UMNO's slogan from *Hidup Melayu!* (Long Live the Malays!) to *Merdeka!* (Independence!).[29] However, in order to attain independence, the Malay elites understood it would need to make some accommodation with the non-Malays.

Municipal elections were held in the early 1950s, and the first major test was the Kuala Lumpur election in 1952. The electorate was overwhelmingly Malay. UMNO expected a strong challenge from the British-favored IMP, and UMNO badly lacked campaign funds. The winner was likely to emerge as the party that would lead the country to independence. Complicating matters by playing a spoiler role, the wealthy MCA indicated that it would put up some non-Chinese candidates. Then came the serendipitous solution. The local leaders of UMNO and the MCA concluded an ad hoc electoral agreement that called for joint candidates and for the MCA to finance the campaign. There was no attempt at a common platform.[30] The election results revealed the utility of such a pact: UMNO-MCA won nine of the twelve seats.

This arrangement was institutionalized at the national level, and in 1953 an alliance was inaugurated as a permanent coalition, with the MIC soon added to it. The elites of the three ethnic parties then worked out, after tough bargaining, a series of compromises that settled some key constitutional problems and became known as "the bargain." It became evident "that the price to be paid by the non-Malays for full participation in the activities of the Federation was acceptance of certain forms associated with Malay traditions."[31] Specifically, the bargain offered liberal citizenship requirements and *jus soli* (citizenship by right of birth in a country) as the major concession by the Malays in return for the acceptance by the non-Malays of the position of the rulers, Malay special rights, Islam as the state religion, and Malay as the sole official language in ten years' time.

Hence, the three pillars of Malayness—language, religion, and royalty—would now have constitutional protection. There was also an informal understanding among the ethnic elites: UMNO and the Malays would be primus inter pares (first among equals) in politics, while in return the business pursuits of the non-Malays would remain free of hindrances or persecution. Although much was purposely left vague, the constitutional bargain and elite understanding satisfied the major claims of each of the communities and led to ethnic solidarity favoring independence. Lijphart considers the arrangement that evolved in Malaysia a "reasonably successful case" of "consociational democracy" until 1969, despite the fact that the Malays were quite dominant.[32]

The degree of support for the Alliance and its elite accommodation was evident at the first general elections in 1955, when the Alliance won all but one seat and 82 percent of the popular vote. All of the non-Malay Alliance candidates won, some of them against Malay opposition, despite a predominantly Malay electorate. The results attested to UMNO's nationalist credentials and the viability of the Alliance concept.

After the elections, progress toward independence was swift, and in August 1957, the Federation of Malaya became independent in a peaceful and cordial transfer of power. The Tunku, whose leadership was undisputed, became the first prime minister and formed a multiethnic cabinet.

Nationalism after Independence

A desire for independence and the threat posed by the communist guerrilla insurrection constituted strong causal factors leading the respective ethnic elites to reach compromises and understandings. However, by the same token, many aspects of state organization and governance were not resolved with independence. As stated in the preceding, it was understood among the elites that the Malays would be the senior partner politically and that the non-Malays would not be hindered in their economic pursuits. But other questions, such as who in ethnic terms was eligible for the top federal and state governmental positions, lacked clearly spelled out answers. Zakaria argues that the younger generation never really understood the tacitly agreed provisions.[33]

Furthermore, some troubling circumstances existed at independence. The Malays were the most feudalistic, least educated, least urbanized, and least economically advanced community in the country despite the fact that the feudal Malay nationalist elites would dominate politically, and Malay culture and traditions, religion and language, were protected in the constitution. The "bargain" seemed to promise protection of the status quo in terms of intergroup relations, except that there were suggestions that the Malays would somehow slowly catch up economically. In fact, the Malays failed to make up ground economically. As the result of compelling the non-Malays to learn the Malay language, its protection as a pillar of Malay identity collapsed. Increasingly, the social marker of substance was Islam.

How Ideas of Nationalism Changed Following Independence

Superficially, one might think that not much has changed concerning nationalism since independence—the ethnic basis of nationalism remains supreme, the parties and party system are largely unchanged, UMNO remains the dominant party in the dominant coalition, and the Malays still control the political process and still enjoy certain special rights. Ethnic divisions have slowed the growth of any unifying nationalism.

In fact, the ideas central to Malay nationalism have evolved from wanting "to save" the race from extinction and gain independence, to protecting Malay political, cultural, and religious symbols, to gaining an equal and more secure social and economic footing with the other communities. In other words, the basis of Malay nationalism has evolved generally, but incompletely, from primordial to instrumental concerns. The ideas that have guided Malay nationalism since 1957 can be divided into rough time periods: the period of being primus inter pares amidst ambiguities from 1957 to 1969; the assertion of Malay hegemony from 1969 to the early 1990s; and now Malay control with some modification by invoking a new, external enemy (the West) and holding out the promise of converting the bases of identification in Malaysia to a nonethnic national identity by the year 2020.

1957–69

The period from 1957 to 1969 was typified by a modus operandi of leaving ambiguous the difficult ethnic demands not easily settled by trade-offs and at the same time trying to maintain the public fiction that the communities were "basically" equal in the ruling Alliance. During this period there were three episodes that served, in different ways, to challenge UMNO and Malay dominance and gradually radicalize Malay nationalism.

The first episode occurred in 1959, when a new group of MCA leaders decided to take a tougher stand with UMNO in order to secure more liberal policies on language and education, as well as a larger allocation of candidacies for the MCA in the upcoming elections. The leaders were stunned at the ferocity of UMNO's response to the challenge to its dominance. The Tunku ordered a withdrawal of all demands, the purging of Chinese "chauvinists," and the authority personally to select all MCA candidates, or else UMNO would rule without Chinese participation. This shattered the myth of equality within the Alliance.

The second episode followed the creation of Malaysia in 1963 and focused on Singapore's tempestuous two years in the federation before it was expelled in 1965. Singapore's People's Action Party (PAP) challenged the entire basis of Malay nationalism and Malay claims to dominance. The

Chinese-dominated but multiethnic PAP called for a "Malaysian Malaysia" based on racial equality rather than a "Malay Malaysia" that gave special rights and privileges to the Malays. It contested seats in peninsula Malaysia, and in 1965 it began putting together an opposition coalition to rival the Alliance.

The PAP challenge alarmed the Malays, stirred up old (supposedly "settled") issues, and heightened the expectations of the Chinese, particularly the youth, for a political realignment. The issue of language became a focal point. The Chinese called for the wider official use of the Chinese language, or even its elevation to co-official status. This move was countered by Malay determination to secure the full implementation of the bargain over language. UMNO Youth threw down the gauntlet: if language was to be reconsidered, so should citizenship. There were nasty race riots in Singapore in the summer and fall of 1964, and UMNO "ultras" called for action against the PAP and the arrest of its leaders. Ethnic outbidding started to erode the leadership of the moderates. The Tunku decided that Singapore must be kicked out of Malaysia. The separation was announced in August 1965.

Singapore's expulsion did not, however, resolve all the problems. The Tunku had alienated the UMNO ultras, who had wanted him to send in the army to take over the island, and now they wanted him replaced. For the non-Malays, a new party, the Democratic Action Party (DAP), which espoused the by now familiar formula of a "Malaysian Malaysia" with ethnic equality, was allowed to register. It is clear that the PAP's actions set off a whole chain of reactions that reverberated through the system for years.

The third episode was Indonesia's limited "war," called *Konfrontasi*, against Malaysia from 1963 to 1966. Because of its territorial enlargement in adding the Borneo states of Sabah and Sarawak, and also Singapore, to Malaya to form Malaysia, Indonesia challenged the new Malaysia as a "neocolonialist plot."[34] Konfrontasi did not constitute much of a military threat, but it posed both a minor problem and an opportunity politically for the UMNO Malay leaders. It was a minor problem because initially it split Malay sympathies. Some of the Malays who supported the small opposition Partai Islam and the Socialist Front were sympathetic to a pan-Indonesian perspective. However, it also provided the government with the opportunity to isolate and discredit (and occasionally arrest) these same small pockets of left-wing and Islamic nationalists. Further, it helped solidify non-Malay loyalties at a time when the government was still fighting the (primarily Chinese) Communists in the jungle and problems with Singapore were beginning that could have alienated the non-Malays. Thus while Konfrontasi did not have much of an effect on Malay nationalism, it contributed mildly to state-building efforts while it lasted. UMNO and the Alliance emerged from the 1964 general election with their dominance strengthened, but this was not to last.

1969–90

The second period began with the May 1969 elections. The elections were conducted in an atmosphere of escalating ethnic militancy. The Tunku was perceived by many Malays as having sold out the country to the non-Malays, and at the same time the Alliance non-Malay leaders found themselves no longer able to keep their followers in line.[35] The election results revealed that the opposition had made considerable gains against the dominant Alliance. The non-Malays were jubilant, while the Malays felt that they were once again in danger of losing control of their country. The tensions generated exploded into serious ethnic rioting and led to a proclamation of a state of emergency and changes in the political system. Under the state of emergency, parliament and the constitution were suspended, and the country came under the de facto rule of a Malay-dominated joint military-civilian National Operations Council under the directorship of Deputy Prime Minister Tun Razak, who would become prime minister in 1970. Clearly this challenge to the ethnic status quo when coupled with growing Malay perceptions that independence had not delivered sociocultural security or economic progress resulted in this watershed event. This led in turn to changes in the political system that ushered in a period of Malay political hegemony and the introduction of preferential policies favoring the Malays.

Razak and his advisers decided that Malay economic grievances were the chief causal factors leading to the riots on May 13. Just protecting the three pillars of Malayness—language, religion, and royalty—was no longer enough for the Malay masses. The brand of Malay nationalism espoused by the UMNO ultras had inflamed the Malays with resentment against the non-Malays, and this frustration was aggravated by a growing belief that the Malay-led government was not doing enough to help the Malays "catch up" to the other groups economically.

Politically, Razak told the country that there needed to be a "new realism" about ethnic relations, that "we have swept these problems under the carpet. Now we must face up to them squarely. . . . We have to have some form of code of conduct or ground rules."[36] Razak's government countenanced no ambiguity: the Malays would openly dominate, although in a spirit of ethnic cooperation. Political competition and debate would be restricted by constitutional amendments and new sedition laws. At the same time, Razak embarked on a coalition-building scheme to broaden representation in the government and thereby reduce "politicking" that might interfere with economic development plans. This eventually resulted in something resembling a grand coalition of parties under a new umbrella organization, the Barisan Nasional (National Front).[37] Although grand coalitions constitute an important conflict management technique in Lijphart's consociational democracy scheme, Lijphart believes that after 1971 Malaysia could no longer be considered a consociational case because the Malays were virtually hegemonic and the state was not democratic enough.[38]

Parallel with political initiatives, the government decided on a set of preferential policies favoring the Malays that was aimed at restructuring society to correct economic imbalances—by reducing and eliminating the identification of race with economic functions—and to eradicate poverty.[39] The key instrument was an elaborate New Economic Policy (NEP) designed to redistribute wealth in the country over a twenty-year period with active government assistance.[40] The most prominent target was for the Bumiputera (Malays and other indigenous people) to own and manage at least 30 percent of the total commercial and industrial activities in the economy in all categories by 1990.

As 1990 approached, the Malay leaders stated that the NEP targets would not be reached and that preferential policies would have to continue. Many non-Malays, including some from the ruling coalition, disputed the government's statistics and contended that the Malays had already reached their targets. They believed that the figures were distorted by a statistical sleight of hand.[41]

It was clear that the NEP experiment produced some dramatic successes in restructuring society. "The NEP . . . was Malaysia's true ideology, at least for Malays."[42] In general, the Bumiputera appeared to have substantially reached their 1990 targets, and poverty was also significantly reduced. There had been a huge increase in Malay university enrollments and graduations, and there were many times more middle-class Malays living and working in urban areas. The cities in Malaysia increasingly reflected a

Malay and Muslim appearance. There was also a new, obvious, superrich, politically well-connected Malay entrepreneurial class that could rival the wealthy non-Malays.[43] Likewise, while many non-Malays resented the preferential policies and some were victimized by them, for most of the non-Malays life was better than had been expected after the riots; many had found ways to survive the restrictions of the NEP.[44] The economy was experiencing consistently fast growth, averaging 6.7 percent GDP growth per year between 1971 and 1990, and there was enough to go around for most everyone to prosper.

All of this had a striking impact on Malay mass attitudes that made them somewhat less receptive to the kind of nationalism that UMNO had always proclaimed as feudal protector of the Malays. There was now a higher percentage of Malays in the population of the country—an important security factor—and many were better educated and more prosperous and self-confident. With years of high economic growth, they had become believers in the culture of success promoted by the government and signified by the slogan *Malaysia oleh!* (Malaysia can!).[45] They no longer felt so threatened, and they were slower to close ranks behind UMNO when it rattled its saber about the threats posed by the non-Malays. As this transpired, criticism grew about official corruption and the use of preferences to enrich party cronies and their clients. In the mid-1980s, disagreements over the distribution of resources and issues of patronage and cronyism resulted in a split in UMNO that threatened its dominance and led to a marked increase in repression and an end to the independence of the judiciary.[46]

The 1990 elections mark the end of the second period. It was a difficult election for UMNO and the Barisan Nasional. Those who defected or were expelled from UMNO formed a new Malay political party and set out to put together a rival multiethnic coalition. The non-Malays were generally dissatisfied that there was not going to be an end to preferential policies. The Barisan Nasional turned in its worst ever performance in this election, losing two states to the opposition, although it retained a clear majority in parliament.

1991 TO THE PRESENT

The third period began in 1991 and continues to this day. Politically, a wounded UMNO needed to hold its share of Malay support by delivering on economic growth while at the same time shoring up flagging non-Malay support. The period is marked by four developments: the gradual easing of some ethnic preferences through the National Development Policy (NDP), the proclamation of "Vision 2020" with its promise of a civic nationalism in thirty years, a shift in the "other"—with the West taking the place of the non-Malays as "the enemy," and the resultant electoral successes in 1995 and 1999 by the Barisan Nasional because of solid non-Malay support.

The NDP became the successor to the NEP in 1991. It retains some of the basic restructuring and poverty alleviation goals of the NEP but has no numerical targets or a specified time frame. The policy is vague and seems focused more on growth.[47] Implementation has been more accommodating to the non-Malays, without seeming to betray Malay interests, and thus it has been less controversial and has helped moderate ethnic tensions.[48] Stafford offers an interesting explanation for what has transpired. He believes that globalization required some liberalization of economic policy, which meant a scaling back of the NEP. So, while the successes of the NEP helped alleviate Malay grievances, its subsequent scaling back helped alleviate the non-Malay backlash it had created.[49]

Vision 2020, Bangsa Malaysia, and the "New Malay": Toward a Civic Nationalism?

The second development is the idea, launched in 1991 by Prime Minister Mahathir Mohamad, of Vision 2020.[50] A document "meant to seize the imagination and to inspire,"[51] it offers some appealing goals and challenges, basically envisioning Malaysia as a fully industrialized state with no ethnic divisions by 2020. By far the most ambitious challenge is the one directed to nation-building: to establish a united Malaysian nation with a sense of common and shared destiny, at peace with itself and living in harmony "in full and free partnership, made up of one '*Bangsa Malaysia.*'"[52] Vision 2020 appears to mean a transformation of the ethnic principles underlying Malaysian society, away from Malay nationalism and toward a civic nationalism with more inclusive membership boundaries.

Part and parcel of the Vision 2020 is the concept of the "New Malay" introduced by Mahathir in 1991. The New Malay has many positive attributes, but these can be pared down to the image of a successful and ethical businessperson or professional, one who has thrown off the feudalistic cultural shackles of the "Old Malay" and can meet all challenges without government assistance. Clearly, if the ethnic bases of the state are going to be discarded, the Malay community must be able to compete successfully on its own with the other communities.

The idea of Bangsa Malaysia has captured the imagination and raised the expectations of many non-Malays, especially the youth.[53] Further, it accompanies a relaxation of some ethnic restrictions—for example in the implementation of the NDP; the opening of the Amanah Saham National Savings Scheme to non-Malays; the Education Act of 1995, which allows for private universities; and the reduction of the quota for university places reserved for Bumiputera after 1985 to 55:45. As Stafford points out, the economic achievements of Malaysia "have created a high level of national pride" for all ethnic groups, which he sees as the basis for creating a Malaysian identity.[54]

However, the notion of Bangsa Malaysia leaves not only critical questions unanswered and vital details unspecified but some contradictory trends as well. The issuance of new identity cards, for example, throws doubt on the government's sincerity concerning working toward a civic nationalism. While the new IDs have eliminated race, they have added the category of religion, a move that the leader of the opposition finds a "retrogressive step" for the nation-building process.[55] So intense were objections by the non-Malays that the government has altered the regulations so that only Muslims will have to state their religion on the cards, an unsatisfactory concession that seems to miss the point about identity and division.[56] In another incident, a government minister said that a prominent opposition leader, the wife of the jailed former deputy prime minister, could not lead the Malays because she "did not have a Malay soul," implying that she was Chinese and therefore unfit. Not only was the accusation untrue, it was offensive and led a Chinese journalist to note, "It's difficult to be a Malaysian in Malaysia."[57]

Meanwhile, the Bangsa Malaysia idea has serious implications for Malay nationalism and Malay hegemony, and it has created a mixed reaction among Malays. The construct of the New Malay, as pointed out by Shamsul, means compromising two of the old central pillars of Malayness—royalty and language.[58] The notion of Bangsa Malaysia—a civic nationalism—has been superficially, or theoretically, endorsed by UMNO Malays. At the same time, when concrete changes have been mentioned, like altering the constitution to remove Malay special rights or opening up UMNO to the non-Malays, there has been no consensus.[59] This leads one to ask whether any withering away of ethnicity can occur without a Malay backlash and whether Malays would really be content to submerge Malay nationalism in favor of a Bangsa Malaysia?

A third development affecting the nature of Malay nationalism has been a shift in the "other"—the enemy—away from the non-Malays and to the West.[60] This has been primarily the work of Mahathir, who has apparently long-harbored anti-Western feelings (although he also viewed the Chinese as "the enemy" and he blamed them for his electoral defeat in 1969[61]). Malaysia itself, including the Foreign Affairs Department and most Malays, has not been particularly hostile to the West, although there has been a rise in anti-Americanism as a result of Muslim perceptions that the United States has launched a war against Islam. What is unclear is whether shifting the target in the 1990s from the non-Malays to the West was a deliberate move to advance the notion of Bangsa Malaysia or simply a domestic political ploy. However, the focus on the West as the enemy has taken considerable pressure off of the non-Malays, who are now only occasionally depicted in the media as a "threat," and this has undoubtedly helped improve ethnic relations.[62]

The final development was the electoral turnaround in 1995—sustained in 1999—after the setbacks in 1990. This reversal of fortunes was largely a result of renewed non-Malay support. The economic climate was good for both 1990 and 1995, and the election issues were basically the same. The difference appears to be the way the non-Malays responded to the easing of the NDP, the idea of Bangsa Malaysia, and the shifting of the target of Malay nationalism away from them. These causal factors help explain why the non-Malays voted so heavily for the Barisan Nasional and helped provide it with its greatest electoral performance ever—winning 65 percent of the popular vote (up 13 percent from 1990). In the November 1999 general election, with the Malays again badly split as a result of the firing and jailing of former deputy prime minister Anwar Ibrahim, the government again needed, and received, the solid support of the non-Malays to offset a considerable loss of Malay votes. To get their vote, government propagandists resorted to frightening the non-Malays with the specter of ethnic violence and/or an opposition-imposed Islamic state. At the same time, the government continued to woo them with the prospect of a not-too-distant end to ethnic distinctions that would open the membership boundaries of the nation to all citizens.

Conclusion: Lessons from Malaysia about Nationalism after Independence

Malay nationalism has shifted from a defensive, almost frantic, posture depicted in such stark terms as the "survival of the Malay race and culture" to an independence goal phase and then, after independence, gradually from a primordial phase to an instrumental phase where Malay nationalism demanded socioeconomic parity. Throughout, successful Malay leaders have presented themselves as protectors. The proclaimed goal of Vision 2020 to achieve a civic nationalism as the next phase is an interesting idea. While nationalism is a normative concept, many would agree that a citizen-oriented notion of national identity with inclusive membership boundaries constitutes a more tolerant brand of nationalism than that of the potentially volatile ethnic nationalisms.[63] The ability of Malay elites to raise ethnic fears and ignite Malay nationalism remains, however, a potent force, and each time it is manipulated for political advantage, the Vision 2020 goal seems farther away.

During the lead-up to the 1999 elections, the cabinet endorsed "in principle" the seventeen points designed to lessen discrimination put forward by Suqui (the Malaysian Chinese Organizations Election Appeals Committee). However, in mid-2000 Mahathir denounced Suqui, likening the group to Communists and religious extremists, and he stated that the seventeen points could not be accepted. Soon after, the government proposed creating integrated "Vision Schools," an idea that was strenuously rejected by the Chinese community as a plot to end Chinese-language education.[64] Following a government by-election loss in a previously safe mixed constituency of Lunas, Kedah, because of the desertion of 60 percent of both Chinese and Malays, the government-controlled Malay press emotionally lambasted the loyalty of the Chinese.[65] This was followed in early 2001 with an impassioned call for Malays to unite to prevent the non-Malays from taking advantage of their disunity. Once again, for a short while, the non-Malays became the enemy.[66] The readiness with which the UMNO elites have been willing to sabotage the goals of Vision 2020 and a Bangsa Malaysia for purposes of political expediency makes one question their seriousness in achieving these aims.

The Malaysian experience suggests that postnationalist concerns may be sequential, in the sense that the defense of primordial characteristics may take precedence until the dangers to these passionate issues seem to subside, and then nationalism may evolve to more instrumental and "rational" concerns. However, the Malaysian case also suggests that primordial passions remain close to the surface and can be rekindled under certain circumstances, thus making ethnic emotions easy for elites to manipulate. Hence, however sequential the route followed, it is not always unidirectional—the intensity of nationalist feelings ebbs and flows, depending on circumstances and elite manipulation.

This case also confirms the merits of taking the middle ground between the cultural theorists and the social constructionists. Nationalism in Malaysia has been largely elite manipulated, but the example of how abruptly the Malays dropped their top leader when he tried to change the direction of Malay nationalism illustrates that elites cannot just bend identities and construct nationalism "out of thin air" without the risk of losing followers. Elites, to manipulate, must construct with the "raw materials" and "building blocks" that they possess. The Malaysian experience also indicates that a policy of ethnic preferences, handled skillfully, *can* work, so long as it is accompanied by rapid growth that expands the economic pie.

Barrington's five variants of postindependence nationalism illuminate some interesting facets of the Malaysian case. His idea of a combination of variants seems relevant as well. Territory was an issue during the first postindependence phase, 1957–69. Malaya became Malaysia in 1963 with the additions of Singapore, Sabah, and Sarawak, and then Singapore was dramatically expelled from the federation in 1965. The expansion of territory in 1963 seems to confirm the "external-territory-claiming" impulse of variant 1, while the expulsion of a valuable piece of territory seems to contradict it. The answer to this apparent paradox is that variant 1 does not really fit the Malaysian case. For a number of reasons (the Communist influence in Singapore, the urging of the British, ethnic considerations, etc.), Malaya somewhat reluctantly incorporated more territory to become Malaysia. But to the Malays, there was no homeland beyond Malaya, and they had no strong attachment to the new territories. This made the expulsion of Singapore in 1965 a reasonably risk-free task for the Malay elites. Thus it could be said that the causal factor of having a perceived homeland outside the original territory of the state did not obtain and did not influence Malay nationalism.

The second ("sovereignty-protecting") variant of responding to internal, external, and mixed threats also has limited applicability to the Malaysian case. Internally, despite constituting 40 percent of the population, the minority communities are territorially dispersed and have never contested the Malay assertion that Malaya is Bangsa Melayu—the rightful homeland of the Malays. Externally, despite the fact that most non-Malays would call Malaysia their "home"—and some desperately want to make Malaysia the focus of their loyalties—it would not be considered by them or by the Malays as their "ancestral homeland." Many Malays think the Chinese and Indians identify with, and perhaps harbor secret loyalties toward, China and India.[67] Certainly the Communist insurgency, comprising mostly Chinese insurgents, impugned the loyalties of all Chinese, but this was basically over before independence.[68]

Variant 5 has some applicability to Malaysia, but only mildly, to the extent that some Malays believe they are entitled to make the treatment of the Malay minority in Singapore their business. However, the Singapore Malays do not look to Malaysia for protection and often bluntly reject Malaysian outbursts on their behalf. It is mainly a ploy in the turbulent foreign relations of Malaysia and Singapore, although Kuala Lumpur is careful to control the extent and duration of "outrage" Malays are encouraged to feel occasionally over events or conditions in Singapore.

There are lessons to be found in variants 3 and 4, both of which concern membership and the question of "Who is the nation?" The "ethnic nation-protecting" variant 4 fits the Malaysia case closely, for all three phases. This can be seen in preferential or "positive-discriminatory" state policies designed to protect and enhance the opportunities of the Malays. Some of these were agreed upon before independence. In return for liberal citizenship provisions, non-Malays agreed to a number of "special rights" and constitutional guarantees for the Malays, Islam as the state religion, Malay as the sole official language in ten years' time, and an understanding that politically the Malays would be primus inter pares. However, the savage May 1969 ethnic riots and state of emergency demonstrated that difficult ethnic issues remained contested and unresolved (including even the language issue, despite earlier agreements). May 1969 was a watershed: after this the Malays strongly asserted their political hegemony. Not only was the Malay language made official but it became the language of instruction in government schools, and its predominant display was required in all public places. Further, as indicated earlier, a number of social, economic, and educational preferential policies were put in place, led by the New Economic Policy.

The third variant, "civic nation-building," is of considerable interest. It fits the Malaysian case only imperfectly, but it seems to indicate possible future directions. Corresponding to the period from 1991, already the severity of preferences has been reduced, the Malay elites have proclaimed a goal of achieving a civic nationalism by 2020, and the target of Malay nationalism has been shifted to a new "other"—the West. As a result, there have been improvements in ethnic relations, and there may be an incipient "Malaysian identity" emerging, existing side by side with, but subordinate to, the traditional ethnic identities.[69] Certainly, the idea has raised non-Malay expectations, especially among the young.

Still, achieving a Malaysian identity will be difficult, and, even if achieved, as Resnick points out, this is "no guarantee of comity."[70] There are huge problems involved in the dismantling of what is a state that is centrally constructed around ethnic institutions and politically based on the principles of Malay hegemony and Malay nationalism. Vision 2020 offers no insight at all into how specific problems related to achieving a Bangsa Malaysia are to be overcome, nor are its economic targets likely to be attained, given the setbacks suffered in the 1997–98 recession. Further, and most significantly, there is no concurrence at all among Malays for major reforms.

The causal factors examined in this chapter show that the nationalist route most strongly pursued in Malaysia is variant 4, although current policy directions indicate the possibility that it may be moving toward variant 3. These are perhaps the most benign of the nationalist patterns. Malay nationalism has escaped the compulsion to exercise control of external territory, the state does not have to contend with secessionist movements, and the role of Malays in seeking to protect ethnic brethren living outside the boundaries of the state is minimal.

A lesson from the Malaysian case seems to be that nationalist aims after independence are unlikely to be static or unidirectional from primordial to instrumental. Rather, there can be an ebb and flow to nationalist emotions and concerns, often constructed, and the possible routes they follow can change over time and backtrack as well. The resilience of nationalism is confirmed. The Malaysian case also shows that, depending on what variant or combinations of variants of nationalism are applicable, sharp divisions along ethnic lines need not always result in persistent violence or instability. Rather, with skillful leadership, it may be possible to arrange a form of the Malaysian "bargain" and, over time, even to pursue a civic form of national identity.

NOTES

1. In 1965, Singapore was expelled from Malaysia after a series of misunderstandings and two race riots.

2. And previously for language, occupation, and urban-rural residence.

3. As noted by Barrington in his introduction, the idea of civic or political nationalism versus ethnic nationalism is not accepted by all nationalism scholars. See Anthony

Richmond, "Ethnic Nationalism; Social Science Paradigms," *International Social Science Journal* 39, no. 111 (1987): 3–18.

4. At independence, the Malays made up only about half the population.

5. Literally, "Malaysian nation," but with the meaning of a civic national identity based on shared citizenship.

6. The cultural theorists would include, among others, Anthony D. Smith, *The Ethnic Origins of Nations* (Oxford: Basil Blackwell, 1986); Walker Connor, *Ethnonationalism: The Quest for Understanding* (Princeton: Princeton University Press, 1994); and Adrian Hastings, *The Construction of Nationhood: Ethnicity, Religion and Nationalism* (Cambridge: Cambridge University Press, 1998).

7. Rupert Emerson, *From Empire to Nation* (Boston: Beacon Press, 1969), 95–96. He writes that perhaps the "simplest statement that can be made about a nation is that it is a body of people who feel that they are a nation; and it may be that when all the fine spun analysis is concluded, this will be the ultimate statement as well" (101). Ernest Gellner, in his last book (*Nationalism* [New York: New York University Press, 1998]), observes that it is "better to try to deal with the conditions which engender nationalism than to preach at its victims and beg them to refrain from feeling what, in their circumstances, it is only too natural to feel."

8. See Benedict Anderson, *Imagined Communities: Reflections on the Origins and Spread of Nationalism* (London: Verso, 1983). He believes that through various media, people acquire a sense of belonging to a larger group, most of whom they have never met. Also see Eric J. Hobsbawm, *Nations and Nationalism since 1780* (Cambridge: Cambridge University Press, 1992), for a neo-Marxist treatment of nationalism. He makes the point that the elites and governments construct nationalism by using language and education particularly.

9. Eric J. Hobsbawm and Terence Ranger, eds., *The Invention of Tradition* (Cambridge: Cambridge University Press, 1983), 6.

10. The social constructionists include Anderson, Hobsbawm, Ranger, and S. and L. Rudolph, "Modern Hate," *New Republic,* March 22, 1993, among others.

11. See Donald Horowitz, *Ethnic Groups in Conflict* (Berkeley: University of California Press, 1985); and Arend Lijphart, *Democracy in Plural Societies: A Comparative Exploration* (New Haven and London: Yale University Press, 1979).

12. Radin Soenarno, "Malay Nationalism, 1900–1945," *Journal of Southeast Asian History* 1, no. 1 (March 1960): 17, 28.

13. W. R. Roff, *Origins of Malay Nationalism* (Kuala Lumpur: University of Malaya Press, 1964), especially chapters 3 and 7.

14. A. B. Shamsul, "The Economic Dimension of Malay Nationalism," *The Developing Economies* 35, no. 3 (September 1997): 240–43. Also see Anthony Milner, *Kerajaan: Malay Political Culture at the Eve of Colonial Rule* (Tucson: University of Arizona Press, 1982).

15. Shamsul, "The Economic Dimension of Malay Nationalism," 243.

16. R. S. Milne and Diane K. Mauzy, *Politics and Government in Malaysia,* rev. ed. (Singapore and Vancouver: Times Books International and University of British Columbia Press, 1980), 26.

17. D. G. E. Hall, *A History of South-East Asia* (London: Macmillan and Co., 1964), 753.

18. Gordon P. Means, "Soft Authoritarianism in Malaysia and Singapore," in *Democracy in East Asia,* ed. Larry Diamond and Marc F. Plattner (Baltimore: Johns Hopkins University Press, 1998), 96.

19. John Kerry King, *Southeast Asia in Perspective* (New York, 1956), 43.

20. Chandra Muzaffar, *Protector?* (Penang: Aliran, 1979), 56.

21. Ibid., 61, from an UMNO Congress resolution in March 1946.

22. Ibid., 59.

23. Shamsul, "The Economic Dimension of Malay Nationalism," 244. Further, the Malay word for "federation" is derived from the base word for "united" (*sa-kutu*).

24. The leftist Malayan Democratic Union Party, led by some Singapore intellectuals, was at this time trying to promote a nonethnic civic nationalism based on loyalty to Malaya. The party hoped to inspire in the Malays a loyalty to the territory that was greater than their natural loyalty to their rulers, while at the same time "weaning the non-Malay races from their nostalgia for their homelands." See Cheah Boon Kheng, *The Masked Comrades: A Study of the Communist United Front in Malaya, 1945–48* (Singapore, 1979), 5, quoted in Barbara Watson Andaya and Leonard Y. Andaya, *A History of Malaysia* (London: Macmillan Press, 1982).

25. See Judith A. Nagata, "What Is a Malay? Situational Selection of Ethnic Identity in a Plural Society," *American Ethnologist* 1, no. 2 (1974): 331–50.

26. See Ishak bin Tadin, "Dato Onn and Malay Nationalism, 1946–51," *Journal of Southeast Asian History* 1, no. 1 (March 1960): 56–88.

27. Muzaffar, *Protector?*, 67–68.

28. Milne and Mauzy, *Politics and Government in Malaysia,* 127.

29. Ibid., 132.

30. For details on the birth of the Alliance, see ibid., 127–31.

31. Ibid., 38.

32. Lijphart, *Democracy in Plural Societies,* 153–54.

33. Zakaria Haji Ahmad, "Malaysia: Quasi-Democracy in a Divided Society," in *Democracy in Developing Countries: Asia,* vol. 3, ed. Larry Diamond, Juan J. Linz, and Seymour Martin Lipset (Boulder: Lynn Rienner, 1989), 354.

34. See J. A. C. Mackie, *Konfrontasi: The Indonesia-Malaysia Dispute, 1963–1966* (Kuala Lumpur: Oxford University Press, 1974). Malaysia had help from British (and Australian and New Zealand) troops in opposing Indonesia's army incursions.

35. Ahmad, "Malaysia," 357.

36. Tun Razak, *A New Realism,* TV and radio speech, June 13, 1969 (Kuala Lumpur: Malaysia Information Department, 1969).

37. For details, see Diane K. Mauzy, *Barisan Nasional: Coalition Government in Malaysia* (Kuala Lumpur: Maricans, 1983); and Milne and Mauzy, *Politics and Government in Malaysia,* 173–91.

38. Lijphart, *Democracy in Plural Societies,* 154. However, conflict management structures in Malaysia still remained closer in spirit to consociationalism than to Ian Lustick's control model ("Stability in Deeply Divided Societies: Consociationalism versus Control," *World Politics* 31 [April 1979]: 325–44). Some analysts have used the term *coercive consociationalism* to describe the situation where the groups are unequal but some consociational techniques are used. See Diane K. Mauzy, "Malaysia: Malay Political Hegemony and 'Coercive Consociationalism,'" in *The Politics of Ethnic Conflict Regulation,* ed. John McGarry and Brendon O'Leary (London: Routledge, 1993), 106–27; and Brendon O'Leary, "The Limits to Coercive Consociationalism in Northern Ireland," *Political Studies* 39, no. 4 (1989), 562–88.

39. For details, see the *Second Malaysia Plan, 1971–1975* (Kuala Lumpur: Government Press, 1971); *Mid-term Review of the Second Malaysia Plan, 1971–1975* (Kuala

Lumpur: Government Press, 1973); and *Third Malaysia Plan, 1976–1980* (Kuala Lumpur: Government Press, 1976).

40. See Just Faaland, J. R. Parkinson, and Rais B. Saniman, *Growth and Ethnic Inequality: Malaysia's New Economic Policy* (Kuala Lumpur: Oxford University Press, 1990).

41. Diane K. Mauzy, "The Tentative Life and Quiet Death of the NECC in Malaysia," in *Managing Change in Southeast Asia: Local Initiatives, Global Connections,* ed. Jean DiBernardi, Gregory Forth, and Sandra Niessen (Montreal: University of Montreal, 1995), 77–92. This included not counting toward Malay ownership any company that was a joint venture, a nominee company, or ethnically mixed. This included most of the largest companies in the country and some of the giant companies owned by UMNO or its proxies. On UMNO's extensive business interests, see E. T. Gomez, *Politics in Business: UMNO's Corporate Investments* (Kuala Lumpur: Forum, 1990); and E. T. Gomez and K. S. Jomo, *Malaysia's Political Economy: Politics, Patronage and Profits* (Cambridge: Cambridge University Press, 1997).

42. R. S. Milne and Diane K. Mauzy, *Malaysian Politics under Mahathir* (London: Routledge, 1999), 51.

43. Ibid., 50–64.

44. James Jesudason, *Ethnicity and the Economy: The State, Chinese Business, and the Multinationals in Malaysia* (Singapore: Oxford University Press, 1989).

45. Chandra Jeshuran notes that there has been "a tremendous build up of national euphoria in the country over Malaysia's achievements." See, "Malaysia: The Mahathir Supremacy and Vision 2020," *Southeast Asian Affairs 1993* (Singapore: Institute of Southeast Asian Studies, 1993), 220.

46. On the mass Internal Security Act arrests in 1987, and the events leading to firing of the chief justice of the Supreme Court and the dismantling of the independence of the judiciary in 1988, see Diane K. Mauzy, "The Corrosion of Checks on Executive Power: Deinstitutionalization in Malaysia," in *The Quality of Life in Southeast Asia: Transforming Social, Political and Natural Environments,* ed. Bruce Matthews (Montreal: McGill University Press, 1992), 1–18; and Mauzy, "Malaysia," 106–27.

47. This can be seen most clearly in the *OPP2,* the *Second Outline Perspective Plan, 1991–2000* (Kuala Lumpur: National Printing Department, 1991).

48. Milne and Mauzy, *Malaysian Politics under Mahathir,* 74.

49. Geoffrey Stafford, "Economics and Ethnicity" (paper prepared for the Second International Malaysian Studies Conference, Kuala Lumpur, August 1999).

50. Mahathir Mohamad, *Malaysia: The Way Forward* (Kuala Lumpur: Centre for Economic Research and Services, Malaysian Business Council, 1991).

51. Milne and Mauzy, *Malaysian Politics under Mahathir,* 165.

52. "Vision 2020: The Way Forward" (keynote address by Mahathir Mohamad at the Vision 2020 National Congress, Petaling Jaya, April 29, 1997), 2–3. Also see Jeshuran, "Malaysia," 203–23.

53. This was impressed upon me firsthand by the keen interest in and high hopes for the idea taken by virtually all of the non-Malay Malaysian students that I have had in class the last several years.

54. Stafford, "Economics and Ethnicity."

55. "DAP Calls on Cabinet to Drop the Retrogressive Step. . . ," media statement by Lim Kit Siang, October 11, 1999, http://www.geocities.com/CapitolHill/3939/sg1971.html. Also see Aliran media statement, "Withdraw Decision to Include Religion in our ICs," October 13, 1999, http://www.malaysia.net/aliran/ms991013.htm.

56. See "A Matter of Identity," *Asiaweek,* November 12, 1999, http://cnn.com/ASIANOW/asiaweek/magazine/99/1112/ed_malaysia.html.

57. S. Jayasankaran, "Spoiling for a Fight," *Far Eastern Economic Review,* May 27, 1999, 18–19.

58. Shamsul, "The Economic Dimension of Malay Nationalism," 257–58.

59. Milne and Mauzy, *Malaysian Politics under Mahathir,* 165–67; and Jeshuran, "Malaysia," 221.

60. See Khoo Boh Teik, *Paradoxes of Mahathirism* (Kuala Lumpur: Oxford University Press, 1995), 88. Khoo sees both continuity and change in Mahathir's nationalism. The continuity can be seen in his penchant for seeing conspiracies against himself or Malaysia all around him. The change was shifting the "target" from the Chinese to the West. Also see Milne and Mauzy, *Malaysian Politics under Mahathir,* 134. The conspirators include the neocolonialists (like the International Monetary Fund and "ethnic Europeans"), the Western press, Zionists, human rights advocates, and, most recently, foreign currency speculators. See, for example, Thomas Fuller, "A Fiery Warning in Malaysia: Mahathir Discerns Threat from 'Ethnic European' Colonizers," *International Herald Tribune,* June 19, 1999.

61. Mahathir Mohamad, *The Malay Dilemma* (Singapore: Donald Moore for Asia Pacific Press, 1970), passim.

62. The November 1999 general election represented a setback. While the non-Malays were not portrayed as the enemy, the specter of ethnic violence and the implication of threat were raised in the ruling party's massive negative advertising that swamped all the media.

63. Philip Resnick, "Civic and Ethnic Nationalism: Lessons from the Canadian Case," in *Canadian Political Philosophy: Contemporary Reflections,* ed. Ronald Beiner and Wayne Norman (Toronto: Oxford University Press, 2001), 282–97.

64. From *Malaysiakini,* an electronic newspaper on November 17, 2000, http://www.malaysiakini.com.my.

65. Media statement by DAP national chair Lim Kit Siang, December 3, 2000, bungaraya@listserv.net-gw.com.

66. Chandra Muzaffar, "Malay Unity—A Shift; Not a Split," January 10, 2001, sangkancil@lists.malaysia.net.

67. In an interview with former prime minister Tunku Abdul Rahman in the 1970s, he told me in all seriousness that Chinese leader and finance minister Tan Siew Sin kept a large map of China hung over his bed. Tan denied this.

68. Interestingly, the most direct postindependence threat to Malaysia's territory came from the Malays' ethnic cousins in Indonesia during Konfrontasi, 1963–66. (Indonesia's nationalism was strongly following variant 1.) It provided an opportunity for the minority communities to demonstrate their loyalty, while the only Indonesian sympathizers were a small number of Malays.

69. However, a large survey of three hundred students at the premier University of Malaya revealed that there is almost no interaction between the different ethnic communities outside of classes. Reported online on October 12, 1999, sangkancil@malaysia.net. University of Malaya professor Sheela Abraham's study also revealed other disturbing findings, including the fact that only 10 percent of the students sampled identified themselves as Malaysians first.

70. Resnick, "Civic and Ethnic Nationalism."

4. Rwanda

Tragic Land of Dual Nationalisms

JOHN F. CLARK

> [The Hutu and Tutsi] are two nations in a single state. . . . Two nations between whom there is no intercourse and no sympathy, who are as ignorant of each other's habits, thoughts and feelings as if they were dwellers of different zones, or inhabitants of different planets.
>
> —Grégoire Kayibanda, president of Rwanda

SINCE THE HOUR of its independence, Rwanda has proven to be a land of horror and fascination. The birth of the independent republic was accompanied by a terrible episode of communal violence, and the Rwandan people have known oppression, fear, and genocide during the postcolonial period. Indeed, the 1994 genocide in Rwanda was an event of historical and global significance, representing as it does one of only three (true) genocides of the twentieth century.[1] Some one-tenth of the entire population of Rwanda died in the killings that took place over about three months in 1994.[2] Given the suffering and tragedy that Rwanda's people have endured—and inflicted upon one another—one feels a strong sense of necessity to understand what forces have given rise to such terrible outcomes. Yet the need for answers about Rwanda surpasses the mere academic: we want to understand the violence there not only as scholars but also as ordinary, moral human beings.

Not surprisingly, the scholarly community, both Africanist and otherwise, has devoted considerable effort to the analysis of Rwanda since the 1994 genocide. Among many other scholarly efforts, a number of journals have given over entire issues to the question of Rwanda and the crises of the "Great Lakes," or of "Central Africa."[3] Similarly, a notable number of books quickly appeared in print soon after the genocide, and many others have continued to appear in subsequent years.[4] All these studies record a natural human revulsion toward the genocide in Rwanda, and many demonstrate a great sophistication about the ongoing dilemmas of reforming the Rwandan polity in such a way as to reduce the possibility of more tragedies in Rwanda's future.

The lessons that one may derive from Rwanda's sad experience are not ones that apply only in Africa, either, as the historical nature of the 1994 genocide suggests. In fact, Rwanda is hardly a "typical" African country, and the "ethnic" violence that has recently unfolded there is most typical of ethnically generated bloodshed elsewhere on the African continent. Only Nigeria, during its civil war, perhaps, has seen ethnically related killing on the scale of Rwanda, but both the context and nature of the killing there were different and perhaps more usual. Unlike most African countries, Rwanda does not have a plethora of ethnic, or "tribal," peoples but rather only three identity communities and only two of major significance.[5] Of these two, the Hutu represented some 84 percent of the population and the Tutsi some 15 percent in the late 1950s; by the early 1990s, following several waves of migration, the Tutsi represented about 12 percent of the population.[6]

Unlike most other African countries, Rwanda is quite densely populated and intensively cultivated. In contrast to many, it has very few resources of international interest. Finally, in Rwanda, those who identify with one of the two dominant identity communities have long lived in near-total interspersion with one another; that it is to say, there are no Hutu or Tutsi "homelands" in Rwanda.[7]

Most studies to date have also treated the Hutu-Tutsi dichotomy in Rwanda as an ethnic phenomenon, which it certainly is, in part. Most (contemporary) scholars have emphasized, however, the incredible fluidity of the fundamental Hutu and Tutsi identities, leaving one to marvel that so much blood could have been spilt on the basis of such apparently fragile social signifiers. Thus, the great paradox of Rwanda is that the bases for Hutu and Tutsi identity are most ephemeral, and yet the Hutu-Tutsi dichotomy is far and away the most important social cleavage in the society, forming the main axis along which political forces in the country divide.

The innovation of this study is to test the limits of a new designation for Rwanda's two outstanding identities; *namely, this chapter proposes that Rwanda is a land of two nationalisms, that of Rwandan Hutu nationalism and Rwandan Tutsi nationalism.* It further proposes that the rival nationalisms first appeared during the political crisis that led to Rwanda's independence and that both were consolidated during the regime of the country's first president, Grégoire Kayibanda. To date, the nature of the Hutu and Tutsi identities has been characterized in a number of different and compelling ways, but never before as *national* identities.[8] Most notably, the Hutu and Tutsi identities have frequently been designated as *ethnic* identities, *caste* identities, or, more problematically, *class* identities.[9] While each of these designations captures some aspects of the identities, providing very useful clues about their origins and evolutions, none acknowledges the ultimate manifestation of the identities as national ones, in the sense adopted in this volume. The designation of these identities as "national" ones will be controversial, and only partly indicative of their overall character, but this need not trouble us.[10] This redesignation in fact captures the most important dimension of the identities and helps us to understand the contemporary nature of Rwandan politics. Most significantly, the specification of (Rwandan) Hutu and Tutsi as *national* identities helps us to understand the violent manifestations of social conflict in the country.

One should hasten to note that the two communities identified here are both *Rwandan* communities. This specification is important because there are indigenous groups of people identifying with the appellations *Hutu* and *Tutsi* both in Burundi and the Democratic Republic of the Congo (DRC) and there are also "ethnically related" peoples in southern Uganda.[11] Despite the possible objective bases for group identity that the two Rwandan groups might have with these extraterritorial peoples, however, no ties of transterritorial *nationalism* have yet emerged, though much communal fealty has been in evidence.[12]

It is also important to clarify that *nationalism* is used here in the sense specified in the introduction to this volume. The Rwandan Hutu and Rwandan Tutsi are nations in that they are each "communit[ies] of people organized around the idea of *self-determination*."[13] The irreducibly tragic reality of Rwandan politics is that the representatives of the Hutu and Tutsi identities have sought *to control the Rwandan state* to protect the fundamental interests of their respective communities. Nationalism is defined at the outset of this volume as "the pursuit—through argument or other activity—of a set of rights and privileges for the self-defined members of the nation, including, at minimum, territorial autonomy or independence." Although I might put it slightly differently, the practical implications are the same: the leaders of the two outstanding identity communities in Rwanda have sought control over a specified territory to protect the "rights and privileges for the self-defined members of the nation."

Despite its explanatory appeal, the idea of dual nationalisms may strike one as odd on a number of counts. First, the demographic, social, and geographic contexts for Rwanda's dual nationalisms are utterly different from those typically imagined for other ethnic or civil communities claiming overlapping territorial spaces. In no other setting do the two national peoples live in such complete interspersion with one another, and in no other setting have two national peoples lived in such long economic symbiosis.[14] In Rwanda, neither of the two identity communities has *typically* envisioned a total expulsion or removal of the other community; only in the extraordinary circumstances of the 1994 genocide did certain prominent Hutu figures in the ruling class undertake a project of eliminating or removing the opposing identity group. For the Tutsi identity community to physically remove the Hutu is virtually unimaginable, but for its leaders to rule the Rwandan state in pursuit of Tutsi interests is certainly not, as the policies of the present government attest. Despite the parallels with Palestine/Israel, and perhaps other multinational territories, the tight symbiosis of the identity communities over a period spanning centuries sets Rwanda apart.

Second, the notion of dual *nationalisms* in Rwanda is odd because there are such excellent objective bases for pan-Rwandan or, better, Banyarwandan nationalism. Rwanda has a "national" language, Kinyarwanda, common to both the Hutu and Tutsi communities, a language only used by the Banyarwanda in neighboring territories. In so many other mixed-identity settings, language has formed such an ineluctable force for creating social cohesion that one naturally expects the same for Rwanda. Both a few Rwandans and many outsiders, particularly scholars, have fervently and long hoped for the emergence of Banyarwanda nationalism, largely based upon language. In fact, a few Rwandans do have such an identity, but they have remained politically marginal, with tragic consequences, due to the social strength of the rival ethnonational identities.

Another source of Banyarwanda nationalism might have been the common colonial experience, but as I argue in this chapter, colonialism did not serve this end. Finally, partly as a result of colonialism, the "national" territory of the Banyarwanda has been well defined for decades and has been recognized among relevant actors including the Banyarwanda themselves, the citizens of neighboring states, and the leaders of more distant global forces, including the great powers and the United Nations.[15] Given these excellent objective bases, it is striking that Banyarwandan nationalism did not emerge in Rwanda.

If we accept that the label *national* can apply to the Hutu and Tutsi identity groups, at least as an ideal type, what implications does this have for explaining Rwanda's tragic postindependence history? Or, to conform with the framework of this volume, we might ask what *caused* the perpetuation of the dual nationalisms in Rwanda after independence. Theoretical approaches to ethnicity (and nationalism) suggest two competing hypotheses. The primordialist approach suggests that the binational conflict was a product of ancient and intrinsic differences between the two identity communities, each of which sought to control the historical Rwandan territory. The instrumentalist approach suggests, on the other hand, that the differences between the groups are largely artificial, created and sustained by the elites for narrow political ends. The instrumentalist approach implies that elite representatives of each identity group sought to create nationalist feelings (i.e., the desire to control the state) in their group in order to maintain themselves in power. This analysis, in turn, sheds light on the preeminent question about Rwanda as more conventionally posed: How can we possibly understand the inhuman hatreds that gave rise, first, to intercommunal mass killing and, finally, to genocide. Although we return explicitly to this causal question at the end of the chapter, the weight of the evidence suggests an answer well in advance.

The Development of Rwanda's Two Identity Communities

Since the Tutsi community, or rather a subset thereof, emerged more than five hundred years ago as the dominant social group in Rwanda, it seems fitting to begin with it in laying out the bases for Rwanda's identity communities. The bases for Rwandan Tutsi identity have included the group's distinctive ethnic origins, economic role, and political institutions, including the *mwamiship* and the chieftaincy. As important as the realities of such distinctive social attributes are the myths associated with each.

The "nuclear cell" of a Rwandan Tutsi kingdom was established by the fifteenth century, and a number of "formerly independent Hutu communities" were absorbed into the kingdom over the following century, beginning a long process of imperial expansion.[16] Meanwhile, Rwanda remained a territorial space occupied by a large but declining number of "microstates," ruled by either Hutu or Tutsi chiefs. This process of expansion culminated only in the early twentieth century, when the rule of Tutsi chiefs was finally established throughout all of the contemporary territory of Rwanda. The process was only accomplished with the explicit, direct, and unflinching support of colonial authorities, first German and then Belgian. During all but the last fifty years of this five-hundred-year period, it must be stressed, only a small fraction of the entire Tutsi community was associated with either the Tutsi monarchy or the institution of Tutsi chieftaincy. The spread of "Tutsi consciousness" to the Tutsi masses only happened as independence neared.

The origin of the Tutsi people has been a matter of intensive debate among European and African scholars for more than one hundred years, and it remains unresolved. It is widely, but not universally, agreed that the Tutsi did originate from a different "ethnic stock" prior to their establishment of dominance in Rwanda.[17] A number of early Belgian anthropologists and colonial administrators speculated about some far distant origins for the Tutsi, including such fantastic places as the lost continent of Atlantis and the Garden of Eden or, somewhat more reasonably, India.[18] Such fantastic notions resonated with late-nineteenth-century and early-twentieth-century European racial prejudices: these observers were able to persuade themselves that the Tutsi ruled in Rwanda because of some genetic superiority associated with race. Most serious scholars, however, seem to believe that the origins of the Tutsi do in fact lie outside of present-day Rwanda.[19]

In the past, the Tutsi apparently had some distinctive physiological features, based on their separate geographical origins. These included a lighter complexion, taller stature, and finer (thinner) noses compared with the "typical" Hutu. To a very limited extent, these physiological differences were occasionally still discernable in individuals at the time of European contact, and even into the twentieth century. Any original physiological distinction between Tutsi and Hutu, however, has largely been obliterated by intermarriage, "caste changing," and other forms of ethnic mixing so that representatives of the two groups are not now reliably distinguishable.[20] Likewise, Tutsi and Hutu cultural practices and beliefs have also blended over the centuries. Thus, ethnicity per se is now a very slight basis indeed for identification with one of Rwanda's two dominant communities.

Besides ethnicity, the traditional political function of the Tutsi in Rwandan society was another basis for the emergence of a Tutsi identity community. Specifically, the institutions of the Tutsi monarch, or *mwami,* and of the Tutsi chieftaincy were vitally important to the process. The Rwandan Tutsi monarchy represented a highly centralized, authoritarian, and unrivaled locus of power in both late precolonial and colonial Rwanda. For purposes of legitimation, the monarchy equipped itself with a ritual code (*ubwiru*) and a cadre of guardians of the code (*biru*). Among the duties of the biru was propagation of the official myths of the monarchy, one of which closely resembles Plato's "myth of the metals."[21] Such myths were one tool that the Tutsi elites employed in their socialization of the Hutu and Twa in their inferior status.

While the Tutsi chiefs of Rwanda had far less autonomy than those of Burundi, where a much looser monarchy emerged, they did exercise a far-flung hegemony over Hutu populations, with the qualifications noted in the preceding. In areas under the control of the central monarchy, they reported to and served only at the will of the mwami, but they had substantial authority over both Hutu and Tutsi populations within their territories. The Rwandan Tutsi chieftaincy was a highly complex institution that involved a tripartite structure.[22] The institution of the chieftaincy, with all of its hundreds of local representatives and myriad subordinates, served to spread the Tutsi identity, associated particularly with social superiority, from the apex down into a substantial part of the Tutsi population.

Yet another basis for Tutsi (and Hutu) identity in Rwanda was economic function, which served to divide the population into "classes," or "castes." The Tutsi who entered the Rwandan territory in the distant past apparently relied heavily for sustenance on cattle herding, rather than agriculture. Having established themselves in Rwanda, the Tutsi frequently put the care of some cattle in the hands of the Hutu, but this did not change the perception of differential economic roles. The *control* of cattle remained largely in Tutsi hands, while the Hutu cared for them and engaged in agriculture. Perhaps the most important socioeconomic institution of Rwanda until the mid-twentieth century was the quasi-feudal *buhake* contract, briefly described as a contract of "pastoral servitude."[23] Under the terms of such a contract, a local patron, usually a Tutsi, would make the usage of cattle and land available to a client, usually a Hutu. More generally, the patron would take on responsibilities for the welfare of the client. In return, the client would render specific goods, including some percentage of his agricultural produce to the patron.

This functional economic differentiation in society paralleled and largely reinforced the cleavages represented by ethnic difference and political control. Whether the resultant cleavages are best viewed as class or caste cleavages depends largely on the degree of movement one perceives to exist between the two identity groups.[24] Early anthropological works documented the possibility of having one's identity change in correspondence with changing economic fortunes. Those Tutsi who lost their cattle and other means of support quite often came to be regarded as Hutu, while those Hutu males who prospered could sometimes marry into Tutsi families and have their offspring be considered as Tutsi.[25] As a result, the ethnic basis for the Tutsi-Hutu distinction eroded, even as identity group distinctions themselves became stronger.

Most of the early bases for Hutu identity can be deduced from the foregoing discussion. Unlike the Tutsi, the Hutu have typically perceived themselves as the "original" inhabitants of the Rwandan territory, as opposed to immigrants from a very distant past; in economic terms, their lives have been more associated with clientage and agricultural work, rather than patronage and cattle herding. Given their overall subordination in the society, the Hutu had little opportunity to develop any sense of collective consciousness, even as victims, until late in Rwandan colonial history.[26] One very important exception to this rule was in those peripheral parts of Rwanda where Hutu chiefs maintained their independence well into the colonial period.[27]

Perhaps the dominant theme of contemporary writing on Rwandan history is the transformation of these sources of identity at the hands of the German, and then Belgian, colonizers. The major effect of colonialism was to reinforce, render static, and rigidify the Tutsi-Hutu identity difference in Rwanda. Both European colonizers found advantage in these practices since both relied on the Tutsi as their local adjuncts in the exercise of colonial hegemony. The Tutsi essentially became the instrument of indirect colonial rule, and for this system to function, it had to be undeniably clear who the Tutsi were and what the nature of their social role was. Among other methods of achieving this end, the Belgians issued identity cards to citizens stating their ethnic origin as Hutu, Tutsi, or Twa.

The rigidification of identities in Rwanda by colonial authorities is observable in a number of areas. For instance, the buhake was altered in several ways to favor Tutsi domination. Whereas in precolonial Rwanda, poor Tutsi often played the client role in the contract, the colonizers turned the institution into one of complete Tutsi domination of Hutu. Moreover, compared to the former terms, the terms of the contract were altered heavily in favor of the patrons. Finally, due to the monetization of the economy and the imposition of taxes, many Hutu were forced into (unequal) buhake contracts in order to meet their obligations.[28] Colonial anthropology, much of which identified the Tutsi as a "superior race" justified and rationalized these changes. Meanwhile, the colonial education system, as it functioned until after World War II, served to reify the abstract notion of Tutsi superiority. The mission schools run by Catholic authorities recruited almost exclusively the sons of Tutsi notables for education, which was the main vehicle for maintaining social superiority.[29] Thus, colonial efforts invested an elite segment of the Tutsi with tangible skills that prepared them for continued social domination and further reinforced their consciousness of superiority.

At a higher social level, the relationship between the monarchy and the chiefs also underwent a transformation under colonialism that reduced the autonomy of the chiefs and bolstered monarchical prerogatives. Colonial authorities also assisted the Tutsi mwami Yuhi Musinga (1896–1931) in putting down revolts in northern regions in 1912, in reasserting authority in Kinyaga in 1917, and in replacing Hutu chiefs with Tutsi chiefs in the second and third decades of the twentieth century.[30] Large areas of northern Rwanda remained under the rule of the Kiga (a Hutu clan) until it was suppressed and brought under Tutsi control through the instrument of a German military expedition in 1912.[31] Similarly, in several areas of the Kinyaga region (of Cyangugu prefect), in the southwestern area of the country bordering on the DRC, Tutsi chiefs were only introduced after conquest by Belgian-led troops in 1925.[32] These areas might well have remained independent of Tutsi rule without the intervention of Europeans in the process. Meanwhile, Tutsi chiefs throughout the country were invested with the formal titles of colonial bureaucrats and given a significant role in administration. Virtually all observers agree that the recrystallization of identities under colonialism set the stage for Tutsi-Hutu confrontation at the moment of independence and beyond.

The Emergence of Rwanda's Two National Communities

The "critical juncture" for the development of Rwanda's dual nationalisms coincided with the crisis of state control occasioned by the end of Belgian colonialism.[33] The revolution in Rwanda between 1959 and 1962 led to a dramatic reordering of social relations in the country, and the Hutu-Tutsi schism was the main axis along which political forces divided. While Belgian colonial rule quietly withered away in the course of that revolution, this change was far from the most important of the transformations that the country witnessed, and it was not the result of Banyarwandan nationalism.[34] In the course of the revolution, a part of the ruling Tutsi establishment fled the country, while others accepted political marginalization.

Meanwhile, ordinary and impoverished Tutsi residents of the country saw themselves implicitly cast as oppressors of the majority of the population by the new Hutu elite that came to the fore. A small segment of this Hutu elite seized power for itself and set up rule over the country in the name of the Hutu masses. As for the Hutu masses themselves, they remained as disenfranchised and exploited as they had been under the "dual colonialism" of European-Tutsi rule. While this set of changes may or may not be termed an "ethnic revolution," the changes did take place despite the absence of primordial, immutable sources of identity for the country's two main groups.[35] Here, though, the main contention is that in the course of the Rwandan revolution the country's two main identity communities took on aspirations of *national* self-determination. That is, large percentages of each community were seized with the desire to gain control over the Rwandan state for the primary reason of protecting the welfare of each group.

If the discussion of the sources of Tutsi group identity should logically precede that of the Hutu's sources, then the discussion of the emergence of Rwandan Hutu nationalism must precede that of Rwandan Tutsi nationalism. Given all of the social advantages that had accrued to Tutsi elites by the 1950s, they most probably took it for granted that they would inherit rulership of the country from the departing colonialists when the time came. Meanwhile, they enjoyed a myriad of advantages that largely reconciled them to colonial rule in the short term. The Hutu, on the other hand, correctly perceived that independence might well mean only continued marginalization for them in the society. Accordingly, they had a strong incentive to mobilize on behalf of a more egalitarian society before the final departure of Belgian authorities. Thus, Tutsi *nationalism* only emerged in reaction to the efforts of the Hutu elites to reorder social relations.

Ironically, given all of the colonial favoritism shown to the Tutsi through the 1940s, it was also colonial policies that allowed Rwandan Hutu nationalism to emerge. Before these changes took place, "the Hutu had little consciousness of themselves as a group."[36] On the one hand, rather abrupt changes in Belgian colonial policy on Tutsi and Hutu status allowed for the emergence of a Hutu elite by the mid-1950s. This new elite quickly came to the fore of the Hutu movement for a reordering of social relations in Rwanda. On the other hand, Hutu peasants played a major role in the revolution at the local level throughout the country. Since Belgian colonial policies had left these peasants feeling overlooked and unjustly subjected to abuse by Tutsi chiefs, they were quite ready to follow their leaders in a campaign of social transformation—and in one of collective confrontation.

Without the creation of a Hutu *elite,* however, it is doubtful that Rwandan Hutu nationalism could ever have emerged. The policy changes that allowed the emergence of this elite took place first in the Catholic Church, particularly in the schools that it ran in the country, and second in the colonial administration itself. As for the local Catholic establishment, its practices toward the two local identity communities appear to have changed because of transformations within the church hierarchy and the arrival of a new class of missionaries after World War II. These new missionaries had "relatively humble social origins" and brought with them ideas of social change.[37] At the other end of the hierarchy, the appointment of a new Swiss apostolic vicar for Rwanda in 1955, Msgr. Perraudin, led to new policies that favored the Hutu. Most important, a greater percentage of Hutu were recruited into the mission schools, and into the clergy, as the 1950s progressed. As a result, by the end of the decade, a sizable cadre of educated Hutu potential leaders was on hand.

In the colonial administration, a slight drift toward more egalitarian social policies was accelerated by the appointment of Vice Governor-General Jean-Paul Harroy, also in 1955. Belgian colonial policies were no doubt affected on a broader scale by the experience of World War II, in which the excesses of "master race" doctrines became evident. The colonial administration began to advance a few Hutu into administrative service, even as it began to curtail the prerogatives of the Tutsi chiefs throughout the rural areas. The colonial administration also sought to thwart the efforts of the United Nation's Trusteeship Council to speed up Rwanda's independence in 1960 because the internal transfer of power was not yet complete. Finally, when the first round of Hutu peasant violence began against local Tutsi, the colonial administration firmly prevented any retaliation. Ultimately, the Hutu were allowed to "seize control of the central machinery of government."[38]

Long before that important event, though, the construction of Hutu national consciousness had to pass through a number of critical stages. A necessary first step was to raise consciousness of Hutu oppression among the literate class of new Hutu elites. Fortuitously for the Hutu cause, the Catholic Church decided to hand over the editorship of the leading Kinyarwanda language paper (*Kimanyateka*) to an important Hutu figure, Grégoire Kayibanda, in late 1956. In the hands of Kayibanda, later Rwanda's first president, this paper became the major voice for the cause of ethnic redress. At virtually the same moment that Kayibanda took over the editorship of *Kimanyateka,* Catholic authorities helped a group of Hutu elites found a coffee cooperative called TRAFIPRO (*Travail, Fidélité, Progrès*) in Kabgayi.[39] This organization provided an opportunity for Hutu elites to sharpen their leadership skills, and it gave rise to other such organizations around the country.

A second logical step was a statement of the philosophical aims of a potential Hutu government, which was aptly supplied by the Bahutu Manifesto,[40] issued in March 1957. The document essentially called for an end to "the political monopoly of one race, the Mututsi." The document frontally assaulted the "feudal" economic system and forthrightly demanded the promotion of Hutu interests. Importantly, the nine Hutu authors of the manifesto strongly opposed the removal of ethnic labels from the identity papers of the citizens.[41] Had such labels been removed, and a strict meritocracy for government service instituted, Tutsi domination would have continued for some time, given that the Tutsi had previously enjoyed so many social advantages. The desire of the Hutu leadership to keep track of ethnic identities after the revolution demonstrates its aspiration for group redress and for rule in the interest of an ethnic majority.

Another critical stage in the development of Rwandan Hutu nationalism was the merger of the divergent northern strain, animated by the memory of a system of Hutu chiefs, who had only recently been disempowered, and the "modern" nationalism of Kayibanda and other educated Hutu elites in the country's central regions.[42] The northern Kiga chiefs looked backward to the recent past when they exercised a feudal control of their own over fellow members of their identity community; meanwhile, the modern Hutu elites in the Gitarama region looked forward to an egalitarian future. Despite their somewhat retrograde political views, the northern Hutu leaders were better connected with peasant populations than those at the center. According to Lemarchand, "the earliest and strongest reaction" against

Tutsi supremacy was in the north. "The revolutionary contagion emanating from the north considerably strengthened Hutu solidarity throughout the country, . . . intensifying inter-caste antagonisms."[43] Kayibanda and his colleagues, on the other hand, were much better connected internationally and drew on a more diverse set of political resources. Thus, according to Lemarchand, "By 1960 . . . these originally very different manifestations had coalesced into a more or less unified revolutionary movement aiming at the wholesale elimination of Tutsi elements from all positions of influence."[44]

The emergence of Rwandan Tutsi nationalism unfolded in two distinct stages leading up to independence. The first stage involved mostly Tutsi chiefs and "modern" elites and was generated by elections to "advisory councils" in 1953 and 1956. These "elections" were in fact a very limited exercise in popular governance since the masses played virtually no role in them.[45] Although a substantial minority of Hutu were elected into the subchiefdom council level, Tutsi representatives dominated at the higher levels. In fact, at the highest level (the Conseil Supérieur du Pays) the percentage of Tutsi actually increased from 90.6 percent in 1953 to 94 percent after the 1956 exercise. In this way, members of the Tutsi elites began to take on some functions—even if advisory ones—in the colonial administration. And as in every other case in colonial Africa, a small taste of power only whetted the appetites of those selected for a more significant role in their state governments. By the end of the decade, the Tutsi elites had developed, in classic anticolonial fashion, a sense of entitlement to power, and pressures for immediate independence began to build.

In the second stage, Rwandan Tutsi nationalism blossomed in reaction to the activities of the Hutu counterelites and, later, those of the Hutu peasantry.[46] Naturally, the Tutsi elites observed with growing anxiety the escalating demands of the Hutu counterelites, and they eventually realized that their only hope for maintaining their superior social standing was to take hold immediately of the reigns of power. Without mass support, however, they had little leverage against the Belgian colonizers. Meanwhile, throughout the country's rural communities, Hutu resentment against Tutsi chiefs was growing, and new political activity among the Hutu evoked a counterresentment. In this environment, the beating near the Kabgayi mission of a Hutu subchief by Tutsi political activists on November 1, 1959, set off a critical round of communal fighting between members of the two identity communities. In the following two weeks, as the fighting spread to other regions, some three hundred people were killed, numerous homes were burned, and a mass exodus of Tutsi out of the country began.[47] The Belgian authorities sympathized far more with the Hutu during this unrest, allowing the Hutu to burn homes and forbidding the mwami to retaliate.[48] While it is important to note that the (Tutsi) monarchy was not a target of Hutu protests at this point, there is no denying the impact that these events had on the crystallization of the two *national* identities. From this point on, the Tutsi masses, who were as impoverished and oppressed as their Hutu comrades, began to identify strongly with their own elite leaders.

For both Rwandan nationalisms a key challenge was to articulate an ideology or program that protected the interests of the emergent nations without explicitly acknowledging the real purpose of the ideas. Particularly for Tutsi national leaders, who only represented a minority of the population by 1960, the appeal took pan-Rwandan (Banyarwandan) form. These Tutsi leaders called for immediate "national" independence for the Rwandan state, a call that attracted considerable international support.[49] Given the strong anticolonial zeitgeist of the era, the justness of the call could hardly be questioned, though its main intent was actually a perpetuation of Tutsi domination.

Meanwhile, those supporting the Rwandan Hutu ideal actually supported a short-term continuation of Belgian rule and decried what they called "Tutsi colonialism." Rather, they called for immediate "democracy," which in fact meant a transfer of power to the Hutu majority. A typical Hutu slogan observed at this hour was "Democracy First, [and] Independence Will Come; Down with Immediate Independence!"[50]

The emergence of political parties and the results of the first elections follow directly from the development of Hutu and Tutsi nationalist feelings. In keeping with their disenfranchised position, Hutu elites were the first to create political parties. The first was the Hutu Social Movement of Kayibanda, founded in June 1957, which later became the Parti du Mouvement et de l'Emancipation Hutu (PARMEHUTU) in October 1959. Both names of this political entity are indicative of its identity-group orientation. The second Hutu party to be formed was the Association pour la Promotion Sociale de la Masse (APROSOMA), founded by Joseph Gitera in November 1957. This organization "claimed to be a class-based party but attracted almost no one but Hutu."[51] Aside from the fact that the two parties were vehicles for the two different personalities involved, hardly surprising in the African context, each also rallied different regional Hutu forces. PARMEHUTU was deeply implanted in the regions of Gitarama and Ruhengeri, while APROSOMA had more support in the southern Butare region.

The hard-core, monarchist Tutsi elements did not counter with a party of their own until August 1959. The Union Nationale Rwandaise (UNAR) "was strongly monarchist and hostile to the Belgians, and defended the idea of immediate independence."[52] The following month, a second largely Tutsi party, the Rwandese Democratic Union (RADER) party, was formed by (Tutsi) Chief Prosper Bwanakweri. The Belgians had encouraged the formation of this party with the idea that it might be able to attract moderate elements from both identity communities, but this was not to be. The party "was frowned upon by the monarchist diehards while the Hutu never quite managed to trust its liberalism."[53] The late formation of these two parties demonstrates the reactive nature of Tutsi nationalism, which responded to the growing activism of the Hutu counterelites.

Despite some local anomalies and instances of cross-ethnic voting,[54] the successive elections in Rwanda demonstrate that the more radical Hutu and Tutsi nationalist parties attracted an increasing percentage of support from their respective identity communities. The first elections were for communal councils and burgomasters for Rwanda's 229 communes in June and July 1960. With these elections, the country's chiefs would become "mere figureheads," and their powers would soon be completely suppressed.[55] PARMEHUTU was the big winner, gaining some 76 percent of the seats on the communal councils and 160 (70 percent) of the burgomaster positions. APROSOMA finished with the second-most votes, winning 7.5 percent of the seats on the communal councils and 51 (22 percent) burgomaster posts. Overall, the two Hutu-oriented parties had won 84 percent of the vote.[56] The legislative elections of September 25, 1961, only confirmed the domination of PARMEHUTU and the final polarization of the two identity communities. In these elections, PARMEHUTU won 78 percent of the vote and thirty-five seats (of forty-four) in the legislative assembly. By this time, the Tutsi vote had swung entirely to UNAR, which gained 17 percent of the vote and seven seats in the assembly. Thus, the two parties that tried in some way to transcend the polarization of the population along communal identity lines were both eclipsed by rivals with purely community-based appeals. In this fashion the ideologies of Rwandan Hutu and Rwandan Tutsi nationalism came to squash any hopes for transcommunity parties or ideologies. Eventually, the great majority of the population chose sides—or was *forced* to choose sides—based on the country's primary identity communities.

For the most part, the national identities were manufactured by elites who sought bases of support in the population. The main hope of Tutsi elites was that Rwanda would quietly succeed to its independence, leaving them in charge. The more liberal among them, such as Chief Bwanakweri, doubtless hoped that the former discrimination against the Hutu would be alleviated and that Hutu representatives would slowly find their way into positions of authority. For the Hutu elites, though, the most apparent path to political power was to instigate a community-wide revolt of Hutu against all Tutsi, elites and disenfranchised alike. Once their campaign had begun, and gained the support of the colonial administration, the only resort of the Tutsi was to retrench around the traditional Tutsi institutions and demand immediate independence as a monarchy. Even the moderate and progressive Tutsi were eventually pushed into the UNAR camp in this way, as RADER disappeared from the political scene.

Rwanda's Nationalisms after Independence

After Rwanda's de facto independence in 1961, the country was in the hands of leaders who may properly be referred to as Rwandan Hutu nationalists through July 1994. Whatever objective good was or was not accomplished for the Hutu masses is scarcely relevant to their actual sources of legitimacy in the eyes of the Hutu public. The long period of Rwandan Hutu nationalism in control of the Rwandan state was punctuated by three major crises—in 1963, in 1972–73, and between 1990 and 1994. The last of these crises ended in a genocide of several hundred thousand Tutsi citizens and the political massacre of many tens of thousands of Hutu opponents between April and July 1994. Since 1994, the Rwandan state has been in the hands of a Tutsi nationalist regime, whose preeminent goal has been to protect the rights and interests of the remaining Tutsi parts of the population.

The Kayibanda Regime

The PARMEHUTU government of Grégoire Kayibanda that succeeded to power in 1961 came to embody the idea of Rwandan Hutu nationalism and staked its legitimacy firmly on the idea of defending and uplifting Rwanda's Hutu population. One can easily argue, and with good reason, that the real purposes of the government were otherwise. Namely, the regime sought above all else to protect in power Kayibanda himself and the group of Hutu elites who formed the core of his supporters. In time, the regime also served to protect those Hutu from a certain region, Gitarama, against rivals from other regions, particularly Butare. One can further argue without real dissent that the PARMEHUTU regime did relatively little to promote or defend the real, material interests of the Hutu peasantry or even middle classes, other than to replace Tutsi members of the civil service with Hutu cadres. Impressive though they are, however, such arguments do not change the fact that the Kayibanda regime ruled with the support of a sizable majority of the country's Hutu population and with virtually no support from the Tutsi population. During its years in power, one main effect of the government was to further harden the two national identities that had emerged in the years leading up to Rwanda's independence, ensuring that any government ruling Rwanda would have to rely on one of the country's two national communities for support.

The real transfer of power in Rwanda did not occur following the legislative elections of 1961 but, rather, earlier that year, at the time of the "coup of Gitarama" on January 28, 1961. By this date, the colonial administration of Rwanda was locked in a quiet battle with the United Nations over the modalities of independence, generated by support for the UNAR position by important members of the United Nations General Assembly and Trusteeship Council. These supporters were now trying to organize a national reconciliation among Rwanda's increasingly fractious parties *before* the organization of elections in late 1961, thus delaying the independence process that they had previously tried to hasten.

In Rwanda, meanwhile, the special resident (Colonel Bem Logiest) and the resident general (Jean-Paul Harroy) both continued to favor the Hutu cause, as they had done since the mid-1950s. The Belgian government, which was initially torn between the two positions, eventually came around to the view of its own colonial administration, partly because of the Congo crisis and the resulting strained relations with the United Nations.[57] In these circumstances, the local administration allowed PARMEHUTU to organize secretly a meeting of all of the country's communal counselors and burgomasters on an assigned date. At this meeting, the representatives, dominated by PARMEHUTU, declared Rwanda a republic, abolished the monarchy, and went on to set up a provisional government with Kayibanda as prime minister. Thus, the subsequent elections of 1961 merely confirmed a political reality that was already well established, and the formal independence that came on July 1, 1962, was a virtual afterthought.

Between early 1961 and 1964 the Kayibanda regime evolved into an exclusionist Rwandan Hutu nationalist dictatorship, but this process happened only slowly. From the beginning, the government did nothing to stop Hutu (PARMEHUTU) militants throughout the country from attacking Rwandan Tutsi citizens, thus encouraging their behavior. Such attacks were typically generated in response to the activities, including border attacks, of the exiled Tutsi communities in Uganda, Congo, Burundi, and Tanzania. The government referred to these exiled Tutsi as *Inyenzi*, or cockroaches, beginning the process of their dehumanization in the eyes of many Hutu. Nonetheless, the government did come to an agreement with UNAR representatives in New York in February 1962 that allowed for the entry of two UNAR ministers into the government. Meanwhile, seven seats in the assembly were in UNAR (Tutsi) hands, and UNAR was initially allowed to criticize the government through its own newspaper, *Unité*.[58]

This limited Tutsi political activity was allowed to continue only until December 1963. In that month, Tutsi exiles based in Burundi and Congo attempted an invasion of Rwandan territory with the aim of overthrowing the Kayibanda/PARMEHUTU regime. In the midst of this fighting, the prominent local members of both the UNAR and the RADER parties, including the liberal Bwanakweri, were summarily executed in Ruhengeri.[59] Following these attacks, whose leaders nearly succeeded in occupying Kigali, national and local PARMEHUTU officials instigated assaults on Tutsi populations in several regions of the country, leading to the deaths of some ten thousand to fourteen thousand ordinary Tutsi. Tens of thousands more fled into exile, joining the thousands who had fled earlier. Following the "Bugesera Invasion," all remaining Tutsi were purged from the assembly, prefect-level political posts, and higher levels of the administration. Only a few Tutsi were allowed to continue working in the lower levels of administration. As envisioned in the Bahutu Manifesto, identity cards listing "ethnic" affiliation were maintained under the PARMEHUTU regime, and the Tutsi were officially limited to no more than 9 percent of the positions in schools, civil service, or any other public sector.[60]

Kayibanda used the threat of the "Inyenzi" to consolidate his power vis-à-vis his potential Hutu rivals and to establish a virtually totalitarian control over the country. This meant, among other measures, that Kayibanda and his government had to extinguish APROSOMA as a rival political movement. A PARMEHUTU delegation in the assembly pointedly asked Gitera, APROSOMA's leader, to retire from politics and return to his business interests in October 1961, which he did. Subsequently, APROSOMA officials were systematically driven from office or "converted" to loyalty to PARMEHUTU by 1966.[61] By this time, Kayibanda had become a kind of Hutu mwami, taking on the airs of a divinely implanted, infallible leader of the Hutu people. According to Prunier, his regime was characterized by "remoteness, authoritarianism and secretiveness." As far as its ideology was concerned, "the intrinsic worth of being Hutu [and] the total congruence between demographic majority and democracy" were emphasized.[62] Indeed, the demographic facts of Rwanda created by the affiliation of most citizens with one of its two dominant identity communities allowed Kayibanda to cloak the practice of Rwandan Hutu nationalism in an enunciated ideology of "democratic" majoritarianism.

In terms of the variants of nationalism described in Lowell Barrington's opening chapter of this volume, Kayibanda's main efforts with regard to territory were of the "sovereignty-protecting" variety. Given the well-established territorial dimensions of the Rwandan state inherited in 1962, the Kayibanda regime did not mount a significant irridentist campaign challenging the territorial integrity of any neighboring state. On the other hand, there were very real internal and external threats to "territorial control," which Kayibanda met with sufficient force to quash. With regard to defining the relevant national identity, Kayibanda took no significant steps to build a civic (i.e., Banyarwandan) nation in Rwanda; rather, he clearly focused his efforts on protecting and defending the interests of the emergent Hutu nation (hence, "nation-protecting"). While Kayibanda and other members of his regime certainly grieved over the fate of Burundi's Hutu, especially during the genocidal massacres of 1972, they took little action in the name of "co-national-protecting," except to welcome the Hutu refugees who flooded into Rwanda in 1972. Kayibanda's main ambition for the Hutu of Burundi would have been for them to seize control of the Burundian state, not for them to live in a common (state) homeland with the Rwandan Hutu. This fact justifies the point made earlier in the chapter that the dual nationalisms of Rwanda pertain solely to the *Rwandan* Hutu and Tutsi identity communities.

The Habyarimana Regime and the Genocide of 1994

The second of the three crises that struck Rwanda under Hutu nationalist rule ended with Kayibanda being driven from power and General Juvénal

Habyarimana seizing power. After the Tutsi nationalism challenge was effectively repressed in 1963, the real politics in Rwanda began to revolve around a different axis, namely the regional rivalries of different Hutu politicians. Kayibanda's core constituency in Gitarama had rivalries both with senior figures from Butare, in the south, and, to a lesser extent, with leaders from Ruhengeri, in the north. The deeper source of the crisis of legitimacy was Kayibanda's failure to stimulate rapid economic development or to articulate any positive ideology to capture the imagination of the citizens of his country. In short, his repression was not justified in the name of any larger discernable project, which became problematic once the Tutsi nationalist "threat" receded.

The actual stimulus for Habyarimana's coup d'état in July 1973 was a failed effort on Kayibanda's part to reactivate the Hutu-Tutsi rivalry beginning the previous year. In May and June 1972, the Tutsi-dominated state in Burundi carried out a massive campaign of Hutu massacres in response to a challenge to its power. Kayibanda, realizing that his regime was failing, sought to capitalize on these events by raising the specter of resurgent Tutsi nationalism. He soon organized vigilante committees of Hutu radicals to ensure a rigid enforcement of his ethnic quota policy in all arenas of Rwandan life. This effort backfired, however, when many of the locally organized committees began to persecute not their putative Tutsi antagonists but rather rival Hutu from other regions.[63] The atmosphere of growing chaos provoked by these events provided the pretext for Habyarimana's coup and ensured its success.

From the time of his coup until the late1980s, Habyarimana ruled without significant challenge and recorded only one failed coup attempt in 1980. Unlike Kayibanda, Habyarimana developed a successful ideology that did engender a certain amount of economic progress, as well as political stability. Habyarimana created his own political party (the Mouvement Revolutionnaire National pour le Developpement—MRND) in 1973 and enshrined it in the constitution as the sole legal party. Political opponents to the regime, including former president Kayibanda (who died in prison), were dealt with ruthlessly. The regime exercised a quasi-totalitarian control over the movement and political activities of its citizens and even required peasants to provide two days of free labor per month.[64] The regime also enjoyed the support of the Catholic Church and encouraged Christian piety and humility in the citizenry.[65] As a result of the order and progress that one could witness in Rwanda between 1973 and 1990, the international aid community lavished the Habyarimana regime with generous support. And despite the restrictions on freedoms, the regime enjoyed the support of the great majority of Hutu and the tolerance of most Tutsi for most of its pre-1990 history.

As in the years of the Kayibanda regime during which the Tutsi nationalist threat was suppressed, the little "politics" that occurred under Habyarimana involved rivalries among various Hutu "political clans" in the country. The activity of Habyarimana's opponents-in-waiting increased during the periodic downturns in the Rwandan economy caused by falling coffee prices in the late 1970s and again in the late 1980s.[66] The nature of Habyarimana's policies with regard to identity community politics was somewhat ambiguous and thus open to interpretation. In that the regime had a kind of "ideology" that transcended the Hutu-Tutsi divide, one may be inclined to agree with Catharine Newbury that the Habyarimana regime made efforts "to dampen ethnic tensions over the period from 1973 to the mid-1980s."[67] Yet one should also bear in mind that the regime continued to equate rule in the name of the majority (i.e., the Hutu) with democracy. Moreover, one must recall, as does Prunier, that "throughout the Habyarimana years there would not be a single Tutsi bourgmestre or préfet, there was only one Tutsi officer in the whole army, there were two Tutsi members of parliament out of seventy and there was only one Tutsi minister out of a cabinet of between twenty-five and thirty members."[68] Most importantly of all, Habyarimana retained the policy of issuing identity cards that listed each citizen's "ethnicity" and the quota policy that restricted Tutsi to no more than 9 percent of the positions in any school, government agency, or business. Such policies may have served to "dampen ethnic tensions," but if they did so, it was by reminding the Tutsi community that they could have no substantive role in the governing of the country and encouraging the Hutu to believe that the government favored them at the expense of the Tutsi.

Due to these ambiguities, the question arises of whether Habyarimana (prior to 1990) was acting as a Rwandan nationalist or as a Rwandan Hutu nationalist. On the question of controlling the "homeland," Habyarimana, like his predecessor, responded to internal and external threats to territorial control but did not claim external territory. On the question of defining the nation, however, there would be disagreement. Newbury, given her emphasis, might well maintain that Habyarimana was engaged in "civic nation-building" (of a Rwandan nation), while Prunier would certainly emphasize that the thrust of his policies served to protect the (Hutu) ethnic nation.

The key to understanding Habyarimana's behavior, however, is to recognize that his most important goal was simply staying in power. To that end, protecting the Hutu identity group and promoting its feeling of enfranchisement was far more important than building a cross-community Rwandan national identity, so one is forced to accept Prunier's emphasis. Like his predecessor, Habyarimana paid lip service to the welfare of non-Rwandan Hutu living abroad, but he did not take substantive steps to annex foreign territory or otherwise protect their interests.

If Habyarimana's policies on identity community politics were somewhat open to interpretation between 1973 and 1989, after the onset of the civil war in 1990, they were clearly and undeniably aimed at protecting the Hutu nation and asserting its right to rule. The late 1980s saw both the onset of a severe economic crisis, occasioned particularly by a drop in coffee prices, and the opening of a new political space in response to global and regional pressures for political reform. Following the outbreak of protests in a number of other African countries, and a decline in support from many foreign donors who now wanted political reform, the pressures for change inside Rwanda mounted dramatically during 1990.[69] The government was forced to free the press and to abandon the single-party state concept. Encouraged by the opening of political space in Rwanda, Tutsi exiles in Uganda had organized an opposition political party, the Rwandan Patriotic Front (RPF), which also gained the support of some Hutu exiles from Rwanda. On October 1, 1990, the RPF launched an attack on the Habyarimana regime from its base in Uganda, but the attack was initially rebutted, and the RPF military commander, Fred Rwigyema, was killed. Although the RPF was publicly seeking the "right to return" for Ugandan political refugees abroad,[70] it certainly had the larger goal of contesting power in Kigali.

Following the attack of the RPF, Habyarimana's government adopted a dual strategy of continuing to open up political space on the one hand and of trying to convince the Hutu population of a grave threat from Tutsi invasion on the other. In the first category, the government began to allow the formation of opposition parties and to negotiate possible power-sharing agreements. It even conceded to the RPF demand that ethnic labels be removed from identity cards.[71] In April 1992, in response to still more popular demands for reform, a new, multiparty transitional government, whose prime minister came from the opposition Mouvement Démocratique Républicain (MDR), was installed.

Nonetheless, Habyarimana remained president. Even as his regime allowed reforms, "it worked simultaneously to diminish the impact of the reforms and to ensure that configurations of power did not change."[72] With the assistance of France, Habyarimana began a massive buildup of the Rwandan army, which increased from five thousand to thirty-five thousand in less than a year after the October 1990 invasion. Meanwhile, the government-controlled radio began disseminating false reports of atrocities at the hands of the RPF, which had again invaded the country in 1992, stimulating fear in the Hutu population. Moreover, the government began to organize massacres of Tutsi by local officials, resulting in hundreds of deaths through 1993. According to Longman, "By raising ethnic tensions, the MRND was able both to appeal to Hutu ethnic loyalty to build support and to frighten most Tutsi from taking an active role in political opposition."[73]

While Habyarimana pursued his dual strategy for defusing the opposition, his grasp on power was slowly slipping away, and the crisis of his regime was growing more severe. Meanwhile, a cadre of extremist Hutu nationalists were drawing up a "final solution" to the threat of Tutsi invasion and Tutsi rule: they were preparing a mass killing of all political opposition to be followed shortly by a genocide of all Rwandan Tutsi within reach. A great many details of the modalities of the genocide, especially the training of Interahamwe militiamen specifically for this purpose, were carefully organized in advance.[74] The plan was then implemented immediately after the downing of Habyarimana's plane on April 6, 1994, an event that itself may have been perpetrated by the *génocidaires*.[75] Some 800,000 Rwandan citizens, including some 750,000 Tutsi, were massacred by a variety of horrifying means over the next three months.[76]

As every serious observer of Rwanda has recognized, the genocide resulted from the active planning of high state officials and not from the "failure" of the Rwandan state.[77] It was a source of tremendous frustration to Rwanda scholars that many press accounts of the genocide accepted the propaganda of the perpetrators that the killings were the result of spontaneous, "tribal" fighting between Hutu and Tutsi elements. In fact, the tragedy represents an extreme form of Rwandan Hutu nationalism in the hands of fanatical state leaders. Essentially, both Habyarimana and his immediate successors pursued the same varieties of nationalism as Kayibanda, but the latter were the first to employ genocide as a means to that end.

Rwandan Tutsi Nationalism: From Exile to Power

As for Rwandan Tutsi nationalism, the flame was kept alive between 1963 and 1994, largely outside the Rwandan state in the various exile communities around the world. Given the near-totalitarian nature of the Kayibanda and Habyarimana regimes, it could also use "democracy" as its official justification. Between 1961 and 1963 Rwandan Tutsi political forces were essentially split between those in exile in neighboring countries and those still trying to operate in the country. As long as UNAR operated within Rwanda, Tutsi nationalism had a voice there, but this was ultimately intolerable to Kayibanda. Insofar as RADER retained some support among better-educated Hutu in certain corners of the country,[78] a glimmer of Banyarwandan nationalism stayed alive, but such an ideology was scarcely more acceptable to Kayibanda. The massacres of innocent Tutsi civilians within Rwanda succeeded in changing the ideologies of many remaining Tutsi inside the country from one of Banyarwandan national to Rwandan Tutsi nationalism, though giving voice to their feelings of pain and disenfranchisement would have been lethal.

After December 1963, Rwandan Tutsi nationalism existed only in the exile community in neighboring countries, where it percolated—or festered—for more than three decades. Prunier estimates that about four hundred thousand Tutsi refugees had fled abroad to neighboring countries by late 1964 and that this number had grown to between six hundred thousand and seven hundred thousand by the early 1990s.[79] The refugee communities kept alive their sense of identity through an array of cultural associations around the world, as Tutsi populations spread far beyond the camps. Many became successful professionals in the Western world, and some contributed money to Tutsi political organizations.

The Rwandan Tutsi might well have languished in exile until they were finally absorbed into the local populations were it not for the onset of the political reform movement in the early 1990s and the fluctuating fortunes of the Tutsi refugee population in neighboring Uganda. Under the second regime (1981–85) of Ugandan president Milton Obote, the Rwandan Tutsi refugee community in Uganda became the target of attacks by certain Bairu militants in Obote's government.[80] As a result, several hundred young Tutsi refugees in Uganda soon joined Yoweri Museveni's National Resistance Movement (NRM), a guerrilla movement seeking to overthrow Obote's government. When Museveni eventually seized power in Kampala in January 1986, some three thousand members of his fourteen-thousand-strong guerrilla army were of Rwanda Tutsi origin; by 1990, the Rwandan Tutsi numbered about eight thousand in Museveni's reinforced, one-hundred-thousand-strong army.[81] As a result of their experience in Museveni's army, these Tutsi exiles gained invaluable military experience, access to arms, and, most important, the good will of President Museveni. At a meeting in Kampala in December 1987 the old Rwandan exile political organ adopted a new name (the Rwandan Patriotic Front—RPF) and a new mission—the return to Rwanda by force.[82]

The vague plans of the RPF leaders were given new life after the onset of the political reform movement in 1989. A number of Hutu political opponents of Habyarimana began to flee Rwanda, and a number came to Uganda and joined forces with the RPF. In the first half of 1990, sensing the growing disarray in Habyarimana's regime, the RPF leaders, including Major General Fred Rwigyema and Major Paul Kagame,[83] planned an invasion of their homeland. When the hour of the invasion came, on October 1, 1990, Kagame was actually in the United States, receiving military training. After Rwigyema was killed on the second day of the attack, Kagame was notified, and he returned home to take command of the RPF force in Rwanda. By the time of his arrival toward the end of October, however, this thrust of the RPF had been repulsed by the Rwandan regular army (the Forces Armées Rwandaises—FAR). The French government soon rushed to Habyarimana's aid, helping him to bolster his army against any new attacks and shielding the regime against "Anglo-Saxon plots."

Over the next three and one-half years, the RPF reorganized itself under Kagame's leadership, while its soldiers hid out in the isolated mountain regions of northern Rwanda and, surreptitiously, in southern Uganda. The army commanders recruited more Rwandan exiles, increasing the size of their military force (the Rwandan Patriotic Army—RPA) from about 2,500 in 1990 to more than 25,000 in April 1994.[84] Tutsi exiles, as well as a few Hutu political opponents of Habyarimana from all around the world, sent financial contributions to the RPF to fund its political and military activities. The RPA leaders acquired arms both from their old comrades in the Ugandan army and from the international arms market.

Throughout this period, the RPA conducted small-scale military operations in the north of the country, including a daring raid on Ruhengeri in January 1991. In February 1993, the RPA launched a major military campaign in response to local massacres and the Habyarimana government's pullout from a political settlement negotiated in Arusha, Tanzania.[85] Local massacres of Tutsi and Hutu political opponents of Habyarimana were rampant in the ensuing months, stiffening the RPA's determination to fight. Meanwhile, the assassination of Burundi's Hutu president Melchior Ndadaye in October 1993 further hardened the hearts of the Hutu hard-liners in Kigali.

The RPA did not launch operations again in earnest until after the death of Habyarimana on April 6, 1994. It soon became apparent to it that an extremist Hutu nationalist faction set on genocide was in control of the government. In late April 1994, the RPA moved into various quarters of Kigali, but the interim government set up by the Hutu hard-liners quickly moved to the city of Gitarama. As the fighting continued, the genocide continued to unfold in areas of the country controlled by the FAR and the militias set up by the genocidal militias, the Interahamwe and Impuzamugambi. On June 13, the RPA took the town of Gitirama, and the rump Hutu hard-liner government again had to flee. On June 23, the French launched a "humanitarian mission" to Rwanda (Opération Turquoise), which failed to save the lives of very many Rwandans but did allow many units of the FAR to escape into exile in Zaire intact. On July 4, the RPA finally captured the remainder of Kigali, after which the resistance of the FAR soon collapsed. On July 19, a new, RPF government was installed in Kigali. Meanwhile, hundreds of thousands of Hutu were fleeing into refugee camps in Zaire, while tens of thousands of Tutsi exiles from Burundi, Tanzania, and Uganda began moving into Rwanda to claim land and vacated homes.

Following its seizure of power in Kigali, the government in Kigali had two major preoccupations: to render justice to the victims of the 1994 genocide and to quash any threat to the regime from the ex-FAR and Interahamwe. In the course of these two activities, the regime, effectively headed by Vice President and Minister of Defense Paul Kagame, committed its own atrocities and grievous human rights abuses. As the RPF occupied outlying areas of the country, there were soon stories of horrifying reprisals against the civilian Hutu population. At least five thousand Hutu refugees were killed at the Kibeho camp in April 1995. In the course of the war that installed Laurent Kabila in power in Kinshasa (DRC) in May 1997, tens of thousands more Hutu civilians fleeing their refugee camps were tracked down and killed, along with some number of Interahamwe militiamen.[86] Meanwhile, some one hundred thousand suspects of the genocide have been packed in the "filthy, human warehouses, the prisons," where thousands have died.[87] The scale of the killings is such that some scholars have even referred to them, albeit controversially, as yet another "genocide."[88] While one may demur from the idea that the regime is bent on the extermination of Rwanda's Hutu, one may infer that it is a Rwandan Tutsi nationalist regime. That is, it controls Rwanda for the primary purposes of protecting the rights and welfare of Rwanda's Tutsi. This is no less true for the fact that a sizable number of prominent Hutu have held important positions in the regime, including the presidency itself, in the person of Pasteur Bizimungu.[89]

Rather contradictorily, the RPF regime has pursued all five variants of postindependence nationalism on behalf of Rwanda's Tutsi at once. Unlike its predecessors, the new regime in Kigali has actually advanced claims over certain parts of territory of the DRC occupied by the (indigenous) Banyarwandan population.[90] This would seem to qualify as "external-territory-claiming," as defined in Barrington's introductory chapter. The real goal of such claims, however, is to justify Rwanda's military presence in Congo, where it has been involved in "co-national-protecting" of the Banyamulenge (indigenous Congolese Tutsi) since 1996. It seems doubtful that Rwanda's leaders will seriously pursue a strategy of incorporating any parts of Congolese territory into that of Rwanda, given the weakness of their claims. The contraction of the current regime's ideology lies in the fact that its practice is transparently one of (Tutsi) nation-protecting, while its rhetoric is that of "civic nation-building." Since the Rwandan Tutsi continue to represent a very small portion of the population, the public appeal to a civic ideal of nationalism, rather than an "ethnic" one, is inevitable. In order to try to resolve this contradiction, the RPF's largely Tutsi leadership has chosen an unusual central value as the centerpiece of "Rwandan" civic nationalism: the ideal of rendering justice to the victims of genocide. The RPF has thus made devotion to the pursuit of the *génocidaires* the highest expression of (putatively civic) nationalism, which happens to serve perfectly the end of protecting the (Tutsi) nation.

The Lessons of the Rwandan Binational Experience

The lessons of the Rwandan binational experience are sobering ones for those who hope that nationalism can be harnessed to liberal goals such as self-determination, democracy, and development. In this case, national identities defined against a communal "other" have been deployed by unscrupulous politicians to propel themselves into office and maintain themselves there. Their power has come at the expense equally of the nation that they represent and of the "other," cast in the role of adversary and threat. In their worst manifestations, these political patterns have set the stage for genocidal campaigns against both national peoples of Rwanda. Moreover, Rwanda's dual national identities have been manufactured despite the exceedingly weak objective bases for Hutu-Tutsi differentiation and the relatively strong objective bases for Banyarwandan nationalism.

The genesis and staying power of national identities in Rwanda are surprising and disturbing to anyone with liberal sensibilities. Liberal Rwandans and outside observers have long hoped for the emergence of a benign Banyarwandan nationalism, which could cultivate a sense of national dignity and serve as a basis for productive economic development. Since the Rwandan territory was well defined, and there were excellent objective bases for the development of such nationalism, such a nationalism might have emerged but for the ambitions of venal politicians. Two opposing national identities were instead created from the two identity communities. Conflict between them has been in the interest of those whose political fortunes have depended upon the support of angry populations, animated by a sense of victimhood and a desire for vengeance.

Rwandan Hutu and Rwandan Tutsi nationalist politicians have sought to control the Rwandan state in the interest of their respective identity communities. Although they typically speak in the name of universal values such as "democracy" (for instance, for a demographic majority) or of "justice" (for the surviving victims of genocide against the Tutsi), their real goals are clear enough in the context: to gain and maintain power by *appearing* to protect or promote the interests of one identity community or the other. The fact that the real interests of neither community are served by such politicians does not change the reality that such appeals have resonated well enough in the identity communities to keep them in power. The fact that the national identities are "artificial" and "created" does not lessen the human devastation wrought in their name.

Between 1959 and 1994, Rwanda's Hutu nationalist politicians sought to polarize people along the lines of the dominant identity communities. The fact that most liberal, Banyarwandan nationalist politicians have disappeared from the scene is a testament to the success of their project. Rwandan Tutsi nationalist politicians have been less interested in polarizing people in the same way, since their community represents a minority of the population. Nonetheless, it is telling that Tutsi exiles were not able to combine forces effectively with opposition Hutu elements during the long years of Hutu domination inside Rwanda. While the current RPF regime in Rwanda had a (token) Hutu as its president, the real power of the country always lay in the hands of Kagame and a few other leading Tutsi. No one can seriously doubt the utter Tutsi dominance of the current regime in Kigali, nor of the army that keeps it in power.

To put matters in terms of the causal hypotheses laid out in the introduction, it is clear that both nationalisms survived in Rwanda due to the actions of elite representatives of each community. In general, this confirms the instrumentalist perspective on the outbreak of intercommunal violence. Interestingly, while this conclusion serves to reinforce one of the main findings of recent scholarship on Rwanda, it challenges another directly. Most recent scholarship goes to great pains to debunk the primordialist mythmaking of both Rwandan Tutsi and Rwandan Hutu nationalist politicians and of ill-informed media sources about the precolonial roots of difference between the identity communities. In their enthusiasm for placing the blame for Rwanda's recent tragedy squarely on colonialism, however, the same scholarship suggests that the recent leaders of Rwanda's identity communities are virtual prisoners of the (colonial) past. Inadvertently, this stance absolves them of blame for episodes of postindependent intercommunal violence and genocide. The present analysis strongly confirms the view that objective, primoridal differences between Hutu and Tutsi have little to do with intercommunal violence. On the other hand, it does suggest that the choices made by power-seeking politicians to create nationalisms out of unformed identity communities were not inevitable or determined by colonial manipulation either. As the constructivist perspective proposes, the structures and the agents in these situations have mutually created ("constituted") one another, but the structures instituted by colonial authorities cannot be said to exercise a determining power over the influence of all Rwandan politicians.

To explain the outbreak of intercommunal violence, as opposed to merely the continuation of dual nationalisms in Rwanda, one has to add one further variable to the causal picture: uncertainty over the control of the state. As long as the Rwandan state was firmly under the control of colonial authorities, aided by their Tutsi adjuncts, Rwandan Hutu nationalism could not even emerge. With the loosening of colonial control, however, and the addition of the idea of the Hutu as a distinctive and oppressed group, Rwandan Hutu nationalism blossomed quite suddenly. While control over the state was uncertain, from 1959 well into the 1960s, intercommunal violence was manifest. During the long years of quasi-totalitarian Rwandan Hutu control, however, such violence was suppressed. It made its reappearance with the return of uncertainty in the era of political reform, the early 1990s. Sensing that they risked losing control over the Rwandan state in 1993–94, extreme Rwandan Hutu nationalists devised a "final solution," hoping to ensure their control in perpetuity. Now that Rwandan Tutsi nationalism has succeeded in dominating the state, and its control is relatively ensured, intercommunal violence has diminished again. Hence, uncertainty of control is a "necessary condition" that can be mated with the "efficient cause" of identity communal nationalism to explain the timing of the outbreaks of intercommunal violence.

As noted in the preceding, most contemporary scholars, and particularly historians, prefer to emphasize the colonial roots of the current national polarization of Rwanda. These years were indeed critical in altering the perceptions of Rwanda's two main identity communities and building the basis upon which nationalisms would later be built. The appearance of these nationalisms themselves sprang onto the political scene in Rwanda with breathtaking suddenness in the final months of colonial rule. At that point, even when colonial authorities sought to address injustices that they themselves had perpetuated in the past, their actions had the effect of further polarizing the political scene. This was the first crisis of state control that wracked Rwanda and began to crystallize the country's two national identity communities. The subsequent crises of control that occurred in 1963, 1972, and 1990–94 all led to abrupt and startling escalations in intercommunity tensions; the last regime crisis led the Hutu nationalists to seek a "final solution" to the challenge of the Tutsi nationalists. The country continues in the grip of these dual nationalisms, with any hope of overcoming the intercommunity confrontation depending on their containment in a larger, pan-Rwanda nationalist framework.

NOTES

The opening epigraph is cited in René Lemarchand, *Rwanda and Burundi* (London: Pall Mall and Praeger, 1970), 169.

1. Alain Destexhe, "The Third Genocide," *Foreign Policy* 97 (winter 1994–95): 3–17.

2. The actual number of those killed in the genocide remains one matter (of many) of intensive controversy surrounding the 1994 genocide. For one discussion of the numbers killed, and their ethnic-national identities, see Gérard Prunier, *The Rwandan Crisis: History of a Genocide* (New York: Columbia University Press, 1995), 261–65.

3. These have included *Issue,* the "opinion" journal of the (U.S.) African Studies Association, *Africa Today,* the *African Studies Review,* and the prestigious French journal *Politique Africaine.* The special issue of *Issue* entitled simply "Rwanda" was vol. 23, no. 2 (1995) and was devoted entirely to Rwanda and to the policies of foreign powers toward Rwanda; the special issue of *Africa Today,* vol. 45, no.1 (January–March 1998), was entitled "Crisis in Central Africa" and contained an introduction and four main articles, three of which were on Rwanda. The special issue of the *African Studies Review* 45, no. 1 (April 1998), contained an introduction and six articles, of which four were on Rwanda or genocide. The special issue of *Politique Africaine* 68 (December 1997), contained two introductory pieces and seven major articles, mostly on the involvement of foreign actors or transnational themes. In 1998 another issue of *Issue* was devoted to the problems of "Central Africa."

4. Among these are Alain Destexhe, *Rwanda and the Genocide,* trans. Alison Marschner (New York: New York University Press, 1995); Prunier, *The Rwandan Crisis;* Howard Adelman and Astri Suhrke, eds., *The Path of Genocide: The Rwanda Crisis from Uganda to Zaire* (New Brunswick, NJ: Transaction Publishers, 1999); and Philip Gourevitch, *We Wish to Inform You That Tomorrow We Will Be Killed with Our Families* (New York: Farrar, Straus and Giroux, 1998).

5. The "third people" referred to here are the Twa, who only represent about 1 percent of the population and whose political presence has been marginal in modern Rwandan history. Of course, the anthropological fascination with the Twa, and other "pygmy" (hunter-gatherer) people, is justified. On the BaMbuti people of Congo, see Colin Turnbull, *The Forest People* (New York: Simon and Schuster, 1962). The role of Rwanda's Twa is not considered further in this chapter.

6. The later figure may be found in Prunier, *The Rwanda Crisis,* 264.

7. As René Lemarchand notes in *Rwanda and Burundi* (London: Pall Mall and Praeger, 1970), 25, "In Rwanda [as opposed to Burundi], Tutsi elements were spread almost evenly throughout the country. The only notable exception was the northern region (Ndorwa, Mutara, Mulra), where the Tutsi never accounted for more than a tiny fraction of the total population."

8. The formulation of former President Kayibanda in the epigraph for this chapter has not been pursued by scholars.

9. The problem with referring to the Tutsi, for instance, as a class, is that the mass of Tutsi was equally as impoverished as the Hutu in 1955. See Phillipe Leurquin, *Le niveau de vie des populations du Ruanda-Urundi* (Louvain, 1961), 203. We might add that the Tutsi were even referred to as a "race" by the authors of the Bahutu Manifesto of 1957, as they were by some colonial administrators and anthropologists of an earlier period. Since this designation is least accurate in characterizing the true nature of the identity community, and reflects an illusory view of social reality, it is not used here.

10. It need not trouble us in the same way that other sociopolitical entities might appropriately go under a variety of labels at the same time. Consider the regime of Mobutu Sese Seko in Zaire (1965–97); this regime might be characterized at once as, for example, *personalistic, military, quasi-totalitarian, statist, one party,* and *kleptocratic.* The relevance of these various labels varied over the course of the regime, but they were not

fundamentally contradictory. Rather, each captured different key aspects of the regime in question.

11. The Banyarwandan populations in eastern Congo (DRC) include one group that had immigrated into the area in precolonial times and other groups that had immigrated more recently. On this topic, see Jean-Claude Willame, *Banyarwanda et Banyamulenge: Violences etnhiques et gestion de l'identitaire au Kivu* (Paris: Harmattan, 1997). On the relatedness of the Banyankole of southern Uganda, see Prunier, *The Rwanda Crisis,* 68 n. 51.

12. Although this is not to say that there have not been intense moments of transnational (transstate, or cross-border) empathy and concern among the Hutu and Tutsi identity communities in the Great Lakes region. For instance, at the moment of Hutu massacres in Burundi in 1972, the Rwandan Hutu leadership viewed events in Burundi with utmost concern. Likewise, the subsequent Rwandan Hutu regime in Kigali expressed similar concerns about developments in Burundi in 1993 when the regime of Mechior Ndadaye was overthrown by Tutsi army officers. For Rwanda-Burundi relations throughout the independence period, see Helen M. Hintjens, "Explaining the 1994 Genocide in Rwanda," *Journal of Modern African Studies* 37, no. 2 (1999): 276–80; and René Lemarchand, *Burundi: Ethnogenocide as Discourse and Practice* (Cambridge: Cambridge University Press, 1994).

13. Ghia Nodia, "Nationalism and Democracy," in *Nationalism, Ethnic Conflict, and Democracy,* ed. Larry Diamond and Marc F. Plattner (Baltimore: Johns Hopkins University Press, 1994), 11, quoted in the introductory chapter to this volume; for a similar view, also see Lowell Barrington, "'Nation' and 'Nationalism': The Misuse of Key Concepts in Political Science," *PS: Political Science and Politics* 30, no. 4 (December 1997): 713.

14. There are some other near parallels, however, such as Palestine/Israel, where two different national peoples are occupying the very same territory. Perhaps the extreme intractability of the Palestinian-Israeli dispute arises for the same reason as the Tutsi-Hutu dispute does in Rwanda: two national peoples vying for control of the same territory makes for the most intensive and dangerous kind of national conflict. Without the line drawn by the United Nations in 1947, in fact, the Israeli-Palestinian dispute might have at some point taken on the genocidal quality of the Hutu-Tutsi clash. In Israel, the Jewish leadership has not generally envisioned a total expulsion of the national "other" from "its" national space (though some elements in both the population and leadership may have happily contemplated such an eventuality).

15. One minor exception to this overall observation is a certain slice of territory in southern Uganda (Bufumbiro), bordering on northern Rwanda. The boundary here was clarified by the International Boundary Commission in 1912 and has not been a matter of serious international contention since then. See Lemarchand, *Rwanda and Burundi,* 99. There has also been a revival of certain irridentist claims since 1994, on which, see the following.

16. Ibid., 20.

17. See, for instance, Prunier, *The Rwanda Crisis,* 5–16, for a concise discussion.

18. See ibid., 8; as late as 1970, a former French ambassador to Rwanda was able to publish a book identifying the primordial Tutsi as a group of "magi" from Tibet. See Paul del Perugia, *Les derniers Rois-Mages,* 2nd ed. (Paris: Phébus, 1978) (1st ed., 1970), 37. Cited in Prunier, *The Rwanda Crisis.*

19. For example, this is the final word of Prunier, *The Rwanda Crisis,* 16. Also see

Lemarchand, *Rwanda and Burundi,* 18. One prominent theory is that the primordial Tutsi came from Ethiopia, where such people as the Oromo seem to have similar economic-cultural patterns and some physical similarities with the stereotypical Tutsi.

20. Given the current climate on race in the Western world, most scholars take great pains to make this point, which is now widely accepted. It is made most emphatically and effectively by Catharine Newbury, *The Cohesion of Oppression: Clientship and Ethnicity in Rwanda, 1860–1960* (New York: Columbia, 1988). Also see Claudine Vidal, *Sociologies des passions: Rwanda, Côte d'Ivoire* (Paris: Editions Karthala, 1991), especially 35; Pierre Tabara, *Afrique: La face cachée* (Paris: La pensée universelle); and Hintjens, "Explaining the 1994 Genocide in Rwanda," 247.

21. According to this foundational myth, the original king of the Tutsi sired three sons, Gatwa, Gahutu, and Gatutsi, but only the last proved himself worthy to be the king's successor—hence the mythical justification for Tutsi rulership. See Lemarchand, *Rwanda and Burundi,* 32–33.

22. According to Lemarchand, "Each province was entrusted to an army chief, and each district to a land chief and a cattle chief who were responsible for the collection of tithes in produce and cattle. Beneath this triumvirate spread a vast network of subchiefs from whom tribute was exacted for the higher chiefs and the kings." See Lemarchand, *Rwanda and Burundi,* 27.

23. Tabara, *Afrique: La face cachée,* 80.

24. Lemarchand, who uses the term *castes* to describe the Hutu and Tutsi throughout his work *Rwanda and Burundi,* represents one school of thought, while Newbury, who explicitly rejects the use of the term *caste* on the grounds that (1) there was no religious grounds for "sanctioning separate between ethnic groups," (2) economic specialization was not so clear-cut as has been suggested, and (3) the categories of Hutu and Tutsi were "flexible" in precolonial times (Newbury, *The Cohesion of Oppression,* 11–12).

25. See Louis de Lacger, *Le Ruanda* (Kabgayi, Rwanda: publisher unknown, 1961) (1st ed., 1939), cited in Newbury, *The Cohesion of Oppression,* 12–13; even Lemarchand, who portrays the Rwandan "caste" system as rigidly inflexible, does acknowledge that wealthy and politically powerful Hutu could be "absorbed into the upper caste." See Lemarchand, *Rwanda and Burundi,* 39.

26. Lemarchand, *Rwanda and Burundi,* 43.

27. In these locations, particularly in the northern regions of the Kiga clan, local Hutu chiefs fought fiercely to resist incorporation into the Tutsi-dominated realm and certainly retained a very different identity as a result. There is no indication, however, that the independent Hutu-Kiga chiefs had any sense of ethnic solidarity with those Hutu who lived under the suzerainty of the mwami.

28. Whereas many Hutu in precolonial times had not submitted themselves to a patron. See Tabara, *Afrique: La face cachée,* 79–83.

29. On the Belgian colonial favoritism shown to the Tutsi in education, see Lemarchand, *Rwanda and Burundi,* 134–36; and Newbury, *The Cohesion of Oppression,* 115–16.

30. See Lemarchand, *Rwanda and Burundi,* 59–60 and 73; and Newbury, *The Cohesion of Oppression,* 130. It is worth noting that Belgian colonial policy initially favored the Hutu before switching definitely to indirect rule through the mwami. See Newbury, *The Cohesion of Oppression,* 129.

31. Lemarchand, *Rwanda and Burundi,* 60.

32. Newbury, *The Cohesion of Oppression,* 183.

33. On the concept of "critical junctures," see Leonardo Villalón, "The African State at the End of the Twentieth Century: Parameters of the Critical Juncture," in *The African State at a Critical Juncture: Between Disintegration and Reconfiguration,* ed. Leonardo Villalón and Philip Huxtable (Boulder: Lynne Rienner, 1998), 3–25.

34. According to Lemarchand (*Rwanda and Burundi,* 81), Banyarwandan nationalism was "never more than an epiphenomenon."

35. Newbury, *The Cohesion of Oppression,* 181.

36. Lemarchand, *Rwanda and Burundi,* 96.

37. Ibid., 107.

38. Ibid., 109.

39. Ibid., 148; and Prunier, *The Rwanda Crisis,* 44.

40. The official name of the document was "Notes on the Social Aspect of the Racial Native Problem in Rwanda." The entire text can be found, in French, in F. Nkundabagenzi, *Le Rwanda politique (1958–1960)* (Brussels: CRISP, 1961), 20–29.

41. See the discussion of this problem in Prunier, *The Rwanda Crisis,* 46.

42. This is an important theme of Lemarchand, *Rwanda and Burundi,* chapter 3.

43. Ibid., 101–2.

44. Ibid., 112.

45. The highly complicated process began with the nomination of "electoral colleges" by regional "subchiefs." These colleges then elected members of subchiefdom councils from among their own members. Subsequently, the members of the councils elected chiefdom councils, which then in turn elected the councils for the territories (region) and the state level. See Jacques J. Maquet and Marcel d'Hertefelt, *Elections en société féodale: Une étude sur l'introduction du vote populaire au Ruanda-Urundi* (Brussels, ARSC, 1959), 22–25.

46. See Lemarchand, *Rwanda and Burundi,* 136.

47. Prunier, *The Rwanda Crisis,* 49–50.

48. Tabara, *Afrique: La face cachée,* 180–85.

49. Especially from left-wing forces, including several Communist countries on the United Nations Trusteeship Council. These countries (ironically) supported the monarchist UNAR party in 1959–60. See Prunier, *The Rwanda Crisis,* 47, and the discussion in this chapter.

50. See the cover photo on Newbury, *The Cohesion of Oppression.*

51. Prunier, *The Rwanda Crisis,* 47.

52. Ibid., 47.

53. Ibid., 48.

54. For instance, Newbury makes much of the fact that an independent party, Intérêts Communaux du Kinyaga (INTERCOKI), and RADER together gained some 32 percent of the vote in Abiiru province (of Cyangugu Territory) in the 1960 communal elections (see Newbury, *The Cohesion of Oppression,* 203–6). After a further analysis of the local vote, she concludes that the vote in the province was "based more on persons and programs than on ethnic orientation and Hutu-Tuutsi polarization" (206). Be that as it may, the increasing polarization of the vote along ethnic lines and in favor of essentially (Hutu and Tutsi) nationalist parties was clear in the 1961 elections.

55. Prunier, *The Rwanda Crisis,* 52; and Lemarchand, *Rwanda and Burundi,* 184.

56. See Lemarchand, *Rwanda and Burundi,* 178; Newbury, *The Cohesion of Oppression,* 198; and Prunier, *The Rwanda Crisis,* 51–52. It is particularly interesting to note

that PARMEHUTU, a forthrightly (Hutu) nationalist party, far outpaced APROSOMA, which initially had some limited support from poorer Tutsi constituents. It is true, on the other hand, that RADER, the more liberal Tutsi-oriented party, outscored the radical Tutsi UNAR party in these elections, though both together only garnered 8 percent of the communal council positions.

57. Lemarchand, *Rwanda and Burundi,* 188–94

58. Ibid., 197.

59. These events are known as the "Bugesera Invasion." Ibid., 216–27; the description of the executions is found on p. 223.

60. Prunier, *The Rwanda Crisis,* 60 n. 35.

61. Lemarchand, *Rwanda and Burundi,* 234.

62. Prunier, *The Rwanda Crisis,* 56, 58.

63. Ibid., 61.

64. Ibid., 79.

65. See Timothy Longman, "Christianity and Democratisation in Rwanda: Assessing Church Responses to Political Crisis in the 1990s," in *The Christian Churches and Democratisation of Africa,* ed. Paul Gifford (Leiden, Netherlands: Brill, 1995).

66. Prunier, *The Rwanda Crisis,* 84.

67. Catharine Newbury, "Ethnicity and the Politics of History in Rwanda," *Africa Today* 45, no. 1 (January–March 1998), 18; also see Timothy Longman, "Rwanda: Democratization and Disorder: Political Transformation and Social Deterioration," in *Political Reform in Francophone Africa,* ed. John F. Clark and David E. Gardinier (Boulder: Westview, 1997), 298.

68. Prunier, *The Rwanda Crisis,* 75.

69. See Longman, "Rwanda," 290–92.

70. As emphasized in ibid., 293.

71. Ibid., 294.

72. Ibid., 296.

73. Ibid., 298.

74. See Michele D. Wagner, "All the Bourgmestre's Men: Making Sense of Genocide in Rwanda," *Africa Today* 45, no. 1 (1998): 29–34; Prunier, *The Rwanda Crisis,* 237–42; and Hintjens, "Explaining the 1994 Genocide in Rwanda," 267–73.

75. See René Lemarchand, "Rwanda: The Rationality of Genocide," *Issue* 23, no. 2 (1995): 10; cf. Longman, "Rwanda," 300.

76. The figures are from Prunier, *The Rwanda Crisis,* 265; for one popular account of the modalities of the killings, see Gourevitch, *We Wish to Inform You.*

77. See especially Alison Des Forges, "The Ideology of Genocide," *Issue* 23, no. 2 (1995): 44–47; this point is a major theme in the writings of, among others, Catharine Newbury, David Newbury, Longman, and Hintjens.

78. As it did; see Lemarchand, *Rwanda and Burundi,* 223.

79. Prunier deducts a percentage for those who had assimilated into their local environments; see *The Rwanda Crisis,* 63.

80. The Bairu are the "low-caste" section of the Banyankole people of southern Uganda, the "high-caste" portion being the Bahima. The Banyankole are historically and ethnically linked with the Banyarwanda, and the "caste" division of the Banyankole parallels the Hutu-Tutsi divide in Rwanda.

81. Prunier, *The Rwanda Crisis,* 70–71.

82. Ibid., 72–73.

83. Rwigyema was a former commander in chief of the NRM's army, and Kagame was then acting head of military security for Museveni.

84. Prunier, *The Rwanda Crisis,* 93, 117.

85. The RPA reached to within thirty kilometers of Kigali before the RPF leadership decided that an assault on the capital would be unwise because of France's determined military support of Habyarimana and because the Hutu population in the capital had rallied to the defense of Habyarimana's regime.

86. René Lemarchand, "The Fire in the Great Lakes," *Current History* 98, no. 628 (May 1999): 196.

87. Wagner, "All the Bourgmestre's Men," 26.

88. René Lemarchand, "Genocide in the Great Lakes: Which Genocide? Whose Genocide?" *African Studies Review* 41, no. 1 (April 1998).

89. Bizimungu's presence at the head of the Rwandan government raises the question of whether a nonmember of a nation could play the role of a leading nationalist for that nation. The answer seems to be affirmative, given not only Bizimungu's example but also that of other state rulers, like Stalin, who served the interests of one nation (the Russians) while having origins in another national group (Georgian/Ossestian).

90. David Newbury, "Irredentist Rwanda: Ethnic and Territorial Frontiers in Central Africa," *Africa Today* 44, no. 2 (1997): especially 214–15.

5. From Irredentism to Secession

The Decline of Pan-Somali Nationalism

PETER J. SCHRAEDER

THE FACT THAT SOMALIA remains synonymous with "ethnic chaos" and "state collapse" makes it a splendid case study for contemporary theorists of African nationalism[1]—not least of all due to the simple reality that Somalia was one of the brightest stars of the galaxy of studies on Africa nationalism at the beginning of the contemporary independence era. In a continent that, in the words of Emerson, was "rich in nationalisms but poor in nations," Somalia stood out during the 1960s as one of three largely ethnically homogeneous African countries (the other two being Lesotho and Botswana).[2] It is for this reason that Somalia was often heralded—one could even say admired—by academics and policymakers alike as having a dramatic head start compared to the vast majority of other, more multiethnic African countries on the "nation-building" goal pursued by the first generation of African nationalists.

Somalia also served as a lightning rod for regional and international condemnation due to the irredentist dimension of Somali nationalism that sought to incorporate the Somali-inhabited portions of neighboring countries into a larger pan-Somali nation-state. For nationalism scholars of the 1960s, the irredentist quest was taken to be a permanent feature of Somali nationalism and therefore one of the greatest challenges for an African continent that considered as "inviolable" the inherited frontiers of the colonial era.[3] The presumed enduring quality of both the domestic nation-building and the international irredentist elements of what can be termed the "pan-Somali nationalist project" was captured in the title *Somalia: Nation in*

Search of a State, one of the classic English-language introductions to Somali politics and international relations.[4]

The primary purpose of this chapter is to examine the rise and decline of the pan-Somali nationalist project during the second half of the twentieth century. An important argument of this chapter is that, contrary to the major assumptions of the nationalist literature of the early independence era, the pan-Somali nationalist project was neither inevitable nor a natural outgrowth of the ethnic homogeneity of Somalis living within the Horn of Africa.[5] Ethnic homogeneity does not, in and of itself, automatically provide the basis for politically inspired and enduring nationalist movements.[6] The emergence of the pan-Somali nationalist project was instead the direct result of the unique confluence of several historically specific developments, most notably the rise of a new generation of Somali political elites during the 1950s and the 1960s who were initially interested in ridding their region of foreign control. Once successful in this regard, however, self-interested and competing groups of elites largely broken down along clan lines employed the rhetoric of nation-building and Somali nationalism to guarantee their quest for and/or hold over power, ultimately squandering whatever degree of pan-Somali nationalism that once existed among the elites and to a much lesser degree the general population as a whole.

This chapter examines a series of political-military events, ranging from the Ogaadeen War between Ethiopia and Somalia in 1977–78 to the Somali civil war of the 1980s and the 1990s, that clearly demonstrate the shallowness of an elite-driven, pan-Somali nationalism that ultimately resonated little with the general population. Somalia's defeat in the Ogaadeen War intensified divisive, clan-based tensions that at a bare minimum historically have been below the surface of this seemingly homogeneous society. The Somali civil war, which culminated in the complete collapse of the Somali state and a series of United Nations–sponsored military interventions from 1992 to 1995, further strengthened clan-based centrifugal forces that, in the words of Adam and Ford, "ripped" the fabric of Somali nationalism.[7] Indeed, northern Somalia's secession and declaration of independence as the Somaliland Republic in 1991 signaled the death knell of both the nation-building and the irredentist components of the pan-Somali nationalist project.

This analysis of the decline of the pan-Somali nationalist project also allows for a modest contribution to the relevance of three major sets of competing theoretical approaches—primordialism, constructivism, and instrumentalism—that have sought to explain the rise and enduring nature of nationalism both in Africa and other regions of the world.[8] Proponents of what is often referred to as the *primordialist* approach have argued that Somali nationalism is the natural outgrowth of historically grounded and enduring affective ties in which individuals recognize their attachment to an overarching Somali ethnic identity.[9] These scholars in particular focus on the ethnic homogeneity of the Somali people as the cornerstone of politically inspired nationalist movements. Proponents of an alternative *constructivist* approach have argued to the contrary that the idea of a unified Somali people in search of a state is essentially an "invented memory" or "myth." The myth was initially propagated by civilian and military rulers of the postcolonial Somali state and ultimately became the cornerstone of both Somali and Western academic scholarship.[10] This myth not only became the basis of the failed pan-Somali nationalist project but also constitutes the essence of internationally inspired attempts to resolve ongoing ethnic conflict and state collapse in Somalia through the resurrection of the unified Somali state originally created in 1960. Finally, proponents of what can be labeled the *instrumentalist* approach have emphasized the voluntarist role of elites in creating and molding politically inspired nationalist movements.[11] In the case of Somalia, these scholars would argue that the pan-Somali nationalist project was generated from above by a diverse group of Somali political elites who perceived the political benefits to be derived from creating a nation-state that transcended traditional clan differences among the Somali peoples inhabiting the Horn of Africa.

The tentative theoretical conclusion of this chapter is that, although each of these three approaches has shortcomings, a reformulated instrumentalist approach that draws upon elements of both its primordialist and constructivist counterparts offers the most promising avenue of research for understanding the death of Somali nationalism and the evolution of similar nationalist projects throughout contemporary Africa. The remainder of this chapter is divided into four sections. After briefly setting out those factors necessary for a comprehensive understanding of Somali nationalism, a second section documents the rise of an elite compact that formed the basis for the historically specific pan-Somali nationalist project of the 1960s. A third section documents how a series of political-military events, most notably the Ogaadeen War (1977–78) and the initial stages of the Somali civil war (1980–91), led to a turning point in Somali nationalist history that signaled the decline of the pan-Somali nationalist project. A final section offers general conclusions and avenues for further research.

Building Blocks of Somali National Identity & Nationalism

Four factors serve as essential building blocks for any comprehensive understanding of the rise and decline of Somali nationalism. The cornerstone of primordialist interpretations of Somali nationalism is the often-stated belief that Somalia constitutes one of Africa's most *homogeneous* countries. The population is composed of two major groups: the dominant Samaale (75 percent of the population), who are descendants of a pastoral nomadic past, and the Sab (20 percent), who traditionally have been distinguished as sedentary or semisedentary agriculturalists inhabiting the interriverine area of the country. Although a social hierarchy exists in which the self-ascribed "noble" Samaale of pastoral descent consider the Sab to be socially inferior, these two groups nonetheless constitute part of an overarching Somali culture.[12] Somalis are further united by a common language, literature, and religion. Despite the lack of an official written orthography until 1973 and the existence of several regional dialects, Somali is spoken throughout the territory.[13] An extremely proud oral tradition places Somali singers and poets in high esteem, with early nationalist leaders being renowned for their oratorical skills.[14] Somalia is also united by religion. An estimated 99.8 percent of the population is Muslim, with most Somalis belonging to the Shafi'i rite of the Sunni sect of Islam, as well as to several Islamic brotherhoods, most notably the Qadiriyyah, Salihiyyah, and Ahmadiyyah.[15]

Somalia's cultural homogeneity is nonetheless challenged by extremely strong and enduring *kinship-based networks* referred to as *clans*. This second building block for understanding Somali nationalism is based on the simple yet powerful reality that individual clans (if not clan members) can usually trace their common lineage back hundreds of years to a specific founding member or ruling family dynasty. As artfully demonstrated in Lewis's pioneering work on Somali clan structure,[16] the Somali ethnic group is divided according to at least six major clan families: four from the predominantly pastoral Samaale (Daarood, Dir, Hawiye, and Isaaq) and two from the predominantly sedentary Sab (Digil and Rahanwayn). These clan families are further subdivided into smaller units that assume responsibility for organizing social, economic, and political activities. The smallest group, known as the *reer* (nomadic hamlet), ranges in size from five to fifty individual Somali families, and the largest, the clan, often includes thousands or tens of thousands of members. The clan remains the cornerstone of Somali society, and its political manifestation is perhaps best captured by the maxim "There are no permanent clan friends or enemies, only permanent clan self-interests."

A third building block for understanding Somali nationalism revolves around the Somali people's classification among anthropologists as a *classic segmented political system.*[17] The term *segmented* refers to a decentralized political system marked by the diffusion of political power. Segmented political systems historically lacked a centralized state and a recognized political authority capable of enforcing a preferred set of policies throughout a territory. Though political authority was diffuse, many communities, such as the Somalis, were nations sharing the same language, customs, and cultural history. The nation simply lacked a central political authority to which the members of that society owed allegiance. In short, a segmented system constituted a nation without a state. This characterization is particularly relevant to the Somali people who, prior to the imposition of colonial rule, were never governed by a centralized political authority. The precolonial history of Somali politics is best described by the rise and fall of clan alliances in the absence of any central government, resulting in alternating periods of peaceful competition and clan warfare. Classic segmented systems typically fostered competition and conflict between extended clan families, especially in nomadic environments when drought and famine diminished already scarce water and food resources.

The *impact of colonialism,* most notably the tendency of colonial powers to draw boundaries that often divided African ethnic groups among numerous colonial states, constitutes the final building block for understanding Somali nationalism. Previously united by a common culture but lacking a centralized authority, Somalia's classic segmented political system was ultimately subjugated and divided among four imperial powers: Britain, France, Italy, and an independent Ethiopia. The northwestern portion of the Somali nation became part of a French colony, Le Territoire Français des Afars et des Issas (French Territory of the Afars and the Issas), which achieved independence in 1977 as the Republic of Djibouti. The western Ogaadeen region was annexed by the Ethiopian empire and remains a province of the present-day country of Ethiopia. The southeastern portion of the Somali nation became part of the British colony (and subsequent independent country) of Kenya and is typically referred to by its original colonial administrative name: the Northern Frontier District (NFD). Two final portions, the British Somaliland Protectorate (often referred to as British Somaliland) and Italian Somaliland, became part of the British and Italian colonial empires. These two portions achieved independence and formed a federation in 1960 that became known as the Republic of Somaliland—the contemporary country of Somalia. The most notable impact of the Somali people's division among several colonial authorities is that it set the stage for what essentially constituted a twofold nationalist project for the elites of the newly independent Somalia: (1) a nation-building goal designed to overcome the divergent colonial pasts of the former British Somaliland Protectorate and Italian Somaliland that were now joined together and (2) the irredentist desire to unite their separated peoples in neighboring territories in one overarching, pan-Somali nation-state.[18]

The Emergence of an Elite-Inspired Pan-Somali Nationalist Project

The emergence and strengthening of the pan-Somali nationalist project in the 1950s and the early 1960s was neither inevitable nor a natural outgrowth of the ethnic homogeneity of Somalis living within the divided Somali-inhabited territories of the Horn of Africa. The Somalis had never sworn allegiance to any centralized political authority nor had their common territories ever been ruled by a centralized political state. A unique confluence of several historically specific developments was instead responsible for the development of what Laitin and Samatar refer to as the "new nationalist climate" of the 1950s.[19]

First, political activists at both the elite and popular levels were inspired by the political exploits of several "heroes" of Somali history, most notably Aḥmed Gurey of the sixteenth century and Sayyid Mahammad Abdille Hasan of the twentieth century. Nicknamed *the left-handed* (a symbol of honor in Somali society), Gurey was a famed Islamic conqueror in Somali folklore who led several Somali-inhabited Islamic sultanates of his era in a campaign against the Christian-ruled Ethiopian empire of Emperor Lebna Dengel. During the twentieth century, the Sayyid (nicknamed *the Mad Mullah* by the British) was renowned for having led the so-called Dervish struggle against the foreign occupying forces of Ethiopia, Great Britain, and Italy.[20] It is important to note, however, that both of these historical figures created regional, clan-based political-military movements rather than territory-wide nationalist movements inclusive of all major clans.[21]

The future basis for the emergence of some degree of pan-Somali nationalism was provided by the temporary unification of significant portions of Somali-inhabited territory under centralized political administration during World War II and its aftermath. The Italians added Ethiopia's Ogaadeen region to Italian Somaliland after occupying Ethiopia in 1935, and in 1940 they added the conquered British Somaliland territory. This latter addition to the Italian empire was short-lived, as Britain reoccupied its territory in 1941. For the next ten years, Britain would place all the Somali-inhabited territories of the Horn of Africa (except for the French colony of Djibouti) under one unified military administration. In both cases, the creation of a centralized political authority allowed for the greater movement of people, trade, and ideas between previously separated territories. "The most notable development under British military rule was the growth of a new and fervent sense of national awareness," explain Laitin and Samatar. "In mosques and markets, in public and private meetings, urban Somalis began to question the legitimacy of colonial rule, to call for political unity, and to help debate large, supratribal issues."[22]

Anticolonial sentiment served as an important rallying point of Somali nationalism. Although Somali nationalists, like their counterparts throughout the African continent, were often sharply divided on political agendas, ideological orientation, and economic programs, they could agree on one point: the necessity and desirability of independence from foreign control. One important turning point occurred in 1946 after British foreign secretary Ernest Bevin failed to win the approval of the wartime Four-Power Commission of Allied nations for the creation of a pan-Somali state to be placed under British trusteeship (the so-called Bevin Plan) in preparation for ultimate independence.[23] The Four-Power Commission rejected the proposal (as well as demands of other Somalis for immediate independence) in favor of redividing the Somali territories, subsequently sending a delegation to Italian Somaliland in 1948 that, with the subsequent endorsement of the United Nations General Assembly, paved the way for a return of Italian trusteeship over the territory from 1950 to 1960. The 1948 visit was marked by a political riot known in Somali as *dagahtur* (literally, "throwing stones") in which at least seventeen Somalis and fifty-one Italians were killed and which was commemorated by the construction of the Dagahtur Monument in Mogadishu in 1970.

The most important contribution to the new nationalist climate of the 1950s, which has served as the basis of instrumentalist interpretations of Somali nationalism, was the emergence of educated elites who were firmly committed to the pan-Somali ideal. In Italian Somaliland, the formation in 1943 of the Somali Youth Club (SYC), later reorganized in 1947 as a political party known as the Somali Youth League (SYL), signaled the emergence of a pan-Somali nationalist party intent on creating a pan-Somali nation-state.[24] The SYL was the most broad-based Somali political party in terms of clan membership, although it only recruited among the four major clans of the pastoral Samaale (Daarood, Dir, Hawiye, and Isaaq). The Hizbia Dighil Mirifle (HDM) political party, later known as Hizbia Dastur Mustaqil al-Somal (HDMS), was also formed in 1947 and sought to serve as a counterweight to the politically dominant SYL.[25] Although the HDMS shared the SYL's pan-Somali political agenda, its recruitment of party members was primarily among the two major clans of the predominantly sedentary Sab (Digil and Rahanwayn). The support for these two parties' nationalist platforms was demonstrated by their success in Italian Somaliland's municipal elections of 1958: the SYL won 63 percent of the seats, and the HDMS won 26 percent.[26]

The formation in 1945 of the Somali National Society (SNS), later reorganized in 1951 as a political party known as the Somali National League (SNL), signaled the emergence of the pan-Somali nationalist movement in British Somaliland.[27] Unlike its southern counterparts, the SNL primarily recruited among one clan group—the Isaaq–which constituted nearly two-thirds of British Somaliland's population. The United Somali Party (USP) shared the pan-Somali dream but nonetheless sought to counter the SNL's dominant influence by primarily recruiting among minority clan groups within British Somaliland, most notably among the Dulbahante and Warsangali in the east and the Iise and the Gadabursi in the west. In the 1960 elections to British Somaliland's legislative council, the domination of the SNL and the USP was demonstrated by their winning of 61 and 36 percent of the seats, respectively.[28]

The emergence of elite-based parties committed to pan-Somali nationalism was more mixed in the three remaining territories inhabited by ethnic Somalis, at least partially due to the determination of colonial authorities to actively suppress such activities. In the case of French-ruled Djibouti, the breakdown of votes related to the 1958 referendum on the *loi cadre* (enabling act) of the Fifth Republic demonstrated a strong commitment to pan-Somali nationalism. Although the referendum was strongly in favor of continued association with France, largely due to a strong yes vote among the Afar ethnic group and resident European populations, the majority of those who voted no were Somalis who supported the pan-Somali platform of Mahmoud Harbi. Harbi was killed in a plane accident in 1960, and a French-groomed Somali alternative, Hassan Gouled Aptidon, who campaigned for a yes vote in the 1958 referendum, not only was elected as a deputy to the French National Assembly in 1959 but also emerged as Djibouti's first president (1977–91) in the contemporary independence era.[29]

In the case of Kenya's NFD region, initial local support for the SYL was quickly quelled by British authorities, who proscribed and closed SYL offices in 1948.[30] During the following decade, a series of pan-Somali organizations, particularly the Somali National Association (SNA), emerged in Kenyan urban areas outside of the NFD, but their links with Somali groups and interests within the NFD were extremely "tenuous."[31] A more activist support for pan-Somali ideals only reemerged in 1960, when it became apparent that the British and Italian Somaliland territories were going to federate and achieve independence as the Republic of Somalia. During this period, increasingly organized political groups in the NFD, most notably the Northern Province People's Progressive Party (NPPPP), offered numerous petitions to British colonial authorities demanding the detachment of the NFD from Kenya and its federation with the Republic of Somalia.[32] These petitions were extremely popular in the NFD, prompting Governor Sir Patrick Rennison to promise the Kenyan Somalis that "they would be consulted on any change in the administration of the area."[33]

Interestingly enough, the Ogaadeeni Somalis did not create a pan-Somali political party prior to 1960 despite the region's historical distinction as a battleground for the sixteenth-century nationalist forces of Gurey and the twentieth-century nationalist forces of the Sayyid.[34] Partially due to Ogaadeeni suspicions that incorporation into a pan-Somali state would deprive them of control over their own resources, as well as a series of ruthless campaigns on the part of the Ethiopian empire to suppress any alternative nationalist political organizations, several events nonetheless demonstrated nascent popular pan-Somali sentiment among the Ogaadeen that would fully blossom in the 1960s and the 1970s. The most notable incident occurred in the Ogaadeeni town of Jijiga in 1948 when the withdrawing British authorities lowered an SYL flag that had been hoisted by pan-Somali nationalists to protest the Ogaadeen region's return the following day to Ethiopian sovereignty. The British action unleashed a popular riot that resulted in dozens of casualties.[35]

The first concrete results of the pan-Somali activities of Somali political elites were realized on July 1, 1960, when the former British and Italian Somaliland territories officially federated as the newly independent Republic of Somalia after months of negotiations primarily between the SYL and the SNL. The federation of these two territories represented the formal launching of the twofold nationalist project shared by the political elites of both countries: the nation-building goal—designed to transform the legacies of British and Italian colonialism in the pursuit of socioeconomic and political-military development—and the irredentist desire to unite their separated peoples in neighboring territories in one overarching, pan-Somali nation-state.

Elite Disillusionment and the Decline of Pan-Somali Nationalism

One of the most remarkable aspects of Somalia's heady nationalist experiment was the degree of agreement and clarity among nationalist elites concerning the nature and ultimate justice of their pan-Somali nationalist agenda. Simply put, elites of the new Republic of Somalia were in agreement as to who theoretically formed the Somali nation (all ethnic Somalis) and which territories theoretically formed part of a larger, natural, pan-Somali nation-state (all neighboring, Somali-inhabited territories). As clearly symbolized by the five-pointed star emblazoned on Somalia's national flag, this irredentist quest envisioned the reunification of all five Somali territories within one pan-Somali state. The Republic of Somalia already included two of these territories (British Somaliland and Italian Somaliland), and the elites of that country were intent on seeking the "return" of the three remaining "lost" territories: the Ogaadeen (Ethiopia), southeastern Djibouti, and the NFD (Kenya). From the perspective of Somali studies specialists, the international politics of the Horn of Africa had been forever transformed. A highly motivated and idealistically infused nationalist elite was on the verge of capitalizing on the varying pan-Somali sentiments of neighboring Somali communities to create a pan-Somali nation-state.

In reality, however, a true, populist-based Somali nationalism was never born. Somali elites, regardless of whether democratically elected or illegally taking power through a military coup d'état, ultimately employed the rhetoric of nation-building and Somali irredentism to guarantee their hold over power—not to promote a pan-Somali nationalism truly capable of overcoming clan-based differences. More than four decades after independence, the domestic and international components of the pan-Somali nationalist project lay in ruins against the backdrop of state collapse, civil war, and the secession and declaration of independence by the north. Three sets of historical events are key to understanding the decline of pan-Somali nationalism.

Military Coup d'État amid Growing North-South Strains, 1960–69

A democratically elected parliamentary regime under the leadership of President Aadan Abdallah Usmaan and Prime Minister Abdirashiid Ali Shermaarke was the first to implement the nation-building goal of the pan-Somali nationalist project. Usmaan, a member of the southern-based Hawiye clan, and Shermaarke, a member of the southern-based Majeerteen subclan of the Daarood, initially oversaw the creation of a clan-based elite compact that ensured proportional representation for individual clans. The regime's first cabinet therefore included four Daaroods (two Dulbahantes, one Majeerteen, and one Mareehaan), two Isaaqs (one Habar Awal and one Habar Yoonis), three Hawiyes (one Habar Gidir and two Abgaals), and three Digil and Rahanwayn.[36] In so doing, the Usmaan/Shermaarke administration was presumably attempting to prevent clan suspicions and competition from subsuming the energies of the new administration by making the equitable distribution of political spoils the bedrock of all future initiatives. Among the many achievements of the new administration were the drafting and adoption of a new constitution, the formulation of a new judicial system that blended important components of the British and Italian (not to mention sharia) legal traditions, and the merging of the northern and southern civil services and security forces.[37]

The newly elected government also lost little time in aggressively pursuing the irredentist component of the pan-Somali nationalist project through a wide variety of interventionist tools ranging from diplomatic demarches to the funding of guerrilla insurgencies in the three "lost" points of the Somali star. In the case of Djibouti, the government actively supported the military activities of the Front de Libération de la Côte des Somalis (FLCS; Liberation Front of the Somali Coast), a pan-Somali guerrilla organization created in 1963 that primarily drew upon the Iise Somali clan for support. In the case of Kenya's NFD region, initial diplomatic overtures were replaced by the funding of guerrilla activities after the British colonial government rejected the results of a 1963 referendum that demonstrated overwhelming support for federation with the Republic of Somalia; instead, the British colonial government favored continued inclusion in a soon-to-be independent Kenya. Guerrilla forces denounced as *shiftas* (bandits) by the Kenyan government were embraced as pan-Somali freedom fighters by the Somali government.

The potential risks associated with the pan-Somali quest, namely the outbreak of direct military hostilities between Somalia and its neighbors, were best demonstrated by Somalia's active support for the Western Somali Liberation Front (WSLF), a primarily Ogaadeeni-based guerrilla organization that was launched in 1963. On June 16, 1963, a full-scale rebellion intent on making the Ogaadeen ungovernable was launched after a meeting of three hundred Somali notables at Hodayo, a watering area north of the Ogaadeeni town of Warder. Numbering over three thousand guerrilla fighters, the Ogaadeeni insurgency became adept at ambushing military convoys and forcing the Ethiopian army to restrict itself to administrative centers within the region. In response, the Ethiopian regime of Emperor Haile Selassie decided to place direct military pressure on Somalia, one of the rightfully perceived instigators and sources of the insurgency. During mid-January 1964, the Third Division of the Ethiopian army, headed by General Aman Adom, launched air and ground attacks against Somali territory at numerous points along the Ethiopian-Somali boundary, including a bombing raid against the northeastern city of Hargeisa, Somalia's second-largest urban area and the former capital of British Somaliland. Mediation efforts on the part of the Organization of African Unity (OAU) ultimately resulted in the establishment of a cease-fire agreement on March 30, 1964, which clearly favored the Ethiopian government.[38]

A shift in tactics occurred after Shermaarke's election as president in 1967 and his subsequent selection of Mahammad Ibrahim Igaal as prime minister. Igaal took the lead in pursuing what was dubbed as a policy of "détente" with his neighbors.[39] With Zambian president Kenneth Kaunda as mediator, Igaal met with Kenyan president Jomo Kenyatta in Arusha. Their talks paved the way for resumed trade and diplomatic relations, along with a "Memorandum of Understanding," in which Somalia and Kenya agreed to examine possibilities for ending hostilities. A similar policy was pursued with Ethiopia, as meetings were held with Emperor Selassie during the same period. The result of these meetings was a communique calling for a joint ministerial Consultative Council to meet periodically for discussion of the many difficulties between the two countries and to make recommendations for their resolution. Similar inroads were made with the French concerning the rights of ethnic Somalis in Djibouti. Although his meetings only amounted to an agreement to begin a dialogue with Kenya, Ethiopia, and Djibouti, Igaal's reception at home was far from warm. Many Somalis viewed these meetings as the Somali government's decision to renege on its promises to ethnic Somalis in neighboring territories.

Despite the lack of progress on the irredentist front—no territories had been "reincorporated"—when compared to the seemingly positive strides being made on the nation-building front, it was this latter portion of the pan-Somali nationalist project that was popularly perceived as having floundered, ultimately contributing to the demise of the parliamentary era. Northern clans increasingly perceived their marginalization within the Somali federation despite the fact that Shermaarke chose Igaal, a northerner of the Isaaq clan, as prime minister. Many northerners considered Igaal to be a traitor to his own clan and "window dressing" for a southern-dominated regime.[40] As a result, Igaal's selection not only was insufficient to quell growing complaints of injustice among the northern clans but also represented the growing intensity of clan-based centrifugal forces at the expense of pan-Somali nationalism. In sharp contrast to the relatively constrained number of political parties that had served as the founding fathers of the Somali union, an incredible sixty-four largely clan-based political parties vied for 123 seats in the legislative elections of 1969. Not surprisingly, political gridlock was one of the most noteworthy outcomes of the intensification of clan-based rivalries. The heady nation-building rhetoric of 1960 had seemingly been lost amidst interminable clan-based political struggles among a political elite that seemed more interested in pursuing than wielding power for the common good.

The growing political stalemate was broken on October 21, 1969, when, in the aftermath of President Shermaarke's assassination six days earlier by one of his bodyguards, Major General Mahammad Siad Barre assumed power in a bloodless military coup d'état. As is often the case with military coups d'état carried out under similar circumstances, Somali public opinion overwhelmingly favored the military's seizure of power.[41] In the days that followed, Siad created a Supreme Revolutionary Council (SRC) composed of twenty-five military officers, replaced civilian leaders at the regional and local levels with military governors and district commissioners, and named senior military personnel to head Somalia's diplomatic missions abroad.

Propaganda of the Siad regime not surprisingly argued that initial popular support for the essentially bloodless coup was fostered by widespread dissatisfaction with the extremely corrupt practices of the civilian governments of the 1960–69 era.[42] The civilian politicians, especially legislators of the National Assembly, were portrayed as primarily driven by the self-interest of financial gain, while the nation's business and the national economy stagnated. This propaganda became the essence of early Western interpretations of the demise of the civilian regime, not least of all due to the fact that it had some basis in reality: political gridlock, inter- and intraelite struggles, a divided National Assembly, and a faltering economy all increasingly characterized the Somali political system at the end of the 1960s.

The propaganda of the Siad regime nonetheless masked the true essence of the civilian regime's demise that also entailed significant implications for the future of Somali democracy and pan-Somali nationalism. As explained by Compagnon, the decline of the civilian era was primarily due to growing clan tensions over the distribution of extremely limited political resources, including political appointments in various government agencies and the ability to bring home to individual clans and subclans a share of the national economic pie.[43] Similar to Schaffer's work on democracy in Senegal,[44] Compagnon argues that popular Somali conceptualizations of the concept of democracy are not centered on Western-focused conceptualizations of formal parliaments, a leading executive, and multiparty elections, but the simple breakdown and distribution of national resources according to traditional clan networks. As a result, pan-Somali nationalism meant little if anything to local populations, whose daily lives revolved around ensuring the equitable distribution of national resources. In the end, argues Campagnon, the promotion of the pan-Somali nationalist project ultimately became an instrumentalist tool of civilian elites to guarantee their continued hold over power and to mask growing clan inequalities in a resource-poor political environment. Indeed, even if one counters that the civilian elites of the immediate independence era were truly interested in fostering a national Somali identity that would transcend individual clan ties, the events of the first nine years of independence demonstrated growing strains between northern and southern clans and their respective elites over the future viability of the 1960 union.

Scientific Socialism and the Ogaadeen War, 1969–78

Major General Siad entered office arguing that the nation-building goal of the pan-Somali nationalist project had floundered due to misguided policies of the parliamentary era and that these policies had contributed to the intensification of clan-based pressures. Unlike his predecessors who essentially pursued a pro-Western capitalist path of development, Siad publicly proclaimed a unique Somali brand of "scientific socialism" patterned after the Soviet Union and its Communist allies as the most effective means for overcoming the destructive tendencies of clan affiliation.[45] Effective nation-building, according to this perspective, could only take place once the country was rid of its "tribalistic" past. In an attempt to legislate such changes from above, the Siad regime outlawed any public reference to clan identities or clan-inspired behavior as a criminal offense and ordered the replacement of clan-based greetings with usage of the term *jaalle* (the Somali equivalent of "comrade"). An extremely close political-military relationship was sought with the Soviet Union and its Communist allies, and a vanguard party—the Somali Socialist Revolutionary Party (SSRP)—was eventually created to ensure effective political control and socioeconomic development. Although Moscow demanded the creation of this party as the means for placing political power in the hands of "true" Communists in Somalia, the party's central committee nonetheless was firmly dominated by Siad and other members of the military junta.[46]

Siad's public adherence to a socialist nation-building project was contradicted by an unofficial regime policy that largely practiced the clan-based policies of earlier years.[47] Although initially careful to include representatives of all the major clans in his government during the initial "honeymoon" period of the military regime, Siad increasingly depended on a more restricted circle of clan relationships that revolved around the clans of his father (Mareehaan), mother (Ogaadeeni), and wife (Dulbahante)—often referred to as the MOD alliance, although no official alliance existed as such. The emergence of political opposition was dealt with through a variety of state-sponsored instruments of repression, such as the National Security Service, the National Security Court, and the Gulwadhayal (Victory Pioneers). State-sponsored repression increasingly became the norm to silence anyone deemed "antisocialist," "antirevolutionary," or "anti-Siad" by the military regime.

Nonetheless, one often-cited early accomplishment of the Siad regime was its adoption of a slightly modified version of the Latin script in 1972 as the official alphabet for the Somali language.[48] Prior to this date, the lack of an official script contributed to a less-than-ideal linguistic mosaic in which the Somali language served as the primary means for oral communication, but all written forms of communication, such as newspapers, government documents, and literature, depended on the uneven usage of three non-indigenous languages: English, Italian, and, to a lesser degree, Arabic. The most curious aspect of this event was not that it took place but that its arrival took as long as it did in a society that has a deep respect and love for its language and bestows great honors on those who can skillfully use its rich poetic heritage in oral discourse.[49]

Siad's greatest gamble, however, revolved around the irredentist dimension of the pan-Somali nationalist project. Attempting to take advantage of the political-military disarray of the Ethiopian state in the aftermath of a bloody revolution (1974–77) that replaced the Ethiopian monarchy with a Marxist regime headed by Mengistu Haile Mariam, Siad ordered the invasion of the Ogaadeen region. On July 17, 1977, nearly thirty-five thousand soldiers of the Somali army coordinated an invasion of the Ogaadeen with fifteen thousand guerrilla fighters of the WSLF and roughly 250 tanks, twelve mechanized brigades, and thirty fighter aircraft and bombers. By mid-November the Somali army had conquered the majority of the Ogaadeen and was laying siege to the strategically located city of Harer. When the Somali army failed to achieve final victory in Harer and the Ogaadeen War became a set battle of attrition, Siad made a series of diplomatic moves at least partially designed to win U.S. and Western recognition of Somali sovereignty over the captured regions. On November 13, he announced the abrogation of the Somali-Soviet Friendship Treaty of 1974, expelled nearly 1,700 Soviet civilian and military advisers and their dependents, and broke diplomatic relations with Cuba.

Any possibility of a negotiated settlement rapidly dissipated at the end of 1977 when Soviet-Cuban intervention in the conflict raised the regional ante and threatened to turn an African conflict into a major East-West confrontation. On December 22, the Soviet Union began a massive airlift of Cuban combat troops from bases in Cuba, Angola, and Congo-Brazzaville in a move designed to break the military stalemate.[50] These troops spearheaded an Ethiopian counteroffensive in late January 1978 that quickly overwhelmed the outnumbered and internationally isolated Somali troops within a matter of weeks, forcing them to flee across the border on March 9.

The Ogaadeen War served as a critical turning point in Somali nationalist history. As Lewis explains, the war was "extremely popular" among Somalis, and Siad's public approval rating—at least when Somali forces seemed poised for victory—was "never higher."[51] The resounding defeat of the Somali army, especially considering that it occurred during one of the historical periods of Ethiopia's greatest weakness and internal disarray, not surprisingly led to "widespread demoralization" and the unleashing of clan-based pressures as "different groups sought scapegoats to explain the debacle."[52] The most logical scapegoat was Siad himself, and some observers of Somali politics correctly suggested that his actions (most notably the execution of numerous officers associated with the battle) significantly tarnished his future portrayal in the historiography of the Somali nation.[53] Rising dissent was perhaps most notably demonstrated in 1978 by a failed coup attempt by disgruntled military officers of the Majeerteen clan.

The most notable, yet still poorly understood, outcome of Somalia's defeat in the Ogaadeen War was its impact on the irredentist dimension of the pan-Somali nationalist project. For the first time during the contemporary independence era, the future viability of pan-Somali nationalism had been severely called into question. A difficult relationship had already existed between the Siad regime and Ogaadeeni guerrilla movements, with many of the latter desirous of outright independence, as opposed to the Siad regime's desire to incorporate the Ogaadeen into Somalia proper. This difficult relationship became even further strained in 1977 when the Siad regime imposed "foreign" governors acceptable to the regime. In the process, traditional Ogaadeeni nationalists were displaced from political power. Many Ogaadeeni nationalists had supported some form of federation with Somalia, but they felt betrayed when it became clear that they would not retain control over their own local affairs within the envisaged pan-Somali nation-state.[54]

The final outcome of the Ogaadeen War further strengthened a sense of betrayal, even among those who had firmly supported the political machinations of the Siad regime. Ogaadeenis who felt betrayed by the Siad regime's decision to withdraw its forces when confronted with a superior Soviet/Cuban/Ethiopian counterattack surely would be more hesitant in the future to seek recourse to military arms—an option that in any case proved disastrous regardless of the willingness of the Siad regime to maintain its forces in the field. Anything less, however, would also prove ineffective, as demonstrated by the absolute unwillingness of any of Somalia's neighbors to entertain the idea of redrawing their colonial-inherited frontiers. In short, the Ogaadeen War unleashed a tremendous amount of national and international debate that no longer automatically accepted either the inevitability or the desirability of seeking to incorporate the Ogaadeen (or its related Djiboutian and Kenyan territories) within an overarching pan-Somali nation-state. Indeed, Djibouti's independence in 1977 under the leadership of Hassan Gouled Aptidon, a Somali of the Iise clan with close ties to France, meant that there now existed two independent Somali states in the Horn of Africa (although a significant portion of Djibouti is inhabited by the rival Afar ethnic group).

Civil Conflict and Secession, 1978–Present

Somalia's defeat in the Ogaadeen War ushered in an era of multiplying guerrilla insurgencies intent on replacing the Siad regime's authoritarian socialist approach to nation-building with a new approach that, at a minimum, would recognize the preeminent rights of clans within their specific regions. After the failed military coup of 1978, Majeerteen military officers who escaped abroad formed the Somali Salvation Front (SSF), which later was transformed into the Somali Salvation Democratic Front (SSDF). These events were followed in 1981 by the rising military successes of the Somali National Movement (SNM), a northern-based insurgency deriving the majority of its support from the Isaaq clan, as well as by the rise of other clan-based insurgent groups, most notably the Hawiye-dominated United Somali Congress (USC).[55]

The Somali civil war entered a new phase when, as part of a "final offensive" designed to topple the Siad regime, SNM guerrillas invaded the northern Somali city of Burao on the evening of May 27, 1988, and assassinated all senior government officials. The guerrillas initially scored stunning successes against the Somali Armed Forces; most notable among these victories was the capture of large portions of Hargeisa, the second-largest urban area within the country. In a wave of terror that followed the initial military assault, the Somali Armed Forces engaged in a "systematic pattern" of attacks against unarmed Isaaq villages, as well as summarily executing an unknown number of suspected SNM supporters.[56] Despite the devastation of the north that bordered on genocide, the Siad regime ultimately was unable to stop the advance of guerrilla armies on the capital of Mogadishu, especially after USC guerrilla forces stepped up their attacks in the central region of the country. On January 26, 1991, the Siad regime was forced to flee when advancing elements of the USC guerrilla army overran Mogadishu.

The initial euphoria surrounding Siad's demise did not mean the end of civil conflict. Choosing to ignore an October 2, 1990, accord, in which the major guerrilla groups agreed to collectively determine the shape of a post-Siad political system, the USC, by virtue of its control of the capital, unilaterally named a Hawiye, Ali Mahdi Mahammad, president of the country. This fateful decision heightened the already tense relations between the Isaaq-dominated SNM and the Hawiye-dominated USC, as well as among scores of other, less-organized clan groupings, ultimately prompting the SNM leadership to declare on May 17, 1991, that the former British Somaliland territory was seceding from the 1960 union and henceforth would be known as the Somaliland Republic. This announcement was followed by the intensification of a second round of clan conflict in the southern portion of the country, which in turn was exacerbated by a reassemblage of Siad's Daarood clan groupings under the banner of the Somali National Front (SNF). In short, once the common political enemy no longer existed, traditional clan differences, exacerbated by the dictatorial divide-and-rule practices of the Siad years, led to the complete collapse of the Somali state and the continuation of an increasingly brutal civil war.[57]

Northern Somalia's secession and declaration of independence as the Somaliland Republic served as a momentous event of contemporary Somali political history due to the simple reality that it signaled the decline of both the nation-building and the irredentist dimensions of the pan-Somali nationalist project. Although SNM elites were clearly willing to maintain the essentials of the 1960 federation in a post-Siad era (albeit with the recognition that the Isaaq would enjoy greater control over their local affairs), the perceived power grab by the Hawiye-based USC simply proved too much. Other factors, of course, played a role, including the spread of stories of atrocities by returning Isaaqs who were forced to flee from the south in what has been referred to as the "great trek," as well as intraclan power struggles among SNM elites.[58] These intraclan struggles are documented elsewhere and in any case are beyond the scope of this chapter.[59] The critical aspect for the purposes of this study is that the perceived power grab by the Hawiye and its aftermath served as an important turning point in the northern elites' perception of the original elite compact of 1960. Indeed, the role of the USC's power grab in the transformation of northern disillusionment into demands for outright independence is best captured in a quotation by Jama Mohamed Ghalib, an Isaaq within the Siad regime, whose memoir is entitled *The Cost of Dictatorship: The Somali Experience,*

> The overwhelming majority of all repressive government personnel, whether civilian or in the armed forces, were southerners who the people came no longer to see as co-nationals, but rather as an alien occupying force. Over the years, there developed a rejection of anything and everything southern. However, despite all the bad feeling among the people of the North, prior to the overthrow of Siad Barre, it had never gelled into a consensus for a unilateral declaration of independence (UDI) before the decision of the United Somali Congress, Mogadishu faction, to usurp power. Before that time, neither the majority of the senior members of the central committee of the SNM, nor their constitution, had contemplated any such separation.[60]

The SNM's decision essentially was based on a strongly held Isaaq belief among both the elites and the general population that the north would continue to be victimized by a southern-dominated government, as had been the case during both the democratic (1960–69) and authoritarian (1969–91) eras. Southern clans had essentially broken the elite compact of the 1960s too many times; as far as the northern elites were concerned, the nation-building goal so enthusiastically supported in 1960 was beyond repair. Equally important, the termination of Somalia's thirty-one-year experiment in nation-building by necessity meant the decline of pan-Somali irredentism. Although nation-building could have been pursued in the absence of irredentism, irredentism is impossible to pursue in the absence of successful nation-building.[61] The de facto existence of two Somalias (northern and southern), not to mention a Somali-dominated regime in Djibouti, has effectively dissipated the elite-driven, pan-Somali nationalist spirit that existed in the 1960s.

Three political developments since Somaliland's unilateral declaration of independence demonstrate the strong unlikelihood that the northern elites will forego separation in favor of some form of reconciliation with their southern counterparts as part of a new Somali nationalist project. First and foremost, it is revealing to note the reaction of northern elites to a further round of fighting that broke out in southern Somalia in September 1991 and, less than two months later, turned into an all-out struggle for control of Mogadishu. Unlike the first round (to overthrow Siad) and the second round (interclan fighting) of the Somali civil war, this round constituted a brutal intraclan power struggle within the Hawiye-based USC guerrilla army between forces loyal to interim president Mahdi (a member of the Abgal subclan of the Hawiye) and those led by General Mohamed Farah Aidid (a member of the Habar Gedir subclan of the Hawiye). According to northern elites, the southern clans, especially the Hawiye, were simply reaping the spoiled fruits of southern-based authoritarianism and the mistreatment of other clans.

Even the three-year intervention (1992–95) by United Nations–sponsored military forces from twenty countries—a development that led to a variety of pan-Somali clan alliances in the south as long as foreign troops remained on Somali soil—failed to garner northern sympathy for the south's plight.[62] Northern elites largely remained aloof and restricted their activities to successfully opposing any United Nations proposals that sought to send peacekeeping troops to the north. Indeed, northern elites, most notably Isaaq members of the SNM, proudly emphasize northern success in creating a functioning government capable of ensuring peace and stability, while the south remains divided among dozens of clan-based fiefdoms.

A final political development revolved around a referendum that was held in Somaliland in 2001. Although ostensibly held to assess public support for a new constitution, the vote essentially constituted a referendum on independence due to the fact that the constitution contains an article on territorial independence. The vote was especially important in that it occurred less that one year after one of a series of conferences in Djibouti had resulted in the reconstitution of a centralized government in Mogadishu that, however weak (as of 2006 it only controls a very small portion of Mogadishu and no outlying areas), continued to stress the illegality of Somaliland's unilateral declaration of independence. The referendum passed by an overwhelming margin of 97 percent in favor, clearly suggesting widespread support for independence—an elusive quest due to the fact that, as of 2006, no single country has been willing to officially recognize Somaliland's independence. Indeed, no discussion with political representatives of the Somaliland Republic ever ends without at least some discussion as to how northern elites can promote international recognition of Somaliland's independence—a much-coveted status that has yet to be bestowed by any other country in the world.[63]

Conclusion: Lessons from Somalia & Implications for the Future

A Somali proverb, "Either be a mountain, or find a mountain to lean on," has been quoted to characterize Somalia's search for external support during the contemporary independence era.[64] This proverb is also relevant to our understanding of the evolution of Somali nationalism. During the decade of the 1960s, the elites of the former British and Italian Somaliland territories decided to lean on each other in their pursuit of both the nation-building and irredentist goals of pan-Somali nationalism. By the beginning of the 1990s, the elites of the former British Somaliland had decided that such a relationship was no longer viable and instead chose to rely on themselves in their country's pursuit of independence as the Somaliland Republic—in essence deciding to be their "own mountain" regardless of the costs that such an action would entail.[65] In the process, one of the most widely cited experiments in African nation-building and irredentism had for all practical purposes come to an end.

The case study of the rise and decline of the pan-Somali nationalist project suggests several tentative conclusions for a wider understanding of nationalism in the contemporary independence era, particularly in those cases where previously separate territories were joined together (e.g., Eritrea and Ethiopia, French and British Cameroon) or where ethnically or racially distinct minority groups in geographically distinguished areas have not been equitably incorporated into existing nation-states (e.g., southern Sudan). First, the emergence of Somali nationalism and its African counterparts during the 1950s was the result of a *unique confluence of several historically specific developments,* most notably the emergence of a first generation of nationalist elites who shared the overriding goal of independence from colonial rule. The heady nationalist era of the 1950s and the 1960s fostered a shared elite image of injustices perpetrated on the Somali people at the hands of the colonial powers and fostered idealistic beliefs in the commonality of the Somali cause, and therefore the attractiveness of unification, in order to restore the dignity of the Somali people. It was precisely for this reason that Somali elites were willing to undertake one of the most ambitious experiments in voluntary nation-building ever witnessed by the African continent. Four decades later, however, the domestic and international contexts within which African nationalisms are evolving have radically changed. The idealism of the immediate postindependence era has largely dissipated, and the international community is less interested in supporting "failed states" in a continent that is perceived to be of marginal economic importance in the post–cold war era. Typically unwilling to actively campaign for the self-determination and ultimate independence of minority regions in existing nation-states, the international community will remain extremely hesitant to recognize the independence of secessionist regions within existing states.

The Somali case also demonstrates the *nation-destroying effects of authoritarianism and civil conflict.* Although the military coup d'état of 1969 and the launching of the Ogaadeen War initially received widespread public support, they both set in motion destructive tendencies for Somali nationalism. The authoritarianism of the Siad regime alienated the elites of increasingly marginalized clan groupings, and defeat in the Ogaadeen War unleashed a variety of clan-based pressures. The extended civil war of the 1980s and the 1990s, most notably the Siad regime's unleashing of what virtually constituted a policy of genocide against northern clans, was particularly destructive for the future of pan-Somali nationalism.

It is interesting to note, however, that authoritarianism and civil conflict have seemingly strengthened a greater sense of national identity in other cases, most notably the Democratic Republic of the Congo and Nigeria. In the case of Nigeria, for example, Igbo elites are now more likely to underscore their commitment to a unified Nigeria despite the fact that they overwhelmingly rallied around the cause of an independent Igbo nation-state (Biafra) during the late 1960s. In the case of Somalia, it is clear that the clan-based structure of indigenous Somali society has remained more internally strong than in other situations where authoritarian regimes emerged. The nation-building and nation-destroying effects of authoritarianism and civil war are thus a topic in need of further research.

A third conclusion of the Somali case is that, in the absence of effective policies, a *"turning point" is reached beyond which elites can no longer conceive of adhering to the nationalist project,* opting instead for their region's pursuit of independence. The SNM's decision to seek independence for the former British Somaliland territory was not made overnight but instead was the result of a series of perceived slights and discriminatory policies ranging from the southern-dominated government of the initial years of the democratic era (1960–67), the policies of repression under the Siad regime (1969–91), and the fateful 1991 decision of the USC to unilaterally name a Hawiye clan member president. Despite the genocidal policies of the Siad regime, the SNM leadership nonetheless remained willing, as late as 1991, to maintain its support for a unified Somalia. After the fateful Hawiye decision of 1991, however, a "point of no return" had been reached beyond which any further consideration of continued adherence to pan-Somali nationalism was impossible. The thoughts of Ghalib are again worth noting:

> It now seems impractical—even impossible—for the people of the newly declared "Republic of Somaliland" to abruptly reverse their verdict *vis-a-vis* the South. Nor does the disintegration of the South offer any encouragement for the exploration of any attempt at such a reversal. The continuation of the *status quo* therefore seems inevitable. . . . In the South some form of a confederation or something similar may emerge. Meantime the opportunity has presented itself, for the first time, for the Somalis in Ethiopia to protect their ethnic interests and play their proper role in the modern state with their rights and obligations recognized by all parties. Political realities have vastly changed and there is no more talk of "Greater Somalia"; but every Somali group in Ethiopia remains genealogically linked with one or other clan in Somalia-proper or Somaliland.[66]

Similar dynamics have been documented in other cases, most notably the decision of Eritrean elites to consider nothing less than independence for their territory (an objective obtained in 1991, after nearly thirty years of guerrilla insurgency) despite a willingness to accept less radical proposals (e.g., regional autonomy) in the 1950s. In short, there is a necessity to understand critical turning points, most notably points of no return, in the development and failure of nationalist projects.[67]

The Somali case further demonstrates the *enduring quality of kinship-based (in this case, clan) networks* even during those euphoric eras, such as the first years of the unified Republic of Somalia, in which nationalist sentiment appears to be on the rise. Indeed, the postindependence history of Somalia offers several examples of seemingly widespread nationalist support, most notably in favor of Somalia's involvement in the 1977–78 Ogaadeen War and, more recently, against United Nations–mandated foreign military involvement during 1992–95. In each of these cases, however, the emergence of nationalist fervor was short-lived, as what appeared to be unified public opinion ultimately dissipated in favor of clan-based disagreements and competition for political power. The policy dilemma for national elites in these and other cases is how best to simultaneously balance the potentially conflicting demands of nationalism and their kinship-based regional alternatives (i.e., self-determination).[68] As witnessed by the evolution of northern suspicions and eventual rejection of the pan-Somali nationalist project, Somali elites ultimately failed in finding such a balance during the second half of the twentieth century.

The case of Somalia also offers some tentative conclusions for assessing several theoretical approaches to understanding the evolution of nationalism in contemporary Africa. Primordialist arguments are partially relevant in terms of their focus on the enduring nature of affective ties in which all Somalis—regardless of clan groupings—recognize their common identity and belonging to some overarching Somali ethnic group. In their purest form, however, primordialist arguments fail to recognize that a common sense of belonging may not transcend the level of clan ties and certainly may not always result in a common yearning for the creation of a centralized political authority or nation-state—the antithesis of the Somali people's segmented, precolonial past.

Constructivist arguments are also partially relevant in terms of their focus on the role of both democratic and authoritarian governments alike in propagating an "invented memory" or "myth" of a unified, trans-Somali nationalist impulse—a myth that transcended clan and subclan ties and relationships and provided the essence of internationally inspired attempts to resolve ongoing ethnic conflict and state collapse in Somalia through the resurrection of the unified Somali state that existed from the 1960s to the beginning of the 1990s. As already noted, however, this argument in its purest form also fails to recognize the degree of common identity that does exist in Somali society—albeit at the level of individual clans and subclans. It also fails to note that some degree of nationalist consciousness did indeed exist during the 1950s and the 1960s, which served as the basis for launching the pan-Somali nationalist project during this same period.

The most important theoretical conclusion of the Somali case is the overwhelming importance of instrumentalist interpretations of nationalism. As already noted, the pan-Somali nationalist project was clearly derivative of shared elite interests at a particular juncture in Somali political history. Extreme critical views suggest that their efforts were doomed to failure from the start due to the overriding importance of clan-based differences. But a more generous conclusion would suggest that the elites of the 1950s and the 1960s were presented with a unique opportunity that was squandered due to a focus on ensuring their own political survival at the expense of facilitating the strengthening of a pan-Somali nationalist identity. It is precisely for this reason that instrumentalist approaches to nationalism can be enriched by the analysis of the destructive tendencies of authoritarianism and civil conflict and, most importantly, critical turning points in the adherence of the diverse elites to an elite-based nationalist compact.

Several questions immediately come to mind. Would the trajectory of increasing north-south elite strains have been minimized during the civilian era if a more regionally based federation respective of regional clan interests served as the cornerstone of governance (as opposed to the more unitary state fashioned after the colonial model)? Would these elite tensions have been minimized if, after the military coup d'état of 1969, a military regime would have handed over power to a newly restructured civilian regime (as opposed to the creation of an authoritarian regime based on personal rule and maintaining power through "divide-and-rule" policies that purposely pitted clan against clan)? Finally, would these elite tensions have been minimized if, after a successful guerrilla struggle to overthrow authoritarian rule in 1991, the elites of the three opposing major clans had stuck to their new elite compact of 1991 and created a decentralized civilian regime that recognized the regional interests of individual clans (as opposed to one clan army—the Hawiye-based USC—unilaterally imposing a national president from the south)? These and other questions can be answered only through comparative research that analyzes similar cases against the backdrop of critical turning points in individual nationalist histories.

A final comment revolves around the vast amount of scholarship devoted to finding a political solution to the Somali crisis. As of this writing, southern clans refuse to accept the self-proclaimed independence of the northern-based Somaliland Republic, which has yet to be officially recognized by any other country in the world. In southern and central portions of the country, a tentative cease-fire has only succeeded in recognizing the political-military supremacy of existing clan leaders in their individual regions. Thousands of Somalis have died in the periodic intensification of clan-based conflict. The cornerstone of any viable proposal designed to resolve ongoing ethnic conflict and state collapse must be the recognition of the death of pan-Somali nationalism and thus international recognition of the sovereignty of the Somaliland Republic. Unfortunately, the vast majority of proposals fail to recognize that northern Somali elites have reached a "point of no return."[69]

Even if the international community is unwilling to extend diplomatic recognition, a policy grounded in local realities must, at a bare minimum, provide official support to the fashioning of an electoral process designed to poll the wishes of those living in the Somaliland Republic. One of the potential electoral models, often cited by proponents of independence, is that which led to Eritrea's independence from Ethiopian sovereignty in 1993: a two-year "cooling-off period" could be followed by a United Nations–sponsored referendum monitored by international observers.[70] "We northern Somalis are not asking for international charity, nor are we asking foreigners to assume responsibility for what we ourselves are capable of accomplishing," explains Ahmed Jirreh, a northern Somali from the Isaaq clan who lives in the United States. "We simply seek international recognition of our sovereign right to withdraw from a union we once voluntarily joined."[71]

NOTES

1. For example, see Somalia's portrayal in David A. Lake and Donald Rothchild, eds., *The International Spread of Ethnic Conflict* (Princeton: Princeton University Press, 1998); and I. William Zartman, ed., *Collapsed States: The Disintegration and Restoration of Legitimate Authority* (Boulder: Lynne Rienner, 1995).

2. See Rupert Emerson's foreword in the first major study of Somali nationalism: Saadia Touval, *Somali Nationalism: International Politics and the Drive for Unity in the Horn* (Cambridge, MA: Harvard University Press, 1963).

3. Such irredentism is, in many ways, a combination of Lowell Barrington's "variant 1" (external-territory-claiming) nationalism and "variant 5" (co-national-protecting).

4. See David D. Laitin and Said S. Samatar, *Somalia: Nation in Search of a State* (Boulder: Westview Press, 1987).

5. For example, see Touval, *Somali Nationalism*. For a later, excellent overview of competing interpretations, see I. M. Lewis, ed., *Nationalism and Self-Determination in the Horn of Africa* (London: Ithaca Press, 1983).

6. See the insightful retrospective by Crawford Young, "Evolving Modes of Con-

sciousness and Ideology: Nationalism and Ethnicity," in *Political Development and the New Realism in Sub-Saharan Africa,* ed. David E. Apter and Carl G. Rosberg (Charlottesville: University Press of Virginia, 1994), 61–86.

7. See Hussein M. Adam and Richard Ford, eds., *Mending Rips in the Sky: Options for Somali Communities in the 21st Century* (Lawrenceville: Red Sea Press, 1997).

8. For an overview of these approaches, see the landmark work by Crawford Young, *The Politics of Cultural Pluralism* (Madison: University of Wisconsin Press, 1976).

9. The scholar most often associated with launching this research agenda within the subfield of Somali studies, although his research is not limited to this approach, is I. M. Lewis, *A Pastoral Democracy: A Study of Pastoralism and Politics among the Northern Somali of the Horn of Africa* (London: Oxford University Press, 1961).

10. This broad label is inclusive of a wide variety of scholarship, including Al Jimale Ahmed, ed., *The Invention of Somalia* (Lawrenceville: Red Sea Press, 1995); and Catherine Besteman, *Unraveling Somalia: Race, Violence, and the Legacy of Slavery* (Philadelphia: University of Pennsylvania Press, 1999).

11. An important proponent of this approach is David D. Laitin, *Politics, Language, and Thought: The Somali Experience* (Chicago: University of Chicago Press, 1977); and Laitin and Samatar, *Somalia.*

12. For a classic interpretation of Somali homogeneity, see I. M. Lewis, *A Modern History of Somalia: Nation and State in the Horn of Africa,* rev. ed. (New York: Longman, 1988). For a more critical understanding that stresses the differences between the Samaale and the Sab, see Besteman, *Unraveling Somalia.*

13. See Laitin, *Politics, Language, and Thought.*

14. See Said Sheikh Samatar, *Oral Poetry and Somali Nationalism: The Case of Sayyid Mahammad Abdille Hassan* (Cambridge: Cambridge University Press, 1982).

15. See I. M. Lewis, *Saints and Somalis: Popular Islam in a Clan-Based Society* (Lawrenceville: Red Sea Press, 1998).

16. See I. M. Lewis, *Blood and Bone: The Call of Kinship in Somali Society* (Lawrenceville: Red Sea Press, 1994).

17. For a general discussion, see Peter J. Schraeder, *African Politics and Society: A Mosaic in Transformation* (Boston: Bedford/St. Martin's, 2000), 66–68.

18. Here again, one could mention Barrington's "variant 1" and "variant 5" nationalism related to irredentism.

19. Laitin and Samatar, *Somalia,* 63.

20. *Dervish* means "one who is dedicated in service to Allah."

21. Gurey's forces largely drew from the Harti and Mareehaan of the Daarood clan and the Habar Magadle of the Isaaq clan, and the Sayyid primarily enjoyed the support of the Ogaadeen of the Daarood clan (and to a lesser extent the Isaaq clan). See Laitin and Samatar, *Somalia,* 9, 12, 56, 58.

22. Laitin and Samatar, *Somalia,* 63.

23. The Four-Power Commission was made up of the United States, the Soviet Union, Great Britain, and France.

24. See Touval, *Somali Nationalism,* 85–100.

25. See Mohamed H. Mukhtar, "The Emergence and Role of Political Parties in the Inter-River Region of Somalia from 1947 to 1960 (Independence)," *Ufahamu* 16, no. 2 (1989): 75–95.

26. See Touval, *Somali Nationalism,* 88.

27. Ibid., 101–8.

28. Ibid., 106.

29. The attraction of Djibouti's Somali population to the pan-Somali dream was also mixed due to the fact that the dominant Somali clan of the country—the Iise–is renowned for an independence streak of its own that, in the extreme, has periodically noted the possibility of creating an independent, Iise-dominated nation-state from the Iise populations in Djibouti, northwestern Somalia, and formerly northeastern Ethiopia (currently Eritrea). Touval, *Somali Nationalism,* 128–29. See also Walter S. Clarke, "The 'Esayi Dream': A Footnote to the Ogaden War" (unpublished paper).

30. Touval, *Somali Nationalism,* 147–53.

31. Ibid., 149.

32. Ibid., 150.

33. Ibid., 150.

34. Ibid., 132–46.

35. Ibid., 135.

36. Laitin and Samatar, *Somalia,* 70.

37. See Paolo Contini, *The Somali Republic: An Experiment in Legal Integration* (London: Frank Cass, 1969); and A. A. Castagno, "The Political Party System in the Somali Republic: A Balancing-Coalitional Approach," in *Political Parties and National Integration in Tropical Africa,* ed. James S. Coleman and Carl G. Rosberg, Jr. (Berkeley: University of California Press, 1964).

38. For discussion, see John Markakis, *National and Class Conflict in the Horn of Africa* (Cambridge: Cambridge University Press, 1987), 169–81.

39. See Raymond L. Thurston, "Détente in the Horn," *Africa Report* 14, no. 2 (February 1969): 6–13.

40. Correspondence with Daniel Compagnon.

41. See I. M. Lewis, "The Politics of the 1969 Coup," *Journal of Modern African Studies* 10, no. 3 (1972): 383–408.

42. For a compilation of some of Siad's early speeches, see Somali Ministry of Information and National Guidance, *My Country and My People: Selected Speeches of Jaalle Major General Mohammad Siad Barre* (Mogadishu, Somalia: State Printing Agency, 1979).

43. See Daniel Compagnon, "Ressources politiques, régulation autoritaire et domination personnelle en Somalie: Le régime de Siyaad Barre (1969–1991)" (doctoral dissertation, l'Université de Pau et des Pays de l'Adour, 1995).

44. See Frederic C. Schaffer, *Democracy in Transition: Understanding Politics in an Unfamiliar Culture* (Ithaca: Cornell University Press, 1998).

45. For a sympathetic overview, see Philip Decraene, *L'Expérience socialiste Somalienne* (Paris: Berger-Levrault, 1977). See also Ahmed I. Samatar, *Socialist Somalia: Rhetoric and Reality* (London: Zed Books, 1988).

46. See Compagnon, "Ressources politiques, régulation autoritaire et domination personnelle en Somalie."

47. For the most comprehensive overview, see ibid.

48. See Laitin, *Politics, Language, and Thought.* See also Hussein M. Adam, "Language, National Consciousness and Identity: The Somali Experience," in *Nationalism and Self-Determination in the Horn of Africa,* ed. I. M. Lewis (London: Ithaca Press, 1983).

49. For discussion, see Adam, "Language, National Consciousness and Identity."

See also B. W. Andrzejewski, "Language Reform in Somalia and the Modernization of the Somali Vocabulary," *Northeast African Studies* 1, no. 3 (1979–80): 59–71.

50. Accompanied by Soviet tactical commanders and nearly $2 billion in Soviet weaponry, the number of Cubans airlifted into Ethiopia by mid-January exceeded 2,500 troops and grew to 15,000 within less than two months.

51. I. M. Lewis, "The Ogaden and the Fragility of Somali Segmentary Nationalism," *Horn of Africa* 13, nos. 1–2 (1999): 57.

52. Lewis, "The Ogaden and the Fragility of Somali Segmentary Nationalism." See also Lee Cassanelli, "Explaining Ethnic Conflict in Somalia," in *High Conflict/Low Conflict: Six Case Studies of Ethnic Politics,* Woodrow Wilson International Center for Scholars (Washington, DC: Woodrow Wilson International Center for Scholars, 1993), 13; and Harry Odada, "Somalia's Domestic Politics and Foreign Relations since the Ogaden War of 1977–78," *Middle Eastern Studies* 21, no. 3 (1985): 285–97.

53. See David D. Laitin, "The War in the Ogaden: Implications for Siyaad's Role in Somali History," *Journal of Modern African Studies* 17, no. 1 (1979): 95–115. See also Abdi Sheikh-Abdi, "Sayyid Mohammed Abdille Hassan and the Current Conflict in the Horn," *Horn of Africa* 1, no. 2 (1978).

54. Correspondence from Daniel Compagnon.

55. For the most comprehensive analysis of the development and role of these and other armed groups, see Daniel Compagnon, "Somali Armed Movements: The Interplay of Political Entrepreneurship and Clan-Based Factions," in *African Guerrillas,* ed. Christopher Clapham (Oxford: James Currey, 1998), 73–90. See also Compagnon's earlier analysis, "The Somali Opposition Fronts: Some Comments and Questions," *Horn of Africa* 13, nos. 1–2 (January–March, April–June 1990): 29–54.

56. See Robert Gersony, *Why Somalis Flee: Synthesis of Accounts of Conflict Experience in Northern Somalia by Somali Refugees, Displaced Persons and Others* (Bureau for Refugee Programs, Department of State, Washington, DC, August 1989); U.S. General Accounting Office (GAO), *Somalia: Observations Regarding the Northern Conflict and Resulting Conditions* (GAO, Washington, DC, May 1989); and U.S. House, Committee on Foreign Affairs, Subcommittee on Africa, *Reported Massacres and Indiscriminate Killings in Somalia,* Hearing, July 14, 1988, 100th Cong., 2nd sess. (Washington, DC: GPO, 1989).

57. See Daniel Compagnon, "Somalie: De l'Etat en formation à l'Etat en pointillé," in *Les Etats d'Afrique Noire: Formations, mécanismes et crise,* by Jean-François Médard (Paris: Karthala, 1991), 205–40; and Daniel Compagnon, "Somalie: L'aube de l'après-Siyaad Barre," *Politique Africaine* 41 (March 1991): 129–34. See also Hussein M. Adam, "Somalia: A Terrible Beauty Being Born?" in *Collapsed States: The Disintegration and Restoration of Legitimate Authority,* ed. I. William Zartman (Boulder: Lynne Rienner, 1995), 69–90; Terrence Lyons and Ahmed I. Samatar, *Somalia: State Collapse, Multilateral Intervention, and Strategies for Political Reconstruction* (Washington, DC: Brookings Institution, 1995), 1–24; and Anna Simons, *Networks of Dissolution: Somalia Undone* (Boulder: Westview, 1995).

58. Primarily between the factions led by Ahmed Mohamed Mahamud "Silanyo" and Abdirahman Ahmed Ali "Tuur."

59. See the analysis of Daniel Compagnon in "Somaliland: Un ordre politique en gestion?" *Politique Africaine* 50 (June 1993): 9–20.

60. Jama Mohamed Ghalib, *The Cost of Dictatorship: The Somali Experience* (New York: Lilian Barber Press, 1995), 216–17.

61. Although Barrington discusses both nation-building and irredentism in his introductory chapter in this volume, the Somali case indicates that he does not make a strong enough connection between the two.

62. See John Drysdale, *Whatever Happened to Somalia? A Tale of Tragic Blunders* (London: HAAN Associates, 1994).

63. Personal interviews with visiting Somaliland dignitaries, Chicago, May 1997.

64. See Peter J. Schraeder, *United States Foreign Policy toward Africa: Incrementalism, Crisis and Change* (Cambridge: Cambridge University Press, 1994), chapter 4.

65. See Gérard Prunier, "Somaliland Goes It Alone," *Current History* 97, no. 619 (1998): 225–28.

66. Ghalib, *The Cost of Dictatorship,* 222.

67. A similar call for such research, which has yet to be realized, was offered by John R. Wood, "Secession: A Comparative Analytical Framework," *Canadian Journal of Political Science/Revue Canadienne de Science Politique* 14, no. 1 (March 1981): 107–34.

68. For example, see Lewis, *Nationalism and Self-Determination in the Horn of Africa.*

69. See, for example, the policy-oriented conclusions included in Ken Menkhaus and Terrence Lyons, "What Are the Lessons to be Learned from Somalia?" *CSIS Africa Notes* 144 (January 1993); Samuel M. Makinda, *Seeking Peace from Chaos: Humanitarian Intervention in Somalia* (Boulder: Lynne Rienner Publishers, 1993); Lyons and Samatar, *Somalia;* and Hussein Adam and Richard Ford, "Removing Barricades in Somalia: Options for Peace and Rehabilitation" (United States Institute of Peace, Peaceworks no. 24, October 1998).

70. Hussein M. Adam, "Formation and Recognition of New States: Somaliland in Contrast to Eritrea," *Review of African Political Economy* 59 (1994): 21–38.

71. Personal interview with Ahmed Jirreh in Chicago.

III. Postcommunist Nationalism

6. The Post-Soviet Nations after Independence

IAN BREMMER

In his introduction to this volume, Lowell Barrington details potential fault lines within nationalist movements, grouped along issues of territory and membership. Nationalists may claim territory of neighboring states based on historical ties or former ownership, while ethnic minorities within the new state may demand their own territory. Nationalists may also dispute membership boundaries, differing about whether national identity is based on ethnicity, language, or shared experience. Ideas of nation change. Moreover, nationalists do not always seek sovereignty as an international state: territorial autonomy or degrees of independence within a federal framework may be sufficient.

The drive to independence often conceals these fault lines or provides insufficient opportunity for their expression. Pursuing independence, nationalist elites mobilize the masses based on shared ideas of nation, homeland, or historical identity and operate under the shared goal of liberation. Following independence, however, the elites of resurrected or recently formed nation-states face new rules, objectives, and constraints, which in turn require new responses. And although nationalist elites must mobilize the masses for nationalism to be successful, Barrington reminds us that "it is misleading to treat nationalists within a state (or within an ethnic group) as a unitary actor." As this volume's authors demonstrate in postcolonial and post-Soviet contexts, elites' competing agendas in the often-unstable environment of new or restored nations generate a wide array of conflict, from social struggles over cultural identity to armed hostility.

Nationalism and Soviet Collapse

The twilight of the Soviet empire witnessed a process of nationalist awakenings that engendered ethnic-based conflict.[1] A large number of non-union-republic-based national groups voiced unequivocal demands for sovereignty, largely following union-republic declarations of sovereignty.[2] These demands sprung from regional movements in the Soviet Union that, due to the logic of Soviet ideas of nationality (*national'nost'*), became national in form, if not in content or even intention. Environmental groups in Uzbekistan, antinuclear groups in Kazakhstan, Belarus, and Ukraine, and workers' movements in non-Union republics within the RSFSR were assailed by Mikhail Gorbachev (and, indeed, Western scholars) as nationalist.[3] In each of these cases it is unclear whether these organizations deserved this title. Suspicion of the Soviet central leadership about all but the most ritualistic manifestations of nationalism in the periphery, however, exacerbated the subjective sense of colonialization felt by local peoples. Additionally, "countermovements" of ethnic Russians in the peripheral autonomous republics, as well as Azeris in Armenia and Armenians in Azerbaijan, challenged the republic-level governments.

Yet despite irredentist Russian minorities, disenfranchised titular minorities, alienated titular elite groups, and an unstable Russian center, the Soviet Union's collapse did not ignite a nationalist powder keg. The myriad levels of nationality enshrined within the Soviet system did not engender the long-term bloody warfare of a Yugoslavia.[4] Ten years ago such conflict was not absent from forecasts formed amidst the chaos and uncertainty of the USSR's disintegration.[5] The massive inventory of the former Red Army, combined with a need for hard currency, for instance, was set to facilitate arms transfers to disenfranchised ethnic groups.

But the conflict never came. Instead, governing elites of the former republics' titular nationalities have hewn close to the Kremlin, with pragmatic civic nationalism trumping ethnic nationalist fervor. Ethnic nationalism, defined as the political ideology aspiring toward the congruency of ethnic group and center, particularly over the right to make decisions on issues perceived as important by the ethnic group, has ultimately not defined post-Soviet relations between Moscow and the former republics. The ongoing integration of the titular nationalities' elites with Moscow following the USSR's collapse has largely eclipsed the varying Soviet legacies of the successor states, reflecting instead the post-Soviet realities of Russia as the most serious regional actor.

The newly independent states' governing elites have avoided ethnonationalist vehemence as a basis for dealings with Russia and foreign relations in general. Departure from civic nationalism incurs specific costs. Russia is the main supplier of energy to the former Soviet republics, the dominant export market and, in the majority of cases, a substantial creditor. The issue of energy supply has kept the titular nationalities of most of the former republics tightly integrated with Moscow. Central Asian republics and Armenia have relied on Russian military support to maintain territorial integrity. In the former republics' dealings with Moscow, economic and defense factors have prevailed upon elites to fashion broadly inclusive nations.

As the former republics downplay ethnic nationalism internationally, they also tend to discourage it domestically. Although ethnic nationalist politics and disputes have not disappeared from the post-Soviet space, they have been driven from the center of the political spectrum. Economic and strategic self-interest, shaped to a large extent by the actions of Moscow, has shaped elites' attitudes and provided constraints and incentives for their behavior.

Lithuania (& Estonia & Latvia)

The Baltic states demonstrate as well as any other former Soviet region the pivotal role of international relations in shaping nationalist attitudes and forms. Empowered by their relatively strong economic position following independence, the Baltic states' post-Soviet path—and their relations with Russia—was initially based on ethnic, exclusionary nationalism, particularly in Estonia and Latvia. Unlike the other cases discussed in this chapter, these states have had little need to cozy up to the Kremlin. Yet due to pressure from the international community regarding NATO and European Union (EU) membership qualification, the Baltic states have also largely moved to models of civic nationalism.

As Terry Clark states in chapter 7, "In the Lithuanian case nationalism has successfully been transformed from one concerned with territorial defense against internal threats to one largely focused on a strategy of building civic consciousness among all of the country's citizens." Although elites in Lithuania granted citizenship to all individuals, regardless of ethnicity or language, anxieties about the national minorities persisted in the early years of independence. Clark notes that the political right represented nationalism in the political system, with the smaller parties more strident in manner, some operating under the slogan of "Lithuania for Lithuanians!"

The ethnonationalist mobilization that led Lithuania, Latvia, and Estonia out of the Soviet Federation found expression in language laws and anti-Russian discriminatory politics as well. Russia has been involved in numerous disputes and protests with the Baltic governments regarding such laws, as well as the general disenfranchisement of ethnic Russian citizens. But these nationalist battles did not generally translate into actual sanctions from Russia, let alone the violent showdown that originally marked Lithuania's exit from Soviet rule. Latvia's treatment of ethnic Russians likely played into the Russian State Duma's refusal to ratify the border treaty signed in 1997, but the tangible consequences of the Baltic states' nationalism-based rejection of Russian channels have been few.

Instead, the blunting of Baltic nationalism, and the effective efforts at shaping Baltic policy provisions, came from the West.[6] Latvia revised its stringent 1994 language law along the recommendations of the Organization for Security and Cooperation in Europe (OSCE) in 1999, in a step toward reconciling with EU requirements and Russian requests. Candidates for local council and parliamentary deputies in Estonia had been required to demonstrate the ability to communicate in Estonian, but in November this language requirement was abolished by Estonia's parliament. When it becomes law, the change will allow Estonia to satisfy OSCE concerns and fulfill EU requirements.

In their relative economic prosperity, historic links to Europe, and progress toward membership in the EU and NATO, Latvia, Lithuania, and Estonia are empowered to reject Russian ties on principle and integrate internationally. In addition to political will and sense of national identity, however, the Baltic states also have historic channels to reactivate: strong pre-Soviet links to Western Europe. The Baltic states not only exited the Soviet Federation on a strong wave of nationalist sentiment, therefore, but also had a destination, both historically and for the future. These circumstances enabled the Baltic states to persist in ethnic nationalism, despite Russian protests, until the middle to late 1990s, when the issue became a roadblock to NATO and EU membership. This international pressure from European states and organizations, much as Russia exerts throughout the other former republics to similar effect, has resulted in a shift to more civic forms of nationalism.

Ukraine

In Ukraine, unlike the Baltic states but similar to the rest of the Eurasian region, the need to maintain connections with Moscow has muted ethnic nationalists. Kiev's integration with Moscow has remained strong, and civic nationalism has captured the political center. The ethnic nationalists of the preindependence Interparliamentary Assembly (IPA), based in western and central Ukraine, and the postindependence successor, the Ukrainian National Assembly (and associated parties), have not succeeded in defining the post-Soviet Ukrainian national discourse.

Ethnic nationalists directed Ukraine's drive to independence in 1989.[7] The Chernobyl disaster radicalized sectors of the population against Moscow preceding the Soviet collapse, and following independence, Ukraine became a foreign policy priority for the West: the largest state in Europe in terms of surface area, fourth largest in population, and highly ranked in natural resources. Indeed, during the first Leonid Kuchma administration (1994–99), Ukraine detached itself from Russian influence and reached out to the West, receiving the fourth-largest amount of U.S. bilateral aid since 1994 and joining NATO's Partnership for Peace program. In addition, Ukraine joined other countries to form GUUAM (Georgia, Ukraine, Uzbekistan, Azerbaijan, and Moldova) in 1996, a strategic grouping pointedly excluding Russia.

The potential for destabilizing splits along territorial or membership lines was thus high following independence. A rapid and severe economic collapse, aggravated by then-president Leonid Kravchuk's reluctance to pursue structural reform, scuttled the polity-wide hopes for postindependence prosperity. Populations in Russian-speaking eastern Ukraine and Crimea—having originally voted in favor of independence—became alienated in the society-wide stress of economic collapse.[8] Likewise, Ukrainian ethnonationalists increased their fervor. The Uniate Catholic and ethnonationalist population of western Ukraine sought integration with the West, while the industrialized and Russian-speaking east called for closer ties to Russia. The lack of economic empowerment following independence demanded that Ukraine pursue a closer relationship with Moscow. Uncertainty surrounding Moscow's intentions for Crimea, the Black Sea fleet, and its headquarters at Sevastopol also led Ukraine to act cautiously, reflecting Moscow's dominance in the post-Soviet space. Ukraine has therefore balanced strengthening ties with the West with the necessity of engaging Russia and has been unmotivated by the ethnonationalist sentiment voiced by some Ukrainian groups.

As Taras Kuzio notes in chapter 8 the ethnic nationalists on the far right of Ukraine's political spectrum "could not convert the energy of the drive for independence into an effective use of the state for implementing ethnic nationalist policies." Ethnic nationalists on the far left, seeking a reunion with Russia and pan–Eastern Slav identity, also have fared poorly. Their interest in the Russia-Belarus union and their hostility to Ukrainian statehood have won few supporters. Ukraine's postindependence weakness determined the outward course of relations with Moscow; simultaneously, Russia's dominance discouraged elites from stirring ethnic nationalism or permitting its expression too systemically.

Ukraine is further constrained by the high level of debts for gas imports that have accrued. As in other former Soviet republics, this energy dependence presents one of Russia's most potent means of reasserting its economic and political control over its neighbors, leveraged more concertedly by the current Russian president, Vladimir Putin, than previously under Boris Yeltsin. And as Ukraine's privatization of state-held assets increased in the late 1990s, and liquidity among Russian enterprises improved, there has been a notable increase in Russian influence in key Ukrainian sectors such as energy and metals. This increased investment and involvement in Ukraine's economy reflects an openness to Russia, driven by both economic and political realities.

Kuchma's dramatic fall into scandal in late 1999 resulted in his isolation from the West, where disenchantment with Ukraine's corruption and institutional transparency reached unprecedented intensity. The Putin administration supported Kuchma through the scandal's fallout, and the appointment in Ukraine of a less pro-Western foreign minister in September 2000 is not unconnected. Additionally, the appointment of Viktor Chernomyrdin, a former Russian prime minister and head of Gazprom, as Russian ambassador to Ukraine signaled both the high levels of engagement between the two countries and the underpinning dependence of Ukraine on Russia's supply of energy. Russia has thus found accommodation among Ukraine's elites, rather than ethnic nationalist resistance to the old Soviet center.

In his chapter, Kuzio states that the far right nationalist groups in Ukraine were "important in framing the question of an independent state in the late Soviet period" but "their unwillingness to abandon ethnic nationalist ideas has left them marginalized and politically irrelevant since independence." This adoption of the civic-nationalist model among the masses may be "a more drawn out process," as Kuzio notes, but Russia's ongoing dominance in post-Soviet affairs only increases the momentum of this development.

Armenia

Ethnonationalist fervor characterized late-Soviet Armenia and the years following independence, but as Razmik Panossian notes in chapter 9, it is no longer the basis of politics in Armenia. The elites' pursuit of economic gains and security guarantees, not mass mobilization of the population on ethnic lines, has heralded the appearance of "postnationalist" politics. Although the nationalist movement following the February 1988 vote by the Nagorno-Karabakh oblast's local soviet to transfer from the Azerbaijani SSR to the Armenian SSR became increasingly anti-Soviet, due to insufficient pro-Armenia sentiment from the Kremlin over Karabakh, following independence Armenia has remained Russia's main ally in the Caucasus region. This ongoing alliance occurs as Armenia has adopted an increasingly civic-based model of nationalism.[9]

This is not to say that the strong ethnic component in Armenia's postindependence nationalism disappeared quickly or quietly. Outside of dealings with Russia, ethnonationalist currents have defined Armenia's foreign policy for much of the period from 1991 to the present. In addition to the ongoing Nagorno-Karabakh conflict with Azerbaijan, tensions with Georgia have arisen from purported discrimination against ethnic Armenians in the Georgian region of Javakheti and concerns for the safety of ethnic Armenians in Abkhazia. Armenian nationalist groups regularly mobilize against Azerbaijan and Turkey, and there has been strong nationalist sentiment in government ranks.[10] Moreover, Armenia also has a large, powerful diaspora in the United States, which has secured significant amounts of aid for Armenia.

Notwithstanding ethnonationalist mobilizations, diasporic groups, and extensive international ties, however, Armenia has remained close to the Kremlin in the past ten years. The essentially pro-Russian direction of Armenia's foreign policy has only grown stronger in recent years. In mid-

September 2001 a ten-year program of economic cooperation was signed between the two countries. Russia has stemmed the security threat from Turkey and has armed Armenian forces in the Nagorno-Karabakh conflict. Armenia has supported the continued presence of Russian troops at a base in Javakheti, despite Georgian opposition, based on concern for ethnic Armenians there. Heavily dependent on energy supply from Russia, and utilizing Russia's weight in the region to balance Azerbaijan and Turkey, Armenia has pursued both economic and political integration with Moscow.[11] Russia is the arbiter of success in the "postnationalist" politics of Armenia. As such, the pragmatism that Russia enforces in Yerevan's dealings with the Kremlin compels Armenia's elites to engage civic forms of nationalism over ethnic ones.

Ethnic mobilization in Azerbaijan and Armenia over the Nagorno-Karabakh dispute drove tensions to new heights in the region. The conflict over the ethnically split Nagorno-Karabakh province was used on both sides to define respective nationhood in the disorder following independence and resulted in a de facto ethnic sorting, with nearly all Armenians exiting Azerbaijan and the Azeri population leaving the disputed Nagorno-Karabakh province. The already complex ethnic relations in the region were complicated by Turkey's support of Azerbaijan in the conflict, adding to Armenia's historical antipathy to the Turkish state, and Moscow's backing of Armenia.

The conflict proved Russia to be a necessary arbiter in maintaining stability in the former Soviet space. Based on a series of military defeats inflicted by Armenia, Azerbaijan realized that sustained fighting would lead to defeat, and sought Russian support in achieving a cease-fire. Secured in 1994, the cease-fire delivered indirect control of the province to Armenia, with Azerbaijan in no position to oppose the Russia-brokered outcome. Russia demonstrated its regional supremacy, transformed the ethnic hostilities into a showcase for Russian security guarantees, and enforced conciliatory stances in both Yerevan and Baku with respect to Moscow. Although ethnic tensions were not erased in such a manner, the elites in Azerbaijan and Armenia were compelled to adopt more civic means of defining their respective nations.

Georgia

Ethnic nationalism in the former Soviet republics did not disappear everywhere. Governing elites deploy exclusionary, ethnic-based nationalism whenever useful, but it has a secondary, selective, and often intrastate role. Thus, where it has occurred, post-Soviet nationalist conflict has been primarily localized: ongoing Azeri-Armenian conflict in Nagorno-Karabakh; ethnic strife in the Fergana Valley in Central Asia; and fighting amidst the autonomies of the troubled North Caucasus—Abkhazia, Ossetia, and Chechnya. Only Chechnya has clashed directly with Russia, a confrontation more economic than ethnic in its origins, and nationalist only in its later manifestations. Ethnic nationalist conflict in former republics is limited largely to conflicts percolating below the titular group's collusion with Moscow: local language laws, vengeful rhetoric, and agitation in the media. Russia's dominance in economic and military affairs has compelled the former republics' elites to deploy ethnic nationalism—or, in turn, sanction its expression—only on the substate level or in conflicts with other former republics. When ethnic nationalism takes the fore in dealings with Moscow, however, or drives the former republic's path toward international integration, the costs can be severe, as the example of Georgia demonstrates.

Georgia's Western-oriented path has brought considerable punishment from Moscow. Georgia's choices in fact demonstrate the costs associated with an ethnic nationalist-based foreign policy in dealings with Moscow, when pursued without the empowerment of economic gains seen in the Baltics. Georgia is the single former Soviet republic to develop ethnic nationalism in this manner, and it illustrates the incentives shaping the foreign policy of post-Soviet states.

Georgia began independence in April 1991 under the leadership of Zviad Gamsakhurdia, a radical ethnonationalist and autocratic ruler who sought to limit Georgia's contact with Russia and the rest of the former Soviet Union. A violent coup in January 1992 ousted Gamsakhurdia and established a military council, which invited Eduard Shevardnadze to return to lead Georgia. Although Gamsakhurdia's policies rejected contact with Russia, isolating Georgia and leading to a proliferation of local militias running near-fiefdoms, Shevardnadze did not seek to reverse matters or reintegrate with Moscow and reconcile with neighboring states. As former Soviet foreign minister, Shevardnadze believed he had the background and will to integrate Georgia internationally, independent of Russia's channels.[12]

In response to Georgia's independent path, Russia has aggressively maintained military bases in Georgia, despite Georgian political protests and an OSCE-brokered agreement to vacate two installations. At a 1999 meeting of the OSCE, Russia agreed to close two of the bases, although only one was closed by the deadline of July 2001. Russia has still not fully vacated the second base (at Gudauta), which is in the separatist region of Abkhazia, where Russian military aid has abetted the proautonomy movement. Russia's resistance to closing the bases is based on multiple geopolitical interests, among them a belief that Georgia tacitly supports Chechen rebels on its territory, which Georgia denies. Additionally, Russia has backed Abkhazia's rejection of Georgia's offer to establish limited autonomy for the territory and simultaneously resisted Abkhazia's request for "associate status" within Russia. By maintaining Abkhazia as an unresolved secessionist movement, Russia is able to exert control on political and defense matters within Georgia.

Among additional means of punishing Georgia, Russia imposed a visa regime upon Georgian citizens traveling to Russia, separate from persons originating in South Ossetia and Abkhazia. Russia also accused Georgia of aiding Chechen rebels by allowing Chechen fighters to seek refuge in the Pankisi Gorge. The Georgian parliament in turn passed a resolution calling for Russia to remove the Commonwealth of Independent States (CIS) peacekeeping force that patrols the border with the breakaway region. Finally, in late 2000 Russia periodically shut off gas supplies to Georgia (partly due to Georgia's perceived softness on Chechnya and also due to failure to pay energy debts). Georgia's efforts at international integration have not brought economic prosperity, and its case demonstrates the explicit costs such a foreign policy incurs from Moscow, revealing incentives that maintain other former republics' pragmatic compliance with the Kremlin.

Stephen Jones observes in his chapter that "Georgian nationalism, despite European pressures and the new elite's pragmatism, will not adopt an integrationist civic model, largely because Georgia's own national minorities find this unacceptable." Making the case for a system that "recognizes and accommodates national group rights," Jones delineates the myths and realities of Georgian nationalism. Yet Russia's punishment of Georgia for its nationalist path in foreign affairs, and ethnic nationalism domestically, demonstrates the role that Moscow plays in the post-Soviet nationalist climate.

The Rest of the Post-Soviet National Legacy

Most successor states realized the need for strong cooperation with Moscow immediately upon independence. Armenia, Belarus, and Central

Asian states (except Turkmenistan) quickly restrained anti-Russian nationalist currents to the occasional rhetorical bluster, instead of a force defining foreign policy. Azerbaijan and Ukraine did so somewhat more slowly but have since stayed the civic course. The relative economic prosperity and strong political ties to Western Europe empowered the Baltic states to leave the Russian sphere. The Baltic states' unique circumstances, particularly pending NATO membership, restrained negative incentives from Moscow.

Even following the September 11 attacks on the United States, which placed the long-standing interest of Central Asian states in containing Islamic fundamentalism directly in line with U.S. foreign policy, the Central Asian states still required Putin's sanction before assisting the U.S.-led coalition. Instead of drifting beyond Moscow's sphere with the passing years of independence and embracing opportunities for new integration internationally and globalizing economic relations, the former republics have largely remained in accord with the Kremlin.

This dynamic has been nearly continuous, regardless of Kremlin leadership and foreign policy regimes. Indeed, Yeltsin's policy in the Russian "near abroad" was fragmented, with different factions of the Russian elite, from the Ministry of Foreign Affairs to LUKoil to defense interests, pursuing different agendas. Putin has consolidated these spheres, unifying Russia's foreign policy and concerting Russia's power in the former Soviet space. Yet under both Kremlin leaders, the former Soviet republics have remained in line with Moscow. As seen throughout the Caucasus (in terms of reward *and* punishment), the Western former republics (where Belarus actively pursues reintegration with Russia), and in the interesting, somewhat diversified foreign policy dynamics of the Baltics (where relative economic success and NATO's overtures adjust the rules), pragmatism in former republics' relations to Moscow persists in trumping nationalism and defining post-Soviet international relations.

Azerbaijan

The potential for instability across the Caucasus states of Azerbaijan, Armenia, and Georgia was a foregone conclusion upon independence from the USSR. Although conflict in the Caucasus region has filled the ten years of post-Soviet independence, with the Nagorno-Karabakh and Abkhazia conflicts unresolved, Iran and Turkey pursuing new regional interests, oil and the risk of religious fundamentalism pressuring the region's unsteady geopolitics, and each Caucasus state mythologizing its nationhood, the tension has not erupted into direct clashes with Russia. Even as strong nationalist trends characterize the region, they have not typified relations with Moscow. Despite no shortage of controversial, unresolved issues, a Russia tilt has largely defined foreign policy.

Such a dominant position for Russia in regional issues is evident even in the case of Azerbaijan, a country that has been less openly hostile to Russia than Georgia but much more so than Armenia. Even with the cease-fire secured in the Nagorno-Karabakh conflict, Russia moved to punish Azerbaijan for signing an oil deal with an international consortium headed by BP and Amoco, imposing a transport blockade of Azerbaijan in 1994. Moscow was displeased with Azerbaijan's move to develop oil prospects without concern for the Caspian Sea's legal status and pointedly retained control of the Gabala early-warning radar station, mirroring the policy of retaining Soviet military bases in Georgia.

In reply to Russian pressure, Azerbaijan acquiesced in October 1995 to transport some crude oil extracted by international companies via Russia. Although mobilizing nationalist sentiment domestically in the conflict with Armenia, Azerbaijan thus submitted to international security and economic interests, acquiescing to (belated) membership in the CIS in 1993, Russia's authority in establishing a cease-fire with Armenia, and Russia's imposition of limits on exploiting oil resources for the international market. The already-limited avenues pursued by Azerbaijan toward international integration, independent of Moscow's terms and motivated by nationalist aspirations, were blocked by Russia.

Moldova and Belarus

Although representing different degrees of pre-Soviet nationalist awakenings and statehoods and diverse experiences in the USSR, both Belarus and Moldova have avoided nationalism in post-Soviet dealings with Moscow. The degree of open cooperation with Moscow, or indeed desire to reintegrate politically with Russia, differs between these two states, yet throughout nationalism has been excluded from foreign policy dictums, in recognition of Russia's power in regional affairs. Indeed, Moldova's early-1990s overtures to closer integration with Romania, with the possibility of political union, and the subsequent action of Russia's Fourteenth Army in Transdniestr, is an illustrative exception proving the rule of Russia's role in the region.

Beyond being a founding member and proponent of the CIS in 1991, and consistently supporting closer ties among post-Soviet states, Belarus has been at the forefront of reintegration with Russia. Thus during the first legislative election following independence, in May–December 1995, voters sanctioned a referendum that approved closer ties with Russia and envisioned increasingly close economic and political links, as well as eventual monetary union. Following this overture, Belarus signed the first Union Treaty with Russia in April 1996, and in May 1997 the two countries signed a Union Charter, aimed at encouraging greater integration and cooperation. A declaration on further unification was signed in December 1998, with all steps culminating in a second Union Treaty approved in December 1999.

This Union Treaty advances the creation of a supranational legislature, the Supreme State Council, and close cooperation on monetary policy, economic, and defense matters. The council is made up of leaders from each country, a joint Council of Ministers, and a union parliament. The parliament is divided into the House of the Union, formed by delegates from Belarusian and Russian legislative bodies, and the House of Representatives, whose delegates are directly elected. The Council of Ministers coordinates foreign and defense policy and is charged with the creation of shared economic space and synchronization of monetary, credit, and fiscal policy. Although the treaty excludes the full assimilation of Belarus into Russia, it provides Russia with use of Belarus's military infrastructure, enabling Russian troops to be stationed on NATO's new eastern border. The treaty allows for a joint military doctrine and armament program. Belarus, in turn, gains easy access to the Russian market for manufactured goods and discounted energy import prices. Implementation of some articles is not due until as late as 2005.[13]

This high level of integration and absence of nationalist rhetoric in foreign policy reflects not only Russia's importance for the economy of Belarus but also the political support that President Aleksandr Lukashenka of Belarus seeks in light of his regime's international isolation. In the ten years following independence, Belarus's foreign trade has continued to be focused on the CIS, with Russia alone comprising more than half of Belarus's export revenue and nearly two-thirds of import expenditure in 2000.[14] This flexibility has allowed Lukashenka to remain in power, based on the economic security he offers citizens relative to other post-Soviet states and despite his regime's poor record on civil society issues. Even without the Lukashenka regime, a high degree of integration would tie

Belarus and Russia based on regional realities in economic and defense measures. However, given Lukashenka's political needs, he drives already close relations with Moscow to a formalized, unified level.

Moldova exited the Soviet Union based on ethnonationalist sentiment and an assertion of the titular group's native language, culture, and traditions, as occurred throughout most former Soviet republics. More unique, however, was that Moldova's ethnonationalism was tied to a neighboring state, Romania. The prospect of renewing historic cultural, linguistic, economic, and political ties maintained Moldova's ethnonationalist momentum longer than a merely anti-Soviet sentiment could achieve. Thus, through the 1990s, Moldova was an unenthusiastic member of the CIS, and although having signed the Almaty Agreement in December 1991 (establishing a wider CIS) and a treaty on economic union in 1993, Moldova's parliament did not authorize the country's membership until 1994. Resisting efforts at monetary integration or collective defense measures, Moldova's government instead emphasized closer ties with the EU, eyeing eventual integration. Moldova has also joined Georgia, Ukraine, Uzbekistan, and Azerbaijan to form GUUAM, an effort intended to balance the Russian-dominated CIS. Moldova's relations with Russia were thus initially defined by nationalism and the aspiration to integrate outside of Moscow's channels.

Nationalist tension came to the fore, however, when the large population of ethnic Russians and Ukrainians in the Transdniestr region perceived Moldovan independence to be a threatening step toward reunification with Romania and voted for autonomy in September 1990 and for independence in late 1991. Civil war resulted in January 1992. A cease-fire in July of that year ended armed conflict, but the political status of the area remains unsettled: Transdniestr is semi-independent, printing its own currency, maintaining a central bank and customs system, and utilizing the Cyrillic alphabet. Unable to settle the conflict militarily, despite Romanian backing, Moldova also perceived that reunification with Romania was increasingly unappealing, given the worsening economic situation there. These developments brought considerable pressure upon Moldova's nationalist groups. Meanwhile, Russia has maintained its Fourteenth Army in Transdniestr, despite 1999 OSCE-brokered promises to withdraw all troops and weaponry by 2002. The Fourteenth Army had sided with fellow Slavs against the Moldovan government and will likely remain stationed in the region. In a situation analogous to the Abkhazia conflict, Russia is the only actor empowered to resolve the issue of autonomy, but it resists, since settlement would mean the withdrawal of troops and loss of influence.

Moldova remains a divided society but has made a dramatic return to Moscow's sphere, reestablishing relations built on pragmatic gain, not nationalist zeal. In February 2001 the renewed, pro-Russia Communist Party of Moldova (CPM) received more than one-half of the votes, marking Moldova as the first former Soviet republic to bring a communist party back to power. The success of the CPM culminated in the election by parliament of Vladimir Voronin as president. Voronin has expressed interest in joining the Russia-Belarus union, and his party plans on reinstating Russian as the official language and reintroducing its mandatory instruction in schools.

Voronin has not dismissed the possibility of joining the EU eventually but has suggested that Moldova would join only when other western CIS states do so also. He has furthermore rejected NATO membership based on the fact that Moldova is a constitutionally neutral state. Despite strong nationalist momentum upon and following independence, Moldova has been compelled to reorient its foreign policy toward the balance sheet of power and away from nationalist aspirations. With this development, Moldova joins Ukraine and Belarus in foreign policy orientation that remains prudently pro-Russian.

Central Asia

The five states of Central Asia are products of the Soviet division of the region in the 1920s into republics loosely correlating with ethnic divisions. Much of Central Asia was formerly a Russian tsarist protectorate, and some scattered nationalist resistance to Soviet rule occurred into the 1920s. Such movements were eliminated, however, and the region was subjected to Soviet modernization programs, large agriculture projects, and—most notably for nomadic tribes—forced collectivization and settlement. Previously lacking borders or statehood, the republics thus experienced modernization and a sense of national identity in strictly Soviet terms. Industrialization in the region brought Russian immigrants, and ethnic Russians dominated the region's political elite. The titular ethnic groups ascended in the Communist Party power structure only later in the Soviet era, generally following Stalin's death, gaining autonomy within strict limits of absolute loyalty to Moscow. Politicians from the titular nationalities obtained leadership in the 1960s and 1970s based on corrupt relations with the Kremlin.

As across regions in the USSR, perestroika brought unrest, demonstrations, and expressions of local discontent and nationalism. The Central Asian states largely gained independence, however, as a de facto development, not as a nationalist endeavor.

The Soviet-gerrymandered borders, designed to both unite and divide coethnics depending on political objectives, set the stage for ethnic conflict in the region. The largest conflagration of the post-Soviet era occurred in Tajikistan, with the substantial Tajik and Uzbek minorities mobilized by their respective governments, intent on asserting cultural rights. In 1992 civil war broke out between opposing regional and ideological groups and claimed as many as fifty thousand lives. Uzbek minorities in the south of Kyrgyzstan, centered around Osh, have been a source of instability for Bishkek, and the Uighur population in Kyrgyzstan compels close relations with Chinese authorities, as Kyrgyzstan cannot confront China.[15] In addition to ethnic-based conflict, Islamic fundamentalism has added to volatility in the region. The armed Uzbek Islamist group the Islamic Movement of Uzbekistan (IMU), based in Tajikistan and Afghanistan, has been active throughout the Fergana Valley. In July 1999 the IMU attempted an attack on Uzbekistan. Although Uzbekistan supported the Tajik government in 1992, it also covertly supported an incursion of one thousand armed men, led by Colonel Mahmud Khudoiberdiyev, an ethnic Uzbek, into northern Tajikistan in 1998 through Uzbek territory. Dealing with separatist movements and border disputes, Central Asian governments have also pursued the creation of ethnonational myths in an attempt to craft pre-Soviet histories to prop up national identities today.

The rise of ethnonationalism, however, has not applied to relations with Moscow. Central Asian states, with the exception of Turkmenistan, have remained integrated with Russia following independence. Russia is the main guarantor of stability in the region and remains heavily involved in regional security and economic matters. With settlement of the civil war in Tajikistan in June 1997, Russian border guards and the 201st army division are based permanently in the country and along the Afghan frontier. Russia's military guarantees are important in easing individual national concerns for security, based on unrest in Afghanistan, Islamic fundamentalist groups (primarily the IMU), and instability in western China. The extent of the region's integration with Moscow was clear following September 11: Central Asian states foresaw the benefit of joining the U.S.-led coalition but needed to clear their cooperation with Moscow first.

Regional alliances among Central Asian states include Russia. In addition to the CIS, to which all Central Asian states have signed, Kyrgyzstan, Kazakhstan, Tajikistan, and Russia (and Armenia) have formed a collective rapid reaction force (CRRF), headquartered in Bishkek. Allying Kazakhstan, Tajikistan, Kyrgyzstan, Uzbekistan, China, and Russia, the Shanghai Cooperation Organization pursues Central Asian security and antiterrorist action, as well as regional economic cooperation. This economic integration is largely based on energy supply, as well as Russia's control of the means of energy export.

The treatment of Russian minorities in Central Asia has not been a source of conflict with Moscow. Russian nationalist groups have only surfaced in Kazakhstan, where ethnic Russians comprised 30 percent of the population in 2001. These groups have been defused by the Kazakh security apparatus, however, and do not represent a serious threat or a Russian foreign policy prerogative. There has been considerable emigration, and Russian minorities remain mostly in urban areas only. Many have left based on a perceived lack of opportunities for ethnic Russians, real instances of discrimination, and the fundamental fact that the rules in the national power structure have changed.

Turkmenistan has been the notable exception in Central Asia to integration with Russia. In March 1991, then–secretary general of the Turkmen Communist Party Saparmurad Niyazov ensured a 95 percent vote in support of preserving the Soviet Union. This referendum, although marked by fraud, indicated the fear of losing Russia's economic support. When the Soviet Federation collapsed, Turkmenistan was forced into independence, which Niyazov has pursued on a nationalist, one-party platform. Under Niyazov, Turkmenistan has isolated itself from other Central Asian states, reintroducing visa regulations for CIS visitors similar to those of the Soviet era and taking little role in the CIS or regional organizations. Turkmenistan pulled out of a border protection treaty signed with Russia in 1993 and has persistently taken contrary positions on the future use of the Caspian Sea. Niyazov's relations with Moscow have been distant since he hedged his bets on the 1996 Russian presidential election. Finally, in 1997 Gazprom effectively cut off Turkmenistan's gas exports.

Niyazov has defined foreign policy largely in terms of energy resources and largely seeks national self-sufficiency and isolation in other matters. He has thus integrated Turkmenistan with Iran, the UAE, and Turkey. Iran has been particularly appealing, as it offers one of the few possible gas export routes not crossing Russian territory. Turkmenistan's alienation of Russia, however, has brought punishment from Moscow upon Turkmenistan's priority sector—gas exports. As the main gas pipeline currently runs to Russia through Kazakhstan, and is controlled by the Russian gas monopoly Gazprom, Turkmenistan's access to Western markets is at Russia's whim. With Niyazov's power based on revenue from gas export and hard-currency inflows, the success of his economic plan and thus control of the country is subject to shocks from Russian energy export decisions.

Conclusion

A dominant theme in the shaping of nationalism after independence in the post-Soviet states has been the "Russia factor." Throughout the region—Ukraine, Belarus, Azerbaijan, Armenia, and most of the Central Asian republics—incipient independence movements that appeared exclusivist and ethnonationalist in content shifted to a more inclusive, civic nationalism as the necessity of a strong relationship with Russia came home to roost.

Notable exceptions were the Baltic states, whose relative lack of economic dependence upon Russia and potential for integration into European and trans-Atlantic security and economic architecture allowed leaders initially to shape a more ethnic nationalist path. In these cases, civic nationalism also emerged, though this time largely due to pressure from the European organizations in which the Baltic states so coveted membership. Criticism from Russia had, at best, an indirect effect on the civic tendencies of countries such as Estonia and Latvia, by getting the attention of Europe.[16] Georgia is the only other country that has made strong efforts to define a more exclusionary national track vis-à-vis Russia, a difference that has only been exacerbated since the 2004 election of President Mikheil Saakashvili. In response, it has been punished severely by Russia, both through economic leverage and implicit military threat.

The policy approaches consistent with civic nationalism have been shaped in large measure by the realities of dependence upon Russia, irrespective of the type of nationalism developed in Russia itself. Many observers express concern that the new Russian minorities—who represent significant percentages of non-Russian populations in all but Armenia—might rise up in revolt against their new governments.[17] Not only were many in the Russian communities from Crimea to northern Kazakhstan uninterested in being the fifth column but many feared they would be.[18] But those Russians who did desire the reestablishment of a union in the Eurasian region were disappointed to find there was little support in Moscow for their cause. Indeed, through much of the Yeltsin era, a power vacuum led to little coordinated action in the "near abroad"—muddled by competing visions of a more exclusivist, Eurasianist bent of the security wing alongside the more civic approach of economic reformers. The more consolidated approach that has developed under President Putin will undoubtedly increase the pressure on some of these states.[19] But whatever the regime in Moscow, Russian economic and strategic influence on the post-Soviet states will continue to have a great impact on the course of their respective nationalisms.

NOTES

1. See Lubomyr Hajda and Mark Beissinger, eds., *The Nationalities Factor in Soviet Politics and Society* (Boulder: Westview Press, 1990); Nadia Diuk and Adrian Karatnycky, *The Hidden Nations: The People Challenge the Soviet Union* (New York: Morrow, 1990); Ian Bremmer and Ray Taras, eds., *Nations and Politics in the Soviet Successor States* (Cambridge: Cambridge University Press, 1993); Stuart J. Kaufman, "Spiraling to Ethnic War: Elites, Masses, and Moscow in Moldova's Civil War," *International Security* 21, no. 1 (autumn 1996): 108–38; and Valery Tishkov, *Ethnicity, Nationalism, and Conflict in and after the Soviet Union: The Mind Aflame* (Thousand Oaks, CA: Sage Publications, 1997).

2. Including the Chechen-Ingush, Chuvash, Karelian, Komi, Mari, Tatar, and Udmurt ASSRs and autonomous regions and areas including Adigei, Chukchi, Gorno-Altai, Karachai, Komi-Permyak, and Koryak. That this nationalist awakening came as a surprise to Soviet citizens and Sovietologists alike is an understatement. The emergence and primacy of nationalist movements in achieving independence for the Soviet titular republics has been well documented since. See Diuk and Karatnycky, *The Hidden Nations;* Geoffrey Hosking, Jonathan Aves, and Peter J. S. Duncan, *The Road to Post-Communism: Independent Political Movements in the Soviet Union, 1985–1991* (New York: Pinter Publishers, 1992); Ronald Grigor Suny, *The Revenge of the Past: Nationalism, Revolution, and the Collapse of the Soviet Union* (Stanford, CA: Stanford University Press, 1993); and Peter Rutland, "Democracy and Nationalism in Armenia," *Europe-Asia Studies* 46, no. 1 (1994): 47–68.

3. John B. Dunlop, "Russia: Confronting a Loss of Empire, 1987–1991," *Political Science Quarterly* 108, no. 4 (winter 1993–94): 603–34.

4. "The myriad levels of nationality enshrined within the Soviet system" is from Lenin's dictum of "national in form, socialist in content" (*korenizatsia,* or nativization) and the Stalinist "merging of nations" (*sliyanie*), to the Brezhnevite "creation of a new historical society—the Soviet people" (*sovetsky narod*) and institutions such as the Soviet passport's designation of a citizen's *national'nost'.*

5. Ted Hopf, "Managing Soviet Disintegration: A Demand for Behavioral Regimes," *International Security* 17, no. 1 (summer 1992): 44–75.

6. For a discussion of the role of European organizations in the evolution of Baltic citizenship laws, see Lowell W. Barrington, "Understanding Citizenship Policy in the Baltic States," in *From Migrants to Citizens: Membership in a Changing World,* ed. T. Alexander Alienikoff and Douglas Klusmeyer (Washington, DC: Carnegie Endowment for International Peace, 2000).

7. Ethnonationalist sentiment continues to be well grounded in Galicia in particular and western Ukraine in general. These areas in fact resemble the Baltic republics, except for the absence of "interfronts" within the population—largely because Russians accounted for only 5 percent of the population of western Ukraine.

8. Ian Bremmer, "The Politics of Ethnicity: Russians in the New Ukraine," *Europe-Asia Studies* 46, no. 2 (1994): 261–83; Alexander Motyl and Bohdan Krawchenko, "Ukraine from Empire to Statehood," in *New States, New Politics: Building the Post-Soviet Nations,* ed. Ian Bremmer and Ray Taras (Cambridge: Cambridge University Press, 1997); Taras Kuzio, *Ukraine under Kuchma: Political Reform, Economic Transformation and Security Policy in Independent Ukraine* (New York: St. Martin's Press, 1997); and Roman Szporluk, *Russia, Ukraine, and the Breakup of the Soviet Union* (Stanford, CA: Hoover Institution Press, 2000).

9. This model did not emerge immediately following independence and instead reflects the interplay of incentives from Moscow regarding Armenia's relations with the Kremlin, selective deployments and expressions of ethnic nationalism domestically, and diminishing hostilities with Azerbaijan. Yet these factors are shaped by the constraints and incentives that the Kremlin has dealt Armenia following independence.

10. For example, when President Levon Ter-Petrossian appeared to accept the OSCE resolution of the Nagorno-Karabakh conflict in January 1998, which provided for the return of conquered Azerbaijani land preceding any agreement on Nagorno-Karabakh's status, he was ultimately forced to resign: the Nagorno-Karabakh leadership and Armenia's prime minister, defense minister, and interior and national security minister were against the deal, leaving Ter-Petrossian without a government.

11. Russia maintains a fighter squadron in Armenia and in 1995 established two full military bases in Armenia as well. Russia has secured a twenty-five-year agreement to base Russian troops in Armenia, which has been an enthusiastic member of the Commonwealth of Independent States (CIS) upon its founding in 1991.

12. Georgia joined NATO's Partnership for Peace program in 1994, for instance, and has leveraged its potential as a transit route for oil and gas exports from the Caspian region, gaining substantial U.S. economic aid. Shevardnadze has actively engaged Turkey as a trade partner, displacing Russian ties.

13. Aleksandr Lukashenka's success in achieving the current level of union with Russia did not occur in a complete absence of nationalist sentiment. As elsewhere in the USSR, nationalism propelled the country's exit, with the Belarusian Popular Front (BPF) appearing in 1988 under the leadership of Zyanon Paznyak and winning 10 percent of the three hundred available seats in the election for the Belarusian Supreme Soviet in 1990 and successfully backing Stanislau Shushkevich as speaker of the Supreme Soviet in 1991. Much of the early nationalist movement was based on dissent stemming from the Chernobyl accident, from which 70 percent of the radioactive fallout landed on Belarus. The nationalist movement quickly lost cohesion in the early 1990s, however, revealing its relative weakness (compared to the Baltics or Ukraine, for example) and fragility when faced with severe economic downturns troubling other former republics. The July 1994 presidential election of Lukashenka set Belarus on a res-

olutely pro-Russian course, with nationalist sentiment largely constrained to the urban intelligentsia and with some strands of disenfranchised opposition groups calling for greater independence from Russia. The BPF has successfully organized demonstrations against Lukashenka and the Union Treaty, but Paznyak's exile in 1996 led to a crisis in leadership and decline in power. Not only is nationalism absent from Belarus's foreign policy with Russia but steps toward reintegration have relegated any sense of nation to tropes utilized by Lukashenka against the West or the hallmark of antiregime groups.

14. Russia is the main supplier of electricity and gas to Belarus and—unlike with other former republics—has regularly accepted Belarus's energy payment problems, allowing write-offs and refinancing of Belarus's energy debt.

15. See Richard Walsh, "China and the New Geopolitics of Central Asia," *Asian Survey* 33, no. 3 (1993): 272–84; Yongjin Zhang and Rouben Azizian, eds., *Ethnic Challenges beyond Borders: Chinese and Russian Perspectives on the Central Asian Conundrum* (New York: St. Martin's Press, 1998); and Anara Tabyshalieva, *The Challenge of Regional Cooperation in Central Asia: Preventing Ethnic Conflict in the Ferghana Valley* (Washington, DC: U.S. Institute of Peace, 1999).

16. Barrington, "Understanding Citizenship Policy in the Baltic States."

17. See Graham Smith and Andrew Wilson, "Rethinking Russia's Post-Soviet Diaspora: The Potential for Political Mobilisation in Eastern Ukraine and North-East Estonia," *Europe-Asia Studies* 49, no. 5 (July 1997): 845–65; Rogers Brubaker, *Nationalism Reframed: Nationhood and the National Question in the New Europe* (Cambridge: Cambridge University Press, 1996); and Vladimir Shlapentokh, Munir Sendich, and Emil Payin, *The New Diaspora: Russian Minorities in the Former Soviet Republics* (Armonk, NY: M. E. Sharpe, 1994).

18. See Lowell W. Barrington, Erik S. Herron, and Brian D. Silver, "The Motherland Is Calling: Views of Homeland among Russians in the Near Abroad" (unpublished manuscript).

19. Though, ultimately, this approach may be diluted by the increasing internationalization of the region through the war against terror. Particularly in the Caucasus and Central Asia, America's expanding role could mitigate some of the influence of coordinated Russian influence.

7. Nationalism in Post-Soviet Lithuania

New Approaches for the Nation of "Innocent Sufferers"

TERRY D. CLARK

MOST SCHOLARS ARGUE that, in contrast to many of the states of the former Soviet Union, Lithuania has had few difficulties with its national minorities.[1] Much of this owes to Lithuanians constituting over 80 percent of the population, while the two largest national minorities comprise approximately 8 percent (Russians) and 7 percent (Poles) respectively. Given these demographics, the new Lithuanian state, unlike its Baltic neighbors, exercised the so-called zero option—granting citizenship to all individuals on its state territory at the time of restoration of independence irrespective of their national identity. This was a major factor in the relatively tranquil relations between national communities in the country.[2]

The argument for comparatively tranquil relations between national communities, however, is not the same as making the case that nationalism as a phenomenon does not exist in the political system. This chapter argues that nationalism has existed in one form or another since the late Soviet era. While it has not led to conflict of the sort seen in the other Baltic republics or parts of the former Soviet Union, it has nonetheless contributed to social difficulties and unrest, particularly in the period leading up to and immediately following the restoration of independence. But, since the immediate postindependence period, nationalism has also been both weakened and transformed. While the Lithuanian national myth remains, its effect on Lithuanian politics and daily life today is not what it had been at the end of the Soviet period when the country's independence was restored.

Early Nationalism

Lithuanian history is marked by an early period of expansionist glory, gradual decline, eventual cultural subjugation, and a prolonged struggle to develop and reassert a national identity. By the end of the fourteenth century, the grand duchy of Lithuania was one of the largest states in Europe. At its zenith it extended from the Baltic Sea to the Black Sea. Following the union with Poland brought about by the marriage of the grand duke of Lithuania with the queen of Poland in 1386, however, the grand duchy entered a long period of decline. While relations between the two states in the Polish-Lithuanian Commonwealth were initially based on no more than the fact that they were under the same ruler, the Treaty of Lublin in 1569 merged what had been separate political and social institutions. As a consequence, the nobility of the two states rapidly fused, converging on the ideal of two peoples with an inseparable past and future.[3] By 1698, Polish culture had become so dominant that Polish was declared the official state language for the entire commonwealth. Lithuanian had been largely relegated to the status of a language spoken by the illiterate peasant population of the Polish-Lithuanian Commonwealth's eastern regions.

The partitions of the Polish-Lithuanian Commonwealth at the end of the eighteenth century brought the Lithuanian lands into the Russian Empire. This was resisted by the nobility and gentry, a resistance that culminated in the Insurrection of 1831. The insurrection, the aim of which was to restore the Polish-Lithuanian Commonwealth, was confined to the largely Polonized upper class and residents of towns.[4] Hence, the tsarist reprisals had little impact on the Lithuanian-speaking peasant population. Such reprisals included executions and deportations of the nobility, land seizures, and the closing of Vilnius University, which had served as a center for the maintenance and spread of Polish culture.

The relative passivity of the lower classes, however, changed radically with the abolition of serfdom in the Russian Empire. The attendant social and educational reforms had the unintended consequence of fueling a Lithuanian national reawakening, something seen in much of east central Europe during the nineteenth century. Taking advantage of the new freedoms and opportunities offered by the reforms, a significant proportion of the Lithuanian-speaking lower classes experienced rapid upward social mobility, entering the ranks of the professions and educated elite. Unlike the Lithuanian nobility and gentry, they rejected both Polish and Russian culture. Many of them quickly formed the vanguard of an independence movement that resulted in yet another uprising in 1863. Unlike that of 1830, the Insurrection of 1863 sought an independent Lithuanian state. Indeed, these new intellectuals and professionals rejected the Polish-Lithuanian Commonwealth and its claim to represent the inseparable interests of the Polish and Lithuanian peoples.[5] Hence, the Insurrection of 1863 can properly be viewed as the start of the Lithuanian national reawakening.

The tsarist response to the Insurrection of 1863 was harsh. In addition to executions and deportations, the use of the Latin alphabet was banned. In essence, no publication in the Lithuanian language was permitted. This policy remained in force from 1864 to 1904. The effect was twofold. First, it helped to identify the language as central to the national identity. Second, it consolidated support for an independent Lithuanian *nation-state* among virtually the entire population. During the period several illegal Lithuanian-language periodicals emerged urging national resistance to assimilation and rejecting reunification with Poland. The intensity of the resistance to the Russian Empire is most evidenced in the willingness of many to school their children in the Lithuanian language despite serious punishments for doing so.[6]

The lifting of the ban on publishing in the Lithuanian language was part of a package of concessions made by the tsar in the wake of the disastrous defeat in the Russo-Japanese War. In response, the independence movement formally organized and continued to press for an independent and national Lithuanian state in which Lithuanian would be the only official language. The vision was achieved on February 16, 1918, when a group of intellectuals declared the creation of the Republic of Lithuania following the collapse of the Russian Empire.

Deep divisions concerning relations with Poland continued to plague Lithuanian society in the interwar period. These divisions were most evident in two events: the Polish seizure of the region surrounding Vilnius in 1920 and the military coup of 1926. The Polish seizure of the heavily Polonized capital region had the support of many of the landowners and townspeople of the region, while the military coup of 1926 forcibly deposed a left-wing government elected with the support of many of the country's Poles and Jews. The Union of Nationalists installed a president in its place, and the president was given near-dictatorial powers. Further, leftist parties were virtually denied the right to political participation for the remainder of the interwar period.[7]

The country's incorporation into the Soviet Union and the replacement of Lithuanian with Russian as the language of political and economic discourse in 1940 once again presented the Lithuanian nation with a challenge to the survival of its identity. However, the lessons learned in the period of the national reawakening and independence struggle helped it to survive. Of particular note were the strong attachment to the national language and the determination to protect it. Also apparent in the independence struggle (and postindependence period) were the efforts to protect the nation from Polish cultural domination and Russian political domination.

Toward Independence: The Struggle to Define National Membership & Gain Territorial Control

The Emergence of Sąjūdis

Responding to the opening provided by perestroika, an initiative group of intellectuals drawn from among discussion clubs, the Lithuanian Writer's Union, and a number of small groups concerned with protection of the environment and historical buildings declared the creation of the Lithuanian Reform Movement, Sąjūdis, in June 1988. The movement's initial goals were largely concerned with the protection of Lithuanian culture, particularly the language. This was reflected in the very first platform, which called for proclaiming the Lithuanian language as an official state language of the republic, strengthening the teaching of Lithuanian in schools, establishing language schools for national minorities, and correcting misrepresentations of Lithuanian history.[8]

These and other demands were adopted at Sąjūdis's Constituent Congress of October 1988, an event of enormous importance. Aired on television and radio, the congress stirred the Lithuanian nation and resulted in a dramatic change in the movement's membership. Almost overnight Sąjūdis was transformed from an intellectual movement to a mass movement. Within a short time, previously prohibited national myths and symbols were once again being displayed throughout the republic. By 1990, Sąjūdis's appeal to the Lithuanian national majority was so deep that the movement captured over 100 of the 140 seats in the republican legislature (the Supreme Council) in elections held that year.

The movement's changing demographics radicalized Sąjūdis. In response, many of the movement's initial founders became some of its harshest critics.[9] The centrality of the cultural concerns that had united the intellectuals of the initiative group gave way to the politicization of nationalism. Within a year, initial demands for economic sovereignty within the Soviet Union were replaced by insistence on the restoration of the country's prewar independence. The Supreme Council, elected in 1990 and dominated by Sąjūdis, declared as its first act the restoration of the independent prewar Republic of Lithuania. The effort to break with Moscow resulted in an economic blockade and several episodes of violence over an eighteen-month-long period. At the end of this period, however, Lithuania regained its independence in the aftermath of the failure by Soviet hardliners to reassert control in the abortive coup of August 1991.

The Crystallization of the Lithuanian National Idea

Much of the activity leading up to the restoration of Lithuanian independence revolved around the membership question "What is the Lithuanian nation?" The self-portrait that emerged was that of a people who had lived in a region traversed by many peoples; hence, Lithuanians had developed a high level of tolerance of others. However, not all of their neighbors had done likewise, imposing their culture and language on the Lithuanians. As a consequence, the Lithuanian nation was also depicted as a heroic people who had suffered for centuries from efforts, made by first the Poles and then the Russians, to dominate and forcibly assimilate them. Yet the Lithuanians had persevered and overcome these efforts.[10] One scholar has called this self-image that of a nation of "innocent sufferers."[11]

Such a self-depiction necessarily required Lithuanians to distinguish themselves from their oppressors. The most difficult task was to define an identity separate from that of the Poles, given the almost four hundred years of union between the two nations in which Polish language and culture had dominated. This mirrored the challenge during the interwar period, during which much of the country's intelligentsia, gentry, and townspeople demonstrated an attachment to Polish culture as well as the idea of union with Poland. Hence, the Lithuanian national revival in the late Soviet period was partially a struggle against Polish culture.[12]

Lithuanians had much less difficulty identifying themselves separately from the Russians. From the Lithuanian perspective, the primary task appeared to be ridding the language of Russian or Soviet-imposed constructions. Indeed, the Soviet period was widely viewed as a time of occupation and forced Russification. Russian political and cultural dominance was supported by the economic dependence of the republic on Moscow, the deportation and liquidation of much of the Lithuanian intelligentsia in 1940 and the postwar period, and Russian immigration. This immigration, which some saw as an attempt at colonization, was most evident as a result of the construction of the nuclear power facility at Ignalina. The Ignalina facility primarily employed scientists and technicians from outside the republic, despite the availability of Lithuanian specialists.[13]

The Minorities Respond

Requiring as it did the rejection of Polish and Russian culture, the articulation of the Lithuanian national idea, combined with the insistence that the Lithuanian language become the primary vehicle for political and economic discourse, gave rise to anxieties among the republic's national minorities. The politicization of the national idea within Sąjūdis led to nationalist exclusivity that further exacerbated these anxieties.[14] The movement's demands that an independent Lithuania be a national state, with priority given to the Lithuanian culture and language, appeared to be a clear threat of oppression or perhaps even forcible assimilation. This was reflected in the fact that Sąjūdis was almost totally a Lithuanian movement. At the Constituent Congress, 980 of the 1,021 deputies were Lithuanian; only 9 were Poles, and 8 were Russians.[15]

The response by many within the national minorities was predictable. Many Russians and smaller Russian-speaking minority groups—including Belarusians, Ukrainians, Jews, and Tatars—formed Edinstvo. This movement, formed with the encouragement of Moscow,[16] stood in open opposition to Sąjūdis, and in particular to demands to make Lithuanian the official state language. But Edinstvo never succeeded in fully organizing the Russian-speaking community. While this was partially due to the organization's open support of the Soviet regime, it also reflected the highly fragmented nature of the Russian community itself. Hardly a community with a common interest, it was divided both socioeconomically and by varying degrees of integration into Lithuanian society. Large numbers of Russians, particularly those living in Vilnius, were descended from families that had lived in the region for centuries. Others were relatively new arrivals who had been brought to the republic to provide a labor force in Soviet factories and projects, including the previously mentioned nuclear power station in the Ignalina region.

Poles, on the other hand, were a good deal more socioeconomically and historically united. Unlike the Russians, who were spread across many of the urban centers of the republic, Poles were largely concentrated in the regions in and around Vilnius that had been forcibly seized and occupied by Poland during the interwar era. The community's major weakness was the lack of an intelligentsia; most of its members were rural peasants with low levels of education. The Polish intelligentsia had fled during and after World War II. Those who had not were in many cases liquidated. Lacking an intelligentsia, and subjected to the Russification efforts of the Soviet era, the Lithuanian Poles spoke a language that was a dialect of Polish with strong Russian and Belarusian influence. In this context, Sąjūdis's demands that Lithuanian be the state language appeared to many as an effort to assimilate the Polish minority. As a consequence, they formed the Union of Poles in Lithuania to counter these efforts and came into direct conflict with Sąjūdis.[17]

The demands of the Union of Poles further contributed to concerns among Lithuanian nationalists within Sąjūdis of a reemergence of Polish cultural dominance or, worse, the loss once again of the Vilnius region. Among such demands were increasing the quality of Polish-language instruction in schools, creating a Polish university, and forming an autonomous Polish region in the area around Vilnius dominated by the Polish population.[18] In pursuit of these goals, the political leadership of the Polish regions openly opposed Lithuanian independence and negotiated with Moscow for greater autonomy from Vilnius.

Given the opposition of both Edinstvo and the Union of Poles to the restoration of Lithuanian independence, both the Russians and Poles were viewed by many Lithuanians as being in clear opposition to the new state when independence was finally achieved. This perception was further fueled by the fact that both communities had elected deputies in the 1990 elections to the Supreme Council who were openly opposed to the restoration of the country's independence. Russians and Russian-speaking groups provided most of the electoral support for the Communist Party,[19] and the Poles had elected eight deputies on the platform of the Union of Poles.

Sąjūdis and the Lithuanian National Idea in the Early Independence Period

The constitution of the Republic of Lithuania, adopted in a national referendum in October 1992, makes it abundantly clear that the new state is a national state. The preamble makes the unambiguous claim that the state is the creation of the Lithuanian nation and that the Lithuanian language is the state language. Further, the national idea of that people as it had emerged during the independence period is laid out. The Lithuanian people, having "established the State of Lithuania many centuries ago" and having "defended its freedom and independence and preserved its spirit, native language, writing, and customs," are nevertheless a tolerant people desiring to foster "national accord" and a "harmonious civil society."

The dilemma for the newly independent state was how to forge national accord and harmony within the context of a national state. Indeed, by focusing on the suffering inflicted at the hands of the Poles and Russians, the national idea contained elements of disintegration instead of integration, particularly since these two peoples constituted the two largest national minorities in the republic. The centrality of language to the Lithuanian self-identity also served to divide instead of unite the citizens of the new state. The paradox was further complicated by the fact that Sąjūdis, as the bearer of the national idea, dominated the national legislature.[20] Without the Soviet Union to struggle against, however, Sąjūdis had by now begun to fragment. As a result, several smaller political parties giving even greater priority to the nationalist idea emerged on the political right. These parties—including the Union of Lithuanian Nationalists, the Union of Political Prisoners and Deportees, the Independence Party, and the Christian Democrats—were largely concerned with the internal threat to the territorial integrity and independence of the new state posed by "disloyal" national minorities.

The nationalist parties and organizations (Sąjūdis had not organized itself as a political party) were particularly concerned at the time with the Polish "threat." Governors of the Polish districts of Vilnius and Šalčininkai had aligned themselves with the Soviet authorities during the independence struggle, going so far as to support the effort by Communist Party hard-liners in August 1991 to reestablish Soviet rule in the republic. Many of these same governors were now making overtures toward Warsaw and demanding autonomy. The fear was that these regions would ultimately sue for independence or union with Poland. Concerns were openly expressed that the Poles might again raise the "Vilnius question."

As a consequence, nationalism in the early independence period was largely of the "variant 2" outlined in Lowell Barrington's introduction to this volume: nationalism in the service of protecting territorial integrity from an internal threat. The constitution declared that the Lithuanian state was a unitary, indivisible state. This left no room for a federalist bargain, which might give vent to demands for autonomy or secession in the regions surrounding Vilnius. Hence, in response to the immediate threat, the government introduced direct rule in these regions in September 1991.

This action led to serious strains in relations with Poland, which—despite its renunciation of any territorial claims on Vilnius or the Polish regions—found itself unable to reduce Lithuanian fears to the contrary. The Lithuanian government further poisoned the atmosphere between the two countries by insisting on a Polish apology for and condemnation of the interwar seizure of Vilnius. While the demand was motivated by Lithuanian concerns that their own claim to the capital was questionable (given that they had regained the city as a "gift" from the Soviet authorities), nationalist yearnings "to correct" the historical record by establishing Polish guilt and Lithuanian innocence was just as apparent. In any event, the Poles would not accede to the demands, fearing that they might provide the pretext for further repression of the Polish minority in Lithuania. When Vilnius reneged on its promise to restore self-rule in the Polish regions, Poland was left with no other option than to engage in formal protest, an action that led to Lithuanian charges that Warsaw was interfering in Lithuania's internal affairs.[21]

The introduction of direct rule in the Vilnius and Šalčininkai regions heightened tensions between the Lithuanian government and the country's Polish population, leading to fears that the new state was bent on assimilating them. The latter was further increased by statements from nationalist leaders—among them the head of the Independence Party, a close personal confidant of Sąjūdis chair Vytautas Landsbergis—that the country's Poles were in reality Polonized Lithuanians who had been deprived of their true identity and culture by centuries of Polish rule, particularly in the regions in which they lived.[22]

Nationalist fears concerning the loyalties of the new state's national minority populations, however, appear not to have been well founded. While sociological surveys of the time indicated a general lack of identity with the new state among Poles and Russians, there was also little indication of disloyalty among these same groups. While leaders in the Polish regions may have supported secession, few Poles did. Russians were largely passive and politically indifferent.[23] Survey results indicated that most Poles and Russians were content to live in an independent Lithuanian state as long as their economic prospects were brighter than elsewhere. Indeed, most of them believed they were.[24] Hence, what was most critical to the social stability of the new state in relationship to its ethnic minorities was the rapid development of its economy.

While it was arguably too much to expect that any government could adequately deal with the challenges presented by the economic crisis in the wake of the Soviet collapse, the economy proved to be the Achilles' heel of the Sąjūdis government. The elections of 1992 were a stunning defeat for the nationalist parties. The former Communist Party, which had transformed itself into the Democratic Labor Party, won an absolute majority in the national legislature (now renamed the Seimas). This was followed by the election of the party's leader, Algirdas Brazauskas, as the first president of the republic (an office created by the constitution of 1992). The electoral victory of the Democratic Labor Party, which was owed in part to the support the party enjoyed with the overwhelming majority of the country's national minorities, helped to greatly reduce ethnic tensions in Lithuania. Entering office at the same time as direct rule was being lifted in the Polish regions, the leftist government placed economic matters as its first priority and greatly deemphasized national issues.

Divisions in, & the Changing Shape of, Lithuanian Nationalism since Independence

Despite the crushing defeat suffered by the nationalist parties in the 1992 elections, they were able to rebound and recapture the national legislature in 1996. By then, however, nationalism had been transformed. If nationalist parties and movements in the early independence movement were of the variant 2 type (being largely concerned with the internal threat to the territorial integrity of the republic), since 1994 they have taken on a more complex, multidimensional form. While many nationalists in Lithuania would claim that the movement has always been of the variant 3 type (nationalism as civic nation-building), the actions taken by the first Sąjūdis government in the Polish regions, as previously described, belie such a claim.

However, since 1994 this variant has indeed been largely pursued by the larger nationalist parties, including the most important of them, the Fatherland Union (Conservatives of Lithuania). The party emerged from the ashes of the electoral defeat suffered by Sąjūdis in 1992 and was the largest of the parties in the Seimas (the national legislature) at the end of the 1990s, just a few votes shy of an absolute majority. However, its popular support waned substantially in the wake of the economic difficulties attending the Russian economic collapse of late 1998. As a consequence, the party suffered a serious electoral defeat in the 2000 national elections, winning only nine seats. Nonetheless, it remains a major contender in the political system, as attested to by its second-place showing in the 2002 local elections.[25] Indeed, the party remained the fourth-most-popular political party in the country by early 2003 (see table 1), and it won 25 seats in the 2004 legislative elections. Given the party's pensioner base, which continues to reflect concerns related to variant 2 nationalism, it has occasionally been compelled to undertake policies reflecting a concern with the territorial integrity of the republic.[26]

TABLE 1. Population Indicating It Would Vote for the Respective Political Parties (in percentages)

Political Party	1999	2001	2003
Center Party	15.9	3.4	5.0
Democratic Labor Party	7.3	—	—
Liberal Democratic Party	—	—	14.0
Fatherland Union (Conservatives of Lithuania)	7.1	6.9	7.8
Christian Democratic Party	6.4	5.9	4.5
Social Democratic Party	6.1	33.1	18.4
National Party of Lithuanians and "Young Lithuania"	3.1	0.9	—
Union of Lithuanian Nationalists	0.4	—	—
"Young Lithuania" and the Union of Lithuanian Nationalists	—	—	0.7
New Union (Social Liberals)	2.9	5.3	5.1
New Democracy/Women's Party	2.1	0.4	—
Peasants' Party	1.9	2.1	—
Union of the Peasants' Party and New Democracy	—	—	3.1
Polish Electoral Action	1.5	0.6	0.5
Democratic Party	1.3	—	—
Christian Democratic Union	1.3	—	
Liberal Union	1.1	9.7	8.1
Union of Political Prisoners and Deportees	0.7	—	—
Union of Russians of Lithuania	—	0.5	0.8
Moderate Conservatives	—	0.6	0.6
Lithuanian Freedom Union	—	0.7	0.5
Modern Christian Democratic Union	—	0.9	0.9
Other parties	1.0	0.4	0.6
Will not vote, unsure, or refuse to answer	39.9	28.6	29.4

Source: For 1999, a Vilmorus public opinion poll conducted in Lithuania in October 1999 and published in *Lietuvos Rytas,* October 9, 1999, 7. For 2001, a Vilmorus public opinion poll conducted in Lithuania in July 2001 and published in *Lietuvos Rytas,* July 14, 2001, 8. For 2003, a Vilmorus public opinion poll conducted in Lithuania in February 2003 and published in *Lietuvos Rytas,* February 15, 2003, 7.

The smaller nationalist parties, on the other hand, have focused almost exclusively on protecting the country from internal and external subversion and threats and have rejected civic nation-building approaches. This is particularly evident in their insistence that Polish and Russian not be given the status of state languages. Their support of Lithuanian nationals abroad is meant to further support these efforts. Thus, the smaller nationalist parties have pursued a mix of a peculiar version of variant 2 (nationalism as sovereignty-protecting) and variant 5 (nationalism as co-national-protecting).[27]

Differences of Opinion among the Nationalist Parties

Concerns about the loyalties of the national minorities persisted among some Lithuanians in the years following independence.[28] These concerns were generally reflected in the positions of Lithuania's nationalist political parties, though not with equal intensity. One can use views on issues such as the perceived loyalty of Lithuania's minorities to distinguish among the nationalist parties. A survey conducted by the Institute of International Relations and Political Science at Vilnius University in 1995 of candidates to the national legislature demonstrates the differences between parties on questions involving the national minorities (see table 2). While the number of respondents is too small to permit detailed statistical analysis, the results confirm the intuitive view on the positioning of the major political parties on the national issue. The two largest parties on the political left, the Democratic Labor Party and the Social Democratic Party,[29] are included in table 2 for comparative purposes.

On questions related to whether national minorities enjoy too many rights or whether they are entitled to enjoy equal rights, the parties on the left took positions in support of the national minorities, while the two largest parties on the right, the Conservatives and the Christian Democrats, were less supportive. However, three small right parties—the Union of Lithuanian Nationalists, the Union of Political Prisoners and Deportees, and Jaunoji Lietuva (Young Lithuania)—were even more strident in their opposition to the rights of national minorities. Candidates from these three small right parties represented the most extreme views. This same pattern is apparent, with some modifications, concerning evaluations of the loyalty of the Russian and Polish national minorities. In the case of the Russians, the Christian Democrats were the most uncertain about the loyalty of this national minority. Concerning the Poles, Christian Democrats were once again the most uncertain; however, Jaunoji Lietuva (the most stridently nationalist party in Lithuania) was the second-least-likely party to question their loyalty.

There is a relatively clear pattern here. While the political right was the bearer of nationalism in the political system, it was the smaller parties (joined by the Christian Democrats in some cases) that were the most stridently nationalistic. This was most certainly the case for Jaunoji Lietuva, which had adopted as one of its political slogans "Lithuania for Lithuanians!"

Interestingly, the other issue on which the nationalist parties have disagreed, at times forcefully, is the pursuit of membership in European organizations, specifically NATO and the European Union (EU).[30] Table 3 reports the ordinal ranking given to Lithuania's membership in NATO and the EU by the candidates of the respective political parties in 1995. There was close agreement among the nationalist parties on NATO membership, though the three small nationalist parties most adamantly supported it. This reflects their fear of Russian subversive and aggressive acts against the

TABLE 2. Attitudes of Political Candidates of Respective Political Parties on Questions Concerning National Minorities

	Average Response			
Political Party (number of respondents)	National Minorities Have Too Many Rights	National Minorities Must Have Equal Rights	Poles are Disloyal	Russians are Disloyal
Average of all respondents	3.24	1.37	2.52	2.77
Large Left Parties				
Democratic Labor Party (57)	3.86	1.19	3.05	3.45
Social Democratic Party (40)	3.64	1.23	2.53	3.15
Large Right Parties				
Fatherland Union (Conservatives of Lithuania) (41)	3.05	1.46	2.33	2.49
Christian Democratic Party (26)	2.58	1.50	1.65	1.96
Small Right Parties				
Union of Political Prisoners and Deportees (19)	2.42	2.05	2.22	2.33
Union of Lithuanian Nationalists (21)	2.29	1.90	1.71	2.19
Jaunoji Lietuva (5)	2.00	2.50	3.00	2.00

Source: 1995 survey of candidates to the Seimas conducted by the Institute of International Relations and Political Science, Vilnius University.

Note: Scores closer to one indicate agreement with the statement; scores closer to five indicate disagreement.

Lithuanian state supported by the Russian national minority within Lithuania (variant 2 nationalism). For them, NATO was the only solution to this security dilemma. The convergence on entry into NATO was also reflected in foreign policy efforts led by the Conservative government from 1996 to 2000 to have an international conference discuss the Russian enclave of the Kaliningrad region. A heavily militarized region adjoining Lithuania's western border, the region is of particular concern to the nationalists.[31] The position of the Conservatives and Christian Democrats on NATO membership was based on more than just security calculations; it was also linked to their desire to "rejoin" Europe in general.

The sense of rejoining Europe was reflected in the similarly high ordinal score that the Conservatives and Christian Democrats gave to Lithuania's entry into the EU. (The two parties merged in 2004.) In contrast, all three of the smaller nationalist parties were adamantly opposed to EU member-

TABLE 3. Attitudes of Political Candidates of Respective Political Parties on Questions Concerning Membership in the European Union and NATO

Political Party (number of respondents)	Average Response	
	Membership in EU	Membership in NATO
Average of all respondents	2.70	3.07
Large Left Parties		
Democratic Labor Party (57)	2.20	3.50
Social Democratic Party (40)	2.29	3.42
Large Right Parties		
Fatherland Union (Conservatives of Lithuania) (41)	2.13	1.90
Christian Democratic Party (26)	2.08	2.22
Small Right Parties		
Union of Political Prisoners and Deportees (19)	2.81	1.88
Union of Lithuanian Nationalists (21)	3.79	1.24
Jaunoji Lietuva (5)	4.00	1.75

Source: 1995 survey of candidates to the Seimas conducted by the Institute of International Relations and Political Science, Vilnius University.

Note: Membership in the organization was placed on a list of ten organizations. Respondents were asked to rank order each in terms of their personal preferences. Scores closer to one indicate greater levels of support for Lithuania entering the organization.

ship, particularly the Union of Lithuanian Nationalists and Jaunoji Lietuva. This reflected a clear division between the moderate nationalism of the Conservatives and Christian Democrats and the more radical form represented by the small nationalist parties.

The small parties' general opposition to entering the EU denoted a novel variety of nationalism in its sovereignty-protecting form (variant 2 nationalism). The threat that these parties perceived from the EU has little to do with national minorities. Instead, it reflected a concern with what were considered to be the insidious effects on both the culture and socioeconomic structure resulting from integration with Europe and opening up to the global economy. Reflecting concerns voiced by left-wing parties as well, the smaller Lithuanian nationalist parties were worried by prospects that these processes might well relegate Lithuania to the status of a third-world economic colony of the West, with little to no control over investment decisions made within its borders. They were also troubled by the possible effects of those decisions on the socioeconomic order. But, unlike the political left, the small nationalist parties were also concerned about the impact that further Western investment would have on the cultural values of the country. This was particularly the case concerning language. Many on the far right voiced fears that English would be de facto imposed on the country by the logic of the global market. Having less than a decade before won their freedom from the Soviet Union, which controlled the country's economic development and placed both its language and culture in a secondary status, these parties represented the concerns of a growing number of Lithuanians that the long-sought sovereignty not be sacrificed.

The expression of such concerns was not new.[32] What was new was the way that efforts of the Conservative government to privatize the economy (and lay the basis for Lithuania's accession to the EU) were increasingly uniting rather disparate forces—pensioners, students, intellectuals, leftists, and the more extreme nationalists.[33] Among the triggering events of the rising chorus of protests were the privatization of the national telephone company to a Scandinavian consortium and the sale of the country's oil industry to an American firm, Williams International. The latter raised particular concern that Lithuania's economic interests would not be well served and that American capital would overwhelm the country's economy, making it virtually impossible for an indigenous industrial and business class to emerge.

While small nationalist parties continued to oppose globalization of

Lithuania's economy in the 2000s, neither they nor the left were able to capitalize on the issue. Instead, populist elements gained the most traction on the issue and were able to mobilize those disillusioned and left behind by the economic reforms. Populism first became evident in the election of a poorly educated anti-Semite as mayor of Kaunas, the country's second largest city, in early 2000. While he left office to become a deputy in the parliament, populism continued to plague the country throughout the early 2000s. Rolandas Paksas was elected president on a populist platform in 2003. Despite his impeachment the following year, the Labor Party won a plurality in the legislative elections. The party had only recently been created by Victoras Uspaskichas, a notorious Russian-Lithuanian businessman who gained his fortune by questionable means and who as a member of the Seimas has demonstrated a willingness to use his political position for economic advantage.

The populism that these elements represent is not part of the nationalist phenomenon in Lithuania. Indeed, they have been opposed by the nationalist parties. They appeal to the disillusioned across ethnic and national lines. Most often they evoke nostalgia for the social guarantees of the Soviet era and often call for closer ties with Russia and a more cautious, if not overtly hostile, attitude toward the West.

The Moderate Nationalism of the Conservatives

As the preceding section indicates, compared to the small nationalist parties the Conservatives were both more pragmatic and more moderate. The greater temperance of the Conservatives on nationality issues gave them room to engage in an effort to build a civic consciousness among the national minorities, placing greater emphasis on a nation-building strategy (variant 3 nationalism). Upon returning to power in 1996, the party pursued such an effort. The main focus of the party was on economic development and integration into European security and economic structures, the latter efforts also largely informed by economic development concerns.

Yet the Conservatives were never able to eschew fully policies reflecting variant 2 nationalism. The pensioner population, an important component of the Conservatives' electoral base, continued to be concerned with the internal threat of secession from Poles in the Vilnius and Šalčininkai regions, as well as that posed by Russian subversive or aggressive behavior. As a consequence, the Conservatives occasionally contributed to a deterioration in the relations with the national minorities, particularly the Poles.

This was most evident in the decision taken by the Conservative-led government in 1998 to change the administrative boundaries of the city of Vilnius. In effect the changes placed large tracts of rural areas from the Polish regions under the city's jurisdiction. The government undertook these reforms without consultations with the Polish government, as required in agreements between the two states,[34] and despite having made promises to the contrary to the visiting Polish head of state the month before.[35]

Causal Factors Shaping Lithuanian Nationalism since Independence

THE PURSUIT OF MEMBERSHIP IN NATO AND THE EU

Thus, by the middle to late 1990s the Conservatives were clearly still a nationalist party, but one that *usually* attempted to deemphasize forms of nationalism focusing on the internal threat to the national integrity. While the pensioners pulled them in the variant 2 direction on occasion, the party's more typically moderate stance owed largely to its aim to enter NATO and the EU. These were both goals that the Conservatives believed Poland could assist in achieving. Indeed, the effort to enter these European structures was behind the 1994 treaty with Poland that finally normalized relations between the two countries and significantly reduced the previous tensions between them. While the treaty was signed by the Democratic Labor Party government, it would not have been possible without the active support and concurrence of the Conservatives.[36] Following Poland's accession into NATO, Conservative leader Vytautus Landsbergis publicly proclaimed that Lithuania should be admitted in the next round given its historic ties with that country. This was indeed a remarkable turnabout for a man who had only several years before argued vehemently that Lithuania was part of an altogether different cultural and historical space from either Russia or Poland.

In addition to the previously discussed idea of NATO and EU membership as part of a larger desire "to rejoin Europe," the Conservatives had rational reasons to pursue membership in both, especially NATO. In addition to the pensioners, the party's political base included some members of the business community. Both the pensioners and the business leaders supported Lithuania's entry into European security structures, but for different reasons. The business community prized the economic stability that NATO membership offered, while pensioners were convinced that the alliance was the only means to ensure against the loss of the country's independence to a reemerging greater Russia.

CHANGES IN MASS ATTITUDES AMONG, AND ABOUT, THE MINORITIES

Both contributing to and resulting from the Conservatives' less strident nationalist attitudes, tensions between the country's national minorities had reduced significantly since the start of the post-Soviet independence period.[37] As early as 1993, public opinion surveys found only a small minority of respondents across the three main national groupings indicated dissatisfaction with living in Lithuania: Lithuanians (13 percent dissatisfaction), Russians (16 percent), and Poles (18 percent).[38] By 1995,[39] surveys indicated even less cause for concern about the loyalties of Lithuania's Russian-speaking community. While ethnic Lithuanians expressed greater support for the legitimacy of the state and its functions, the Russian-speaking population was only marginally less supportive. Responses to the questions listed in table 4 demonstrate that Russian speakers were slightly less likely than Lithuanians to feel that everyone living in the country should perform military service, pay taxes, and respect the national flag. There was no significant difference of opinion on whether residents should respect the law. These general patterns remained relatively unchanged in 2000, as the data in table 4 indicate.[40] The only differences of note in the 1995 and 2000 responses were increases in the numbers of citizens from both groups indicating support for the legitimacy of the state and its functions, with Russian speakers significantly more likely to support military service in 2000 than in 1995 and both Lithuanians and Russian speakers more likely to believe that paying taxes was a civic duty.

These data suggest that there was very little difference in levels of satisfaction with Lithuanian citizenship from 1993 to 2000 among the country's ethnic groups. They also indicate that the kind of reactive nationalism among the ethnic majority seen in other Eurasian countries (Azerbaijan, for example) was much less likely in Lithuania. There was no violent ethnic conflict of the kind seen in the Caucasus, there was much less perception of cultural threat than in the other Baltic states, and the perception of territorial threat was declining among all but the most extreme nationalists. These factors, combined with the push for membership in NATO and the EU, gave nationalist elites little reason to push an occlusive (variant 2) nationalist agenda.

The only source of any significant degree of disagreement among

Lithuania's major ethnic communities revolved around the language issue. Not surprisingly, given that Lithuanian national identity is primarily defined along this dimension, an overwhelming majority of ethnic Lithuanians (95 percent) in 2000 continued to insist that all citizens had a civic responsibility to learn the national language. In contrast, only three-fourths of Russians and Poles held to this view.[41] This served as a primary means for right-wing nationalists in the smaller parties to mobilize support. However, the amount of support was relatively small.

Conclusions: Lessons about Lithuania, Lessons from Lithuania

Perhaps the most important conclusion to be drawn *about* Lithuania is that the core of the Lithuanian identity is neither the national myth nor symbols

TABLE 4. Comparison of Attitudes toward Civic Duties (in percentages)

	1995 Survey		2000 Survey	
Duty	Lithuanians	Russians	Lithuanians	Russians
Military service				
Always	57	46	57	51
Usually	22	30	21	26
Unimportant	10	12	13	14
Not at all	9	8	9	7
Don't know	1	4	0	2
Pay taxes				
Always	59	48	71	58
Usually	26	29	20	25
Unimportant	10	11	7	12
Not at all	3	7	2	5
Don't know	1	4	0	0
Respect flag				
Always	88	79	94	80
Usually	10	18	5	17
Unimportant	1	1	1	3
Not at all	0	2	0	0
Don't know	0	2	0	0
Obey laws				
Always	76	75	78	76
Usually	19	21	18	21
Unimportant	3	2	4	3
Not at all	0	1	0	0
Don't know	0	2	0	0

Source: "New Baltics Barometer II" (Centre for the Study of Public Policy, University of Strathclyde, 1995), questions 89–93; and "New Baltic Barometer IV: A Survey Study" (Centre for the Study of Public Policy, University of Strathclyde, 2000), questions D.1.A., D.1.C, D.1.D, and D.1.E.

related to the myth. More so than most nations, language is central to determining inclusion. This is not surprising given the forty-year-long effort by the Russian Empire to abolish the language in its written form. Indeed, the Lithuanian language serves more than as a means for transmitting culture. It is itself virtually the only way of identifying that one is or is not culturally Lithuanian. Different regions of the country demonstrate wide variation in traditions and even symbols. Even religion does not unite the nation. While a plurality are professed Catholics, a large part of the nation is Protestant or even pagan, holding to the earliest traditions of the grand duchy of Lithuania as the last pagan state in Europe.

Nonetheless, the national myth is not unimportant. While it does not serve as a means for determining inclusion, it helps to define Lithuanian culture and attitudes to the outside world. What is interesting about the myth is that while Lithuanian nationalism has evolved sometimes over short periods of time, and even taken more than one form at any given time, the national myth has remained relatively stable. Indeed, despite the evolution of the strategies pursued by Lithuanian nationalists since 1988, the idea that Lithuanians are a nation of "innocent sufferers" has continued to persist, at times in the face of contradictory evidence. The charge of national complicity in the Holocaust, for example, has posed a challenge to the very heart of the national myth. It calls into question both the image of a nation of innocent sufferers as well as that of a tolerant nation. It is therefore not at all surprising that many Lithuanians have had difficulty in addressing the issue.[42] Indeed, the response by some has been outright denial or countercharges that the Jews were implicated in the genocide of the Lithuanian nation during the Soviet occupation. Nonetheless, despite substantial popular resistance, formal apologies have been rendered, and the country's schoolbooks have for the first time addressed Lithuania's involvement in the Holocaust.[43]

Although it is less important than at the time of the restoration of independence, the image of a nation of "innocent sufferers" continues to manifest itself in the form of a distinct distrust of outsiders. While not resulting in overt hostility—indeed Lithuanians are outwardly quite tolerant—the distinctive form of xenophobia that is reflected here is more than mere national pride. It is informed by a sense that all foreigners, not just representatives of historically repressive nations such as the Poles or Russians, have little to contribute to Lithuania.[44] Indeed, there is a pervasive belief that the Lithuanian nation is so unique that it defies understanding by outsiders. Hence, there is a decided resistance to advice or assistance proffered by foreigners.

Yet there is nothing about the Lithuanian national myth that demands retribution or aggressive behavior toward others. While the idea of innocent suffering calls for vigilance in defense of the nation, the choice for aggressive behavior is just that, a choice. There is nothing in the context of the development of the Lithuanian state and society from 1988 to the present that suggests that such a choice has been made or is likely to be made. To the contrary, perhaps the healthiest aspect of the Lithuanian social and political system has been the steady breakup of the nationalist movement itself. Sąjūdis in its early stages represented a nearly monolithic nationalist movement. However, it quickly began to fragment. It has since given birth to a number of splinter parties directly or indirectly related to the initial movement. Indeed, until very recently the core of virtually every party in the country with the exception of the Social Democratic Party (the new Social Democratic Party having formed as the result of the merger of the Democratic Labor Party and old Social Democratic Party in 2000) is drawn from the movement.

While most such parties continue to hold onto the national idea, they disagree on what the national interests are and the strategies best employed for achieving them. The resultant political competition has not only placed a healthy check on the emergence of more destructive expressions of nationalism but has contributed immeasurably to the development of a sense of loyalty to the young state among all national groups.[45] As a result, the transformation of postindependence nationalism has assisted the formation of a stable, consolidated, and democratic Lithuanian state. This, in turn, argues that nationalism need not be a destructive force. Indeed, it can and does play an important role not only in state-building but in the transition to democracy, a point made in much of the earlier literature on development and democratization as well as the more recent literature on nationalism.

Lithuanian nationalism offers some lessons about the general phenomenon as well. First, as Lowell Barrington points out in his introductory chapter, nationalism has a resilient quality to it. This owes largely to the fact that political elites find it a useful tool for mobilizing segments of the public in support of their political aspirations. In the Lithuanian case nationalism has successfully been transformed from one concerned with territorial defense against internal threats to one largely focused on a strategy of building civic consciousness among all of the country's citizens. At the same time, however, political elites are not unconstrained in their efforts to mold nationalism to their purposes. This is evidenced by the relative inability of Lithuania's small nationalist parties to convince the larger part of the Lithuanian population of the continued need for vigilance against an internal threat posed by the country's ethnic minorities. In contrast, the larger parties were successful in responding to *both* the opportunities and limitations of the moment.

A second set of lessons concerns the degree to which territorial integrity and the inclusivity of the national ideal serve as causes for the continued survival of nationalism. Both remain at the core of the smaller parties' political programs. These parties stress the threat posed by the Polish and Russian minorities and demand that the state increase disincentives for engaging in discourse in any language other than Lithuanian. This lies at the heart of their concerns about membership in the EU. The larger nationalist parties on the other hand are content with the status quo, which de facto (although not de jure) establishes a working knowledge of Lithuanian as a prerequisite to enjoying fully the economic and social benefits of citizenship.

The third and final lesson is that external forces, particularly those related to globalization, can have a profound effect on nationalism. For some, such as Lithuania's smaller parties (not including populist parties), globalization can present a threat to the nation. That threat can encompass assaults on territorial integrity, as global economic changes may increase the number of foreigners owning property or voting in local elections. For others, however, globalization may well introduce incentives to make the national community more inclusive by eroding the dominance of the national language in economic discourse and establishing a mutually beneficial dialogue with a wider community.

NOTES

1. An exception is Vesna Popovski, *National Minorities and Citizenship Rights in Lithuania, 1988–1993* (Basingstoke: Palgrave, 2000).

2. See, for example, Vesna Popovski, "Citizenship and Ethno-politics in Lithuania," *International Politics* 33 (March 1996): 45–55; and Tamara J. Resler, "Dilemmas of Democratization: Safeguarding Minorities in Russia, Ukraine and Lithuania," *Europe-Asia Studies* 49, no. 1 (1997): 89–116.

3. Jack J. Stukas, *Awakening Lithuania: A Study on the Rise of Modern Lithuanian Nationalism* (Madison, NJ: Florham Park Press, 1966).

4. Ibid.

5. Ibid.

6. Ibid.

7. Alfonsas Eidintas, "The Nation Creates Its State," in *Lithuania in European Politics: The Years of the First Republic, 1918–1940,* ed. Edvardas Tuskenis (New York: St. Martin's Press, 1997).

8. Arvydas Juozaitis, "The Lithuanian Independence Movement and National Minorities" (Peace Research Reports, Peace Research Institute, Frankfurt, Germany, December 1992), 7–8.

9. Ibid.

10. See, for example, Thomas Venclova, "The Heirs of Gediminas," in *Personal Freedom and National Resurgence: Lithuanian Philosophical Studies I,* ed. Alexandr Dobrynin and Broniua Kuzmickas (Washington, DC: Paideia Press and the Council for Research in Values and Philosophy, 1994), 7–16; and Vytautas Kavolis, "The Second Lithuanian Revival: Culture as Performance," in *Personal Freedom and National Resurgence: Lithuanian Philosophical Studies I,* ed. Alexandr Dobrynin and Broniua Kuzmickas (Washington, DC: Paideia Press and the Council for Research in Values and Philosophy, 1994), 149–60.

11. Tim Snyder, "National Myths and International Relations: Poland and Lithuania, 1989–1994," *East European Politics and Societies* 9, no. 2 (1995): 317–43.

12. Ibid.

13. A. Matulionis, "Tautines mažumos ir tautinės problemos Lietuvoje," in *Tautinės Mažumos: Etnosocialinių̧s problemų̧ seminaro 1991–1992 m. medžiaga,* ed. Natalija Kasatkina, Vida Kasparavičienė, and Arvydas Matulionis (Vilnius: Filosofijos, sociologijos ir teisės institutas, 1992), 11–15. It should be noted, however, that this influx of Russians was significantly less in Lithuania than in its Baltic neighbors to the north, Latvia and Estonia. The larger numbers of such Russian speakers in the other Baltic countries created a perception of threat to the cultural survival of the nations there that was much greater than in Lithuania.

14. Popovski, "Citizenship and Ethno-politics in Lithuania."

15. Juozaitis, "The Lithuanian Independence Movement and National Minorities."

16. It is almost a certainty that the movement was formed at the instigation of the KGB to help undermine political stability in the breakaway republic.

17. Juozaitis, "The Lithuanian Independence Movement and National Minorities."

18. Ibid.

19. In late 1989, the Communist Party of Lithuania (CPL) formally declared its independence from the Communist Party of the Soviet Union (CPSU). As a result, two communist parties nominated candidates in the legislative elections of 1990: the newly independent CPL, which later that year became the Democratic Labor Party, and the CPL that remained a part of the CPSU (CPL[CPSU]). The former won twenty seats and the latter four seats in the Supreme Council.

20. The republican legislature elected during the Soviet era, which had declared the restoration of Lithuania's independence, became the first legislature of the Republic of Lithuania and remained so during the first year of independence.

21. Snyder, "National Myths and International Relations."

22. Popovski, "Citizenship and Ethno-politics in Lithuania."

23. Irena Maryniak, "The Uncomfortable Commonwealth," *Index on Censorship* 21, no. 10 (October 1992): 26–27.

24. A. Eigirdas, "Pilietybės priėmimo procesas pietryčių Lietuvoje: Socialinė politinė gyventojų tipologija," in *Tautinės Mažumos: Etnosocialinių problemų seminaro 1991–1992 m. medžiaga,* ed. Natalija Kasatkina, Vida Kasparavičienė, and Arvydas Matulionis (Vilnius: Filosofijos, sociologijos ir teisės institutas, 1992), 19–24.

25. The party won the second-largest number of deputies in the December 2002 elections to local councils.

26. See the following discussion.

27. A peculiar version of variant 2 because it included a desire to protect Lithuania from EU dominance (see the following).

28. In response to the question on the 1995 "New Baltics Barometer II" whether there is any potential for minority conflict between Lithuanians and Russian residents, Lithuanians were statistically less sanguine on the issue (chi-square significance = 0.0001, Cramer's V = 0.16495). Forty-two percent of Russian speakers answered "definitely not," compared to only 28 percent of Lithuanians. Further, 29 percent of Lithuanians responded "definitely" or "possibly" in comparison to 18 percent of Russian speakers. See "New Baltics Barometer II" (Centre for the Study of Public Policy, University of Strathclyde, 1995), question 72.

29. These two parties have since merged into a new Social Democratic Party.

30. Lithuania became a member of both NATO and the EU in 2004.

31. Among other efforts was the signing of agreements with Kaliningrad to provide general economic aid as well as cultural and educational support for Lithuanians in the region. The latter reflects variant 5 nationalism, nationalism as co-national-protecting. It was further apparent in similar agreements for the cultural support of Lithuanian national minorities in Poland and Belarus.

32. See, for example, Leonidas Donskis, "Lithuania at the End of the Twentieth Century: The Creation of an Open Society and Culture," in *Personal Freedom and National Resurgence: Lithuanian Philosophical Studies I,* ed. Alexandr Dobrynin and Broniua Kuzmickas (Washington, DC: Paideia Press and the Council for Research in Values and Philosophy, 1994), 75–82.

33. See, for example, Kęstutis Gečas, "Mitinge-raginimai Lietuvai prisikelti iš naujo," *Lietuvos Rytas,* October 23, 1999, 7; and Rúta Grinevičiūtė, "Pono 'Williams' naftos jausmas," *Veidas,* October 14–20, 1999, 30–32.

34. Related to the treaty, the two countries signed a number of agreements promising to respect the rights of national minorities in their respective countries and to consult one another on policies affecting these minorities. In this regard, it should be noted that Poland has a substantial Lithuanian minority.

35. While many saw in this an effort to reduce the number of regions dominated by the Polish minority, others viewed the move in more economic terms. Placing these rural districts under the jurisdiction of the Vilnius government required the Poles to submit their claims for the restoration of prewar properties to a largely non-Polish jurisdiction.

36. Snyder, "National Myths and International Relations."

37. Public opinion surveys indicated that the percentage of Lithuanians perceiving a degradation in relations between the republic's minorities decreased from 8 percent in 1989 to 5 percent in 1993. The corresponding figures for Poles were 18 percent in 1989 and 13 percent in 1993. The smallest decrease was reported among Russians, from 9 percent in 1989 to 8 percent in 1993. During the same period, those reporting they had participated in altercations between different nationalities decreased from 21 percent in

1989 to 12 percent in 1993, with corresponding decreases reported among Lithuanians (23 percent to 12 percent), Poles (16 percent to 9 percent), and Russians (21 percent to 11 percent). See Vida Kasparavičienė, Eugenija Krukauskienė, and Arvydas Matulionis, eds., *Vilniečio portretas: Sociologiniai metmenys* (Vilnius: Filosofijos, sociologijos ir teisės institutas, 1995).

38. Ibid.

39. The "New Baltics Barometer II" was conducted in Lithuania in April 1995 by Vilmorus. It overrepresents the Russian-speaking population to permit comparisons between ethnic Lithuanians and the Russian-speaking community, many of whom are Poles. Of the 870 respondents to the survey, 239 were self-identified Russian speakers.

40. The "New Baltics Barometer IV: A Survey Study" was conducted in Lithuania in April 2000 by Vilmorus. It overrepresents the Russian-speaking population to permit comparisons between ethnic Lithuanians and the Russian-speaking community, many of whom are Poles. Of the 1,112 respondents to the survey, 212 were self-identified Russian speakers.

41. "New Baltics Barometer IV," question D.1.B.

42. Before the war, Vilnius was home to one of the most thriving Jewish communities in the world. Ninety-six percent of that community was liquidated in the Holocaust, in which many Lithuanians participated. On May 8, 1990, the Supreme Council passed a declaration of regret for the nation's involvement in the extermination of Jews, and President Algirdas Brazauskas apologized in a speech before the Israeli Knesset in February 1995. Nevertheless, many in the international community doubt whether these apologies reflect the attitudes of most Lithuanians. See Vytautas Paulauskas, "Erscheinungen des Rechtsextremismus und Nationalismus in Litauen," *Berichte des Bundesinstituts fur ostwissenschaftliche und internationale Studien* 21 (1996); and Laisvė Radzevičienė, "Išniekinta tautiška giesmė–tik autentiškas folkloras?" *TV antena* 39 (October 2–8, 1999): 10–12. These doubts were heightened when a radical politician who had made several statements with overtly antisemitic overtones was elected mayor of Kaunas, the country's second-largest city, in early 2000.

43. Paulauskas, "Erscheinungen des Rechtsextremismus und Nationalismus in Litauen."

44. The previously noted opposition to privatization is partly motivated by the notion that the sale of state assets to foreigners suggests that Lithuanians are not capable of managing them.

45. The more radical nationalist parties on the political right are small. They do not have enough public support to meet the requirement for gaining seats in the national legislature that are allocated on a proportional basis. And while there is a fascist party, the central government refuses to register it, as it violates laws against sowing social discord and national enmity. The party itself comprises no more than two hundred individuals.

8. Kravchuk to the Orange Revolution

The Victory of Civic Nationalism in Post-Soviet Ukraine

TARAS KUZIO

UKRAINE'S 2004 PRESIDENTIAL election and Orange Revolution was facilitated by the role of civic nationalism. The inability to mobilize civic nationalism in sufficient quantity in 1991–92 permitted the election of sovereign Communist Leonid Kravchuk and later centrist Leonid Kuchma. The growth of a civic nationalist Ukrainian identity from 1992–2004 transformed the political landscape, permitting Viktor Yushchenko to be elected president.[1]

Civic and ethnic nationalists in Ukraine can be differentiated fairly effectively based on their views on two issues, corresponding to the idea proposed by Lowell Barrington in this volume's introductory chapter that nationalism involves both membership boundaries and territorial boundaries. First, they have different definitions of the state, as either inclusive (civic) or exclusive (ethnic). Second, they either support Ukraine's inherited borders (civic nationalists) or harbor a desire to change them (ethnic Ukrainian, Russian nationalists, and Sovietophiles). This chapter is divided into two sections, which deal separately with ethnic and civic nationalism before and after independence.

Prior to independence, ethnic nationalists grouped within the Interparliamentary Assembly (IPA) demanded independence from the moment of its arrival on Ukraine's political scene in 1989. After Ukraine became an independent state, the IPA transformed itself into the Ukrainian National Assembly (UNA). As an ethnic nationalist movement, it was joined by several new parties.[2] Civic nationalism only appeared as a phenomenon in 1990–91, although the Ukrainian Popular Movement for Restructuring

(Rukh) was created in 1988. Rukh was composed of two wings (national democratic political parties created by former political prisoners and the cultural intelligentsia) and adopted a platform of independence only in October 1990. Rukh was joined in 1989–90 by the Democratic Platform of the Communist Party of Ukraine (CPU), which created the centrist Party of Democratic Revival and New Ukraine bloc. In 1990–91, the "Sovereign Communists" also peeled off from the CPU. These two wings of the CPU backed the transformation of the USSR into a confederation of sovereign states until August 1991, after which they supported Rukh's program of independence. During 1988–91 civic nationalism in Ukraine therefore expanded from a narrower to a wider base by incorporating all CPU supporters except " Imperial Communists."[3]

In the post-Soviet period, ethnic nationalists on the far right of the political spectrum could not convert the energy of the drive for independence into an effective use of the state for implementing ethnic nationalist policies. Instead, the far right nationalists were marginalized following independence, while civic nationalist parties in the center and center right borrowed from them when convenient on issues of language, culture, and history. Ethnic nationalists on the left were likewise unsuccessful in their pursuit of reunion with Russia and the development of an Eastern Slav identity based on Russian language and culture. Instead, a civic nation-building approach became paradigmatic, with broad consensus about the need to balance Ukrainian cultural revival with protection of minority cultural rights.

This does not mean that civic nationalists agreed on the details of the nation-building program. As in other former Communist states, the civic nationalist movement divided into its ideological wings once independence was achieved. But the central ideas of civic nationalism spread across the political spectrum. Rukh narrowed into a center-right political party and was joined by other national democratic offshoots (the Republican, Democratic, Reforms and Order, Christian Democratic, and other political parties). In the March 2002 elections both wings of the now-divided Rukh were members of a wider, patriotic (civic nationalist), reformist Our Ukraine bloc led by former National Bank governor and prime minister Viktor Yushchenko, which came first in the proportional half of the elections with 23.57 percent.

During the first half of the 1990s, the national idea extended to the center ground of Ukrainian politics within which the Sovereign Communists congregated. Hence, Ukraine's "parties of power" (i.e., parties close to the authorities) are to be found among centrist (or "oligarchic") parties. During the second half of the 1990s, the civic national idea continued moving to the left and incorporated center-left and left-wing political parties committed to state independence, many of which were offshoots from the CPU during its period of illegality (the Socialist and Peasant parties). After more than a decade of independence only the radical left is in favor of Ukraine joining the Russian-Belarusian union. The center left now holds similar views to the center right on state independence for Ukraine and Russia. This could be clearly seen in the 1999 presidential election, when a majority (52.2 percent) of those who supported CPU leader Petro Symonenko also backed a union with Russia. Among supporters of Oleksandr Moroz's Socialists and President Leonid Kuchma, this figure was only 30.2 and 26.7 percent respectively.[4]

This brief overview of the various components of nationalism in Ukraine highlights its evolutionary nature, in both the late-Soviet and post-Soviet periods. It also points out the necessity of thinking carefully about one's categorization of political parties as nationalist, both in general and in terms of their civic and ethnic leanings. Scholars of Ukraine—and scholars generally—face potential pitfalls when attempting to employ the label *nationalist* either to a broad political movement or to a particular political party. Parties on the left can be nationalists, and parties on the right need not be ethnic nationalists. In this chapter, I outline a wider understanding of nationalism in Ukraine than is commonly discussed (see fig. 1 in the appendix to this chapter). I explore these various themes and conclude with lessons from the case of Ukraine about understanding nationalism after independence.

Nations & Nationalism prior to Independence

Nationalism is a multifaceted concept that incorporates many different definitions. A central claim of this chapter is that it should be differentiated before, and after, a state achieves independence. Although the tendency among scholars has been to define nationalism in Ukraine as one continuous process from the second half of the 1980s until the present, this approach has serious flaws. Nationalism prior to independence sought to establish a newly independent state (e.g., Ukraine from the former USSR). But nationalist movements for self-determination can be defined as either civic and inclusive, ethnic and exclusive, or—as is usually the case—incorporating both elements.

Although scholars and journalists have defined as nationalists those who defend a state from disintegration and oppose self-determination (e.g., Serbia in the former Yugoslavia), this serves merely to confuse the issue. Those who seek to defend a multinational state or empire are best defined as imperialists—not nationalists—for they oppose both the self-determination of their own core state and that of the nonimperial nations.[5] That which has been commonly defined as Russian nationalism is therefore, as Motyl points out, a myth.[6]

Ukraine's movement for self-determination evolved from two groups—former dissident political prisoners and the cultural intelligentsia—after Rukh was established in 1988. Rukh declared its support for self-determination, and thus became de facto a nationalist movement, but not until its October 1990 congress. Prior to that, Rukh had supported the transformation of the USSR into a confederation of sovereign republics (Boris Yeltsin's preference even in December 1991). Rukh defined itself as civic and inclusive, and the Ukrainian nation as encompassing all of Ukraine's ethnic groups. The civic nationalist approach adopted by Rukh was a product of three factors. First, the dissident-political prisoner wing of Rukh had a long tradition, dating back to the 1960s, of support for human rights. Ukraine was home to the largest Helsinki Group of any of the Soviet republics. In the Gulag, Ukrainian political prisoners, who were proportionately the largest of any Soviet ethnic group, developed close working relations with Jewish and other prisoners. Second, the conservative, anti-Gorbachev Ukrainian Communist leader Volodymyr Shcherbytsky ruled the republic from 1972 to 1989. Rukh and religious movements only developed into mass movements after his resignation in September 1989. Finally, the large number of Russian-speaking Ukrainians and ethnic Russians in Ukraine influenced Rukh's adoption of an evolutionary and nonradical program.

Not all political parties agreed with the evolutionary and civic approach of Rukh. Radical nationalist parties and movements emerged in western and central Ukraine by 1989 and immediately championed self-determination and maximum opposition to the Soviet regime and all Soviet institutions. These groups united in the IPA and opposed Rukh's participation in the 1989 Congress of Peoples Deputies and the 1990 Ukrainian parliamentary and local elections as "collaboration" with an occupying regime.[7] The

IPA remained a minority movement and changed into a radical nationalist party (the Ukrainian National Assembly) after December 1991.

Alongside the evolution of Rukh, the CPU began to divide into three groups, particularly during 1990 and 1991. The first group was the Sovereign Communists. Led by Leonid Kravchuk, it championed Ukraine's sovereignty over all-union institutions. In the March 1991 referendum, Kravchuk added a question that obtained higher support for republican sovereignty than the Mikhail Gorbachev question regarding a "renewed federation." The former Sovereign Communists remained unaffiliated in the first half of the 1990s, earning the group the label of *party of power.* After 1994–96, this group naturally gravitated toward newly created centrist parties that had close ties with the establishment (Agrarians, Labor Ukraine, Party of Regions) or took over existing ones (United Social Democrats, Democratic Party, People's Democratic Party [the former PDRU]). As these were also the natural home of the Leonid Kuchma camp, there was a convergence of groups one and two (the Sovereign Communists and the CPU Democratic Platform) in the second half of the 1990s. In the October–November 1999 presidential election, Kravchuk backed Kuchma, and in 2000 Kuchma led the nonleft majority in parliament with his former parliamentary speaker, Ivan Pliushch, as the new speaker until it dissolved during the "Kuchmagate" scandal after November 2000.[8]

The Democratic Platform comprised the second group. The young, radical, democratic wing of the CPU—with the support of the Komsomol—broke off and formed the Party of Democratic Revival of Ukraine (PDRU). The PDRU backed the transformation of the USSR into a confederation of sovereign states, the same position as that of the Sovereign Communists until August 1991. The PDRU created the New Ukraine bloc to unite other smaller civic groups and political parties of a centrist orientation. New Ukraine stood in "constructive opposition" to President Kravchuk (December 1991–July 1994) and thereby became the ideological base, together with the Union of Industrialists and Entrepreneurs, that mounted the successful challenge on behalf of Kuchma in the summer 1994 presidential elections.

Members of the former Democratic Platform peeled away from supporting Kuchma in the late 1990s because of his support for a new oligarch class and the increasingly authoritarian nature of the regime, a process hastened by the revelations found in the "Kuchmagate" tapes made by a presidential guard in Kuchma's office from 1998 to 2000. By the 2002 elections many of them were either members of the radical anti-Kuchma opposition (Yulia Tymoshenko's Forum for National Salvation) or Yushchenko's Our Ukraine.

The third faction of the CPU was the "Imperial Communists." As the ideological heirs of Shcherbytsky, this group detested both groups one and two *and* Gorbachev. After the CPU was banned for supporting the putsch in August 1991, it reformed as a new CPU in October 1993. The CPU remains an orthodox, Sovietophile party that finds it difficult to come to terms with Ukrainian independence. During its period of illegality, the Socialist Party (SPU) and Peasant Party (SelPU) emerged as moderate offshoots that supported state independence. Their heyday was in 1994–99, when their leaders (Oleksandr Moroz for the SPU and Oleksandr Tkachenko for the SelPU) were parliamentary speakers. The CPU, SPU, and SelPU opposed Kravchuk and Kuchma. In 2000, a pro-statehood Communist Party of Ukraine Revived was established, probably with backing from the presidential administration.[9]

Thus, prior to independence, the Ukrainian nationalist movement that *supported* self-determination was composed of three groups: (1) the radical right (from 1989 on) adopted a platform of independence immediately in 1989 and espoused an *ethnic,* exclusive program of "Ukraine for Ukrainians!"; (2) Rukh (from 1990 on) adopted a platform of state independence in October 1990 based on a *civic,* inclusive program that linked national and human rights;[10] and (3) the Sovereign Communists and Democratic Platform (from 1991 on) championed a confederation of sovereign republics until the August 1991 putsch (eleven months after Rukh dropped this program). On August 24, 1991, the Sovereign Communists, led by parliamentary speaker Kravchuk, moved into the Rukh camp and supported the parliamentary declaration of independence by an overwhelming constitutional majority vote.[11]

Between October 1990 and August 1991 the Ukrainian nationalist movement for self-determination became a mass movement. The banning of the CPU in August 1991 removed the last obstacle to taking Ukraine out of the USSR and led to a united nationalist movement for self-determination from August to December 1991 that produced a 91 percent endorsement in the December 1 referendum.[12] If we define as nationalists those that sought to establish an independent state, then radical nationalists, Rukh, and the Sovereign Communists all joined the nationalist movement at different times during the three years leading up to independence. Of these three groups, only the radical nationalists had an ethnic, exclusive program. The other two (Rukh and the Sovereign Communists and Democratic Platform) always backed a civic, inclusive definition of the nation. The Ukrainian example, therefore, shows how a broad-based nationalist movement for self-determination can simultaneously encompass both ethnic and civic nationalist ideologies (ethnic nationalism within the IPA and national [civic] democracy within Rukh).

Nationalist Ideas in Ukraine after Independence

Who Are the "Nationalists"?

After a country achieves independence, the nationalist movement has achieved its goal. In other words, as Ukrainian scholars and political party activists are fond of pointing out, "the national idea has been fulfilled."[13] What next? How should the national idea in an independent state be defined? Who are the "we" and who are the "others"?[14] Defining who are "nationalists" in the independent state is more complicated than defining nationalism for self-determination prior to independence. If we accept a definition that all of those who actively support the continued independence of the state are by definition nationalists, then this group of people includes, as it did in the preindependence era, both civic *and* ethnic nationalists.

Civic (also called *pragmatic* or *state*) nationalists are those who support an inclusive definition of the nation and range from the pro-statehood left (SPU, SelPU) to the center right (national democrats such as Rukh). In the West this has been described by Billig as "banal nationalism" because it has become ingrained within societal culture and public consciousness, as seen in the aftermath of the terrorist attacks on the United States in September 2001.[15] This spectrum is large and incorporates the former Sovereign Communists and "Democratic Platform Communists" who have congregated in the center (Kravchuk, Kuchma), as well as national democrats and offshoots from the CPU (SelPU, SPU).[16]

Wilson argues that it is impossible for a "nationalist" to win the presidency in Ukraine.[17] Using our definition of civic (pragmatic) nationalists, we can see how such a definition is too narrow and flawed. Civic nationalists have, in fact, won *every* presidential election in Ukraine (December

1991, July 1994, November 1999, and 2004). In the first two cases civic nationalists were pitted against each other: V'iacheslav Chornovil versus Kravchuk (December 1991) and Kravchuk versus Kuchma (June–July 1994).[18] In the last, a civic nationalist, Kuchma, faced off against a Sovietophile, Petro Symonenko, the head of the CPU. In 2004, two civic nationalists faced each other—Yushenko and Yanukovych.

Civic nationalists have been divided over aspects of the national idea, but as discussed in more detail in the following, they remain united in defense of national interests such as territorial integrity. A study of Russian politics argued that "pragmatic nationalism represents the standard view one might expect the foreign policy elite to hold in any country."[19] Pragmatic nationalism has increasingly dominated Russian reformist circles since 1993, with a program of Commonwealth of Independent States (CIS) integration, promotion of Great Russia, and defense of national interests.[20]

A similar development emerged in Ukraine. D'Anieri's study of Ukrainian security policy in the 1990s found that the ruling elites defended sovereignty over and above any benefits of economic integration in the CIS. Elites from all regions of Ukraine and different civic nationalist political parties were similarly concerned with "foreign economic penetration of Ukraine and the potential for neocolonialism."[21] D'Anieri continues, "The coalition of forces that sees sovereignty as a preeminent goal is strong in particular because it cuts across Ukraine's other major political schisms."[22] In the October–November 1999 presidential elections the "pragmatic nationalist" call to rely on one's own national forces dominated the programs of most of the contenders.[23]

Unlike Malcolm, Pravda, Allison, and Light on Russia, D'Anieri does not define Ukraine's ruling elite's as pragmatic nationalists. Instead, D'Anieri falls into the traditional trap of only defining as nationalists western Ukrainian national democrats, which serves to confuse readers as to who the "nationalists" are in Ukraine.[24] He cannot argue that nationalism in parliament cuts across regions and parties and at the same time claim that nationalists only exist in western Ukraine among Ukrainophone national democrats.

Such a division of Ukrainian politics and parliamentary affairs into "nationalists" and "Russophiles" is common among Western scholars.[25] Ethnic nationalism, using this author's definition and that most commonly found in Ukraine, is weak throughout Ukraine, including in its western region.[26]

The Ideas of the Ethnic Nationalists, Ukrainian and Russian

Ethnic nationalists are the same as those who were defined as such in the preindependence era (radical right parties such as the IPA [UNA]). But while scholars writing on nationalism in Ukraine usually adopt a similar framework to that used by D'Anieri,[27] I argue that the ethnic nationalists also include Russian and Soviet nationalists. Russia's policies of "external-territory-claiming" were matched by ethnic Russian nationalists and Sovietophiles within Ukraine arguing that Ukraine had no right to exist as an independent state but only in a vaguely defined Eastern Slavic union or a revived USSR. Sovietophiles saw an Eastern Slavic union as a stepping stone to a revived USSR. The homeland for Russian nationalists in Ukraine and Russian imperialists in Russia was clearly neither Ukraine nor the Russian Federation but an Eastern Slavic union, USSR, or tsarist empire.

Ethnic Russian nationalists include pan–Eastern Slavic and Russophile parties that usually align themselves with the CPU, Progressive Socialists, and internationalist fronts in regions such as the Donbas and Crimea.[28] The presidential program of Oleksandr Bazyliuk, head of the Slavic Party (successor to the Civic Congress and organizer of the Congress of Russian Organizations of Ukraine), defined Ukraine as part of the Slavic world and his party as patriotic.[29] Although Bazyliuk denies that Ukrainians are a separate ethnic group,[30] Wilson does not deem this sufficient to warrant defining him and his party as nationalist, only Russophile.[31] Clearly double standards are at work here, as Ukrainians making similar comments about Russians would be undoubtedly defined as ethnic nationalists, or worse, by these same scholars.

Russian nationalists in Ukraine have difficulty in accepting Ukraine's right to exist as an independent state. They vacillate between a belief that the three Eastern Slavs are merely regional branches of one Russian nation or recognizing that a Soviet Ukrainian republican identity now exists that harmed the "natural" unification of the three Eastern Slavic "Russian" peoples prior to 1917.

In arguing for the unity of the three Eastern Slavs, they are as much pan-Russianists as German nationalists in the 1930s were pan-Germanists in seeking to unite all German speakers in one state. Russian nationalists in Ukraine see the three Eastern Slavs as all "Russians" (*Russkii*). The aim of the Slavic Party "is identical to what nationalists strive for in Russia."[32]

In both the German and Eastern Slavic cases, nationalism is ethnic and primordial, not civic, although a civic path to power can be used (e.g., Adolf Hitler in Germany in 1933 and his admirer, Alyaksandr Lukashenka, in Belarus in 1994).[33] Lukashenka's ideology, Kolstø points out, is an "expression of skewed ethnic nationalism."[34] Other scholars have similarly defined the CPU in Ukraine as "Soviet national-socialism."[35]

Russian ethnic nationalism in Ukraine is weak because many CPU supporters are Russified Ukrainians and ethnic Russian nationalism is weak throughout the former USSR.[36] In the 2002 elections, the two Russian nationalist blocs (the Russia Bloc and For a Union of Ukraine, Belarus, and Russia) obtained a combined total of only 1.12 percent.[37]

As tables 1 and 2 show, the proportion of ethnic Ukrainians increases as one moves across the political spectrum from left to right. Ethnic Ukrainian representation in the radical left is half that of ethnic Russians. The ethnic Ukrainian to ethnic Russian proportional mix is 2:1 (radical left), 3:1 (center left), 5:1 (center right), and 18:1 (radical right).[38]

Russian nationalism in Ukraine has other defining attributes, many of which are jointly held with the radical left:[39]

denounces liberal values traditionally as "un-Russian";
supports anti-Westernism;
supports anti-Semitism;[40]
sees Russia as the natural leader of the Eastern Slavs;
defends the inherited postcolonial status quo and denounces as "nationalist" any attempts at affirmative action for Ukrainian culture and language;
fears a decline in the hegemony of Russian culture and language in Ukraine and accuses the authorities of discrimination in policies aimed at upgrading Ukrainian culture and language;
saw, and still sees, no need to learn the titular language;
describes the decline of the titular languages in republics such as Ukraine as "natural" and Russians are therefore not guilty for the Russification of other peoples;
believes Russians suffered more than others in the former USSR and they never undertook any negative actions; and
holds that the former USSR was never fully a Russian empire.

Ironically, Ukrainian ethnic nationalists share one idea with the ethnic Russian nationalists in Ukraine: the rejection of post-Soviet Ukraine as the homeland for Ukrainians. They, like all their counterparts in other European states, want to expand the borders of the state to its "ethnographic borders." As with Russian nationalists they seek to unite all those whom they define as belonging to one ethnic group within one state. Such a policy would bring confrontation with all of Ukraine's neighbors. Ethnic Ukrainian nationalists seek to incorporate territory in Poland, Slovakia, Moldova, Belarus, and Russia into a "greater Ukraine." Ethnic Russian nationalists and Sovietophiles would like to see Ukraine included within the Russian-Belarusian union or a revived USSR.

Ukrainian ethnic nationalists strongly oppose pan–Eastern Slavism. Nevertheless, one party, the UNA, turned the pan–Eastern Slavic framework on its head by arguing in favor of it as the basis for a Ukrainian empire centered upon Kyiv—not Moscow (a city six hundred years younger)—as a modern successor to the medieval state of Kyiv Rus'.

The Ideas of the Civic Nationalists

After independence is achieved, the unity of the nationalist movement, even a civic nationalist movement, can come under stress. Different groups have alternative approaches to dealing with key questions for the state—how to define the nation and how to establish full control over its terri-

TABLE 1. Ethnic Self-Identification of the Electorate (in percentages)

	Radical Left	Center Left	Center Right	Radical Right
Ukrainian	62.9	70.2	80.1	91.4
Russian	33.9	23.6	14.9	5.0
Other	3.2	6.1	5.0	3.6

Source: O. Haran and O. Mayboroda, *Ukraiins'ki Livi: Mizh Leninizmom I Sotsial-Demokratieu* (Kyiv: KM Academia, 2000), 204.

TABLE 2. Language Group and Political Affiliation (in percentages)

Language Group	Radical Left	Center Left	Center Right	Radical Right
Ukrainian	31.7	39.5	52.7	76.3
Russophone Ukrainian	30.9	30.7	27.1	14.6
Russian	29.8	20.7	12.1	3.7
Other	7.6	9.0	8.2	5.5

Source: O. Haran and O. Mayboroda, *Ukraiins'ki Livi: Mizh Leninizmom I Sotsial-Demokratieu* (Kyiv: KM Academia, 2000), 204.

tory—which lead to clashes over policy, programs, and frames of reference. Civic nationalists in Ukraine differ on how to deal with foreign and domestic threats to territorial integrity, how much to participate in European integration, and whether to grant territorial autonomy to minorities in an otherwise unitary state. The biggest differences, however, concern how to define the "we" (nation), as based upon one or two titular nations or one or two state languages.

Dealing with External Threats

Civic nationalists remain divided over how to deal with external threats. Although they remain committed to defending in the last resort Ukraine's territorial integrity by any means (the president is, after all, the guarantor of the state's integrity), they differ over how to deal with threats. National democrats adopt a tougher line against these threats than centrists and the center left, particularly if they emanate from Russia.

Nevertheless, Ukraine's civic nationalist elites have consistently rejected Russian proposals for maintaining ill-defined "internal" CIS borders by treating them in the same manner as external borders; they have also opposed dual citizenship and demanded that the borders be defined as integral not only within the context of the CIS. Employing Barrington's nationalism variants presented in the introduction, Ukraine, during 1991–97, therefore adopted a policy of "sovereignty-protecting" vis-à-vis Russian claims to its territory (Crimea) and Russia's refusal to accept its inherited borders. Ukraine has consistently denounced Russian attempts at "co-national-protecting" in the former USSR and has rejected any attempts by Moscow to speak on behalf of its Russians or "compatriots" (Russophones).

DOES UKRAINE NEED EUROPE TO BE MODERN?

Ukrainian nationalism was originally a reaction against modernization that was tantamount to assimilation for Ukrainians. In the Soviet era, attacks on Ukrainian "bourgeois nationalism" included anybody or anything nationally conscious, or culturally, ideologically, and politically different from the Communist Party line. In independent Ukraine, civic nationalists are in the process of developing a nationalism that is an "ideology of national solidarity" but also a "doctrine of modernization."[41]

Attempts have been made since the late 1990s to make civic nationalism into a doctrine of modernization that would lead to Ukraine's reintegration into Europe.[42] Linking modernization to the diffusion of civic nationalism and integration from the center to the periphery would be consistent with the Karl Deutsch diffusionist model popular until the 1960s. Such a model has been elaborated by Viktor Medvedchuk, head of the United Social Democrats and former deputy speaker of parliament.[43] A modernization doctrine that links political and economic reform to a foreign policy of returning to Europe is obviously not to the liking of left-wing civic nationalists, such as the Socialists. This is because it rejects much of the Soviet legacy and supports the creation of a Western-style liberal democratic market economy.

TERRITORIAL AUTONOMY FOR MINORITIES?

In Ukraine, the center right, as in other liberal democratic states (except in the United States, Canada, and Germany), opposes federalism and territorial autonomy for minorities. Its support for a unitary state is premised upon a vision of the French Jacobin state that recognizes only individual, not collective, rights. Centrists and the left are more willing to countenance territorial autonomy as a quid pro quo to take the heat out of the separatist movement but remain divided over federalism. Federalism is largely opposed by Ukraine's elites, and plans to establish an upper parliamentary chamber (which was allegedly backed by a majority in the April 2000 referendum) are not popular across the entire political spectrum (as seen in discussions in 2003 and 2004 over presidential political reform proposals to introduce an unelected upper Council of Regions in parliament). Civic nationalists all remain united on the question of state- and institution-building, which is closely tied to expanding the center's control over its territory and ensuring that its policies are implemented at the local level.

WHO ARE "WE"? NATION-BUILDING AND THE DIFFICULT ISSUES OF RELIGION AND LANGUAGE

The civic definition of the nation has dominated state policy in Ukraine since independence, with Russian and Ukrainian ethnic nationalists and Sovietophiles marginalized from the policy process. Nevertheless, civic nationalists within the ruling elite in Ukraine only reached a consensus on nation-building during the course of the second half of the 1990s. Civic nationalists all desired some kind of nation-building and national integration, but they differed over how this should be undertaken.[44] Both the consensus on the need for nation-building and these differences over it in practice are a reflection of the country's regional disparities, the influence of Russian-speaking Ukrainians, and the colonial legacy.

A divided titular nation inevitably led to evolutionary, moderate policies, and a certain level of agreement developed. Few civic nationalists, for example, supported the definition of Ukraine as a state with two titular nations (Russians and Ukrainians), as this would transform Ukraine into an Eastern Slavic state. Those that supported such a definition stressed the benefits of Ukrainian-Russian biculturalism.

Liberal Russophiles who defended such a definition united in the Social-Liberal SLON election bloc in the 1998 elections with the slogan "Let's Defend Russian Culture for the Peoples of Ukraine."[45] Such a rallying cry, however, attracted the support of only 0.91 percent of the voters.[46] The July 1996 constitution defined Ukraine as a country with only one titular nation, following the long tradition of the Soviet nationality policy of assigning a republican homeland to each major ethnic group with a foreign border.

The inculcation of common values, myths, and customs also proved to be unproblematical for civic nationalists in Ukraine. The only alternative to a Ukrainian national historiography that stressed Ukraine's distinctiveness from Russia and its Europeanness was that espoused by ethnic Russian nationalists and Sovietophiles from the nineteenth century to the 1980s, with a brief interlude in the 1920s when the Soviet regime pursued a policy of indigenization.

A Russian nationalist or Sovietophile historiography and myths rejected the very idea of a Ukrainian ethnic group or an independent existence from Russia and therefore could not be used by Ukrainian nation-builders. Western scholars, though, have been quick to negatively label this national historiography as *nationalist,* while defining Russophile historiography as merely the "traditional Russian interpretation" or "Soviet version."[47] Laitin calls Mykhailo Hrushevs'kyi, the doyen of Ukrainian national historiography, the author of a "nationalist bible."[48]

One of the nation-building questions surrounds religion. Ukraine has sought to create an autocephalous, united Orthodox Church as an attribute of independence. Efforts to make the Ukrainian Orthodox Church—Kyiv Patriarch the basis for such unity failed in 1992–94. The largest of the three Orthodox Churches in Ukraine, in terms of parishes, remains the Ukrainian Orthodox Church, which is under the jurisdiction of the Moscow Patriarchate, though polls give the Ukrainian Orthodox Church—Kyiv Patriarch far greater popular support.

After 2000, efforts were again underway to unite all three Orthodox Churches in Ukraine into an autocephalous church. Such a move was backed by the Constantinople patriarch, who does not recognize the cannonity of the transfer of the Kyiv Metropolinate from Kyiv to Moscow in 1686 or the Russian Orthodox Church's jurisdiction over Ukraine. Not surprisingly, the main opponents of an autocephalous Ukrainian Orthodox Church are ethnic Russian nationalists and Sovietophiles, who see this as further evidence of Ukraine cutting its ties to Russia.[49]

But it is language that has proven to be the most divisive and complicated issue for civic nation-builders in Ukraine. A consensus was reached by Ukrainian civic nationalist elites that an independent state needed its own language. The loss of a national language is widely held to lead to the loss of national identity and independence, as seen most starkly in Belarus. The alternatives for Ukraine's nation-builders and civic nationalists are as follows:

1. Ukrainian as the sole state language: Russian would be squeezed out completely in favor of Ukrainian by removing the colonial legacy of Russification. Such a policy, similar to that adopted in the Baltic states, was never seriously contemplated and was only applied in western Ukraine.
2. Ukrainian as the sole state language applied differently by region: This policy was adopted in the 1989 Soviet Ukrainian law "On Languages" and reaffirmed in the 1996 constitution.[50] Such a policy foresaw the continued use of Russian but at the same time allowed for the continued expansion of Ukrainian. Although some of the postcolonial legacy would be tackled through affirmative action, the legacy would never be completely removed except in western Ukraine. The provision of Ukrainian in education has gradually expanded throughout the 1990s in all regions except the Donbas and the Crimea.[51]
3. Ukrainian and Russian as two state languages: Such a policy was only ever backed by ethnic Russian nationalists and Sovietophiles, particularly the CPU.[52] Russian nationalists and Sovietophiles saw it as an attempt to "maintain the hegemonic status of the (Russian) minority

in the linguistic-cultural sphere."[53] Precisely for this reason, Ukrainian civic nationalists opposed the introduction of two state languages because they understood that such a fictional equality, as in Belarus, would maintain the domination of Russian. The attitude of different political parties to the language question can be ascertained from tables 3 and 4.

Some in Ukraine, and many Western scholars, have defined a policy of only one state language—Ukrainian—in a country with a large number of Russophones as "ethnic" and tantamount to Ukraine pursuing "nationalizing" policies that deviate from its proclaimed aim of building a civic state.[54] But a civic state, if it has an inclusive citizenship and franchise, can be based on a Ukrainian *or* Ukrainian-Russian ethnocultural core. Either policy decision and framework could be defined as civic.

The definition of a civic state rests not on whether a state has one or two state languages or indeed if it has one or two titular nations. Most scholars define how civic a state is in terms of the inclusiveness of a state's citizenship laws and the electoral franchise. All civic states are not purely civic but constructed on the basis of an ethnocultural core (in the case of some, two cores [Belgium]).[55]

TABLE 3. Support for Languages within the Ukrainian Political Spectrum (in percentages)

	Radical Left	Center Left	Center Right	Radical Right
Russian as a second state language	37.4	26.4	15.7	1.9
Russian as an official language	36.4	31.0	25.6	10.2

Source: O. Haran and O. Mayboroda, *Ukraiins'ki Livi: Mizh Leninizmom I Sotsial-Demokratieu* (Kyiv: KM Academia, 2000), 204.

Note: Russian as a second state language would make it on a par with Ukrainian, which has been the sole state language since 1989. As an official language it would have recognition only in some restricted fields and in some regions of Ukraine.

TABLE 4. Languages Used within the Ukrainian Political Spectrum (in percentages)

	Radical Left	Center Left	Center Right	Radical Right
Ukrainian	36.8	44.0	58.1	79.4
Russian	63.2	56.0	41.9	20.9

Source: O. Haran and O. Mayboroda, *Ukraiins'ki Livi: Mizh Leninizmom I Sotsial-Demokratieu* (Kyiv: KM Academia, 2000), 204.

In the Ukrainian case, scholars have been tempted to characterize the state as "ethnic" because it only has one constitutionally defined state language and titular nation. A Ukrainian state defined in such a manner that simultaneously adopts affirmative action for Ukrainian language and culture, has a Ukrainian ethnocultural core, and respects national minority rights and regional differences can still be defined as civic.[56]

The Nation & Nationalism after Independence: Political Parties

National Democrats on the Right: Are They the Only "Real" Nationalists?

In Ukraine, the center-right parties are often disparaged by scholars as "nationalists."[57] What such scholars mean by this is ethnic nationalists, with all the negative connotations this type of nationalism carries. Of particular relevance here is Rukh, which Kubicek claims is "the largest party with a nationalist orientation in Ukraine today."[58] Are then only Ukrainophone political parties such as Rukh to be defined as nationalists?

Laitin thinks so and argues that only "nationalist deputies" opposed the definition of "peoples of Ukraine" (*narod Ukraiiny*). These Ukrainophone "vigilantes" allegedly use "nationalist threats" and "provocations" against Russophones that "instills shame and guilt in many russophone Ukrainians."[59] "Ukrainian nationalists," Arel believes, see Russophones as victims of Soviet nationality policies (which they are) and thereby believes that they will only reacquire national consciousness through becoming Ukrainophones (which is not the case).[60] Arel believes that Kravchuk's policies undermined his commitment to a civic state so that by 1994 "Kravchuk was widely seen as a partisan of the nationalizing state." Therefore, Kravchuk lost the 1994 presidential elections to ascendant left-wing forces and a "fierce anti-nationalist campaign."[61]

This use of the label *nationalist* to associate the center-right parties with (bad) ethnic nationalism is a loose use of the term. Labeling all center-right parties as *nationalist* (and only Ukrainophones as nationalists) places them in the same camp as the extreme right. Rukh and the other center-right policies have been labeled (*bad ethnic*) *nationalists* because of their support for righting some of the wrongs committed against the Ukrainian language and culture during tsarist and Soviet rule through affirmative action.

This is a common policy position in all postcolonial countries. It also need not be ethnic nationalism but rather can be one wing of civic nationalism. As Barrington's introduction makes clear, all national identities—whether civic or ethnic—need common cultural features to help unify groups. Pursuing policies designed to resurrect particular features need not be ethnic nationalism, especially when considered as part of a broader set of policies favorable to minority rights and pursued within an inclusive framework.

Downplaying the positions of Rukh and the center right on minority rights also means that such labeling is factually incorrect. Rukh and center-right parties have always been strong advocates of polyethnic rights for national minorities and group rights for those who live compactly in defined territories (e.g., Tatars in the Crimea, Hungarians in Transcarpathia, and Romanians in Chernivtsi oblast). The Ukrainian center-right parties do not advocate the disenfranchisement of ethnic Russians or the total removal of Russian language and culture from Ukraine.

Even many former political prisoners (who dominated the commanding heights of new national democratic parties) have always been strong advocates of minority rights. Rukh has supported a definition of the nation that defines everybody in Ukraine as a citizen regardless of their nationality.[62] While supporting the introduction of Ukrainian into all walks of life (as stated in the June 1996 constitution) Rukh also "guarantee[d] the development of the Russian language, the languages and cultures of all nationalities."[63] Indeed, Jaworsky believes that one of the two factors that prevented the outburst of interethnic conflict in Ukraine was its political parties, "which quickly reached a consensus on the need to provide guarantees for the rights of ethnic minorities in Ukraine."[64]

In addition, Ukraine's national democrats do not espouse the policies that are commonly promoted by Europe's new nationalist right. These include hostility to the European Union, xenophobia, anti-immigration policies, racism, distrust of parliamentary politics, neocorporatist economic policies, and state intervention. Ukraine's center right (i.e., Our Ukraine) would never support the "Third Way" of Europe's nationalist right. Third Way politics in Ukraine can be best summarized with the nationalist slogan of "Neither Moscow nor Washington!" Such views are the preserve of two groups in Ukraine: "pragmatic" oligarch centrists and the populist-right Yulia Tymoshenko bloc. The Tymoshenko Bloc includes the populist-right Fatherland Party, led by Tymoshenko. Her party split from the populist-left Hromada Party after it went into decline when former prime minister Pavlo Lazarenko fled abroad in 1999. Tymoshenko's

Fatherland Party gained adherents and a political niche in 1999–2002 from those who had backed Yevhen Marchuk's failed 1999 presidential campaign, such as veteran dissident Levko Lukianenko. The Fatherland Party merged with Stepan Khmara's populist-right Conservative Republican Party in 2002.

Ukraine's center-right parties are the staunchest advocates of Ukraine's full integration into transatlantic and European structures and espouse moderate free market economic policies.[65] These policies are to be found within Yushchenko's Our Ukraine 2002 election bloc that incorporates Rukh and other center-right parties and in Yushchenko's presidential program.[66]

Centrists and the National Idea

Centrists only came on the scene after Ukraine achieved independence. They grew out of the "Democratic Platform" and "Sovereign Communists" wings of the CPU, regional interests, and industrialist groups. The earliest centrist groups were those linked to the PDRU and its New Ukraine bloc that backed Kuchma in the 1994 and 1999 presidential elections. Other political parties have adopted either regional titles (Crimean Party of Economic Revival and the Party of Regions) or social democratic and liberal labels.

After 2000, parliament was led by a speaker, first deputy speaker, and deputy speaker from centrist parties with close ties to the local or national establishment and therefore termed *parties of power*. These include the Party of Regions in the Donbas, Agrarians (renamed People's Party) in western and central Ukraine, and Social Democratic United Party (SDPU) in Kyiv and Transcarpathia. The Party of Regions is led by former Donetsk governor and prime minister Viktor Yanukovych.

Centrist political parties that backed Kuchma in the 1999 presidential elections see "centrism" as an ideology that backs Ukraine's independence (i.e., civic nationalism), the "consolidation of Ukraine as a modern European state," and accelerating political and economic reform.[67] In other words, centrist political parties defer to the national democrats on questions of symbols, myths, and ethnocultural attributes of the state, while seeking to build a new civic nationalism that both integrates nationally and modernizes economically and politically. This centrist "unification ideology" is pro-statehood and pro–economic reform, providing "the basis to achieve general national consensus."[68] While economically liberal, centrist political parties may also be authoritarian politically, a feature common to "parties of power" in Russia.

In contrast to national democrats, centrist political parties give greater emphasis to individual over collective or state rights, including those of any ethnic group. They often deny that the state needs to possess any ethnocultural character, opening them to charges of cosmopolitanism. The equality of all ethnic groups is championed, and they therefore do not like the terms *titular nation* and *national minorities* because these divide Ukraine into ethnic Ukrainians and others. They also recognize the multinational character of the state, something Kuchma championed after 1994. Federalism was originally popular among them but has declined in favor of a decentralized unitary state that is the current policy of the state.[69] They support flexible language policies that take into account the inherited ethnocultural situation in the regions (whereas national democrats would like to change the postcolonial situation through affirmative action throughout Ukraine). Language problems, they believe, can be resolved locally, taking into account the views of the local inhabitants.[70]

These policies are clearly recognizable as those that have been backed by Ukraine's ruling elites during the 1990s. At the same time, centrists do support the gradual expansion of the Ukrainian language in education and would like Russophone Ukrainians to at least know Ukrainian. They do not oppose the national historiography, myths, and legends backed by national democrats. The national hymn, symbol, myths, and flag are also elements of nation-building that centrists have been happy to accept from the national democratic camp. Their quarrel with the national democratic camp is largely over language policies, although both camps recognize the value of language to national identity.

The Left and the National Idea

Discussions of nationalism in Ukraine tend to ignore the left. But a large section of the Ukrainian political spectrum on the left is supportive of Ukrainian state independence and can also therefore be defined as civic nationalist. This left-wing tradition has long historical roots in Ukraine going back to the late nineteenth century. Patriotism and civic nationalism can, after all, be defined in different ways. Kas'ianov points out that the first calls for Ukrainian independence came from the Ukrainian Marxist intelligentsia in Galicia and the socialist intelligentsia in eastern Ukraine.[71]

In Ukraine, the center left is now composed of four competing social democratic parties, one of which had close ties to the "party of power" establishment (USDPU). In addition, the oligarchic, antipresidential Hromada and the propresidential Agrarian Party can also be included within this spectrum. To the immediate left of these parties, the Socialist and Peasant parties can be defined as pragmatic and are evolving away from the communists toward civic nationalist positions. Their evolution toward civic nationalist positions has occurred since the 1994 elections.

THE OPPOSITION OF THE LEFT TO NEOLIBERAL ECONOMICS AND NEOLIBERAL INTERNATIONAL ORGANIZATIONS

Left-wing nationalism in Ukraine is similar to that espoused by Mustafa Kemal Atatürk in Turkey, Gamel Abdel Nasser in the Middle East, and traditional anti-American left-wing nationalism in Latin America. The left in Latin America, like in Ukraine, is critical of neoliberal policies not only for socioeconomic reasons but also because of the damage it inflicts on the "nation." Criticism leveled at international financial institutions rests on the impact of their policies on society, sovereignty, and "the ability of the nation to determine its own fate."[72] Patriots should not only shout how much they love Ukraine (i.e., national democrats), former parliamentary chairman Oleksandr Tkachenko argues, but should learn how to do "everything that is the most advantageous for the state."[73]

The Ukrainian left parties, as in all postcolonial countries, remain critical of international financial institutions, a factor influenced by decades of anti-Western Soviet propaganda. The Progressive Socialists believe that international capital is leading Ukraine to "a total national catastrophe, the loss of statehood, enslavement and colonization." After this, "the colonization of Ukraine will be completed by the hob nail boots of NATO troops."[74] Protesting against the latest economic program sponsored by the International Monetary Fund (IMF), the Communists believe that it "threatens the existence of our state as an independent and sovereign state." Condemning the Ukrainian government's "capitulation to world capitalism," it called upon the parliament "to protect our people and Ukraine from the encroachment of national and foreign enslavers!"[75] This is indeed rich coming from a party that seeks itself to subvert Ukrainian independence.

This ruining of Ukraine by Kuchma on behalf of the IMF (or "international capital") is a common theme within left-wing civic nationalism and Soviet and Russian ethnic nationalism.[76] Socioeconomic reforms in Ukraine, conducted with the assistance of the IMF and "Western advisers" led to a "satanic blitzkrieg" that has resulted in a decline in Ukraine's population from fifty-two to forty-eight million. "We are now being presented with genocide against our own people," Communist leader Symonenko claimed.[77] Socialist leader Oleksandr Moroz's aide, Ivan Bokyi, believes that it is Kuchma's socioeconomic policies "which are destroying independence, sowing social tensions."[78] Moroz's 1999 presidential election program denounced the "immoral ruination of one's motherland and the physical extermination of millions of citizens." Ukraine's revival would be undertaken by "liquidating the banditocratic regime" and placing "trust in one's people, its talents and traditions, and in the potential of the Fatherland."[79] The Progressive Socialists also issued a statement, "On Political Genocide in Ukraine," with a call to commemorate the "memory of the victims of genocide in Ukraine."[80] They are here, of course, not referring to the artificial famine of 1933, which led to the deaths of seven million people under Joseph Stalin, but to the decline in Ukraine's population during the 1990s.

Such policies, aided and abetted domestically, are "transforming Ukraine into a colonial state"[81] and into a "protectorate of international financial oligarchs and NATO's puppet."[82] The IMF, the left believes, is undertaking a "veiled form of colonisation and economic plunder."[83] Symonenko believes that Ukraine has already lost its economic independence and is forced to do the bidding of international financial organizations, NATO, and "overseas lords." Government programs and presidential decrees "are only translations into the Ukrainian language of demands by the IMF in return for successive financial-narcotic injections." The main outcome of this is that "the colonization of Ukraine continues."[84] Symonenko argues that "our elite acts like a colonial administration" that robs from a colony to provide for a future luxurious lifestyle in the West.[85] These denunciations turn Kuchma's arguments on their head by accusing him (not the left) of endangering Ukraine's sovereignty and thereby promoting the left as defenders of Ukraine's state independence (civic nationalism). For the radical left, Ukraine would be better served with republican sovereignty within a revived USSR.

In the ideological arsenal of the left, *international capital* can refer to Western, domestic, *and* Russian capital. The left claims that the West is attempting to "eliminate Ukraine as a potential competitor," yet it has also been distrustful of Russian oligarchs, particularly of those close to former Russian president Boris Yeltsin.[86] Obeying the dictate of the IMF and the

West threatens Ukraine's sovereignty because "positions in the Cabinet of Ministers are not decided by the President of Ukraine but some Washington uncle."[87] The left is also a strong supporter of the protectionism of domestic industry. Such policies are not only found in Ukraine. Protectionism is a "quintessentially nationalist discourse," a study found of the era in France of the Socialist president François Mitterand.[88]

THE LEFT AND TIES TO RUSSIA

Contrary to what is usually perceived, the left parties are not in favor of a militarily weak Ukraine. The pro-statehood, civic nationalist wing (SPU, SelPU) supports Ukraine's nonbloc status and does not want Ukraine to join *either* the CIS or NATO military bloc. Soviet nationalists (CPU, Progressive Socialists) seek to join with Russia and Belarus in a "common (nuclear) shield" against NATO.[89] Tkachenko is critical of the destruction of sections of Ukraine's military industrial complex because "now, powerful neighbors do not want to reckon with our country as a weak state."[90]

Tkachenko has strongly denied any comparison between himself and Lukashenka.[91] Lukashenka minimizes differences between Belarusians and Russians and thereby sees no need for a border between both states (or with Ukraine; Belarus refuses to ratify the Ukrainian-Belarusian border treaty). Tkachenko, on the other hand, insisted that the Russian Duma ratify the May 1997 Ukrainian-Russian treaty—which it did in December 1998, followed by the Federation Council two months later. This legally codified the inherited borders from Soviet Ukraine. Tkachenko therefore argues that he "dotted the i's on the question of Ukrainian independence."[92] The ratification of the treaty led to the arrival of an "independent country (Ukraine) with its own borders and territory."[93] This meant, Tkachenko argues, that Russian-Ukrainian cooperation could advance between both independent countries.

Tkachenko believes, with some justification, that Russia's acceptance of Ukraine as an independent state began only after both houses of its parliament ratified the treaty and thereby accepted the inherited territorial status quo from the former USSR. Tkachenko rebuts accusations that he favors a revived USSR, which, he believes, is contradicted by his insistence that Russia ratify the treaty with Ukraine, thereby recognizing the border as a prerequisite before cooperation could progress between them.[94] Tkachenko is therefore convinced that "the Ukrainian people will never turn away from this glorious achievement [of an independent Ukraine] and have a chance to impart with it."[95] The left parties turn the argument around and argue that it is Kuchma, and his ruling elites, who are likely to lose Ukraine its independence.

Moroz's party, established in October 1991 when the Communists were still banned (August 1991–October 1993), has grown into what it defines as "a pro-state party."[96] The gulf between the pro-statehood SPU and the Soviet nationalist, antistatehood CPU grew during the "Kuchmagate" crisis. The SPU played a central role in exposing the misdemeanors found on the tapes and remained in radical opposition to Kuchma. The CPU, on the other hand, saw a greater threat in Yushchenko than from Kuchma and the oligarchs. Only after the 2002 elections, which saw the CPU presence in parliament halved, did the CPU join the radical antipresidential SPU and Yulia Tymoshenko bloc.

Moroz has emphasized a belief that the policies pursued by Kravchuk and Kuchma have led to disunion in society. Support for independence was strongly linked to the degree to which citizens have faith and trust in their state. Independence was therefore being undermined by Kuchma's policies, even though it was "historically justified," and if these policies were continued, it would lead to the loss of Ukrainian independence. The October 1999 presidential elections were "a chance to choose independence." "Independence," as defined by the left, would be "real," no longer dependent upon "foreign advisers" (i.e., the IMF and other international institutions) who have conducted "economic and social experiments by political maniacs." Moroz's 1999 election program called upon Ukrainians to resist "turning Ukraine into a colony, an appendage to NATO." Although it welcomed "good neighborly fraternal economic and political relations" with Russia, Belarus, and other Slavic states, it fell far short of sacrificing Ukraine's sovereignty in a union.[97] According to Moroz, Ukraine should not be assigned to any kind of "special zone" (i.e., a Russian "sphere of influence").[98]

To save Ukraine, the left proposed that a "coalition of national patriotic forces" be established "who can take upon themselves the responsibilities for the fate of both the state and the people."[99] The skills of "patriotic" Ukrainians should be pooled to produce a national program for Ukraine's revival in order to reject foreign advisers.[100] In such a program, "national interests must dominate in the work of all branches of government."[101] Achieving a "genuine independent state" required "a steadfast majority of true patriots and true people placed in the highest legislative body of the state."[102] A national program should be advanced that would unite Ukrainians on the basis of patriotism in order for Ukraine to be truly "a sovereign and economically independent country."[103] The continued decline in the economy "was a threat to our state sovereignty" and would be rescued by "true experts and patriots" whose duty would be to "rescue the state." "The president must become an example of honor, diligence, and patriotism for the people," Tkachenko told Mykolaiv oblast leaders.[104]

The evolution of the left toward civic nationalism was evident in the joint appeal by four presidential candidates (Moroz, Tkachenko, Yevhen Marchuk, and Volodymyr Oliynyk) on the August 24, 1999, anniversary of Ukraine's independence. The joint appeal was made symbolically in Kaniv, the birthplace of Ukraine's national bard, Taras Shevchenko. The appeal is noticeable in that it never once mentions socialism, yet it is permeated by civic nationalism. They felt that a new executive needed to be elected as a "rescuer of the state": "It is visible that, if the current president remains, our state will be finally ruined and Ukraine will lose its sovereignty." They therefore called upon Ukrainians to unite because "the Fatherland is in danger!": "We will rise together and make Ukraine a rich, strong, and respected country in the world."[105]

THE LEFT AND CULTURE IN UKRAINE

A common misconception among scholars is that the Ukrainian left is opposed to nation-building, Ukrainian language, and culture. To what degree is this the case? The left and the "Kaniv-4" bemoan the lack of national consolidation and unity under Kuchma. They therefore place great emphasis upon building greater unity not only between different branches of the ruling elite but also between different regions of Ukraine. Thus, they propose that different regions should be harmonized within an overall common national identity and national idea. The language problem would be "solved," Moroz promised if he was elected president, and Ukrainians would become "united and consolidated."[106]

A national idea that unites social, economic, political, and national factors could therefore be developed as a means of uniting and mobilizing Ukrainians to rally around a program developed as a left-wing Third Way. It would have to "enrich nation wide values" and "incorporate our Ukrainian mentality."[107] The revival of Ukrainian culture and language is a central plank of Ukraine's national and economic revival in order that "our people will never become the fertilizer of the future, or anonymous Ivans who do not remember their ancestry."[108]

A "union of popular and patriotic forces" with the Socialists as its core could develop a national idea, Moroz believes.[109] A national idea that promoted ethnic hatred or forcefully inculcated Western ideas would not work, Socialists argue. Instead, a national idea incorporated within state-building, which maintains "national traditions" and maintains one's "originality" (i.e., language and culture), "will never lose its actuality, its value."[110] All decisions by Ukraine's leaders should therefore be based upon the "Ukrainian people's will," which includes national interests, historical experience, and traditions.[111]

Conclusion: Civic Nationalism in Ukraine and Lessons from Its Victory

In this chapter, I have divided the discussion of nationalist ideas and parties between a nationalist movement *prior* to independence (seeking self-determination) and the civic nationalists who have attempted to engage in nation-building and integration *after* independence. The two periods of Ukrainian nationalist development are clearly different and should not be confused.

In the Ukrainian case, the preindependence nationalist movement expanded from radical right ethnic nationalists in 1989 to the civic nationalist Rukh and the Sovereign Communists and Democratic Platform of the CPU in 1990–91. Civic nationalism was confined to the center-right movement Rukh until 1991, spread to the center in 1992–95, and then to the left beginning in the middle to late 1990s (see fig. 2 in the appendix to this chapter).

I therefore have defined civic nationalists in the post-Soviet period to include those political parties from the left to the center right committed both to independence and to a civic definition of citizenship and the franchise. As in all civic states, civic nationalists define the "we" differently depending upon their place within the political spectrum—not depending on the language they speak or the region they hail from, as is commonly the view among scholars.

The ethnic nationalist option never received widespread popular support in Ukraine, either before or after independence was achieved. Prior to independence, both wings of the nationalist movement (civic and ethnic) were able to mobilize only one-third of Ukrainians. Independence was only made possible by defections from the Sovereign Communists and the Democratic Platform of the CPU joining this nationalist movement. The addition of these two elements pushed support for independence to a majority of the population and forced this nationalism to be moderate to appease different linguistic and regional constituencies.

If Ukraine's titular population was not divided by language, as in the Baltic states, the ethnic-civic nationalist movement would have achieved a majority without assistance from these two defecting wings of the CPU. Such a scenario would have led to the victory of Rukh leader V'iacheslav Chornovil in the December 1991 presidential elections, not Kravchuk.

Events in the post-Soviet space show that postindependence nationalism may have then led to either of two scenarios, the Baltic or Transcaucasian. In the former, the nationalist movement evolved from ethnic to civic in Estonia and Latvia after international pressure and the reestablishment of the hegemony of the titular nation where German-style ethnic exclusive policies were initially applied. In Lithuania, the nationalist movement evolved into a civic variant quicker. In the Transcaucasus, on the other hand, the victory of ethnic nationalism led to civil and interstate wars and the eventual removal of nationalists in all but Armenia.

In Ukraine the only region where ethnic nationalism had—and still has—a presence is in its western region, the only area of Ukraine where ethnic Ukrainians and the Ukrainian language dominate urban centers. The ethnic, regional, and linguistic diversity of the remainder of Ukraine influenced the evolution of nationalism in post-Soviet Ukraine into a civic variant that gradually spread during the course of the 1990s from the center right through the center to the center left. After a decade of independence only the radical left still remains hostile to Ukrainian statehood.

These steps in the evolution of Ukrainian nationalism are not peculiar to Ukraine, although their study within a comparative perspective is still to be undertaken.[112] The Baltic and Transcaucasian scenarios show how defining nationalism only in a negative manner fails to provide us with the full picture. Ukraine's post-Soviet nationalism has been forced to balance an uneasy alliance between the national democrats and centrist oligarchs that disintegrated during "Kuchmagate." This alliance had a positive and negative side to it. Ukraine escaped ethnic conflict and did not go down the Transcaucasian path. At the same time, Ukraine "muddled" along indecisively throughout its first decade as an independent state because (again, unlike in the Baltic states) the former Sovereign Communists turned centrist oligarchs are ideologically amorphous and unable to chart a clear domestic or foreign policy course.[113]

In the independent Ukrainian state, the wide-embracing political spectrum of civic nationalism incorporated a wide variety of policy proposals as to how the national idea (i.e., the nation) should be defined. The most complicated question relates to language, whereas others (symbols, historiography, myths, etc.) were accepted by both centrists and national democrats.

There was simply never an alternative to a civic, inclusive definition of the Ukrainian state. A concession to the Crimea, the only region in Ukraine with an ethnic Russian majority, of territorial autonomy has been the exception rather than the rule, as Ukraine's civic nationalists have consistently opposed federalism.

Ukraine's control over Ukraine's borders and defense of territorial integrity has always been a central plank of its nation-builders, and consensus in support of territorial integrity has remained high. Ethnic Russian nationalists and Sovietophiles have disagreed with the boundaries of the state and nation, looking to either a pan–Eastern Slavic or Soviet homeland for Ukraine. Ethnic Ukrainian nationalists, on the other hand, seek, as do extreme nationalists elsewhere, to incorporate all Ukrainians in one state through the annexation of Ukrainian ethnographic territory in neighboring states.

One of the main lessons from the case of Ukraine is not to equate ethnic nationalism with nationalism. This leads scholars to produce an overly wide list of "nationalist" parties and leaders, and it feeds into the perception of nationalism as something negative—leading to chauvinism and ethnic tensions. Nationalism can be either good or bad and has existed in all nation-states since the late eighteenth century. This is especially important in the period following the establishment of independence. Groups supporting the pursuit of independence are easy to label *nationalist.* Once nationalism is achieved, it becomes more important for scholars to think carefully about those they consider—and, especially, do not consider—nationalists.

Another, related, lesson for scholars is to be careful about how they portray the nationalism of parties on the right and the left of the political spectrum. In Ukraine, Rukh has been criticized for supporting ethnic nationalist policies and therefore labeled (again, in the bad ethnic sense) *nationalist.* But as described in detail in this chapter, Rukh's policies are much more accurately labeled as *civic nationalism,* particularly given the group's strong support for polyethnic rights for national minorities, its rejection of any anti-Semitism, and its backing for automatic citizenship.[114]

This makes Rukh an unusual bedfellow to its center-right allies in the West, such as Britain's Conservatives or Republicans in the United States, who are opponents of multiculturalism, polyethnic rights, and regional devolution.[115] Yet, ironically, it is the center-right parties in Ukraine that are labeled as *nationalists,* while similar parties in Western liberal democracies who are *opposed* to regional devolution and polyethnic rights rarely receive this label. They are, simply, *conservatives.*

On the other hand, scholars have been to quick to label parties of Ukraine's left as *antistate,* seeking reunion of Ukraine and Russia. This has been particularly misleading since the late 1990s. The 1998, 1999, 2002, and 2004 parliamentary and presidential elections witnessed the evolution of Ukraine's political spectrum toward a left committed to state independence. Although President Kuchma attempted to portray himself as the only defender of independence (as, ironically, Kravchuk had in 1994 against Kuchma), the reality was that only three of the thirteen presidential candidates in the 1999 election supported Ukraine's integration into another union.

Scholars should not look to political leaders for guidance on how to label a country's political parties. Like it or not, left-wing civic nationalists have arrived on the Ukrainian political scene, and they can build upon a wealthy tradition of Ukrainian socialist thought, going back over one hundred years, that links social, economic, political, and national issues.

There is much that could have been covered in this chapter but was not. I have discussed in greater detail elsewhere the far right nationalist groups in Ukraine in the post-Soviet period.[116] While important in framing the question of an independent state in the late Soviet period, their unwillingness to abandon ethnic nationalist ideas has left them marginalized and politically irrelevant since independence. I leave to further study the question of the acceptance of the civic nationalist project at the mass level, especially in a setting of continued political and economic difficulty.[117] The creation of an integrated civic nation is slowly progressing in Ukraine, and consensus is growing among the ruling elites as to its outlines and policies.[118] By 2002, two years after the Ukrainian economy began to grow for the first time since the late 1980s, support for Ukrainian independence had returned to the high levels recorded in the December 1991 referendum.[119] During Ukraine's independence the political landscape changed sufficiently to facilitate mobilization in the 2004 Orange Revolution and Yushchenko's election: civic nationalism had emerged victorious in Ukraine.

NOTES

1. See Taras Kuzio, "Kuchma to Yushchenko: Ukraine's 2004 Elections and 'Orange Revolution,'" *Problems of Post-Communism* 52, no. 1 (March–April 2005): 29–44.

2. Including the Federation for the State Independence of Ukraine (known by its abbreviation DSU), the Social National Party, and the Congress of Ukrainian Nationalists (ideological heirs to the Stepan Bandera faction of the Organization of Ukrainian Nationalists).

3. With 3.5 million members the CPU was the largest republican party in the USSR until the Russian SFSR created its own republican communist party in 1990. Imperial Communists had no political representation during the illegality of the CPU (August 1991–October 1993).

4. O. Haran and O. Mayboroda, *Ukraiins'ki Livi: Mizh Leninizmom I Sotsial-Demokratieu* (Kyiv: KM Academia, 2000), 212.

5. For an elaboration of this argument see David. G. Rowley, "Imperial versus National Discourse: The Case of Russia," *Nations and Nationalism* 6, pt. 1 (January 2000): 23–42; and Oleksandr Mayboroda, *Roiys'kyi Natsionalizm v Ukraiini (1991–1998rr)* (Kyiv: Kyiv Mohyla Academy, 1999), 4.

6. See Alexander J. Motyl, "The Myth of Russian Nationalism," *Sovietology, Rationality, Nationality: Coming to Grips with Nationalism in the USSR* (New York: Cambridge University Press, 1990), 161–73. In the former USSR, no Russian dissident group agitated for self-determination. Hence, the dissident groups' demands for the Soviet state to uphold human rights were less threatening than those of Ukrainian, Estonian, and other national democrats who sought to defend human *and* national rights (including self-determination), an ideology that was closer to nineteenth-century liberal nationalism than to universalist liberalism (see Bear F. Braumoeller, *Deadly Doves: Liberal Nationalism and the Democratic Peace in the Soviet Successor States* [Washington, DC: National Council on Eurasian and East European Research, 1996], as well as Richard Sakwa, *Russian Politics and Society* [London: Routledge, 1993], 98). The Russian SFSR was the only Soviet republic *not* to declare independence from the USSR, and it celebrates its "independence day" on the day it declared republican sovereignty in May 1990. The Russian SFSR was led by a democrat—Boris Yeltsin—and therefore it accepted the replacement of the USSR with the CIS (unlike Serbia, which was led from 1988 by a former Communist turned ethnic nationalist, Slobodan Milosevic). Nevertheless, Russia disagreed with Ukraine over the definition of the CIS as either a new confederation dominated by Russia or a "civilized divorce" as advocated by Ukraine (see chap. 1 in Paul D'Anieri, Robert Kravchuk, and T. Kuzio, *Politics and Society in Ukraine* [Boulder: Westview, 1999], 10–44).

7. See T. Kuzio, "Radical Nationalist Parties and Movements in Contemporary Ukraine before and after Independence: The Right and Its Politics, 1989–1994," *Nationalities Papers* 52, no. 2 (summer 1997): 211–42.

8. See T. Kuzio, "Ukraine One Year after 'Kuchmagate,'" *RFE/RL Newsline* 5, no. 224, pt. 2 (November 28, 2001).

9. See I. V. Diyak, *Khto Zakhystyt; Nash Narod I Derzhavu: Komunistychna Partiya Ukrayiny chy Ukraiins'ka Komunistychna Partiya? Shtrykhy do Istorii ta S'ohodennia Kompartii Ukraiini* (Kyiv: Naukova Knyha and Nova Literatura, 2000). On presidential clone parties see T. Kuzio, "The 2002 Parliamentary Elections in Ukraine: Democratisation or Authoritarianism," *Journal of Communist Studies and Transition Politics* 19, no. 2 (June 2003): 24–54.

10. Prior to December 1991, Rukh was supported by the PDRU in parliament in the Democratic Bloc.

11. The "Imperial Communists" also jumped ship and backed the parliamentary vote, but in this group's case it was out of fear of the anti-Communist Yeltsin leadership in Moscow.

12. The Gorbachev era is covered in T. Kuzio, *Ukraine: Perestroika to Independence,* 2nd ed. (London and New York: Macmillan and St. Martin's Press, 2000).

13. Z. V. Kas'ianov, "Ukrayins'kyi natsionalizm: Problema naukovoho pereosmyslennia," *Ukraiins'kyi Istorychnyi Zhurnal* 2 (1998): 39–54.

14. See T. Kuzio, "Identity and Nation Building in Ukraine: Defining the 'Other,'" *Ethnicities* 1, no. 3 (December 2001): 343–65.

15. Michael Billig, *Banal Nationalism* (London: Sage, 1995).

16. Such a wide definition of civic nationalism is consistent with Kas'ianov's study of Ukrainian nationalism that defines it from the center-left through centrist parties to the center-right. I agree with Kas'ianov's framework, which defines Ukrainian nationalism in a broader manner to that of integral nationalism. See Kas'ianov, "Ukraiins'kyi natsionalizm."

17. Andrew Wilson, "Ukraine: Two Presidents and Their Powers," in *Postcommunist Presidents,* ed. Ray Taras (Cambridge: Cambridge University Press, 1997), 83.

18. As Paul D'Anieri points out, "Compared to most other states in the world and in the region, Ukraine's politics is still a very nationalist one." See Paul D'Anieri, *Economic Interdependence in Ukrainian-Russian Relations* (Albany: State University Press of New York, 1999), 201. It is consequently unclear why "nationalists" are only to be found among Ukrainophones in western Ukraine.

19. Neil Malcolm, Alex Pravda, Roy Allison, and Margo Light, *Internal Factors in Russian Foreign Policy* (Oxford: Oxford University Press, 1996), 87.

20. Malcolm, Pravda, Allison, and Light, *Internal Factors in Russian Foreign Policy,* 131.

21. D'Anieri, *Economic Interdependence in Ukrainian-Russian Relations,* 176.

22. Ibid., 203.

23. Oleh Derhachov, "Presidential Elections and Foreign Policy of Ukraine" (Center for Peace, Conflict and Foreign Policy of Ukraine, Kyiv, October 1999).

24. For an early discussion see T. Kuzio, "Nationalism in Ukraine: Towards a New Framework," *Politics* 20, no. 2 (May 2000): 77–86.

25. The only exception is Stephen Shulman, "Nationalist Sources of International Economic Integration," *International Studies Quarterly* 44, no. 3 (September 2000): 365–90. The more common viewpoint of defining nationalism in a very narrow sense is to be found in Paul Kubicek, "Regional Polarisation in Ukraine: Public Opinion, Voting and Legislative Behaviour," *Europe-Asia Studies* 52, no. 2 (March 2000): 273–74; Sarah Birch, *Elections and Democratization in Ukraine* (London: Macmillan, 2000), 29;

and Andrew Wilson, *The Ukrainians: Unexpected Nation* (New Haven, CT: Yale University Press, 2000), 163, 182, 184, 203.

26. As Molchanov points out, Ukraine has experienced "selective nationalism" while "popular nationalism," which might have led to ethnic nationalism, has been mooted. Mikhail A. Molchanov, "Post-communist Nationalism as a Power Resource: A Russian-Ukrainian Comparison," *Nationalities Papers* 28, no. 2 (June 2000): 283. But who better to quote than the leader of the CPU, Petro Symonenko, who argues that ethnic nationalism is weak throughout Ukraine, including in western Ukraine (*Tserkalo Tyzhnia,* September 16, 2000). The image of a nationalist western Ukraine does not square with the ethnic Ukrainian nationalist election bloc National Front obtaining only slightly more votes than the left and pro-Russian organizations in L'viv oblast in the 1998 parliamentary elections. See Volodymyr Kulyk, *Ukraiins'kyi Nationalizm u Nezalezhniy Ukraiini* (Kyiv: Kyiv Mohyla Academy, 1998), 58.

27. See Kubicek, "Regional Polarisation in Ukraine"; and Anatol Lieven, "Russkoyazychnye Regiony Ukrayiny: Troyanski Kon'?" in *Ukraina I Rossiya: Obshchestva I Gosudarstva,* ed. D. E. Furman (Moscow: Prava Cheloveka, 1997), 224, 226, 233, 246, 253.

28. Oleksandr Mayboroda points out that the main political force in support of the "Russian great power idea" in Ukraine is the CPU. See Mayboroda, *Rosiys'kyi Natsionalizm v Ukraiini (1991–1998rr),* 27.

29. Ukrainian Television-1, October 4, 1999.

30. "Russian and Ukrainian culture, despite language and local differences, represent a single whole," Bazyliuk told the convention of his Civic Congress. Quoted from Shulman, "Nationalist Sources of International Economic Integration," 386.

31. Andrew Wilson, *The Ukrainians,* 309. On Russian perceptions of Ukrainians see Tor Bukkvoll, "Off the Cuff Politics—Explaining Russia's Lack of a Ukraine Strategy," *Europe-Asia Studies* 53, no. 8 (December 2001): 1141–57; and Vera Tolz, *Russia: Inventing the Nation* (London: Arnold; New York: Oxford University Press, 2001), 209–34.

32. Mayboroda, *Rosiys'kyi Natsionalizm v Ukraiini (1991–1998rr),* 19.

33. On the Lukashenka phenomenon see Steven M. Eke and Taras Kuzio, "Sultanism in Eastern Europe: The Socio-Political Roots of Authoritarian Populism in Belarus," *Europe-Asia Studies* 52, no. 3 (May 2000): 523–47.

34. Kolstø, Pål, *Political Construction Sites: Nation-Building in Russia and the Post-Soviet States* (Boulder: Westview, 2000): 162.

35. *Den',* May 22, 1997; Andrew Wilson, "The Long March of the Ukrainian Left: Backwards towards Communism, Sideways to Social-Democracy or Forwards to Socialism?" *Masaryk Journal* 3, no. 1 (January 2000): 130.

36. Interview with the sociologist Yevhen Holovakha in *Den',* October 24, 2000. Birch disagrees: "Russian ethnicity can thus be expected to be a more distinct determinate of voting behaviour than Ukrainian ethnicity." Birch, *Elections and Democratization in Ukraine,* 28.

37. On the weakness of Russian nationalism see T. Kuzio, "Russians and Russophones in the Former USSR and Serbs in Yugoslavia: A Comparative Study of Passivity and Mobilisation," *RFERL East European Perspectives* 5, nos. 13, 14, 15 (June 25, 2003; July 9, 2003; July 23, 2003).

38. Haran and Mayboroda, *Ukraiins'ki Livi,* 206.

39. President Lukashenka has promoted these policies since 1994 in Belarus.

40. In December 2001 the Prosecutor's Office in the Crimea launched criminal proceedings against the *Russkii Krym* newspaper, organ of the ethnic nationalist Russian Movement of the Crimea, because of anti-Semitic articles it had published. The charges could have led to the newspaper being banned.

41. Kas'ianov, "Ukraiins'kyi natsionalizm," 49.

42. Mikhail A. Molchanov believes that Ukraine's and Russia's elites use nationalism less for modernization than in a struggle over resources. See Molchanov, "Post-communist Nationalism as a Power Resource," 284.

43. *Holos Ukrayiny,* December 25, 1998.

44. See T. Kuzio, *Ukraine: State and Nation Building* (London: Routledge, 1998).

45. SLON was created by the Constitutional Democrats and Interregional Bloc of Reforms (IRBR). The latter had been an ally of Kuchma's in 1994. Its leader, Vladimir Grynev, was a former leading member of New Ukraine. The IRBR merged with the oligarch People's Democratic Party in 2001.

46. See Anatol Lieven, "The Weakness of Russian Nationalism," *Survival* 41, no. 2 (summer 1999): 53–70.

47. D'Anieri, *Economic Interdependence in Ukrainian-Russian Relations,* 22. See also T. Kuzio, "Historiography and National Identity among the Eastern Slavs: Towards a New Framework," *National Identities* 3, no. 2 (July 2001):109–32.

48. David D. Laitin, *Identity in Formation: The Russian-Speaking Population in the Near Abroad* (Ithaca, NY: Cornell University Press, 1998), 291.

49. See the interview with Patriarch Filaret, head of the Ukrainian Orthodox Church—Kyiv Patriarch in *Tserkalo Tyzhnia,* August 5–11, 2000.

50. See Dominique Arel, "Language Politics in Independent Ukraine: Towards One or Two State Languages?" *Nationalities Papers* 23, no. 3 (September 1995): 597–622.

51. See Jan Janmaat, *Nation-Building in Post-Soviet Ukraine: Educational Policy and the Response of the Russian-Speaking Population* (Amsterdam: Netherlands Geographical Studies, 2000). See my review article in *Journal of Ukrainian Studies* 25, nos. 1–2 (summer–winter 2000): 200–213.

52. The language question has never even been straightforward for the CPU. At its second congress in 1995, 159 (or 40 percent) out of 390 delegates opposed supporting Russian as a second state language. Many of those who opposed this policy were from western Ukraine.

53. Mayboroda, *Rosiys'kyi Natsionalizm v Ukraiini (1991–1998rr),* 25. "The final goals of the communists and Russian nationalists are the same," Ukrainian authors believe. See Yu. M. Alekseyev, S. V. Kul'chytskyi, and A. H. Sliusarenko, *Ukraiina na zlami istorychnykh epokh (Derzhavotvorchyi protses 1985–1999rr.)* (Kyiv: Eksor, 2000), 145.

54. Laitin, *Identity in Formation,* 100, 101, 141, 142; and Dominique Arel, "Ukraine: The Temptation of the Nationalizing State" in *Political Culture and Civil Society in the Former Soviet Union,* ed. Vladimir Tismaneanu (Armonk, NY: M. E. Sharpe, 1995), 294. For an alternative view see T. Kuzio, "Nation Building or Nationalizing State? A Survey of the Theoretical Literature and Empirical Evidence," *Nations and Nationalism* 7, pt. 2 (April 2001): 135–54.

55. See T. Kuzio, "The Myth of the Civic State: A Critical Survey of Hans Kohn's Framework for Understanding Nationalism," *Ethnic and Racial Studies* 25, no. 1 (January 2002): 20–39.

56. Jack Snyder, *From Voting to Violence: Democratization and Nationalist Conflict* (New York: W. W. Norton, 2000), 25, 199, 250, 257, 258–59; and Teresa Rakowska-Harmstone, "Nationalism and Communist Multi-Ethnic Polities: The Legacies of Ethnicization," in *Cultures and Nations of Central and Eastern Europe: Essays in Honor of Roman Szporluk,* ed. Zvi Gitelman, Lubomyr Hajda, John-Paul Himka, and Roman Solchanyk (Cambridge, MA: Harvard University Press, 2000), 504–5.

57. The exception is scholars and political leaders in Ukraine. Rukh, Democratic, Reforms and Order, and Christian Democratic parties are usually labeled as *center-right,* not *nationalist,* ones. See O. M. Volkov, *Politychna Ideolohiya* (Kyiv: Stylos, 1999), 81–83, 127. Jack Snyder agrees with this commonly used definition in Ukraine. See Snyder, *From Voting to Violence,* 25, 199, 250, 257, 258–59. Andrew Wilson disagrees and argues that they are better defined as ethnic nationalists. See his *Ukrainian Nationalism in the 1990s: A Minority Faith* (Cambridge: Cambridge University Press, 1997), 137, and *The Ukrainians,* 79.

58. Paul Kubicek, "Dynamics of Contemporary Ukrainian Nationalism: Empire-Breaking to State Building," *Canadian Review of Studies in Nationalism* 23, nos. 1–2 (1996): 39–50; and Paul Kubicek, "What Happened to the Nationalists in Ukraine?" *Nationalism and Ethnic Politics* 5, no. 1 (spring 1999): 29–45.

59. Laitin, *Identity in Formation,* 100–101, 141–42.

60. Arel, "Ukraine," 294.

61. Wilson, *Ukrainian Nationalism in the 1990s,* 112, 114.

62. *Kievskiye Vedomosti,* September 2, 1997.

63. Quoted from the election program of Hennadiy Udovenko, head of one wing of Rukh, in *Uriadovyi Kurier,* September 23, 1999.

64. John Jaworsky, "Nationality Policy and Potential for Inter-ethnic Conflict in Ukraine," in *Managing Diversity in Plural Societies: Minorities, Migration and Nation-Building in Post-Communist Europe,* ed. Magda Opalski (Ottawa: Forum Eastern Europe, 1998), 117–18.

65. The new nationalist right in Western Europe includes the Freedom Party (Austria), Northern League (Italy), Flemish Bloc (Belgium), People's Party (Switzerland), Republican Party (Germany), and National Front (France). This definition of nationalist parties does not include conservative or Christian Democratic parties but parties whose policies toward citizenship, the franchise, and minorities are not civic or inclusive. See Ian Hall and Magali Perrault, "The Re-Austrianisation of Central Europe?" *Central European Review* 2, no. 13 (April 3, 2000).

66. The only exception is the Congress of Ukrainian Nationalists, which, after much initial hesitation, was finally allowed to join the Our Ukraine bloc. On centrist parties see T. Kuzio, "Reformers Face Limited Choices," *Kyiv Post,* July 2, 2002.

67. Quoted from the speech by Prime Minister Valery Pustovoitenko to the congress of the All-Ukrainian Democratic Forces Association (*Uriadovyi Kurier,* September 7, 1999).

68. Ibid.

69. See T. Kuzio, "Centre-Periphery Relations in Ukraine: Regionalism, Federalism and National Integration," in *Federalism and Decentralization in Eastern and Central Europe,* ed. Jurgen Rose and Johannes Raut (Frankfurt: Carl Lang Verlag, 2002), 329–48.

70. Via'acheslav Shved, "The Conceptual Approaches of Ukrainian Political Par-

ties to Ethno-Political Problems in Independent Ukraine," *Journal of Ukrainian Studies* 19, no. 2 (winter 1994): 69–84.

71. H. Kas'ianov, *Teorii Natsii ta Natsionalizm* (Kyiv: Lybid, 1999), 326. In 1917–21, Ukraine's various independent governments were socialist (except for the conservative monarchist government of 1918), supporting initially federal ties with Russia and then independence. Such a civic nationalist tradition within socialism was a result of the strong interconnection in Ukraine between the socioeconomic and national questions. The Communist Party (Bolshevik) of Ukraine (CP[B]U) had only 4,300 members in the whole of Ukraine in mid-1918. As Magosci points out, "The party itself was foreign to Ukraine." See Paul R. Magosci, *A History of Ukraine* (Toronto: University of Toronto Press, 1996), 531. The establishment of the Ukrainian SSR by invading Bolshevik forces created a territorial entity devoid of national content. This forced the Bolsheviks to agree to a policy of indigenization that was promoted by the Borotbists (Ukrainian Social Revolutionaries), who had merged with the CP(B)U. In the 1920s the Soviet regime's policy of indigenization allowed for Ukrainianization, which was supported by Ukrainian national Communists seeking to link socialism with the national idea. On national communism in Ukraine, see Bohdan Nahaylo, *The Ukrainian Resurgence* (London: Hurst, 1998), 11, 31–32, 263, 281, 316, 339, 341. Nahaylo points out that in the 1920s Ukraine's national Communists supported a confederal USSR (as they did between March 1990 and August 23, 1991), the "unfinished business of nation-state building," the de-Russification of cities, and the Ukrainianization of education (p.11). By 1933–34 the policy had been halted with an artificial famine, great terror, and reimposition of traditional Russian historiography. Ukrainian national communism was never totally extinguished but reappeared during times of liberalization in the 1960s and the late Gorbachev era in the form of "sovereign communism."

72. "The Latin American Pressure Cooker," *STATFORCOM, Global Intelligence Update,* December 30, 1999, http://www.stratfor.com.

73. O. Tkachenko, interviewed in *Holos Ukrayiny,* March 31, 1999.

74. *Holos Ukrayiny,* September 18, 1998.

75. *Holos Ukrayiny,* December 26, 1998.

76. See the comments by speakers at the left speakers' rally on May 1 (*Interfax,* May 1, 1999).

77. Nahaylo, *The Ukrainian Resurgence,* 495.

78. Interviewed in *Sil'ski Visti,* September 10, 1999.

79. *Holos Ukrayiny,* September 8, 1999.

80. *Holos Ukrayiny,* December 26, 1998.

81. Appeal of the left-center parliamentary faction (*Kievskiye vedomosti,* May 21, 1999).

82. Heorhiy Kruchkov, Communist and former head of the parliamentary commission on defense and security (*Holos Ukrayiny,* June 8, 1999).

83. *Ukrainian Weekly,* July 11, 1999.

84. Petro Symonenko, "Kolonizatsiya Ukrayiny: Rik S'iomyi," *Holos Ukrayiny,* November 21, 1997; *Holos Ukrayiny,* May 23, 1998; and *Intelnews,* November 16, 1999

85. Petro Symonenko, "Novitne Istoriya Ukrayiny: Pochatok Vidrodzhennia chy Prodovzhennia Natsional'noii Trahediia?" *Tserkalo Tyzhnia,* September 16, 2000.

86. Natalia Vitrenko, leader of the Progressive Socialists, quoted on Ukrainian Television-1, September 23, 1999.

87. V. Semeniuk, "Samovbyvcha polityka menshovartosti," *Holos Ukrayiny,* June 30, 1999. Tkachenko said on Ukrainian Television-1 (September 20, 1999) that Ukrainians "are now deprived from ruling the country and are playing someone else's tune."

88. Julius W. Friend, "Nationalism: The Guiding Thread in French Policy, 1981–1996" (paper prepared for the American Political Science Association, Washington, DC, August 28–31, 1997).

89. Comments by Natalia Vitrenko, leader of the Progressive Socialists, in *Kyiv Post,* September 9, 1999.

90. ITAR-TASS, October 9, 1999.

91. He rose to his position from that of first deputy chairman of the Council of Ministers, whereas Lukashenka became president from his post as director of a collective farm. See ibid.

92. Ibid.

93. O. Tkachenko on Ukrainian Television-1, September 20, 1999.

94. *Zerkalo Nedeli,* August 28–September 3, 1999.

95. *Holos Ukrayiny,* August 21, 1999.

96. *Holos Ukrayiny,* January 16, 1998.

97. *Holos Ukrayiny,* September 8, 1999.

98. Oleksandr Moroz, "Nam ne potribna ani 'spetsial'na' ani prosto 'zona,'" *Holos Ukrayiny,* August 26, 1999.

99. Left-center parliamentary faction statement in *Holos Ukrayiny,* September 9, 1998.

100. O. Tkachenko in *Holos Ukrayiny,* September 24, 1998.

101. O. Tkachenko in *Ukraiina moloda,* October 15, 1998.

102. Left-center parliamentary faction statement in *Sil'ski Visti,* January 15, 1998. Symonenko, leader of the Communists, also denounced the fact that Ukraine "has virtually lost its economic and political independence" (*Holos Ukrayiny,* September 1, 1999). After the victory of Kuchma in the October–November 1999 presidential elections, defeated Communist leader Symonenko warned that Ukraine "will begin to quickly lose its economic independence" (*Intelnews,* November 16, 1999).

103. O. Tkachenko on his "National Program for Ukraine's Revival" (*Holos Ukrayiny,* May 27, 1999).

104. *Holos Ukrayiny,* August 19, 1999. Tkachenko blamed the "destructive experiment" and "senseless reforms" conducted in the former USSR and Ukraine over the last fifteen years for the "economic collapse" that led to a "threat to its existence" and Ukrainian statehood (*Holos Ukrayiny,* September 8, 1999). Ukraine therefore needed to elect a "savior of the Motherland" (ITAR-TASS, August 21, 1999).

105. *Holos Ukrayiny,* August 26, 1999.

106. Ibid.

107. O. Tkachenko, addressing Odesa deputies (*Holos Ukrayiny,* December 9, 1998).

108. Interview with O. Tkachenko in *Nezavisimost,* September 16, 1998.

109. O. Moroz, to the sixth congress of the Socialist Party (*Ukrayina moloda,* June 16, 1998).

110. *Holos Ukrayiny,* April 30, 1996.

111. O. Moroz, "Livyi Marsh," *Viche* 9 (1999): 22.

112. See Philip G. Roeder, "Peoples and States after 1989: The Political Costs of Incomplete Revolutions," *Slavic Review* 58, no. 4 (winter 1999): 854–81; T. Kuzio, "Stateness and Institutions in Ukraine: A Theoretical and Comparative Introduction" in *State and Institution Building in Ukraine*, ed. T. Kuzio, R. S. Kravchuk, and P. D. D'Anieri (New York: St. Martin's Press, 1999), 1–24; and T. Kuzio, "Transition in Post-Communist States: Triple or Quadruple?" *Politics*, September 2001, 169–78.

113. See T. Kuzio, "Muddling Along: The First Decade of Ukrainian Independence," *Harriman Review* 14, no. 3 (fall 2001). On Ukraine's multiparty system see T. Kuzio, "Ukraine's Approaching Elections and Fractured Multiparty System," *RFE/RL Newsline* 5, no. 220, pt. 2 (November 20, 2001).

114. See Lowell Barrington, "The Domestic and International Consequences of Citizenship in the Soviet Successor States," *Europe-Asia Studies* 47, no. 5 (July 1995): 731–63; and Yuri I. Shevchuk, "Citizenship in Ukraine: A Western Perspective," in *State and Nation Building in East Central Europe: Contemporary Perspectives*, ed. S. J. Micgiel (New York: Institute on East Central Europe, Columbia University, 1996), 351–69.

115. In addition, while Rukh is commonly defined as nationalist, the Polish Solidarity movement is not. At the same time, Rukh supports many nationality policies more commonly associated with social democratic and liberal parties in Western democracies.

116. T. Kuzio, "Radical Nationalist Parties and Movements in Contemporary Ukraine before and after Independence"; and T. Kuzio, "Radical Right Parties and Civic Groups in Belarus and Ukraine," in *The Revival of Right-Wing Extremism in the Nineties*, ed. Peter H. Merkl and Leonard Winberg (London: Frank Cass, 1997), 203–30.

117. Lowell Barrington found that the most popular identity in Ukraine at the mass level was citizenship (i.e., state or civic), followed by ethnic and linguistic. See his "Russian-Speakers in Ukraine and Kazakhstan: 'Nationality,' 'Population,' or Neither?" *Post-Soviet Affairs* 17, no. 2 (April–June 2001): 129–58.

118. See W. Zimmerman, "Is Ukraine a Political Community?" *Communist and Post Communist Studies* 31, no. 1 (1998): 43–55.

119. See T. Kuzio, "Support for Independence Returns to 1991 Levels," *RFERL Poland, Belarus and Ukraine Report* 5, no. 2 (January 21, 2003).

APPENDIX: VIEWS OF ETHNIC AND CIVIC NATIONALISM IN UKRAINE AND THE GROWTH OF UKRAINIAN CIVIC NATIONALISM

In this appendix, I use two figures to summarize the arguments presented in the chapter about civic and ethnic nationalism in Ukraine. Figure 1 is a model of the way scholars have traditionally thought about political parties in Ukraine and where they fall on a political spectrum from ethnic Russian and Soviet to ethnic Ukrainian. As the text of the chapter points out, while some scholars have had an even more narrow version of nationalism in Ukraine—only considering Ukrainian ethnic nationalist parties to be "nationalist"—many have also recognized the "nationalist" features of the ethnic Russian parties.

But even this understanding of ethnic Russian parties as nationalist has missed the extent to which the major political parties in Ukraine came to accept the basic ideas of the civic nationalist approach during the 1990s. Figure 2 charts what I describe in the chapter as the development of attachment to the principles of civic nationalism by the major parties in Ukraine from the late Soviet period through thee first half-decade of independence. It is, therefore, a graphic representation of the victory of civic nationalism in Ukraine.

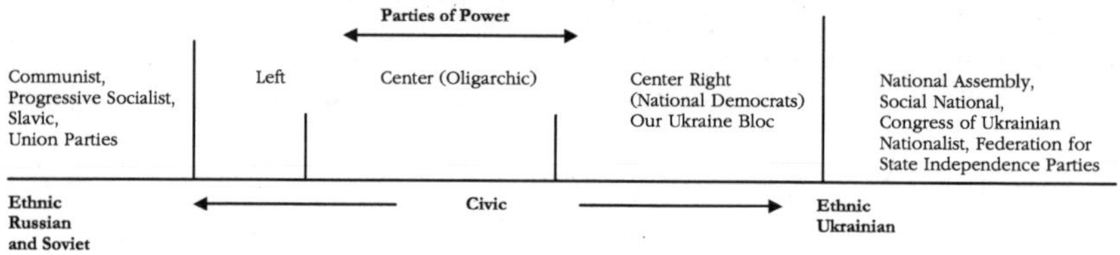

Fig. 1. A spatial model of the traditional view of civic and ethnic nationalism of the major political parties in Ukraine

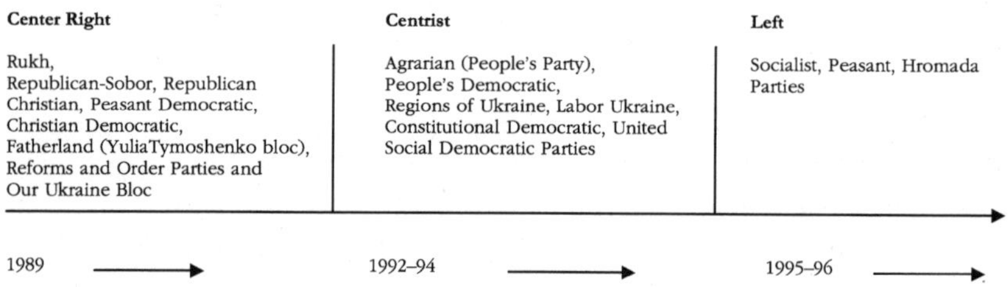

Fig. 2. The acceptance of civic nationalism in Ukraine by the major political parties in Ukraine

9. Post-Soviet Armenia

Nationalism & Its (Dis)contents

RAZMIK PANOSSIAN

THE NATIONALIST FERVOR that engulfed Soviet Armenia in early 1988 was one of the major flash points that led to the eventual collapse of the USSR. The resulting ethnic conflict over the enclave of Nagorno-Karabakh (*Lernayin Gharabagh* or *Artsakh* in Armenian) evolved into a major undeclared war between Armenia and Azerbaijan. Following the cease-fire of 1994, passions cooled somewhat, and nationalist discourse declined. While ethnonational sentiments still exist in Armenia, they are no longer the basis of politics.

This chapter does not evaluate Armenian nationalism in toto. Diasporan nationalism and politics, for example, are not covered. Rather, the chapter focuses on the politics of nationalism in Armenia since 1988. I argue that nationalist considerations and ideology are no longer prevalent in Armenian politics. Instead, an era of "postnationalist" politics has emerged, in which elites are preoccupied with issues of power and economic gain and the main issues in the political sphere relate to socioeconomic policies and day-to-day concerns. There is a difference between the "politics of nationalism"—that is, policies and acts that emanate from concerns regarding the interest of the nation (however defined)—and the use of nationalism to advance narrow political interests and gains. In Armenia, the shift from the former to the latter occurred between 1992 and 1995. It was epitomized with the September 1996 presidential election, in which nationalist rhetoric, symbols, and slogans were instrumentally used for electoral purposes. Three years later, the parliamentary shootings on October 27, 1999, killed the spirit of nationalism. On that day, the era of 1988 metaphorically came to an end.

This analysis of the (d)evolution of Armenian nationalism is divided into three parts. The first section provides a brief historical overview of nationalism under Soviet rule. The second deals with the 1988–91 period. The third and longest part covers the postindependence period.

Background: Nationalist *and* Soviet

> The Communists first saved Armenia from guaranteed destruction in 1920. They took it out of the mouth of the lion or the crocodile and saved it. After, they began to build it up. By the 1930s, the Communist leadership of Armenia had already developed a sense of national identity and [the drive for] national development. Subsequent first secretaries and other leaders continued this and strengthened it. We prepared the country for independence, to be a strong republic. Hence, we did two things: (a) kept national identity unique and developed it further and (b) built a strong economic base; we developed the country. This was very obvious by the 1960s. . . . I am very proud that as First Secretary, 20 percent of the history of Soviet Armenia belongs to me![1]

This statement from Karen Demirchian, who led Armenia from 1974 to 1988, is indicative of the prevalence of nationalist sentiments within the Soviet Armenian political elite. Needless to say, it was easy for Demirchian to claim to be a nationalist in 1997, and he overstated the point in an ostentatious manner. Nationalist opponents of the Communist regime in 1988 had a long list of grievances and arguments as to why the Communist Party of Armenia was not defending national interests. Nevertheless, Demirchian presented a view that is quite widely accepted in postindependence Armenia: that the Soviet Armenian leadership *used* communism to build the nation and that most Armenian intellectuals, political leaders, and even some party apparatchiks—especially after Stalin's death—pursued nationalist goals within the confines of the USSR.

Until 1988, Armenians did not tend to contrast communism with a strong projection of national identity. Karlen Dallakian, another member of the pre-1988 Communist Party elite, puts it forcefully in the preface of his memoirs: "I reject with anger any attempt to contrast the Armenian with the Communist. All the Communists, be they members or leaders, have been the most real and the most authentic Armenians during the entire 70 year period of Armenia's development [and] the construction of its national character."[2] Even the anti-Communist nationalist leader, Vazgen Manukian, agreed with this point. In a speech during a 1995 visit to the United States, he said that communism was buried in Armenia long before the July 1995 parliamentary elections (which ousted the last remnants of delegates elected under Soviet rule). He then explained that the leadership in Soviet Armenia knew how to successfully "Armenianize" communism by applying it to the Armenian character.[3]

By 1988, Armenians had a clearly articulated and strong sense of national identity.[4] Armenian nationalism was linked to and expressed through culture, historiography, architecture, demographic trends, and other seemingly benign forms. It was clear who belonged to the nation: those who were *ethnically* Armenian—wherever they lived. It was a blood-based definition, incorporating within it, at least partially, linguistic and religious characteristics. The threat of survival came from "The Turk." Anti-Turkishness was rooted in the official Soviet view, popular culture, and sense of history. Importantly, *Turk* and *Azeri* were used interchangeably by the Armenians. In general, Armenians were not anti-Russian, although there emerged an anti-Russian phase in the nationalist movement between 1989 and 1990.[5] Most Armenians had internalized the view that Russia was indispensable to the survival of the country for security reasons. The "quiet nationalism" in Soviet Armenia envisioned the nation to be the ethnic group.

But it also had a powerful territorial component to it, either in the form of land claims or desire for autonomy.[6] The boundaries of the Armenian SSR were clear-cut, but they were not acceptable to many Armenians. The most immediate concern was Nagorno-Karabakh, the predominantly Armenian enclave in Azerbaijan. There was also Nakhichevan (in Azerbaijan as well), the Javakheti region (in Georgia), and, of course, western Armenia (the "lost lands" in Turkey). The Armenians could not raise some national issues without incurring the wrath of Moscow. If "cultural" nationalism was permitted, territorial demands against other Soviet republics were strictly "off limits." Soviet Armenian authorities, therefore, did not raise the issue of land claims, at least officially, on these territories.[7] But they were not forgotten, particularly Karabakh.

1988–91: The Storm Begins

The "quiet nationalism" became a very loud explosion on February 20, 1988, when the local Soviet of the Nagorno-Karabakh Oblast voted to request its transfer from the Azerbaijani SSR to the Armenian SSR. This unleashed pent-up frustrations and led to the Armenian-Azerbaijani conflict, which mostly involved the territorial dispute over Karabakh. The politics of nationalism dominated the Armenian political process between 1988 and early 1992. All other considerations were subjected to the logic of "national interests" and the struggle for Karabakh.

Using Mikhail Gorbachev's reforms as their basis, and the slogans of glasnost and perestroika, Armenian protestors, one million strong, demanded the unification of the Karabakh Oblast to their republic. This first wave of nationalism was *not* anti-Soviet or anti-Russian. It did not at all advocate independence. It simply sought to redress a perceived historical injustice and demanded the change of boundaries within the USSR. In the absence of a favorable response from central authorities, and due to the emergence of a non-Communist leadership within the movement, the scope of the demonstrations widened. More general and radical issues were incorporated (democratization, corruption, environmental degradation and other social problems) as part of the nationalist demands. Then the legitimacy of Soviet rule began to be questioned, the nationalist leadership started to vie for political power, and demands for autonomy and eventually independence were articulated—all within a period of two years. In August 1990, the nationalist counterelite assumed power and issued a Declaration *on* Independence, outlining Armenia's *intention* to secede from the USSR.[8]

The Emergence of Nationalist Organizations

Organizationally, a loose "Karabakh Committee" emerged to guide and coordinate the movement. Some of the early pro-Communist popular leaders and spokespersons (Igor Muradian, Zori Balayan, Sylva Kaputikian, etc.) were pushed aside, and a group of mostly non- or anti-Communist intellectuals (Vazgen Manukian, Rafael Ghazarian, Levon Ter-Petrosian, Babken Ararktsian, Vano Siradeghian, etc.) took over. In the fall of 1988, the committee reorganized itself into the Hayots Hamazgayin Sharjum (Armenian Pan-National Movement [ANM]). Its leaders were arrested in December 1988, during the chaotic weeks after the devastating earthquake in northern Armenia. Released six months later, they returned to Yerevan as heroes. Between 1990 and 1998, the ANM was the ruling political force in Armenia, with its candidate, Levon Ter-Petrosian, the president of the republic.

In addition to the ANM, two other parties had strong nationalist credentials and were factors in the movement. The first was Paruir Hairikian's Azgayin Inknoroshum Miavorum (National Self-Determination Union), which had its roots in the late 1960s anti-Soviet dissidentism. Hairikian had spent many years in Soviet jails for demanding independence for Armenia. Even though he always remained consistent with his demands for self-determination, his party never caught the imagination of the masses. Hairikian came to be known as "Mr. 5 percent" for consistently polling in the range of 5 percent during elections. In 1988, when the "mainstream" nationalists were not yet advocating independence, Hairikian was publishing pamphlet after pamphlet calling for Armenia's secession from the USSR.[9] This enabled him to maintain that he had always been "ahead of the times."[10]

The other important party was the main diaspora-based Hai Heghapokhakan Dashnaktsutiun (Armenian Revolutionary Federation [ARF or Dashnak]).[11] The ARF did not have a presence in Armenia until August 1990, when it formally registered in the country with much fanfare. It was not, therefore, involved in the nationalist mobilization. However, the party had great symbolic value, as the "vanguard" of Armenians' anti-Turkish and anti-Soviet struggle for national rights. It embodied the idea of independence and the "national cause"—including land claims.

In truth, the ARF was no more than a paper tiger. It had long dropped its sharp anti-Soviet stand and in fact came out against the mass protests and work stoppages in 1988. Nevertheless, many people in Soviet Armenia believed in the party's mythical strength and took its nationalistic rhetoric to heart. Forbidden ARF symbols (including the tricolor flag of the 1918–20 independent republic), past heroes, and (revolutionary) songs and literature provided much of the visual and ideological basis of the nationalist movement between 1988 and 1990.[12] Because of this, in the words of one commentator, "the feelings of the people toward the Dashnaktsutiun [ARF] in 1988–1989 had reached the level of religious reverence."[13] Even Levon Ter-Petrosian, who banned the ARF in December 1994, had earlier said that "if in 1988 the ARF had embraced the Armenian National Movement which had come into being on the [basis of an] ideology of independence [*an ex post facto assessment*—R.P.], it is highly probable that the Movement would have become assimilated into the ARF. . . . But the Dashnaktsutiun did not do that, and rejected us."[14] Despite the symbolic link between the ARF and the nationalist movement in Armenia, the relationship between them was problematic largely due to the ARF's incapability to come to terms with the indigenous Yerevan-based leadership of the ANM and its brand of pro-independence nationalism. From 1988 to 1998, relations between the two organizations were almost always adversarial.[15]

Nationalism in the Streets

The nationalist movement initially took the form of demonstrations in Yerevan. Up to a million people marched through the streets of the capital in the first week of the protests in February 1988. These were peaceful and orderly events, and they imbued a tremendous sense of solidarity among the participants and the entire nation. Everyone who took part in them spoke of a magical sense of unity and purpose.[16] The slogans were in line with glasnost and perestroika, with portraits of Gorbachev being paraded. People were not demonstrating against the USSR, or against Azerbaijan, but in favor of Karabakh's unification with Armenia, in the firm belief that justice was on their side and that the central authorities in Moscow would eventually redress past wrongs. The central stage of the demonstrations was Opera Square (eventually renamed Freedom Square), where various unofficial publications with nationalist themes were widely circulated.

As the months passed, it became obvious that Moscow was not going to solve the problem in favor of the Armenians. Even worse, central authorities denounced the Armenian protestors as "extremists" and "hooligans." Consequently, the demonstrators became more radical in their demands. Anti-Communist sentiments were expressed, Gorbachev was denounced, and forbidden nationalist symbols began to emerge. The means were radicalized as well, with mass work stoppages and hunger strikes becoming common.[17] To the credit of the Armenians, riots and anti-Azerbaijani pogroms did not take place in Yerevan or other Armenian cities, even though anti-Armenian pogroms had taken place in Azerbaijan.

This is not to say that all was well for the Azerbaijanis in Armenia. In late 1988, the entire Azerbaijani population (including Muslim Kurds)—some 167,000 people—was kicked out of the Armenian SSR. In the process, dozens of people died due to isolated Armenian attacks and adverse conditions. This population transfer was partially in response to Armenians being forced out of Azerbaijan, but it was also the last phase of the gradual homogenization of the republic under Soviet rule. The population transfer was the latest, and not so "gentle," episode of ethnic cleansing that increased Armenia's homogenization from 90 percent to 98 percent.[18] Nationalists, in collaboration with the Armenian state authorities, were responsible for this exodus. In addition, there were armed skirmishes between Azerbaijanis and Armenians in and around Karabakh, as well as at various border points (with scores of casualties). During this period, volunteer militias were formed by nationalists who went to defend Armenian villages in the Oblast and at the Azerbaijani border.[19] From the summer of 1988 onward, armed skirmishes became common, as central authorities were unable to stop them. Two years later, Gorbachev threatened to declare martial law in Armenia if these militias (most notably the so-called Armenian National Army) were not brought under control. Soon after he was elected chairman of the Armenian Supreme Soviet in August 1990, Levon Ter-Petrosian managed to assert some degree of authority over the militias.

In short, the nationalist movement in Armenia started in the form of peaceful demonstrations in solidarity with Karabakh Armenians. But in the absence of a favorable solution, Armenian nationalism was radicalized. Anti-Soviet sentiments emerged, and anti-Azerbaijani feelings were further entrenched. Initially, violence crept in in the form of the murder of Azerbaijanis in Armenia and border skirmishes. Eventually, violence escalated to a full-scale but undeclared war between Armenians and Azerbaijanis in and around Karabakh (i.e., within Azerbaijan).

The mass movement from below, with its alternative and non-Communist leadership, put the Communist Party of Armenia in a very difficult position. First Secretary Karen Demirchian was dismissed in May 1988, and Suren Harutiunian was appointed in his place. Harutiunian tried to appease the protestors by allowing certain freedoms and legalizing nationalist symbols such as the tricolor flag. He sought to bridge the gap between Moscow and the protestors on the streets. His basic approach was that national demands could and should be met through existing Communist structures. But it was increasingly clear to Armenians that as long as the ultimate decision lay in Gorbachev's Kremlin, their demands would not be met.[20]

In conclusion, four out of the five variants of nationalism mentioned in Lowell Barrington's introductory chapter applied to Armenian nationalism at the eve of the country's declaration of independence. First, there was a claim to *external territory* (the Karabakh Oblast). Second, Armenian nationalism was a response to *threats of territorial control* insofar as it was challenging Azerbaijani control over the enclave and demanding autonomy from Moscow. Third, the Karabakh movement was clearly driven by *the desire to protect co-nationals* in the Oblast. And, finally, the overarching characteristic of Armenian nationalism was *ethnic nation-protecting.* The only variant that did not apply was nationalism as civic nation-building; there was a strong democratization current between the summer of 1988 and 1991, but this was not about "nation-building" per se since it took the ethnic nation as its basis. At the time of independence, Armenian politics was almost exclusively based on national(ist) goals and interests. This trend—and the nationalism variants mentioned in the preceding—continued into the early postindependence period before giving way to postnationalist, "normal" politics.

1991–2001: The Emergence of Postnationalist Politics

Armenia's declaration of independence from the Soviet Union came after the failed August coup in Moscow, and it was solidified by the results of the September 21, 1991, referendum (which was scheduled in March to take place in September, i.e., it was planned before the coup attempt). Voter turnout was 95 percent, and the vote in favor of secession was 99 percent.[21] Although declared in September, Armenia's independence was not recognized by the international community until late December 1991, once the USSR had formally expired.

Soon after independence, it became clear that the unity around nationalist goals was indeed very fragile. As early as 1991, clearly visible tensions emerged within the elite of the ANM. Prime Minister Vazgen Manukian, one of the key founding members of the organization, and generally considered its ideologue, split from the party just before the 1991 presidential elections and formed the National Democratic Union (NDU). He agreed in 1992 to return and serve in the ANM government as defense minister until the summer of 1993, but he then resigned and became one of the fiercest opponents of Ter-Petrosian.[22] Another founding member, Ashot Manucharian, also quit the ANM and joined the ranks of the opposition.

The sharpest political battle up to 1996 was between the ANM and the ARF. The two organizations were at odds with one another from the very beginning of the nationalist movement. They disagreed over such fundamental issues as Armenia's independence, the direction of its foreign relations, the meaning of the Armenian Cause, the solution to the Karabakh conflict, the political and economic system that the country should adopt, and the diaspora's role.[23] These disagreements were manifested through drastic political measures. For example, when Dashnaks began to agitate for a coalition government in 1992, despite their disastrous performance in the 1991 presidential election,[24] Ter-Petrosian responded by expelling the leader of the party, the Athens-based Hrair Marukhian, from Armenia. As antagonisms sharpened, the most severe blow to the ARF came when Ter-Petrosian banned the organization and its press outright in December 1994, accusing it of assassinations, terrorist activities, drug trafficking, and attempts to destabilize the ANM government. The ARF remained officially banned because it was considered a "foreign organization." A dozen or so of its prominent members, as well as others, were jailed, with charges ranging from the possession of false documents to murder. The ARF was relegalized by Robert Kocharian, and most of its members released from prison, after Ter-Petrosian's forced resignation in February 1998.

Even though there were clear ideological and policy differences between the ANM and the ARF, their struggle was really about power and arrogance, and it was indicative of what was to replace the politics of nationalism of the 1988–92 period. It became clear between 1994 and 1995 that a shift had indeed taken place that led to "postnationalist" politics insofar as (1) the predominant goal in intraelite competition focused exclusively on obtaining or maintaining power, rather than "national interests," and (2) the main issues around which people mobilized related to social problems, economic crisis, corruption, and the impunity of the leadership; nationalism became, at best, a prism through which other issues were often expressed. At this point, nationalist symbols and rhetoric began to be *used* for political advancement rather than being the *basis* of political activity.

By using the term *postnationalist politics* in contrast to the politics of nationalism, I am not at all suggesting some sort of approval or disapproval, or implying a dichotomy of democratic/nondemocratic or good/bad. Postnationalist politics is about "everyday" politics, and it is about power and the administration of society (and in the post-Soviet setting, personal gain). In this sense, it is "normal" politics, as extraordinary or as corrupt as some of its means actually are. Political processes based exclusively or primarily on nationalist considerations, similar to revolutions, are not part of the "normal" politics because day-to-day (mundane) considerations are suspended or they are made subservient to the nationalist "logic."

The mass nationalist movement put "everyday" politics on the back burner in Armenia between 1988 and 1992. When normal politics began to reemerge soon after independence, it was kept in check due to the Karabakh war. During the first three years of independence, Armenia suffered the hardships resulting from the dual crisis of near total economic collapse and war with Azerbaijan (including the initially devastating economic blockade imposed by Azerbaijan and Turkey). National solidarity was maintained, people retained their resolve and hope, and nationalism remained the dominant paradigm of politics in the face of war over Karabakh, despite the many political tensions and divisions. Once the war ended (victoriously for the Armenians) and a cease-fire was signed in May 1994, political disagreements led to the fragmentation of national solidarity. Nationalism lost its unifying force and became a political tool.

Elections and the Intensification of Postnationalist Politics

The clearest way to demonstrate the victory of postnationalist politics over the politics of nationalism (and the latter's instrumentalization) is to analyze the 1996 presidential election,[25] the most important political event in between 1991 and the parliamentary assassinations of October 27, 1999. But, before I examine the presidential election, it is important first to mention briefly the 1995 parliamentary election; this was the precursor to the 1996 vote. The election was far from "clean." It was manipulated to ensure that the ANM and its supporters won enough seats to control the chamber. Simultaneous to the National Assembly election, the new Armenian constitution was accepted in a referendum. Opposition parties cried foul, but they were powerless to stop both the passing of the constitution (by 68 percent of the vote) and the irregularities, which ensured the victory of pro-ANM candidates.[26] For the opposition, and most Armenians, the irregularities of the 1995 election became the prism through which they approached the 1996 presidential vote. By 1995, the politics of idealism already had given way to the politics of party interests and material gain.

The September 22, 1996, election signaled the end of the politics of nationalism and the emergence of "normal" or "ordinary" politics. Maintaining power was considered above all else, and it was justified, as always, as being in the "benefit" of the nation. More than a presidential vote, the election was seen as a referendum on Ter-Petrosian's presidency. When the campaign officially began on August 23, there were seven candidates: Ter-Petrosian and six opposition leaders. On September 10, twelve days before the election, four of the six candidates, plus the officially banned ARF, joined together and formed a united front—the National Unity Pact (NUP), headed by Vazgen Manukian.[27] The hitherto lackluster campaign became an intense two-horse race between Manukian and Ter-Petrosian, two men who had made their political careers as colleagues in the Karabakh movement. The Communist Party's Sergei Badalian was a distant third.

What united the opposition was not a common program or a similar ideology, but simply the desire to unseat Ter-Petrosian and the ANM. It was made up of ideologically unlikely allies—from the right-wing approach of Paruir Hairikian to the nationalist and socialist Dashnaks—all held under the precarious leadership of Vazgen Manukian. The NUP put forth a vague common program, which stressed social issues, and promised to dissolve the National Assembly and to hold new parliamentary elections, as well as to rewrite the constitution in order to reduce the powers of the president. Other promises included increasing wages tenfold. More specifically, the key issues raised by the opposition included:

Corruption in government (viz., using public office for personal gain).

Impunity of state officials and members of government (viz., being above the law due to connections). This was a widespread and highly visible problem.

The very obvious discrepancy of income between the new economic elite (with close government ties) and the overwhelming majority of the population.

Issues of social welfare and the terrible economic conditions of the people.

The destruction of the industrial and productive capacity of the country as a consequence of privatization (often labeled as *looting*), as well as the squandering of Armenia's intellectual and academic resources due to neglect.

And, related to the preceding, the mass exodus of the population from Armenia in order to seek work abroad.

Note that these key issues were not related to nationalism, the Karabakh war, independence, national rights, or any of the other key nationalist issues. The election campaign centered on socioeconomic factors. The opposition capitalized on people's pent-up anger against the government and against Ter-Petrosian—who was blamed for all of the problems of the country and accused of only looking after his ANM cronies. The opposition leadership promised to put on trial those who had abused their office, and it promised "to clean house."

The key issues stressed by Ter-Petrosian in his campaign were captured in his election slogan: "Victory, Stability, Progress." The message was very clear: Yes, there are many problems, including corruption in government and difficult socioeconomic conditions. But there are no quick solutions, conditions are slowly improving, and the economy is growing. We should be realistic about our capabilities and resources. Look how well we have done in the past five years, given our difficult situation: we have won the war in Karabakh and provided some fundamental services, such as restoring a regular supply of electricity. People have more money to spend, and this is obvious with the number of new cars and cafes in Yerevan. A new middle class is emerging, and eventually all will benefit from this prosperity. Armenia is going forward, surely, securely, and with a cool head. We know what we are doing, and it is for the benefit of the country. The theme emphasized the most was stability and the dangers of "rocking the boat" in difficult conditions. The opposition was attacked for being a motley crew of adventurists who wanted power for its own sake, for making false promises, and for the guaranteed instability that would ensue if "extreme" nationalists like Vazgen Manukian came into power.

Despite the nonnationalist *issues,* almost the entire campaign, especially on the opposition side, was couched in the *terminology* and *imagery* of nationalism. The whole debate was put in terms such as *traitors, anti-nation* and *anti-Armenian, betrayers of national interests,* and so forth. Opposition leaders often said that the government was selling "national treasures" and the country's wealth to foreigners under the guise of privatization or that government leaders were "agents" of external powers under the guise of politicians and (diasporan) advisers. Of course, the same was said of the opposition by Ter-Petrosian supporters, as they accused the opposition of being "fascist," "extreme nationalist," and even taking money from Azerbaijani sources! Before the election, Vano Siradeghian of the ANM commented that whoever does not support the ANM is anti-Armenia. Both sides also used images from the nationalist movement of the past. The theme repeated most often by the opposition at its rallies was the similarities between its campaign and the 1988 movement; it maintained that people should unite for the sake of the nation and for the sake of democracy. Ter-Petrosian posters carried images of the 1988 rallies and of the victorious war in Karabakh.

The malicious nature of the vocabulary employed by the opposition reached its peak immediately after the military crackdown on the opposition (discussed in the following). The statements are indicative of the passions roused. On September 25, Paruir Hairikian declared at a rally: "Today, it is being decided who is Armenian and who is anti-Armenian. Whoever is not with us today is not Armenian." At another point, in a rally on November 1, he went further, saying of the government, "not only are they not Armenian, they are not human." Another opposition figure, Samvel Harutiunian, claimed on September 25 that the Armenian government was not different from the rule of Abdul Hamid (the "Red Sultan" responsible for hundreds of thousands of massacred Armenians in the 1890s) and Kemal Ataturk. Others equated Ter-Petrosian to Talaat Pasha, the architect of the 1915 Genocide and the epitome of evil for the Armenians. Of course, the rhetoric of the progovernment and pro-ANM side did not fall too far behind.

The use of such vocabulary was an attempt to redefine the unifying nationalism of 1988–92 in a way that excluded political opponents. Nationalism was made contingent on narrow political interests; who was in the "nation"—that is, who is the "us" versus the "them"—was reduced to the sharp political divisions.[28] People did not necessarily believe that their opponents were not actually Armenian, but the discourse utilized to explain internal political antagonisms, which had nothing to do with "core" national issues, was based on nationalistic categories.

Following Ter-Petrosian's dubious "victory" with 51.75 percent of the vote in the first round of the election,[29] the NUP organized a series of mass rallies. The opposition was not willing to allow Ter-Petrosian and the ANM to get away with stealing the election as they had done in the 1995 parliamentary vote. On September 25, the largest of these rallies turned violent as the opposition crowd, led by *some* of the leaders of the NUP (e.g., Arshak Sadoyan and Kim Balayan), attacked the Armenian parliament building. An unprecedented recourse to extralegal and violent means to obtain political power was thus introduced into Armenian politics. Parts of the National Assembly were ransacked, and the speaker and his deputy were beaten and taken hostage for a few hours. The government responded with a military crackdown: soldiers fired in the air, water cannons and tear gas were used on the night of the attack, and tanks and soldiers were stationed in the streets of Yerevan for weeks to come. Although the violence was limited, and there were no deaths, a taboo—that Armenians would not resort to violence against one another for political purposes—was broken on September 25, 1996. Power politics, in its brutal form, had clearly replaced national solidarity and nationalist goals, once considered "above" narrow political interests.

From Ter-Petrosian to Kocharian

Ter-Petrosian attempted to normalize Armenian politics between 1996 and 1998. His primary goals were to regain some legitimacy for his rule and, directly related to this, to improve the economic situation of the country. He appointed Armen Sarkissian as prime minister in November 1996, giving him a "carte blanche" to govern Armenia. Sarkissian, Armenia's ambassador to the United Kingdom, was a popular choice because of his clean image, his international connections, and his status as an "outsider" to the tarnished political process in Yerevan. However, Sarkissian had to resign within four months due to ill health.

In March 1997, Ter-Petrosian appointed Robert Kocharian, the president of the Nagorno-Karabakh Republic, as prime minister of Armenia. This surprised many Armenians, but Kocharian's appointment was welcomed as well. Being from Nagorno-Karabakh, he too was an "outsider" to the Yerevan scene. Whatever he lacked in terms of administrative experience, he made up for in terms of impeccable credentials as a war hero, although the political logic in Armenia at that point was that Kocharian's long-term success or failure was to be determined by his ability to deliver the "economic goods."

Kocharian's appointment proved to be Ter-Petrosian's undoing. Part of the latter's calculation in appointing Kocharian to a high office in Yerevan seemed to be related to his desire to negotiate a permanent peace settlement with Azerbaijan. Hence, it would have been useful to have Karabakh's popular leader as part of the team that would sign a potential peace agreement. The job of "selling" an accord with Azerbaijan—clearly based on compromises—to the Armenians of both Armenia and Karabakh would be easier if Kocharian, the prominent Karabakh leader, was backing it as prime minister. This calculation, however, backfired on Ter-Petrosian.

Kocharian was unwilling to compromise on Karabakh and astute enough to orchestrate the removal of Ter-Petrosian from office.

Ter-Petrosian was forced to resign in February 1998, less than a year after Kocharian's appointment. The intraelite power struggles, combined with the "core" nationalist issue of Nagorno-Karabakh, was a potent mix. Although politics had ceased to be about nationalism, compromise on Karabakh was still a potential pitfall for any politician, especially one whose legitimacy was so severely questioned. The pressure on Ter-Petrosian came from within the political elite and, more important, from within his own entourage: Kocharian, Interior Minister Serge Sargsian (from Karabakh as well), and the "kingmaker," Defense Minister Vazgen Sargsian (not related to Serge). It was made clear that neither the army nor the interior ministry troops would bail out Ter-Petrosian this time. Sensing which way the mood of the top officials had swung, the majority of the parliamentarians—former supporters of Ter-Petrosian—turned against him as well. With not much of a support base, the president had no choice but to resign.[30]

It is important to note that the pressure on Ter-Petrosian did not come from a mass movement, although most Armenians were happy to see him go. He resigned due to "palace intrigues" that were aptly labeled "a velvet coup." Nevertheless, the events that forced him to leave office were precipitated over, and justified by, considerations of Karabakh's well-being—in other words, the most fundamental nationalist issue. The president's opponents claimed that he was getting ready "to sell out" Karabakh by agreeing to a permanent peace accord that would have left the enclave in official Azerbaijani jurisdiction.[31] Although nationalism was no longer central in Armenian politics, it was both the reason and the instrument for some elites to dislodge Ter-Petrosian and his ANM supporters. No one doubted Kocharian's (and some of his supporters') total commitment to the enclave's security. But it is also clear that, to an important extent, the Karabakh issue was instrumentalized and nationalism *used* to legitimate a fundamental political change.

In March 1998, presidential elections were held once again. The main race was between Robert Kocharian and Karen Demirchian, the former first secretary of the Armenian SSR (1974–88), who emerged—rather suddenly and surprisingly—out of political retirement. Kocharian won the election in the second round, with close to 60 percent of the vote. Once again, the main election issues were not related to nationalism (e.g., Karabakh) but socioeconomic considerations. Demirchian was running a populist campaign, based on the nostalgia of the "Soviet days of plenty." The election did not rouse much passion.

A significant outcome of the 1998 election—and affirmed by the May 1999 parliamentary election—was the almost complete disappearance of the ANM from the Armenian political landscape. It did not place a candidate in the presidential race, and in the parliamentary election it received only 1.17 percent of the vote. Its chairman, Vano Siradeghian (formerly a high-ranking ANM minister), was the only ANM member elected to the National Assembly through the majoritarian system.[32] This election provided further evidence of the end of nationalist politics based on the popular movement of 1988.

Vazgen Manukian and his organization ceased to be a major political force as well. As the mirror image of Ter-Petrosian, Manukian's presence at the center of Armenian politics no longer made sense. He ran as a presidential candidate in 1998 but came in third with 12 percent of the vote in the first round. In general, Dashnaks supported Kocharian (the ARF was relegalized by Kocharian in February 1998), but the ARF too became a "normal" party, with limited participation in the government and having dropped a good part of its nationalist discourse.

October 1999: The Death of Vazgen Sargsian and of Armenian Nationalist Politics

The last of the nationalist politicians who remained a prominent figure in the Armenian government was Vazgen Sargsian.[33] He was the defense minister in both the Ter-Petrosian and Kocharian administrations. A man of tremendous power and charisma, he was also known for his brutality, temper, and nonchalant attitude toward the law. On the one hand, he embodied Armenian nationalism in his words and deeds; on the other, he was, par excellence, the master at the game of power politics. After the Republican Party, which he had come to patronize, in alliance with Karen Demirchian's People's Party,[34] won the most seats in the National Assembly (63 out of 131), Sargsian was appointed prime minister in June 1999. His combination of everyday political concerns with the discourse of nationalism is clear in the following toast-speech:

> Our fate is in our hands. Let us not blame anyone for our failure. So let us drink to this country, the country which we had dreamt about in

> 1988. If in 1988, at the Square, when we were demanding the freedom of Artsakh, and Armenia's independence, and the unity of Armenians, a prophet had appeared and said that in seven to eight years Armenia is to be independent, Artsakh is to be independent and liberated, Artsakh is to be with Armenia, but because of this you are to have difficult social conditions, not enough sausages, less gas, less water, would you agree to this? We would all have responded: yes! So now Armenia is independent, Artsakh is independent, and together [with Armenia], and recognized by the world [*sic*]. So what's wrong? All that has remained is the lack of sausages? We can overcome this too, and there will be plenty of sausages![35]

A month after this speech, on October 27, 1999, Sargsian was assassinated in the National Assembly, along with Demirchian (the speaker of parliament) and six other deputies. The murderers, led by Nairi Hunanian, were extreme nationalists who were hoping that their act would instigate a popular uprising. They referred to the Armenian leadership as the "bloodsuckers" of the nation and in their statement declared, "Under our very eyes, during several years, our country was being tormented and turned into a country that's being left by everybody. . . . Everything that happened [in the National Assembly] was provoked by our filial desire to protect our homeland from final destruction and to recover the infringed rights of the nation."[36] But there was no mass uprising, no nationalist fervor in favor or against the terrorists. Armenians were shocked that such a thing could happen but remained mostly passive. Ironically, it took an extremely violent act, in the name of the nation, to finish the process in Armenia of the transformation from the politics of nationalism to normal politics.

The shootings were both symbolic of the death of nationalism, and its literal death—killing the last significant nationalist politician whose commitment to Karabakh *and* Armenia—was not doubted by anyone. Prior to the parliamentary election of 1999, a new, overtly nationalist force had emerged under the leadership of Vazgen Sargsian. This organization, the Yerkrapah Union of War Veterans,[37] was directly tied to the Karabakh *war* rather than the movement. Essentially an organization of soldiers, with limited intellectual leadership (unlike the early ANM and other parties), the Yerkrapah has been militant in its views on national issues and Karabakh. Yerkrapah members failed to generate a mass support base, and their input in politics after Sargsian's death decreased considerably.

Kocharian's skillful manipulation to diffuse the threat posed by the Yerkrapahs, and the latter's incapacity to see politics as anything more than a power struggle against the president, meant that their brand of fierce nationalism has not taken root beyond their limited constituency of people directly related to the war against Azerbaijan. Moreover, the Yerkrapah Union of War Veterans has fragmented into various camps loyal to, neutral to, or against President Kocharian.

Thus, by the end of 2000 and beginning of 2001, there was no longer a nationalist political force in Armenia of any significance. There were nationalist individuals, parties, and a president and defense minister (Serge Sargsian) who were unlikely to compromise much on Karabakh. But the dominant political discourse was no longer about nationalist issues, and no leading individuals or organizations were willing to subsume their interests for the sake of nationalism. The postnationalist mood was epitomized by Kocharian's appointment in May 2000 of Andranik Margarian of the Republican Party as the new prime minister. Once an "extreme" nationalist with "Nzhdehian" views,[38] he and his party nevertheless supported Ter-Petrosian because it was beneficial for the Republican Party to be close to the center of power. Upon Ter-Petrosian's resignation, the Republican Party supported Kocharian. As prime minister, Margarian has been preoccupied neither with ideological concerns nor with nationalist issues. His main task has been to maintain political power and to deal with the everyday issues of running the country and benefiting his supporters. In other words, he has been a perfectly "normal" politician driven by pragmatic issues.

Conclusion

The case of Armenia demonstrates that nationalism is a complex ideology and political phenomenon. It does not emerge or disappear suddenly. It can coexist with other ideologies, and of course, it is quite compatible with power politics. The years between 1988 and 2001 can be divided into two periods in Armenia, based on the balance between nationalist politics and "normal" politics. The 1988–92 period was clearly in favor of the nationalist side of the scale—with all other interests being subordinated for the sake of the nation. After 1992, the balance began to shift, and "normal" politics, preoccupied with power and specific interests, started to become more and more prominent. After the 1994 cease-fire with Azerbaijan, the causal factor of the "external threat" weakened significantly. There was no longer an explicit nationalist project to prevent the victory of postnationalist politics.

Nationalist considerations did not die out completely. They were behind Ter-Petrosian's resignation in early 1998. However, the assassination of Vazgen Sargsian, Karen Demirchian, and the six other parliamentarians was the final blow, killing the spirit of nationalism aroused in 1988. The *politics* of nationalism had arguably died much earlier, with the 1996 presidential election. October 27, 1999, will be remembered by Armenians as day when the *dreams* of the nationalism of 1988 and 1991 were assassinated as well—ironically by someone who claimed that he wanted to resuscitate those dreams.

In 2002, for better or worse, a period of postnationalist, "normal" politics has been solidified in Armenia. Party and individual interests dominate the political landscape and power politics drives Yerevan. The economy is the declared main concern of all in government, but as elsewhere, everyone wants to hold onto his (or her) position for as long as possible. This, after all, is the best guarantee for economic well-being for the holder of the position.

I am not suggesting that Armenian nationalism has disappeared entirely from the political scene. Armenians, on the whole, remain profoundly committed to their country and people. But this drive is no longer manifested in their politics. A major crisis, another war, or too much compromise on the Karabakh issue could, for example, once again rekindle passions and lead to the politics of nationalism. But this is an unlikely scenario for the time being. In the foreseeable future, politics in Armenia will remain "normal," mundane, and nonnationalist. Nationalism will be used in imagery to justify the power of certain individuals, but it will not be the driving force of the system.

NOTES

I would like to thank Dr. Ara Sanjian for his helpful suggestions on this chapter.

1. Karen Demirchian, interview with author, Yerevan, December 3, 1997.

2. Karlen Dallakian, *Hushapatum* (Memoir) (Yerevan: n.p., 1999), 6–7. All translations from Armenian sources are the author's.

3. As reported in *Armenian Reporter International* (New York), November 11, 1995, 10. Similar sentiments and views were expressed to me during various interviews I conducted during my research in Yerevan. Some examples from November 1996 interviews include Vazgen Manukian, who elaborated on the above-mentioned point: the postwar generation of Communist leaders "were pragmatic people. They did not share Communist ideology so deeply—they were not Khanchians or Miasnikians [i.e., the first generation of leaders]. They did not feel a contradiction between the national

and the Communist." Sergei Badalian and Tital Tavrishian (of the Communist Party) naturally lionized the role of the Communists in nation-building but without giving too much credit to the actual leaders, especially Demirchian. Razmik Davoyan, a poet with Armenian Revolutionary Federation (ARF) sympathies, said that despite the awful system, in the past twenty to thirty years "leaders realized that Soviet ideology was a veil . . . underneath which national culture and values were being built." In addition to the elite, there was almost universal appraisal of Demirchian, and before him Kochinian, as "nation-builders" among the general populace.

4. For further analysis of Armenian nationalism under Soviet rule, see Vahakn Dadrian, "Nationalism in Soviet Armenia: A Case Study of Ethnocentrism," in *Nationalism in the USSR and Eastern Europe,* ed. George Simmonds (Detroit: University of Detroit Press, 1977); Ronald Suny, *Looking toward Ararat: Armenia in Modern History* (Bloomington: Indiana University Press, 1993); and Razmik Panossian, "The Evolution of Multilocal National Identity and the Contemporary Politics of Nationalism: Armenia and Its Diaspora" (Ph.D. dissertation, London School of Economics and Political Science, 2000).

5. The clearest articulation of this view is found in Rafayel Ishkhanian, *Yerrord uzhi patsarman orenke* (The Law of Excluding the Third Force) (Yerevan: Azat Khosk, 1991), 49–73, 128–35 (a collection of essays from 1988 to 1990); and in Vazgen Manukian, "It Is Time to Jump off the Train," in *Armenia at the Crossroads,* ed. Gerard Libaridian (Watertown: Blue Crane Books, 1991), 51–86 (originally published in Armenia in May–June 1990).

6. The territorial demands of Armenian nationalism were expressed forcefully in April 1965 when thousands of protesters marched in Yerevan on the occasion of the fiftieth anniversary of the Genocide, shouting, "Our Lands! Our Lands!" After 1965, the Soviet regime allowed Armenians more freedoms to express "officially" sanctioned ethnocultural nationalism; the Soviets calculated that this would deflect attention from nationalist issues related to independence and territorial claims.

7. In the context of post–World War II geopolitical posturing, Stalin demanded the historical Armenian territories of Kars and Ardahan from Turkey between 1945 and 1948. Of course, the Armenian leadership fully supported these claims. The demands came to naught, and they were formally withdrawn in 1953 after Stalin's death.

8. The best source on the early stages of the Karabakh movement (based on an eyewitness account) is Mark Malkasian, *"Gha-ra-bagh!" The Emergence of the National Democratic Movement in Armenia* (Detroit: Wayne State University Press, 1996). Two studies that explore the links between identity and the nationalist movement are Nora Dudwick, "Memory, Identity and Politics in Armenia" (Ph.D. dissertation, University of Pennsylvania, 1994); and Stephanie Platz, "Pasts and Futures: Space, History, and Armenian Identity, 1988–1994" (Ph.D. dissertation, University of Chicago, 1996). See also Michael Croissant, *The Armenian-Azerbaijan Conflict: Causes and Implications* (Westport, CT: Praeger, 1998); and Levon Chorbajian, ed., *The Making of Nagorno-Karabagh: From Secession to Republic* (Basingstoke: Palgrave, 2001).

9. Some of these hard to find "samizdats" include the weekly newsletter called *Ankakhutiun* (Independence), which Hairikian began to publish in October 1987. He also published the journal-like monthly called *Hairenik* (Fatherland) from May 1988 onward. These were printed and sold illegally, although the "price" of being caught no longer entailed imprisonment, especially after February 1988. Other pro-independence

organizations were also established at this point (e.g., National Independence Party of Armenia), but they were mostly short-lived and insignificant.

10. Interview with author, August 20, 1996.

11. The ARF is one of the "historical" Armenian political parties. It was founded in Tiflis (Tbilisi) in 1890. It became an exclusively diasporan organization after the elimination of the Armenians in the 1915 Ottoman genocide in western Armenia and the sovietization of eastern Armenia in 1920.

12. The samizdat literature is full of ARF slogans, images, and biographies of its heroes. One ARF figure from the first half of the century, Garegin Nzhdeh, was particularly revered and written about. Nzhdeh was a staunch nationalist, to the point of being kicked out of the ARF in 1937 for his extremism, racist views, and sympathy for fascism. He was captured by Soviet troops in 1945 in Bulgaria and perished in 1954 as a prisoner in the USSR. The ARF rehabilitated Nzhdeh in the 1960s. Two other diaspora-based parties established themselves in Armenia in the summer of 1990: the liberal Ramkavar party and the socialist Hnchak party. These organizations did not have any significant impact on Armenian nationalism or politics.

13. S. Melik-Hakobian, "Establishment of the Second Republic of Armenia and the Dashnaktsutiun (ARF)," *Nor Gyank* (New Life), November 28, 1996, 51.

14. As quoted in ibid. Original quote comes from *Nor Gyank,* October 3, 1992.

15. I have analyzed the ARF-ANM relationship elsewhere, and in the context of Armenia-diaspora relations. See Razmik Panossian, "The Diaspora and the Karabagh Movement: Oppositional Politics between the Armenian Revolutionary Federation and the Armenian National Movement," in *The Making of Nagorno-Karabagh: From Secession to Republic,* ed. Levon Chorbajian (Basingstoke: Palgrave, 2001). See also Razmik Panossian, "Between Ambivalence and Intrusion: Politics and Identity in Armenia-Diaspora Relations," *Diaspora* 7, no. 2 (fall 1998) (particularly pp. 165–75).

16. Dudwick makes this point quite clearly in her study. For example, she examines the protests as a form of "communion" (p. 180) and as "rituals of purification" (p. 195ff.); see Nora Dudwick, "Memory, Identity and Politics in Armenia," particularly chapter 4, 144–98. See also Nora Dudwick, "Armenia: The Nation Awakens," in *Nations and Politics in the Soviet Successor States,* ed. Ian Bremmer and Ray Taras (Cambridge: Cambridge University Press, 1993), 275–76; and Malkasian, *"Gha-ra-bagh!"* 35, 43, 47.

17. Malkasian, *"Gha-ra-bagh!"* 95ff.

18. Generally, this homogenization process is seen as a positive development in Armenia. As one intellectual—who was not even a nationalist politician—put it, "One benefit of this war [over Karabakh], despite its many hardships, is that Armenia was cleaned [or cleansed] of this weed [i.e., of Azerbaijanis]." Gurgen Geghamian, an economist at Academy of Sciences, interview with author, November 28, 1997.

19. See, Malkasian, *"Gha-ra-bagh!"* 143–47. Throughout his book, he speaks of other skirmishes in 1988.

20. For example, Yegor Ligachev declared in Baku (in May 1988) that Karabakh's unification with Armenia was a closed issue—that is, it was not going to take place. See Malkasian, *"Gha-ra-bagh!"* 82.

21. Joseph Masih and Robert Krikorian, *Armenia: At the Crossroads* (Amsterdam: Harwood, 1999), 34.

22. The main difference between Manukian and Ter-Petrosian lies in their attitudes toward the relationship between politics and nationalism. According to Manukian, the

uniqueness of the nation must be the basis of its politics, whereas Ter-Petrosian would reject this "national ideology" as false and insist that Armenia is like any other nation (Vazgen Manukian, interview with author, November 2, 1996).

23. For further elaboration see Panossian, "The Diaspora and the Karabagh Movement." Some of the key articles in the ARF organ *Droshak* (Banner) (published in Athens) *before* Armenia's independence set the tone of the oppositional politics to come; see, for example, July 5, 1989, 6–11; November 22, 1989, 7–12; January 16, 1991, 3–14; June 19, 1991, 10–12; and August 14, 1991, 2.

24. The first direct election for the position of president took place in October 1991, during the euphoria of independence. Ter-Petrosian won with 83 percent of the vote. Paruir Hairikian polled at 8 percent, and the ARF candidate, popular actor Sos Sargsian, was humiliated with less than 5 percent of the vote. This was a major blow to the (self-) image of the ARF as the "vanguard" of the nation. Ter-Petrosian's victory was also a victory for the ANM, which consolidated its control over the political process in Armenia.

25. As far as I am aware, no systematic analysis of the 1996 election has yet been published in the academic press. The discussion that follows is based on my own research notes and interviews in Armenia before, during, and after the election.

26. Some of the irregularities were noted by international observers, although the overall results of the election were not dismissed. *Armenia: Assessment and Observations on the 5 July Elections by the United Kingdom Observers Attached to the UN/OSCE Joint Operation* (London: Electoral Reform Society, July 1995).

27. The National Unity Pact was composed of five organizations: National Democratic Union (led by Vazgen Manukian), Union for National Self-Determination (led by Paruir Hairikian), Democratic Party of Armenia (led by Aram Sargsian [not related to Vazgen Sargsian]), Artsakh-Hayastan union (led by Lenser Aghalovian), and Armenian Revolutionary Federation (led by its central committee in Armenia). Two opposition parties did not join the NUP: Ashot Manucharian and Rafael Ghazarian's Scientific Industrial Union and the Communist Party of Armenia (led by Sergei Badalian).

28. This sentiment was also echoed in the views of ordinary citizens. One lamented that "this was 'our' city, now it is 'their' city. We no longer belong to this country."

29. Ter-Petrosian cleared the 50 percent mark (to avoid a second round of voting) by approximately twenty thousand ballots. This was almost exactly the number of ballots missing in the final count. For a report on the election, see International Foundation for Election Systems, "Technical Assessment, Armenian Presidential Election" (Washington, DC, October 8, 1996).

30. For an interpretation of the crisis sympathetic to Ter-Petrosian, see Gerard Libaridian, *The Challenge of Statehood: Armenian Political Thinking since Independence* (Watertown, MA: Blue Crane Books, 1999), particularly chapter 2.

31. Ter-Petrosian laid out his position on Karabakh to the Armenian public in the autumn of 1997. He called for a "public debate" on the issue, but he was severely criticized by many (opposition) commentators for "giving in." His key ministers and the leadership in Karabakh also made it clear that they did not approve of his compromises. The first of his pronouncements was in the form of a lengthy press conference; the second, in the form of an article. See Levon Ter-Petrosian, "Hajord serundneri gaghaparakhosutiune petk e lini mer petakanutian amrapndume" (The Ideology of the Next Generation Must Be the Strengthening of Our Statehood), *Hayastani Hanrapetutiun* (Republic of Armenia) 187 (September 27, 1997): 1–3; and Levon Ter-Petrosian, "Pat-

erazm, te khaghaghutiun? Lrjanalu Pahe" (War or Peace? The Moment to Get Serious), *Hayastani Hanrapetutiun* 212 (November 1, 1997): 1–2.

32. Siradeghian is currently a fugitive who has fled Armenia. He is implicated in the murder of opponents—that is, for ordering the killings as interior minister.

33. This is not to suggest that President Kocharian is not a nationalist. He certainly is. But his nationalist outlook is confined to Karabakh's security. In all other respects, he is much more of a pragmatist than a nationalist in the style of 1988.

34. The two had formed the "Unity Bloc." Sargsian was the "senior" partner in the alliance because of his control of the defense ministry and the Yekrapah Union.

35. This is part of a toast-speech given at the closing reception (at Sardarapat) of the Armenia-Diaspora conference on September 24, 1999. As far as I am aware, it has not appeared anywhere in print. Author's audio recording.

36. As read out to the Armenian media and reported (in translation) on Armenian News Network Groong (e-mail news service), October 28, 1999.

37. *Yerkrapah* means keeper or defender of the country. The organization was led by Vazgen Sargsian when he was defense minister, and its members were personally loyal to him. It had been set up as a nonpolitical organization promoting the interests of the war veterans. However, it was politicized, and a substantial chunk of its members merged with the Republican Party to become Vazgen Sargsian's support base in the 1999 parliamentary election.

38. Andranik Margarian, interview with author, November 12, 1997 (see n. 12 on Nzhdeh). Margarian is not a charismatic individual, and he did not have much experience with government at the time of his appointment. He was very much a second-tier politician who had become the leader of the Republican Party—an insignificant political organization at that point in 1997—upon the death of its founder, the former Soviet-era dissident Ashot Navasardian. Margarian rose to national prominence due to Vazgen Sargsian's patronage of the Republican Party. Margarian was appointed as prime minister after the Sargsian assassination because he represented, by default, the largest bloc of parliamentarians.

10. Georgia

Nationalism from under the Rubble

STEPHEN JONES

WHAT HAPPENS TO nationalism after it has attained its putative aim: a self-governing territory under the nation's control? A glance at the ex-USSR suggests there is no pattern. The Soviet system—standardizing, homogenizing, and a powerful legacy for all the nations that were part of it—has been an important but unpredictable variable in shaping nation- and state-building among former Soviet peoples.

It was clear even before statehood was achieved that the nationalist movements in the USSR had different goals and tactics, shaped in part by specific histories and demographics, but also by different experiences under Soviet rule. As Slezkine puts it, the Soviet regimes in Ukraine, Kazakhstan, Lithuania, Georgia, and elsewhere were united by a state that allocated them separate rooms in a communal apartment, but the tenants arranged these rooms differently and dealt with the landlord in cleverly varied ways.[1] Brubaker is right to stress, as did Rakowska-Harmstone over twenty-five years ago, that the Soviet state reinforced or created nationalism by prescribing national identities and establishing national borders.[2] But the internal design of the rooms, "landlord-tenant relations," the nature of the neighborhood, and the psychology of the new bosses all contributed to variations in post-Soviet nationalism and why some tenants proved better at managing their newly independent "rooms" than others.

Georgian Roommates: Can They Behave?

Georgians, and more generally Caucasians, are perceived as bad roommates. Since 1991, Georgia has undergone two wars of secession, a civil war, a number of failed (and badly planned) coups, and at least two assassination attempts on former president Shevardnadze. Western commentators often suggest that, like their Balkan confreres (if the Serbs, Croats, Bosnians, Slovenes, Macedonians, and Albanians can be treated as one group), Georgians cannot shake their bloody past or inclination to violence.[3] Georgian history is conflict, and therefore conflict is Georgian. But nationalism in Georgia today, when put in context, is more "modern" and "normal" than most Western analysts—still reeling from the heated rhetoric of Georgia's militant nationalist pamphleteers of the early 1990s—suggest. Our focus on national conflict and violence in Caucasia distorts our understanding of Caucasian history and Caucasian nationalist movements and raises broader questions as to what exactly we mean by terms like *ethnic conflict* and *nationalism.*

Caucasian history is not just one of conflict; it has other traditions too, including interethnic cooperation. The recovery of the Caucasian past should not be equated with only "the revenge of the past." Western academic studies of Caucasia show an overwhelming bias toward national conflict and its resolution, perhaps in part because such studies are more likely to obtain financial support.[4] But this narrow focus leads to incorrect assumptions about the relationship between nationalism and politics in the region.

Walker Connor has pointed out that Western scholarship is confused about the concept of nationalism.[5] Nationalism covers the broadest spectrum of popular movements and states dedicated to maintaining the identity, unity, and autonomy of the nation, however conceived.[6] Defining *nation* and *nationalism* is not the central concern of this chapter; there are many worthy studies on this issue,[7] and the terms have been defined in the introductory chapter of this volume. But as I argue in this chapter, at a minimum one needs to distinguish between the core beliefs of nationalism, on the one hand, and the methods, style, and emphases of nationalist movements and states, on the other. At the first level, most people share the aspirations of nationalism—the pursuit of autonomy, unity, and common identity—but on the second level they differ considerably. Some, but not all, nationalists have an exclusive view of identity, promote popular mobilization around political and cultural homogeneity, and consider autonomy an insufficient guarantee of self-rule free of foreign influence. These nationalists—on the more extreme spectrum of nationalism—are more likely to scapegoat minorities and use force. Yet there are other nationalist movements characterized by inclusive views of the nation, political tolerance, and civil rights. The more extreme forms of nationalism can develop into moderate, constructive nationalisms, and liberal nationalisms can metamorphose into radical jingoism. However, the distinction between different forms of nationalism is crucial. Many scholars and Western analysts when discussing Caucasia do not differentiate and as a result fail to see the major changes in nationalist values and style in the region over the last decade.

Former deputy secretary of state Strobe Talbott presented a typical outsider's view of Caucasia in a speech in Bucharest in 1998. He declared:

> We can all say good riddance to Marxist-Leninist dictatorship, to the Iron Curtain and to the self-styled geniuses who ruled by brute force and primal fear. But the collapse of these modern evils has, in many parts of the post-Communist world, been accompanied by the eruption of medieval struggles over blood and culture. From Bosnia, Croatia, Albania, and Kosovo in the Balkans to Chechnya, Abkhazia, South Osetia, and Nagorno-Karabakh in the Caucasus, more Europeans have died violently in the last five years than in the previous forty five.[8]

There are four assumptions here, all of which misrepresent nationalism in Georgia and in Caucasia more generally. National conflicts in Georgia (specifically in Abkhazia and South Osetia) are neither medieval nor about blood. Such overly historicist interpretations simplify the causes of the post-Soviet crisis and reflect a crude primordialist view of nations in the region, a view that nationalism was always present and is now, after a period of repression, back with a vengeance. This view, fueled by the media, suggests that politics in Georgia and Caucasia is driven by the past and is always "national," rarely local.[9] Thinking nationally ourselves, and drawing on our own obsession with "ethnic identity" in the United States, we fail to explore the many other perspectives that can determine political behavior in Caucasia, whether they are generational differences, gender, class and economic interests, local and regional identities, or institutional loyalties.

Second, nationalism in Georgia cannot be blended, as Talbott supposes, into a Balkan pot. Superficial similarities ignore vital differences between the two regions and overestimate the importance of violent conflict in Georgian nationalism. Far too often, nationalism and violence in Georgia are considered partners in crime, whereas nationalism—talking more generally—is no more inherently violent than most other ideologies and its contemporary form in Georgia today has much less to do with the centuries of violent imperial competition in Caucasia than is often suggested.[10]

Frequently, liberalism is presented as a rational enterprise based on a social contract between the state and its citizens, and is counterposed as a peaceful ideological alternative to nationalism in Caucasia. But liberalism's early strivings at statehood during a period of major economic restructuring (the industrial revolution) and domestic adjustment—similar to Georgia's position today—were characterized by violence and social unrest. A glance at national anthems shows that most of today's liberal democracies were born out of war.[11] Mill, Smith, Nodia, and others, have pointed out that the philosophical roots of nationalism and liberal democracy are intertwined.[12] When scholars differentiate between nationalism and liberalism, it is worth remembering that nationalism, based on nineteenth-century principles of popular sovereignty, citizen equality, democracy, and self-determination, defined—and still does—the historical, territorial, and cultural parameters of modern liberalism. Quebec is the most obvious example of a polity where liberalism and nationalism serve as a common source of "statehood." Trying to introduce an ethnically neutral liberalism as an alternative to nationalism is both conceptually confusing and overrates its power to eradicate "ethnic" conflict.

But Georgian nationalism *is* different from "ours" in the United States and Western Europe.[13] Yet the difference is often exaggerated and becomes a crude demonstration of the superiority of our own "civic" form of nationalism. This is reflected by Talbott's third (implied) assumption that *we* have a "civilized" ("civic") nationalism, and *they* in Georgia and Caucasia have an atavistic ("ethnic") nationalism. In his speech, Talbott does not mention Northern Ireland, the Basque region, the successful right-wing parties in Europe, or the growth of violent militias in the United States, all of which show that some nationalisms in the West, superficially at least, have no fewer "ethnic" roots than their counterparts in the East. Germany's official concept of citizenship is still ethnically determined, and even the cosmopolitan French do not accept all national groups resident in France as French, even when those groups want to be.[14] Restrictive immigration and asylum laws in most Western democracies show a continued fear of foreigners. There is a suspicious Orientalism to Talbott's selection of countries where "ethnic violence" occurs, despite his generous use of the term *Europeans*. Mestrovic, in his book *The Balkanization of the West*, argues convincingly that the civic-liberal and ethnic-illiberal paradigms are misleading. In his view, popular sentiments in liberal democracies are "ethnic," "emotional," and tradition-bound too, and the attempt to deny it tells us more about Westerners' self-perception than it does about the Balkans.[15]

Fourth, Talbott implicates whole countries in the "crimes" of nationalism. Just as one would not expect public and congressional opinion to coincide in the United States, so in Georgia and other countries of the former Soviet Union—where there are particularly strong traditions of hierarchy, regionalism, and long-standing cultural and economic divisions between leaders and the led—we need more discernment in judging the depth of "ethnic" nationalism. In the Abkhazian and South Osetian conflicts, the majorities on both sides were the victims of national conflict, not the progenitors.

Nationalism defines our categories of thinking. Most of our citizens—with the exception of a few cosmopolitans—are firm believers in the national idea. Arguably, the violent extension of American national interests into Grenada and Panama reflects an even more militant nationalism than Georgia's attempt to hang on to its internationally accepted state borders. But comparisons of the two nationalisms would almost certainly lead to the opposite conclusion among U.S. citizens. This is because many politicians (and scholars) who talk about the resurgence of nationalism in the late twentieth century focus not on large established states like the United States but rather on small nations like Georgia, challenging already-existing states, or on weak states like Russia, characterized by an absence of consensus and by serious internal conflicts.[16]

The violence that may accompany these conflicts is often thoughtlessly interpreted as "ethnic." But violence between "ethnic groups" is not necessarily ethnic. Even if we establish that the violence is *ethnic,* the term is used too loosely and blurs the many sources and expressions of conflict—whether they are employment, representation, participation, the environment, or legislative changes that threaten to change the status of national groups. Hroch, Gellner, and Nairn have all stressed the importance of understanding the economic, political, and educational sources of national identity and mobilization, but many of us seem to have forgotten this.[17]

To understand nationalism in places like Georgia (and in Armenia, Azerbaijan, and Chechnya), we need both a broader perspective and a finer focus. Mestrovic points out there are "good" (compassionate and peaceful) and "bad" (egoistic and megalomaniacal) nationalisms.[18] They coexist both within a country and between countries. Nationalism, like most other *-isms,* is diverse and adaptable. Within a few years, new conditions may overturn its champions, transform its goals, and dramatically alter its modes of expression.

This is the case in Georgia. Georgian nationalism cannot be defined simply by the experience of the last decade. The imperial breakup of the 1990s produced specific circumstances: socioeconomic crisis, state disintegration, and challenges to territorial and political legitimacy. Georgian nationalism during this period *was* violent, state challenging, and ethnically based, but our focus on this period distorts our understanding of what came before and what followed. Georgian nationalism cannot be caricatured as "tribal" or "medieval," because nationalism in Soviet and post-Soviet Georgia, like our own nationalisms, has not always been state challenging, violent, or ethnic. Nationalism in Georgia today, understood as a part of the state-building process, is arguably constructive, legitimate, and stabilizing. It can be used as a source of cohesion, much as it was in Germany after the fall of the Berlin Wall.

The focus on nationalist violence in Georgia excludes the "valleys" in favor of the "peaks." It encourages an anachronistic vision of crises and nationalist tensions, which are then incorporated into a "pattern" of a dedicated struggle for national liberation. A review of Georgian history suggests a much more complicated and less heroic path. Georgian nationalism has been and is now only part of a wide complex of political, economic, and power relationships. It is one factor—and not always the most important—that we have to consider in our assessment of pre- and post-Soviet developments. For most Georgians today, as in the past, it is the economy and social conditions, not radical nationalism, that determines political behavior.

The Weakness of Georgian Nationalism

Georgia's route to nationhood was not unusual. Before the nineteenth century, Georgian elites were multiethnic and multidenominational, and the Georgian state absorbed Armenians, Osetians and Abkhazians into the country's ruling class, representing what Brubaker calls an "assimilationist" culture.[19] In the second half of the nineteenth century, under the influence of a Russian modernizing state (Georgia was annexed by the Russian Empire in the first decades of the nineteenth century) and a Europeanized Georgian intelligentsia, a modern sense of nationhood spread among

Georgian elites. Ethnicity became the focus of a new secular intelligentsia, and switching or combining identities became increasingly difficult.[20] The new emphasis on "ethnic ancestry" (what Brubaker calls a "differentialist" culture) increased competition between emerging national groups in the towns and cities. Georgian nationalists bemoaned the demographic imbalance in the capital (Georgians were a minority in Tbilisi until the 1920s) and campaigned for more political power. But despite inspiring struggles by newly formed Italians, Hungarians, and Greeks against imperial overlords, by the end of the nineteenth century, Georgians were flocking not to nationalism but to the internationalist ideology of socialism as the means to a better life. It was socialism in Georgian colors with priority given to the defense of national culture, but it is significant that no single Georgian party before 1917—even those opposed to the new "internationalism"—advocated independence from Russia.[21] Georgia became independent in 1918, led by a socialist government. But independence was more by default than design and in much the same circumstances as 1991 (imperial collapse, economic crisis, and military defeat).

Like all socialist states, the newly created Georgian Democratic Republic was a nationalist/socialist hybrid. It was a nationalizing state, standard for all new states seeking legitimacy in the twentieth century. The Georgianization program—in education, the courts, and administration—encountered resistance from many non-Georgian minorities, fearful of economic and political domination by the new Georgian elite. There are many examples of Georgian excesses during this period, such as the Georgian government's refusal to admit Armenian refugees fleeing the Ottoman Empire into Tbilisi in May 1918, its bloody suppression of Osetian revolts in 1918, 1919, and 1920, and of Abkhazian insurrections in 1918 and 1919. But in a country experiencing economic collapse, surrounded by a civil war, and facing threats of invasion by the volunteer army, Bolsheviks, and neighboring Armenia, such military solutions were as much about security as about settling ethnic scores (there were in fact no ethnic scores to settle). The Bolsheviks—after 1920 a major threat to Georgian sovereignty—exploited justified dissatisfaction among Georgia's national minorities and turned them into major challenges to the state's survival.

Much of the resistance to the Georgian central government—there were revolts among Georgian peasants as well—was land related, driven by economic as well as ethnic concerns.[22] This is not to deny the brutality of the Georgian National Guard during these years, which by its action foolishly turned economic and social demands into secessionist ones. But to argue that the Georgian government's repressive actions in 1918–21 were part of a pattern of ancient and, by implication violent, animosities is wrong. They were related more closely to state collapse, economic chaos, and foreign threats to security, all of which generated extreme economic and political insecurities among Georgians and their minorities.

In the Soviet period, the West's image of Georgian nationalism was transformed. From the negativity it had acquired in 1918–21, it became a brave anti-Soviet movement compatible with Western norms of self-determination.[23] But both the chauvinist image of 1918–21 and the courageous image of Georgian national resistance from 1921 to 1991 ignore history and context. After the Soviet invasion of 1921, Georgian nationalism either went underground (Georgian nationalist groups practically disappeared after a failed 1924 revolt to regain Georgian independence) or was rechanneled into cultural frameworks provided by the Soviet state—what Rakowska-Harmstone has called "orthodox nationalism."[24]

"Orthodox" Georgian nationalism focused on primarily cultural issues, such as language, education, the restoration of monuments, literature, film, sport, and, in the last two decades of Soviet power, the church. During World War II there was no armed anti-Soviet national resistance movement as in the Baltics and Ukraine (although if the Germans had reached Georgia, that might have been different[25]), and although Georgians were singled out by Western commentators as the most passionate nationalists, their nationalism rarely spilled onto the streets or directly challenged the Soviet regime. Georgian dissidence, unlike that of Lithuania, was represented by a dozen or so prominent, but largely unknown, figures, with no mass base. Even nationalist dissent in Ukraine, weak though it was, was more of a challenge to the Soviet regime than in Georgia.

There were only two significant occasions between World War II and 1980 when Georgian nationalism openly expressed its discontents.[26] The first in 1956, when twenty to thirty Georgian demonstrators were gunned down by Soviet interior forces, was a reaction to Nikita Khrushchev's de-Stalinization campaign. The mass protest, sparked by the absence of celebrations on Stalin's birthday, had weak nationalist credentials, although the Soviet government's brutal reaction "posthumously" made the demonstration into a nationalist one. The second occasion was in 1978 when Georgians, primarily students from Tbilisi, demonstrated against the Soviet government's decision to remove Georgian as the official language of the republic.[27]

This is not to suggest that Georgian nationalism was feckless—individual Georgians made great sacrifices for their beliefs—but it was rarely a mass protest movement, and its focus was neither on territory (like continuing Armenian protests and petitions over Nagorno-Karabakh in the Soviet period) nor on the exclusion of national minorities. Before perestroika, Georgian nationalism had adapted itself to the colonial framework. It fully exploited what Scott has called "everyday forms of resistance," and without directly challenging the Soviet state, it usurped its power.[28]

The Soviet context partly explains Georgian nationalism's benign focus. There was little opportunity for open protest. But the Soviet empire shaped Georgian nationalism in other important ways. First, it maintained and promoted Caucasian traditions of ethnic intermixing. Georgians, Abkhazians, Osetians, Armenians, and others shared villages, yards, schools, and places of employment. Intermarriage between Georgians (more specifically Mingrelians, a Georgian subnational group living in West Georgia) and Abkhazians (at least those living in the southern regions of Ochamchire and Sukhumi) was common, and social intermixing and intermarriage, promoted by the process of migration to major Georgian towns, were evident among Georgians and other groups such as South Osetians.[29] This is not to deny the prejudices that existed between Georgians and non-Georgians at all levels of interaction or to romanticize, as Georgians do, their history of tolerance (Serbs claim the same tradition). The Soviet state, by allocating Georgians a union republic, also helped reinforce Georgians' sense of cultural and historical superiority. But at the same time, it enhanced Georgia's inclusive traditions. Second, the Soviet state successfully maintained Georgian nationalism's traditional focus on cultural issues, especially language and literature. Georgian nationalism remained, as it did in the nineteenth century, a cultural phenomenon, and it was only with perestroika and the threat of Abkhazian and South Osetian secessionism that Georgian nationalism became a political movement that challenged the Soviet state.

Georgian Nationalism: From Populism to Pragmatism

Gamsakhurdia and the Rise of Populist Nationalism, 1989–92

Zviad Gamsakhurdia was a radical nationalist. Brought to power by a wave of popular nationalism in the October 1990 Supreme Soviet elections, he was not simply an ethnic entrepreneur who, using nationalist slogans to gain authority, manipulated a formerly moderate Georgian populace into a chauvinistic mob. Resource theories of nationalism, which stress manipulation by elites, are inadequate explanations of nationalisms' successes. Gamsakhurdia, after eight months as chairman of Georgia's Supreme Soviet, was elected president in May 1991 with 87 percent of the vote. His success was based on ideas and anxieties that resonated among Georgians—the threat of Georgia's disintegration, the fear of Russian military power, and the perceived neglect of Georgian interests. In contrast to 1918, almost every party by 1989–90 was advocating independence, the great panacea for Georgian ills. This was a time of national trauma; twice in 1989 Georgians had been killed in conflict with Soviet interior troops—on April 9 at a popular demonstration outside parliament advocating independence and on July 15 in clashes with Abkhazians in Sukhumi.[30] Georgians, in Gamsakhurdia's view, were being victimized in their own state. The reaction of both Georgians and the minority Abkhazians and Osetians to Gamsakhurdia's militant nationalist rhetoric was understandable. In a time when physical and economic security was unprotected, national solidarity and self-reliance were the obvious answer. In circumstances like those of 1990–91, with the threat of dissolution of the state, economic collapse, and hostile declarations from a still militarily powerful imperial overlord, it is hard to imagine even "civic" European nations, let alone newly independent states led by inexperienced elites, abjuring militant nationalist ideas.

But a closer look at Georgian nationalism from 1989 to 1992 shows this was neither the resurgence of latent ethnic hatreds nor the expression of a violent political culture. Rather, it was contingent on extraordinary economic, political, and physical insecurities brought about by the collapse of Soviet power. It is worth remembering that from 1989 to 1990 those leading the Georgian national liberation movement tried to divert popular focus from national minorities. Representatives of the Kurdish and Armenian communities, among others, took part in the early rallies for Georgian independence (there was a similar pattern in the Baltics), and Georgian radicals in these early years saw the "ethnicization" of Georgian politics as a deliberate Kremlin provocation.[31] At the April 9, 1989, public demonstration, few of the painted banners or chalked slogans mentioned Abkhazia, despite a March 1989 call at Lykhny in Abkhazia for secession.[32] The focus was on Georgian independence.

Gamsakhurdia, who split with the radical opposition in May 1990 in preparation for the October/November Supreme Soviet elections, by contrast focused on the demographic threat from within. This is what Lowell Barrington refers to as "sovereignty-protecting" nationalism. Driven by a mystical vision of Georgian unity and the threat of multiple enemies, Gamsakhurdia's radical nationalist rhetoric helped shape a psychological state of siege. Leaders like Vladislav Ardzinba (Abkhazia) and Torez Kulumbegov (South Osetia) followed suit. They used the demographic card even more effectively, defending communities that numerically were in a far worse situation than the Georgian.[33] To Georgians, the anti-Georgian statements of national minority leaders, fed by Gamsakhurdia's own threats, proved their disloyalty.

However, even Gamsakhurdia in his most intense moments of nationalist apoplexy did not advocate the forcible expulsion of national minorities or question minorities' cultural rights in Georgia.[34] And although his government abolished South Osetia's regional status in December 1990 in response to a South Osetian declaration of independence and unsanctioned elections to the South Osetian Supreme Soviet a few days before, he did not question Abkhazian autonomy. In 1991 he negotiated a consociationalist agreement with the Abkhazians which put Georgians living in Abkhazia at a political disadvantage. The Abkhazians, who made up only 17 percent of the autonomous republic's population, received twenty-eight seats in the sixty-five-seat Abkhazian parliament; the Georgian community (46 percent) received twenty-six seats; and the remaining population (37 percent), consisting mainly of Armenians, Greeks, and Russians, received eleven seats. No constitutional change was possible without two-thirds of the vote, which gave Abkhazians relatively secure protection of their existing legal rights.[35]

Gamsakhurdia's differential treatment of the Abkhazians and South Osetians was based on an official Soviet paradigm: the former were autochthonous, the latter, nonindigenous.[36] The rights of other immigrants were covered by different legislative acts.[37] Whatever Gamsakhurdia's motivation—calculation that things would change in Georgia's favor or that the alternative would lead to a conflict with Abkhazia and ultimately Russia—the consociationalist policies in Abkhazia show inconsistencies with Gamsakhurdia's reputation as an uncompromising nationalist who believed in "Georgia for the Georgians." The argument is not that Gamsakhurdia was a liberal nationalist; he was not. He threatened, bullied, and belittled Georgia's national minorities. But the evidence of these years, including the expulsion of Gamsakhurdia in January 1992, suggests that Gamsakhurdia, though a bully, was capable of pragmatic calculation. Not all national groups were equally bad or unacceptable as partners in the Georgian state.

Finally, and important to remember, Gamsakhurdia's support was not based solely on his nationalist credentials. Like Boris Yeltsin, Juan Perón, and other populist leaders, Gamsakhurdia's appeal was as much about defense of the little man, anticommunism, rejection of privilege, and support of blue collar state-subsidized jobs as it was about national glory. One cannot understand the Gamsakhurdia phenomenon without going outside the nationalist framework. Gamsakhurdia was an authoritarian populist who scapegoated not only national minorities but Georgian groups too, such as the "red intelligentsia" and university students. His promotion of state paternalism, emphasis on personal loyalty, centralization of power in a strong executive, appeal to provincial voters, cultivation of charisma, and use of plebiscites and public rallies tell us more about post-Soviet society between 1989 and 1991 than does a narrow focus on nationalism. In fact, the theoretical framework of an illiberal radical populism is a more useful tool for analyzing the Gamsakhurdia phenomenon than nationalism, which, though a vital part, was only a part.[38]

Shevardnadze and the New Pragmatism

After he came to power in March 1992, Eduard Shevardnadze slowly shifted Georgian politics from Gamsakhurdia's illiberal democratic populism toward a more stable, elite-mediated "civic" nationalism. There have, of course, been setbacks. Shevardnadze's government continued to experience serious problems integrating Georgia's national minorities into the political system. There was little coherent strategy and poor implementation of policies on national minority rights. The Georgian parliament did not pass any important laws on the national question; a controversial bill on national minorities, under discussion in parliament since 1996, was never passed. The same was true of a language law.[39] The new electoral systems introduced in 1992, 1995, and 1999 produced few national minority deputies to represent Georgia's 25–30 percent non-Georgians.[40] Due to the continued postponement of Georgia's territorial organization, the status of non-Georgia areas remained undecided (too much decentralization was seen by many parliamentarians as an encouragement to secession). Few resources were allocated to teaching non-Georgians the Georgian language.

Non-Georgians in the regions continued to complain of police "targeting," and large numbers of Azerbaijanis, Russians, Greeks, and Armenians emigrated, although mostly for economic reasons.

But there have been noteworthy successes. Shevardnadze's government established the basic legal and constitutional framework for a democratic multinational society. The law on citizenship, passed in March 1993, in contrast to Latvia and Estonia, granted unconditional citizenship to all Georgia's residents. No special qualifications were required, including knowledge of the state language. The constitution, criminal code, code of criminal procedure, the Law on Public Associations of Citizens, the Law on Education, and the Law on Culture all laid the basis for civil and national minority rights, nondiscriminatory protections, the right to receive education (up to the secondary level) in one's native language, the right to a translator in the courts, and the right to set up political organizations based on national culture (though political parties cannot be based on a single region and have to have an all-national character).

Georgian legislators ratified OSCE (Organization for Security and Cooperation in Europe) and United Nations conventions such as the United Nations Convention on the Elimination of All Forms of Racial Discrimination, as well as the Council of Europe's Convention for the Protection of Human Rights and Fundamental Freedoms. A parliamentary committee on human rights and a national ombudsperson (also known as the "public defender") were established to protect minority rights.[41] Shevardnadze appointed regional and district representatives from among the local national groups, and his speeches, which extolled the concept of citizenship, helped diffuse much of the chauvinistic hysteria that dominated the 1992–95 parliament. Undoubtedly, the reality does not reflect legislative ambition, but the political context has changed radically since Gamsakhurdia. Under Shevardnadze, Georgia's revolution moved from a Jacobin to Girondist stage and, officially at least, from a differentialist emphasis to more of an assimilationst one, or, to put it in Lowell Barrington's words, from a "sovereignty-protecting nationalism" to a "civic nation-building" nationalism. The language of militant nationalism was expunged from the official lexicon, replaced by concepts of citizenship and minority rights.

Georgian nationalism—if one accepts it is related to the depth and sustainability of mass support—today seems weaker than many European nationalisms. It is quite extraordinary, given the scale of military threats to Georgian national integrity, how restrained Georgians have been regarding the loss of Abkhazia and South Osetia. This may partly be explained by political fatigue, but even during the war in Abkhazia, few Georgians were willing to risk their lives for a campaign that to many was distant and irrelevant. Most fighters (though not all) were local Georgians from Sukhumi defending their livelihoods and homes. Other local Georgians, who supported ousted President Gamsakhurdia (mostly Mingrelians) refused to fight "Shevardnadze's" war.

That is not to suggest Georgians are unpatriotic, but the picture is more complex than the analysis proffered in the West—a mass-based conflict motivated and sustained by militant nationalist passions and historical wrongs. The vast majority of Georgians were not engaged in militant nationalist struggles, and if militant nationalism was so pervasive in Georgia, it is surprising that after Georgia's military defeat Georgians did not rise up against the government that led the country into such catastrophic national humiliation. This needs explanation. One wonders how Americans would have reacted to a comparative loss of U.S. territories and blatant internal interference from a powerful neighboring state. I suspect they would not have shown the Georgians' coolness.

Georgian Nationalism: Continuity or Discontinuity?

Georgian nationalism has a long and varied history. To ignore this changeable and often contradictory history, which included at times tolerance for different national groups in the pre-Soviet and Soviet periods, would result in a partial history and make the prognosis for civil peace in Georgia a much dimmer prospect. The interesting question for the researcher into Georgian nationalism is not so much the "continuities" of violence and ethnic conflict but the discontinuities and contradictions. What was it that made the new Georgian state in 1991, supported by the majority of its population, a violent threat to some (again, not all) of its minorities upon the establishment of independence?[42] What made these fairly good neighbors into bad ones over the years 1989–93, when Georgia became embroiled in two wars of secession and a civil war? And what led to the movement away from radical nationalism in the years that followed, as postindependence Georgian nationalism was weakened and transformed?

At least five factors come to mind: the Soviet legacy, the role of Zviad Gamsakhurdia, state disintegration, economic collapse, and Russian intervention. The Soviet legacy is complex, but two issues in particular contributed to the breakdown in national relations. The collapse of the USSR left Georgia with a "multicolored" map, divided into nationally or religiously based territories, each one assigned to a titular group. These were the Abkhazian and Ach'aran Autonomous Republics and the South Osetian Autonomous Region. The territories of these republics and regions were "sacralized," with their own borders, "national" institutions, popular assemblies, and symbols. Nations were seen as fixed entities despite official rhetoric about their ultimate disappearance. On gaining independence Georgia faced small "domestic states" within its borders, or, as Lowell Barrington puts it, the existence of "overlapping homelands." Titular nations conceived of these autonomous units as "their own." The local elites in Abkhazia and South Osetia feared the removal of Russian protection after Georgian independence threatened their political, economic, and cultural privileges as well as their security. The Georgian government of 1990–92, inexperienced and chauvinistic, confirmed their fears.[43]

The Soviet Union also left behind a radical, polarized view of politics, a theatrical cast of heroes and enemies. The pseudopolitics of the Soviet state left the narrowest space for development of a critically engaged public that could experience negotiation, compromise, and process. Leaders, institutions, and the law were seen either as oppressive and corrupt or as conspiring against Georgian interests. The instruments of change would have to come from outside, uncorrupted by the Soviet system. In a time of national crisis, Gamsakhurdia–a former political prisoner, young, religious, son of a great patriot—fit the heroic anti-Communist bill perfectly. At the same time, he was a Soviet product—ideological, intolerant of opposition, conspiratorial, a seeker of enemies within.[44] His populist rhetoric stimulated Georgians' own anxieties about demographic decline and loss of control in their own republic. Add to this the other three factors mentioned above—the state's rapid disintegration, economic collapse, and Russian intervention, which deprived the Georgian government of institutional stability and legitimacy, as well as economic resources and control, and offered a strong (Russian) patron to disaffected national minorities—and the pattern of conflict in Georgia in the immediate postindependence years is not surprising. Rather, it is almost inevitable.

Under Shevardnadze, Georgian history was put into service once more, but this time as an example of how Georgia's nations could live in peace.[45] Militant nationalist organizations such as the National Independence

Party, Merab Kostava Society, and St. Ilya the Righteous Society disappeared from the political scene. The absence of public support for these parties needs explanation. Why did they become marginalized, and why did militant nationalism lose its appeal? First and foremost, the illiberal populism of the Gamsakhurdia leadership was dysfunctional for most Georgians; it brought economic chaos, civil war and disorder, a crisis of identity, regional fragmentation, and isolation from Europe. Put simply, Gamsakhurdia's populist nationalism failed to bring results. The repression of national minorities and civil strife between Georgians was cathartic—it led many Georgians to reassess their image of themselves as united and tolerant and created a nostalgic yearning for the Georgian tradition of multinational cooperation.

The disorder of the Gamsakhurdia era led to accelerated political maturity among Georgians. In his book *The End of History and the Last Man*, Fukuyama projects a "final political neutralization" of nationalism. He argues that as a national group becomes secure in its identity, it will become—like European religions in the past—"defanged and modernized."[46] While I do not entirely agree with this generalization, a process of deradicalization quickly developed in Georgia, especially after its defeat in the Georgian-Abkhazian war of September 1993 and the civil war that followed. Popular exhaustion with the symbolic hyperbole and infighting of militant nationalist parties led to a widespread desire for stability and more moderate goals. The strong anti-Russian feelings inspired by Gamsakhurdia gave way to a realization that the country's northern neighbor had to be accommodated. As a result, Shevardnadze was initially welcomed as someone who could "deal" with Russia.

Equally important in the deradicalization process was the increasing role of Europe and international organizations in Georgia. Gamsakhurdia's alienation of European and American leaders irritated Georgians who always thought of themselves as Europeans and deserving members of the Western cultural community.[47] Georgians' desire to be European required conformity with European ideas of civil and minority rights and the rule of law and opened them to new and more flexible interpretations of sovereignty (a reassessment of federalism, for example). Official acceptance into the Western community, which followed precipitously on Shevardnadze's return to Georgia in March 1992, also brought recognition of independence, the hope of financial support, and an influx of international nongovernmental organizations (NGOs). Today, there is considerable disillusion with the NGOs, but they helped establish a nongovernmental sector and provided new depoliticized avenues of social activism.

A third strand in the deradicalization process was a shift in the power elite. Gamsakhurdia removed and alienated much of Georgia's traditional cultural, political, and economic elites. In contrast, Shevardnadze's Soviet background and pragmatic approach to administrative needs led to the restoration of Georgia's former nomenklatura—the old regional party secretaries, Komsomol officials, enterprise managers and moderate nationalist intellectuals transformed into governors, entrepreneurs, and presidential advisers. Young pro-European modernizers, often educated abroad and known as the "Mississippdaleulni" (literally, "those who have drunk from the Mississippi"[48]), joined this elite and helped mediate Georgian economic and political life. Direct action, popular participation, and street politics withered away. Shevtsova in her book on the Yeltsin era, suggests the former nomenklatura, enriched and ambitious, is probably "the most solid shield against a return to the Soviet past."[49] In Georgia, it was also the best guarantee against a return to the militant nationalism of Gamsakhurdia.

Shevardnadze did not abandon nationalism but "reframed" it from a state-seeking activity to a state-building activity.[50] His "institutional" nationalism avoided popular mobilization and aimed to attach both the Georgian nation and national minorities to the state through a redefinition of history and citizenship. When Shevardnadze came to power, Georgia was a state on the verge of collapse. Strong regionalist movements and civil war underlined fundamental disagreements on what constituted "Georgianness," and disputes over national symbols and history, territorial structures and majority-minority relations, showed nation-building in Georgia, despite its claim to deep roots, was incomplete. Georgians were fighting among themselves over the "national project" as much as they were with non-Georgians. In this context, nationalism became an important focus for unity based on reconciliation, a strong and independent state, a restored self-image of multinational tolerance, and a return to Christian Georgia's traditional alliance with Europe. This "defanged" nationalism is usually accompanied, as Brubaker puts it, by "declining curves of mobilization."[51] This was the case in Georgia under Shevardnadze.

One cannot, of course, omit history and ethnicity from this analysis, although in the case of the Georgian-Abkhazian and Georgian–South Osetian disputes, both were mainly weapons of choice used to mobilize support. The use of the term *ethnic conflict* is too blunt and unambiguous to describe the conflict between Georgians and their national minorities. It assumes that all stages of the conflict were "ethnic" (focused on cultural, religious, historical, or linguistic differences) and that all members of the opposing groups unanimously supported the objectives and strategies pursued by their leaders.

"Ethnic conflict" simplifies the picture. It ignores the stages of conflict and the saliency of other issues that contribute to collective action and resistance, such as ideology (fear of political and economic change), self-interest (protection of privilege), intragroup differences, and the interests of powerful neighboring states. Violence between national groups can defy all models and predictions, but the Georgian-Abkhazian and Georgian-Osetian cases suggest that the "ethnicization" of a dispute is not entirely spontaneous and may follow the mobilization of the population rather than precede it. As Smith has pointed out, conflict and war can produce nations and nationalism as much as the other way round.[52]

In the Georgian-Abkhazian and Georgian-Osetian cases, ethnic differences existed, but they were not always the most salient sources of conflict. The conflicts in Georgia began with questions of parliamentary competency, self-government, and territorial status between numerically small elites on either side. With the formation of new state institutions, differences focused on representation, participation, and territorial control. Even Gamsakhurdia did not reject Abkhazian claims to special political and cultural rights; the issue was rather the preservation of Georgian national sovereignty in Abkhazia. But as the conflicts intensified, especially after the outbreak of violence in July 1989 in Abkhazia and in 1990 in South Osetia, the rhetoric of the disputes shifted to "deeper" ethnic issues of cultural and historical incompatibilities and hatreds. The conflict became self-sustaining with each confrontation, reinforcing a sense of injustice, exclusion, and insecurity on all sides. The trigger to mass violence in both cases came with the intrusion of armed outsiders from Tbilisi.[53]

Thus, the link between ethnic conflict and violence in Georgia and elsewhere is the result of three mistaken assumptions: (1) that if the groups are ethnic, then the conflict's source must be ethnic, (2) that ethnic conflict is an explosion waiting to happen (without an appreciation of the different stages and intensities that precede or accompany the conflict), and (3) that all ethnic conflicts are irrational and therefore likely to end in violence. All three premises lead us to an uncomplicated emphasis on ethnicity as the sole source of the conflicts in Georgia.

Conclusion

What did post-Soviet Georgian nationalism look like under Shevardnadze? It was not exclusive, antimodernist, or illiberal (but neither could it be described as entirely inclusive, modernist, or liberal). Defining Georgian nationalism depends on where you look and when. We might draw different conclusions based on when we polled, where we polled, and whom we polled. Focusing on the early 1990s would have given us a very different picture of Georgian nationalism than in the late 1990s. As with other nationalisms, Georgians' "ethnic" passions wax and wane, depending on political and economic circumstances.

Lowell Barrington's five variants provide an excellent model for the numerous patterns of nationalism in post-Soviet states. It helps us understand the difference between the Gamsakhurdia era of "sovereignty-protecting" and Shevardnadze's "civic nation-building." His point that "postindependence nationalists" can pursue many of these variants simultaneously, or that "different nationalist elites may support different nationalist variants," is particularly appropriate in the Georgian case. Four of the five variants—nationalism as sovereignty-protecting, civic nation-building, ethnic nation-protecting, and co-national-protecting—could be used to describe aspects of Georgian nationalism at different stages of its development since independence. The first variant, however—nationalism as external-territory-claiming—though not alien to Georgian nineteenth-century nationalism, was not a significant part of the postindependence nationalist movement

Yet, overall, the issues that dominate Georgian newspapers today are not nationalist ones—though secessionist Abkhazia is a constant feature—but the economy, crime, corruption, and scandal. In a public opinion survey taken in September 1999 by SOCIOGEO, 66 percent declared economic and social problems to be the most serious facing Georgia today, and only 17 percent mentioned ethnic and territorial issues.[54] Alternative militant nationalisms still gain high visibility but are weak. A good example is MP Guram Sharadze's party—Georgia First of All—which has almost no organization but attracts national attention when it demands the retention of nationality in the Georgian passport and takes Jehovah's Witnesses to court for antistate propaganda.[55] One might cite as more radically nationalist the electoral platforms of the Labor and Socialist parties (or the party Industry Will Save Georgia), which have a strong populist, antiforeign ring to them, in particular on the questions of resistance to International Monetary Fund (IMF) directed economic policies.[56] But these parties received support not because of their nationalist platforms but due to their economic and social programs or because of the personalities of the men leading them.[57]

Just as I would not judge American nationalism by the statements of militia leaders, populist politicians, electoral platforms, or violent shooting incidents, so I would make no assumptions about the importance of militant nationalism in Georgia from reports picked up by Reuters or Associated Press. Many in the Georgian elite continue to voice strong anti-Abkhazian, anti-Osetian, and, less openly, anti-Armenian sentiments, but as Lieven points out in his intelligent dissection of Chechen nationalism, "the world is full of nations which regularly indulge in outbursts of nationalist rhetoric, and still more of elites who use such rhetoric to mask their real and ugly motives for holding onto state power. How many, though, actually have the ability or will to carry out their rhetoric in reality?"[58]

This does not mean Georgian nationalism has no distinctive features but that they are mixed, neither exclusively illiberal nor fully inclusive, a combination of—in Georgia's case—four of the variants of Lowell Barrington's model. Georgians share with other nations what Nairn has called nationalism's "Janus-like face," looking both backward and forward.[59] Resentful of the impact of globalization, Georgians want to become part of the modern global world; sharing a largely ethnocultural conception of nationhood, they also support pragmatic, multicultural policies, based on a historical self image of national tolerance. Strong believers in national sovereignty, Georgians yearn to become members of the European Union, an organization that promotes integration.

Under the leadership of Gamsakhurdia, and in the context of imperial collapse, Georgian nationalism resembled a combination of the sovereignty-protecting and ethnic nation-protecting features described in Lowell Barrington's introduction, common among the defensive and exclusionary movements of the late twentieth century tabulated by Eric Hobsbawm in his book *Nations and Nationalism since 1870*.[60] It was revolutionary and integral to Gamsakhurdia's populist, egalitarian, and anti-establishment policies. But the loss of Abkhazia and South Osetia, regional divisions, civil war, economic collapse, and isolation from the West created the context for the more constructive, civic nation-building nationalism of Shevardnadze. Under Shevardnadze nationalism became an instrument for stabilizing the state. It was a mechanism for redefining membership of the nation, reintegrating national minorities, establishing consensus and controlling the opposition.

Georgia under Shevardnadze did not become a fully "civic" state where, in theory at least, ethnicity has no relevance to citizenship rights (a rare achievement anywhere in the world). The special role given to the Georgian church in the constitution, the semiofficial persecution of new religious groups such as the Jehovah's Witnesses, the state's ambivalence as to whether national origin should remain in passports, the reluctance to specify and implement national minority rights in a comprehensive law on national minorities, arguments over the flag, and continued tensions in the regions with national minorities such as the Armenians in Javakheti—all testify to the ethnocultural core of Georgian national identity.

But at the same time, the traditional self-image of Georgia as a tolerant multinational state, while not accepted by many non-Georgians, has become part of Georgians' own political discussions in the postindependence period. Aspirations to join Europe have stimulated Georgian elites to consider federalism an appropriate territorial division and to incorporate international norms protecting minority rights into their legislation. Ethnic concerns are no longer uppermost in Georgian minds and compete unfavorably with economic and social issues such as employment, health, and corruption. Ethnocultural issues play no significant role in foreign policy. Turkey, for example, although not fully trusted by ordinary Georgians, has been transformed from a Muslim threat into a friendly NATO ally that will help Georgia itself get closer to Europe.

Georgian nationalism, despite European pressures and the new elites' pragmatism, will not adopt an integrationist civic model, largely because Georgia's own national minorities find this unacceptable. They want to be treated as separate national groups and preserve a system that Karklins, among others, has termed *ethnopluralism,* a system that recognizes and accommodates national group rights.[61] Georgians' multinational tradition—historically more significant than the "tradition" of national conflict—is an important base for such a model. But this model's effectiveness depends on greater state authority (an end to Georgia's massive corruption is an essential step to achieving this), a stable and friendly regional environment (while Russian intervention persists, reconciliation between the Abkhazians and Georgians will be difficult), and a reversal of Georgia's social and economic decline.

In short, as I have suggested throughout this essay, Georgia's "ethnic" problems are neither deeply rooted nor "autonomous." They cannot be isolated from a complex mix of Georgian legacies and attitudes or separated from vital economic and social issues. Georgia's legacies are not those of ethnic conflict. The tradition of multinational coexistence has greater longevity. The question is whether this tradition can be successfully incorporated into a new national ideology acceptable to all Georgia's national groups.

Postscript

This chapter was completed prior to the revolutionary change in November 2003, the peaceful ouster of Eduard Shevardnadze, known as the "Rose Revolution." This peaceful revolution confirms the argument of this essay. Post-Soviet politics in Georgia has become a complex process that cannot be confined within the parameters of ethnonationalism. Georgians' demands in November 2003 led to a dramatic example of how post-Soviet politics—not only in Georgia—has changed in the last decade from simplistic ethnocentric claims to "ordinary" demands for clean government, fair representation, decent economic standards, and better protection of rights. Political authoritarianism is the dominant pattern in the Newly Independent States, but post-Soviet societies are rapidly changing into pluralistic entities that should move Western scholarship beyond its traditional focus on postcommunist "vacuums" and "fundamentalisms."

NOTES

1. Yuri Slezkine, "The USSR as a Communal Apartment, or How a Socialist State Promoted Ethnic Particularism," *Slavic Review* 53, no. 2 (summer 1994): 414–52.

2. Teresa Rakowska-Harmstone, "The Dialectics of Nationalism in the USSR," *Problems of Communism* 22, no. 3 (May–June 1974): 1–22; and Rogers Brubaker, *Nationalism Reframed: Nationhood and the National Question in the New Europe* (Cambridge: Cambridge University Press, 1996), especially chapter 2.

3. One in a long line of such commentaries is Robert Kaplan's "Where Europe Vanishes" (*Atlantic Monthly* 286, no. 5 [November 2000]: 67–81), in which he writes, "The story of the Republic of Georgia illustrates that the peoples of the Caucasus may prove as incapable of self-rule as they were resistant to rule by outsiders." See also David Rieff, "Nagorno-Karabagh: Case Study in Ethnic Strife," *Foreign Affairs* 76, no. 2

(March 1997): 118–32, where Armenians in Nagorno-Karabakh are characterized as little less than mad. The article seems to be based on a limited number of interviews.

4. This is not to suggest that these articles are unimportant, only that the study of Caucasia needs to address other issues. To give a bibliography of all the articles published on "ethnic conflict" in Georgia over the last ten years would take up tens of pages, but articles addressing, say, local government, legislative power, the constitution, and political parties could be counted in the tens. For interesting examples of work on ethnic conflict in Caucasia, see Ronald G. Suny, *The Revenge of the Past: Nationalism, Revolution, and the Collapse of the Soviet Union* (Stanford, CA: Stanford University Press, 1993); Stephan Astourian, "The Nagorno-Karabagh Conflict: Dimensions, Lessons, Prospects," *Mediterranean Quarterly* 5, no. 4 (fall 1994): 85–109; Bruno Coppieters, ed., *Contested Borders in the Caucasus* (Brussels: VUB University Press, 1996); and Bruno Coppieters, Ghia Nodia, and Yuri Anchabadze, eds., *Georgians and Abkhazian: The Search for a Peace Settlement* (Cologne: Bundesinstitut fur ostwissenschaftliche und internationale Studien, 1998). For articles on other issues in Georgia over the last five years, see in particular the United Nations Development Program discussion paper series. Papers include Revaz Gachechiladze, "Population Migration in Georgia and Its Socio-Economic Consequences" (no. 1, UNDP, Tbilisi, 1997); Erekle Natadze, "Taxation and the Economic Consequences for Georgia in Transition" (no. 2, UNDP, Tbilisi, 1998); and George Tarkhan-Mouravi, "Poverty in a Transitional Society: Georgia" (no. 6, UNDP, Tbilisi, 1998). On democratization, see Karen Dawisha and Bruce Parrott, eds., *Conflict, Cleavage, and Change in Central Asia and the Caucasus* (Cambridge: Cambridge University Press, 1997). See also my "Democracy from Below: Interest Groups in Georgian Society," *Slavic Review* 59, no. 1 (spring 2000): 42–73.

5. Walker Connor, "A Nation Is a Nation, Is a State, Is an Ethnic Group, Is a . . . ," *Ethnic and Racial Studies* 1, no. 4 (1978): 379–88.

6. Anthony Smith, *National Identity: Ethnonationalism in Comparative Perspective* (Reno: University of Nevada Press, 1991), chapter 4.

7. The list could be enormous. Some of the most prominent include Benedict Anderson, *Imagined Communities: Reflections on the Origin and Spread of Nationalism* (London: Verso, 1983); Eric Hobsbawm, *Nations and Nationalism since 1780: Programme, Myth, Reality* (Cambridge: Cambridge University Press, 1990); Ernest Gellner, *Nations and Nationalism* (Ithaca, NY: Cornell University Press, 1983); John Hutchinson, *Modern Nationalism* (London: Fontana Press, 1994); Tom Nairn, *The Break-up of Britain: Crisis and Neonationalism,* 2nd ed. (London: Verso, 1981); Geoff Ely and Ronald G. Suny, *Becoming National: A Reader* (New York: Oxford University Press, 1996); Anthony D. Smith, *The Ethnic Revival* (Cambridge: Cambridge University Press, 1981); Brubaker, *Nationalism Reframed;* and John Breuilly, *Nationalism and the State* (Chicago: University of Chicago Press, 1985).

8. The complete March 19, 1998, address from Bucharest University, Bucharest, Romania, is available from the State Department Web site at http://www.state.gov/www/policy_remarks/1998/980319_talbott_bucharest.html.

9. This is a reference to the famous quip by Tip O'Neil, Speaker of the U.S. House of Representatives from 1977 to 1986, that "all politics is local." I am suggesting that the explanations for political behavior in Caucasia should be as complex as they are in the United States, that much of what we perceive as "national" in Caucasia is also determined by local and regional interests. We need to investigate the devilish details behind the big picture.

10. On the complex links between violence and nationalism, see the articles in Christopher Dandeker, ed., *Nationalism and Violence* (New Brunswick: Transaction Publishers, 1998). For the viewpoint of a Caucasian scholar, see Levon Abrahamian, "Typology of Aggressiveness and National Violence in the Former USSR," in *Divided Europeans: Understanding Ethnicities in Conflict*, ed. Tim Allen and John Eade (The Hague: Kluwer Law International, 1999), 59–75. Abrahamian does not assume an automatic link between violence and ethnic conflict. He prefers to talk about the different "cultures of violence," a better way of explaining why and in what form violence in the Caucasus occurs.

11. See George Mosse, *Confronting the Nation: Jewish and Western Nationalism* (Hanover: Brandeis University Press and University Press of New England, 1993), especially chapter 1, "National Anthems: The Nation Militant."

12. John Stuart Mill, *Considerations on Representative Government*, chapters 16 and 18, crucial chapters on the relationship between nationalism and liberalism, are reprinted in Omar Dahbour and Micheline Ishay, *The Nationalism Reader* (Atlantic Highlands, NJ: Humanities Press, 1995), 98–107; and Anthony Smith, *Nations and Nationalism in a Global Era* (Cambridge, MA: Polity Press, 1995). See also Ghia Nodia, "Nationhood and Self-Recollection: Ways to Democracy after Communism," in *Towards a New Community: Culture and Politics in Post-Totalitarian Europe*, ed. Peter Duncan and Martyn Rady (Hamburg: School of Slavonic and East European Studies, LIT Verlag, 1993), 53–63; and Michael Lind, "In Defense of Liberal Nationalism," *Foreign Affairs* 73, no. 3 (May/June 1994): 87–99.

13. Though to talk of a single type of nationalism in the West that we can compare to Georgian nationalism is also simplistic.

14. Rogers Brubaker, *Citizenship and Nationhood in France and Germany* (Cambridge, MA: Harvard University Press, 1992). See chapter 7, "Etre Francais, Cela se Merite: Immigration and the Politics of Citizenship in France," where Brubaker discusses the debate of the mid-1980s in France concerning the right of nonethnically (in particular North African) French residents to acquire citizenship.

15. Stjepan Mestrovic, *The Balkanization of the West: The Confluence of Postmodernism and Postcommunism* (London: Routledge, 1994).

16. In his testimony to the Senate Select Committee on Intelligence, George J. Tenet, former director of central intelligence, declared: "This new world harbors the residual effects of the Cold War which had frozen many traditional ethnic hatreds and conflicts within the global competition between two superpowers. Over the past 10 years they began to thaw in Africa, the Caucasus, and the Balkans, and we continue to see the results today." See the February 2, 2000, statement by Director of Central Intelligence George J. Tenet before the Senate Select Committee on Intelligence, "The Worldwide Threat in 2000: Global Realities of Our National Security," *Turkistan Newsletter* 4, no. 34 (February 9, 2000), available at http://www.turkiye.net/sota/sota.html. Tenet's suggestion is that nationalism not only is rooted in the past but also occurs only in small and weak states.

17. Gellner, *Nations and Nationalism;* Nairn, *The Break-up of Britain;* and Miroslav Hroch, *Social Preconditions of National Revival in Europe: A Comparative Analysis of the Social Composition of Patriotic Groups among the Smaller European Nations*, trans. Ben Fowkes (Cambridge: Cambridge University Press, 1985).

18. Mestrovic, *The Balkanization of the West*, 8–10.

19. Brubaker, *Nationalism Reframed*, 88, and especially chapter 4.

20. On the rise of nationalism in Georgia, see Ronald G. Suny, *The Making of the Georgian Nation* (Bloomington: Indiana University Press, 1988), especially chapters 6–9.

21. Georgian parties did, however, call for greater autonomy. On this period in Georgian history, see Firuz Kazamzadeh, *The Struggle for Transcaucasia (1917–1921)* (New York: Philosophical Library, 1951), chapters 1–3; Ronald G. Suny, "The Emergence of Political Society in Georgia," in *Transcaucasia, Nationalism and Social Change: Essays in the History of Armenia, Azerbaijan and Georgia,* rev. ed., ed. Ronald G. Suny (Ann Arbor: University of Michigan Press, 1996), 109–40; and Stephen Jones, "Georgian Social Democracy in 1917," in *Revolution in Russia: Reassessments of 1917,* ed. Jonathan Frankel, Edith Rogovin Frankel, and Baruch Knei-Paz (Cambridge: Cambridge University Press, 1991), 247–73.

22. On the relationship between nationalism and socialism among non-Russians during the Russian Revolution of 1917, see Stephen Jones, "The Non-Russian Nationalities," in *Society and Politics in the Russian Revolution,* ed. Robert Service (New York: St. Martin's Press, 1992), 35–63.

23. In the Soviet period, Georgians became fighters against Soviet oppression. Resistance to totalitarianism was identified as a fight for the values and freedoms of Western democracies. Only after the collapse of the USSR did it become clear that dissidents like Zviad Gamsakhurdia were concerned not with human rights more generally but with national rights more specifically. For a balanced assessment of the Georgian dissident movement in the 1970s, see Ludmilla Alexeyeva, *Soviet Dissent: Contemporary Movements for National, Religious and Human Rights,* trans. Carol Pearce and John Glad (Middletown, CT: Wesleyan University Press, 1985), 106–20. Yet even Alexeyeva does not highlight the tensions between national and human rights in Georgia, already evident in Gamsakhurdia's writings, but sees them as essentially compatible.

24. Rakowska-Harmstone, "The Dialectics of Nationalism in the USSR."

25. The nearest the Nazis got to Georgia in their push for Baku's oil was Nalchik, currently situated in the North Caucasian republic of Kabardino-Balkaria.

26. After 1980, the number of protests in defense of Georgian culture and language increased among students and intellectuals. Although there was general sympathy among Georgians for anti-Russification protests, they did not take to the streets. There were anti-Soviet demonstrations in 1981 and 1983 of up to two thousand (mainly students), but it wasn't until 1988 that mass demonstrations took place, protesting a proposed railway link between Russia and Georgia crossing the Greater Caucasian Range (see Stephen Jones, "The Caucasian Mountain Railway Project: A Victory for Glasnost?" *Central Asian Survey* 8, no. 2 [1989]: 47–59). On the rise of Georgian nationalism in the 1980s, see Stephen Jones, "Glasnost, Perestroika and the Georgian Soviet Socialist Republic," *Armenian Review* 43, nos. 2–3 (summer/autumn 1990): 127–52.

27. There is little information in English on either of these events. On 1956, see Alexeyeva, *Soviet Dissent;* G. Charachidze, "Les emeutes de Tiflis et leur signification," *Est et Ouest* 153 (June 1956): 15–17; and Elizabeth Fuller, "Georgia, Stalin and the Demonstrations of 1956," *Radio Free Europe/Radio Liberty Research* 190, no. 88 (May 3, 1988). On the 1978 events, see Ann Sheehy, "The National Languages and the New Constitutions of the Transcaucasian Republics," *Radio Free Europe/Radio Liberty Research* 97, no. 78 (May 3, 1978); and, more generally on language issues, Stephen Jones, "The Georgian Language State Program and Its Implications," *Nationalities Papers* 23, no. 3 (September 1995): 535–48.

28. James Scott and J. Tria Kerkvliet, eds., *Everyday Forms of Peasant Resistance in South-East Asia* (London: Frank Cass, 1986). See also Stephen Jones, "Old Ghosts and New Chains: Ethnicity and Memory in the Georgian Republic," in *Memory, History and Opposition under State Socialism,* ed. Rubie Watson (Santa Fe, NM: School of American Research Press, 1994), 149–65.

29. Between 1959 and 1979, the Osetian proportion of the Georgian population decreased from 3.5 to 3.2 percent. This combined with Georgian population gains above their natural growth rate (taking into consideration net migration and mortality rates) leads Anderson and Silver to suggest Georgians assimilated considerable numbers of Osetians during this period (B. A. Anderson and Brian Silver, "Estimating Russification of Ethnic Identity among Non-Russians in the USSR," *Demography* 20, no. 4 [November 1983]: 461–89). This does not mean this was a process accepted by all non-Georgians with equanimity. In the 1970s, there were a number of Abkhazian protests against Georgian demographic gains and perceived pressures to assimilate. See Darell Slider, "Crisis and Response in Soviet Nationality Policy: The Case of Abxazia," *Central Asian Survey* 4, no. 4 (1985): 51–68.

30. Abkhazians, too, were victims of the clashes in Sukhumi. One of the better works on the manipulation of the Georgian-Abkhazian conflict is Chervonnaya, *Conflict in the Caucasus Georgia, Abkhazia, and the Russian Shadow,* trans. Ariane Chanturia (Glastonbury, UK: Gothic Images, 1994).

31. Ghia Nodia, "Political Turmoil in Georgia and the Ethnic Policies of Zviad Gamsakhurdia," in *Contested Borders in the Caucasus,* ed. Bruno Coppiters (Concord, MA: Paul and Company Publishers), 73–89.

32. This is a result of my own observation. See also Alexei Zverev, "Ethnic Conflicts in the Caucasus, 1988–1994," in *Contested Borders in the Caucasus,* ed. Bruno Coppieters (Concord, MA: Paul and Company Publishers), 40–41, which presents a slightly different explanation for the absence of anti-Abkhazian slogans.

33. According to the 1989 census, the Abkhazians in the Abkhazian Autonomous Republic numbered 93,267, or 17.8 percent (they made up 95,900 in the Georgian republic as a whole). The South Osetians in the South Osetian Autonomous Region (oblast) numbered 65,000 (66 percent), although generally in Georgia they were more numerous at 164,000. For these figures, see Revaz Gachechiladze, *The New Georgia: Space, Society, Politics* (London: UCL Press, 1995), 73–104.

34. Although expulsions did occur among South Osetians and Armenians in Georgia during the war in South Osetia in 1990–91.

35. Nodia, "The Conflict in Abkhazia: National Projects and Political Circumstances," in *Georgians and Abkhazians: The Search for a Peace Settlement,* ed. Bruno Coppieters, Ghia Nodia, Yuri Anchabadze (Cologne: Bundeinstitut für ostwissenschaftliche und internationale Studien, 1998), 30–31.

36. We see a similar sort of differentiation in other states. In Hungary, for example, a law on national and ethnic minorities was passed in 1993 that gave special rights only to those groups that had lived in Hungary for more than a century.

37. Guram Svanidze, "National Minorities in Georgia" (International Centre for Peaceful Caucasus, n.d.), 7.

38. For fuller exposition of these arguments, see Stephen Jones, "Populism in Georgia: The Gamsaxurdia Phenomenon," in *Nationalism and History: The Politics of Nation Building in Post-Soviet Armenia, Azerbaijan and Georgia,* ed. Donald Schwarz and Razmik Panossian (Toronto: University of Toronto Press, 1994), 127–49.

39. I have an unofficial translation of the "Draft Law on National and Ethnic Minorities," written by G. V. Zhorzholiani and A. Ch. Abashidze. It was considered overly favorable to non-Georgian minorities by many Georgian parliamentarians. The language law, to supplement a language program passed in 1989, is also still under discussion at the time of this writing.

40. In the 1995 elections, four ethnic Armenians, four Azerbaijanis, two Russians, two Greeks, one Osetian, one Jew, and one Kurd were elected as MPs. In 1999, based simply on my identification of MPs by their last names (admittedly highly suspect), the new parliament included six Armenians, six Azerbaijanis, one Russian, two Abkhazians, and one Osetian. There are a total of 235 MPs.

41. The full name of the parliamentary committee dealing with human and minority rights under Shevardnadze was the Committee for Human Rights, Petitions by Citizens, and the Construction of a Civil Society. Four of its fourteen members were national minority representatives. The ombudsperson, or public defender, of Georgia was Nana Devdariani. Because she was a member of the Socialist Party, many parliamentarians felt she was not sufficiently objective to dealing with the rights of national minorities and other dissenting groups.

42. It is important to note that Georgian nationalism in the 1990s did not mean hostility to all resident national minorities. The Greek, Jewish, and, before 1990, South Osetian communities were on good terms with the Georgians. On the other hand, for historical and demographic reasons, the Abkhazians (they numbered ninety thousand and had no external homeland to protect them) and Armenians (the traditional merchant class in Georgia) were viewed by Georgians with greater hostility. Brubaker, in his discussion of Poland as an example of a "nationalizing state" (*Nationalism Reframed*, 79–106), notes similar differentiation. Some national minorities were considered by the Poles to be unassimilable (the Germans and Jews), while others were considered autochthonous and assimilable (the Ukrainians and Belorussians).

43. On the early years of Georgian independence under the leadership of Zviad Gamsakhurdia, see Jonathan Aves, "The Rise and Fall of the Georgian Nationalist Movement, 1987–1991," in *The Road to Post-Communism: Independent Political Movements in the Former Soviet Union, 1985–1991*, ed. Geoffrey A Hosking, Jonathan Aves, and Peter Duncan (London: Pinter, 1992); Ghia Nodia, "Georgia's Identity Crisis," *Journal of Democracy* 6, no. 1 (January 1995): 104–16; and Stephen Jones, "Georgia: A Failed Democratic Transition," in *Nations and Politics in the Soviet Successor States*, ed. Ian Bremmer and Ray Taras (Cambridge: Cambridge University Press, 1993), 288–310.

44. Jones, "Populism in Georgia." For Gamsakhurdia's writings, see *Sakartvelos resp'ublik'is p'rezident'i zviad gamsakhurdia* (Tbilisi: Khma erisa, 1995), especially "Mimartva javakhetis somekh mosakhleobas," 69–71, and "Sakartvelos resp'ublik'is uzenaesi sabch'os tavmjdomaris bat'on Zviad Gamsakhurdias gamosvla," 82–99, for examples of his view of national minority issues in Georgia. See also *22 shekhvedra* (Tbilisi: Khma erisa, 1995), a collection of interviews with Gamsakhurdia.

45. See, for example, Eduard Shevardnadze's "state of the union" address to parliament in May 1997. He declared that Georgia's "national philosophy must be based on, and take into account, the Georgian state's multinational population, the specifics of our state, and the many centuries we have experienced of people of different faiths living peacefully side by side." See "Sakartvelos p'rezident'is eduard shevardnadzis

mokhseneba sakartvelos p'arlament'is 1997 ts'lis 27 maisis skhdomaze," *P'arlament'is uts'q'ebani,* Tbilisi, May 31, 1997.

46. Francis Fukuyama, *The End of History and the Last Man* (New York: Free Press, 1992), 266–75.

47. On Georgians' identification with Western Europe, see Ghia Nodia, "The Georgian Perception of the West," in *Commonwealth and Independence in Post-Soviet Eurasia,* ed. Bruno Coppieters, Alexei Zverev, and Dmitri Trenin (London: Frank Cass, 1998), 12–43.

48. In the nineteenth century, Georgian intellectuals and reformers who were educated in Russia were known as the "tergdaleulni" or "those who had drunk from the river Terek," the traditional border between Georgia and Russia. The term *Mississippdaleulni* refers to those young Georgians who since independence in 1991 have received an education in the United States and returned with reformist zeal.

49. Lilia Shevtsova, *Yeltsin's Russia: Myths and Reality* (Washington, DC: Carnegie Endowment for International Peace/Brookings Institution Press, 1999), 282.

50. See Brubaker, *Nationalism Reframed,* chapter 4, where he discusses the nationalism of "nationalizing states" as distinct from the nationalism of state-seeking nations.

51. Rogers Brubaker, "Myths and Misconceptions in the Study of Nationalism," in *The State of the Nation: Ernest Gellner and the Theory of Nationalism,* ed. John Hall (Cambridge: Cambridge University Press, 1998), 272–306. This is a masterful summary and critique of many of the assumptions we make about nationalism. Reading this article made me reflect on Western assumptions about nationalism in the Caucasus and had a significant influence on this article.

52. Anthony Smith, *Theories of Nationalism,* 2nd ed. (London: Duckworth, 1983), xxxii–xxxvi.

53. On the Abkhazian conflict, see Nodia, "The Conflict in Abkhazia"; and Viacheslav Chirikba, "The Georgian-Abkhazian Conflict: In Search for Ways Out," in *Georgians and Abkhazians: The Search for a Peace Settlement,* ed. Bruno Coppieters, Ghia Nodia, and Yuri Anchabadze (Cologne: Bundesinstitut für ostwissenschaftliche und internationale Studien [BIOst], 1998), 14–62.

54. "Georgians Hope for Better Days Ahead," *Opinion Analysis* (Office of Research, Department of State, M-205–99, November 22, 1999).

55. On the court case, see *South Caucasian Human Rights Monitor,* Caucasian Institute for Peace, Development, and Democracy, Tbilisi, series no. 3 (November and December 1999 issues), available at cipdd@access.sanet.ge. In November 1999, Guram Sharadze took both the Union of Jehovah Witnesses and the Pennsylvania Guard Tower Association to court, claiming they were registered illegally. He demanded a ban on their activities and claimed they were antistate, antinational, and anti-Orthodox (*Akhali taoba,* no. 330 [November 30, 1999], 4, 6).

56. For the manifesto of Industry Will Save Georgia, see "P'olit'ik'uri modzraoba: Mrets'veloba gadaarchens sakartvelos; Dziritadi sap'rogramo p'rintsip'ebi," Tbilisi, 1999, especially 4–7. I have a copy of the political platform of the Socialist Party (Sotsialist'uri part'ia: Dziritadi p'rintsip'ebi). It is a draft version given to me by its chairman, Vakht'ang Rcheulishvili. Unfortunately, these platforms are no longer available on the Georgian parliament Web page (http://www.parliament.ge). In an interview I conducted with Rcheulishvili in August 1998, he blamed Shevardnadze for poor Georgian-Russian relations and subservience to the IMF. Rcheulishvili advocates a "semiprotec-

tionist" industrial policy for Georgia and a fairer redistribution of wealth. The Socialist Party and Industry Will Save Georgia both stress active government intervention in the economy, a more egalitarian wages policy, better employment, and an immediate improvement in living standards.

57. In the 1999 parliamentary elections, only three parties managed to surmount the 7 percent barrier required for party representation based on the proportional system—the Citizens Union of Georgia (41.75 percent), Industry Will Save Georgia (7.04 percent), and Revival of Georgia (25.18 percent). However, members of the Labor and Socialist parties were elected from individual constituencies. There were twelve members of the Socialist faction in the 1999–2003 parliament, although only two members of the Labor Party were elected. The Labor and Socialist parties were much more successful in the local elections of November 1998, when they captured a number of Georgia's major cities. For official results of the October 1999 national parliamentary elections, see *Sakartvelos tsent'raluri saarchevno k'omisia: Sakartvelos p'arlament'is 1999 ts'lis 31 ok't'ombris archevnebis shedegebis shemajamebeli okmi,* Tbilisi, November 9, 1999.

58. Anatol Lieven, *Chechnya: Tombstone of Russian Power* (New Haven: Yale University Press, 1998), 7.

59. Nairn, *The Break-up of Britain,* 329–63.

60. Eric Hobsbawm, *Nations and Nationalism since 1870,* especially chapter 6.

61. Rasma Karklins, "Ethnopluralism: Panacea for East Central Europe?" *Nationalities Papers* 28, no. 2 (2000): 219–41.

IV. Conclusion

11. Nationalism, Nation Making, & the Postcolonial States of Asia, Africa, & Eurasia

RONALD GRIGOR SUNY

I HAVE BENEFITED ENORMOUSLY from Lowell Barrington's clarifying essays on ethnicity and nationalism. His distinction insisting on territoriality for the nation but not for ethnicity is very useful. At the same time, in our many discussions, I have argued that his definition of the nation remains, for my money, too objectivist. So I have amended the definitions he offers in his introductory chapter as a prelude to my own discussion of nationalism after independence. My additions are in brackets. "What makes nations different from other groups," writes Barrington, "is that they are *collectives* [who feel they are] *united by shared cultural features (such as language, myths, and values) and the belief in the right to territorial self-determination.* Put another way, they are groups of people [who believe they are] linked by unifying cultural characteristics and the desire to control a territory that is thought of as the group's rightful homeland."

My amendments here are meant to emphasize the unease I have about too concrete a notion of "cultural features" or "cultural characteristics." Having heard all my life about the importance of preserving ethnic culture and remaining unsure about what that entailed, I subscribe to a notion of culture as a "a system of symbols possessing a real but thin coherence that is continually put at risk in practice and therefore subject to transformation."[1]

In this chapter, *nation* is employed to mean a group of people who imagines themselves to be a political community distinct from the rest of mankind, deserving self-determination, which usually entails self-rule, control of their own territory (the "homeland"), and perhaps a state of their own. Nations, therefore, have to be made; they are not simply given by God, nature, history, or ethnic origins. And they can only exist in their full modern form when a discursive environment has been established in which cultural communities, however defined, are understood to have legitimate claims to political recognition, autonomy, independence, statehood, and control of a piece of geography.

Although arguably there were precocious instances of culture endowing power to leaders, such a discursive universe did not exist persistently and hegemonically anywhere in the world before the late eighteenth century. By the twentieth century, nations were the name of the game in politics, and the days of empires, dynastic realms, or class-derived polities were numbered. Even as they continued in various forms to coexist with nation-states, empires and non-nation-states spoke the language of the nation, dressed in national costume, and, joined by late-arriving theocratic challengers, defended the people in the form of the nation against rival forms of modernity and transnational predators.

Finding the "Radical Middle" in Ideas about the Nation

As several authors in this volume mention, our usual understanding of nations and nationalism is based on irreconcilable opposites, binarisms, or dichotomies. There is the good nationalism of the West, often referred to as *civic*, and the bad nationalism elsewhere, referred to as *ethnic*. There is the dichotomy between theories of nationalism that consider the nation to be ancient and primordial, natural and organic, and those—now hegemonic—that consider nations to be modern and constructed. Some see the nation as spontaneous, popular, and folkloric, while others talk about it as something created from the top down, elite generated, and manipulated by those in power. To those who see nationalism as inevitable, permanent, and relatively unchanging are counterposed those who see it as situational and constantly shifting.

Here, I propose a radical middle position. For me the nation is (1) modern and constructed *but* built on prior associations, communities, and identities, which in turn were constructed, though at a different time and in a different way. Ethnicity itself, for all the primordialism that accompanies its spokespersons, is like every other human category or group, a social construction—though one with deep roots and considerable longevity—and it evolves and changes over time, is contested by its members and outsiders, and requires effort by actors to maintain some coherence or make changes.

The nation is (2) certainly influenced, shaped, often driven, even created by elites, *but* on the basis of themes, traditions, and symbols that resonate in the population. "Experience," as understood and explained, is the context for the creation of the nation. "History" is doubly implicated: what is remembered as having happened, and what historians, journalists, and politicians select and promote as collective or official memory.

The nation is (3) more often both civic and ethnic than either one exclusively. As Barrington mentions, these forms of nationalisms are useful, perhaps, as ideal types but seldom exist in isolation from one another. They overlap and blend into each other. For one thing, civic requires a stable community, which in some sense is a culture, though the markers of it may be different from those more easily recognized as ethnic.

The nation is (4) both situational and constantly shifting. At the same time, it is much more persistent and indelible than many constructivists would have it. If nations are successful and maintain themselves, imagined communities are soon institutionalized communities.

The Postindependence Nationalisms of the Cases Covered in This Volume

As the chapters in this volume show, in many cases these various nationalisms operate simultaneously and in combination with one another. One might see the Yugoslav-Bosnian conflict as a clash between a nationalizing state nationalism (of Yugoslavia/Serbia) and a state-seeking nationalism (of the Bosnians), as well as the result of imperialist nationalisms (of Croatia and Serbia), not to mention the diasporic nationalism of Bosnian Serbs and Bosnian Croats. In Africa, Asia, and Eurasia, such a mixing of nationalism variants has been common.

There is one additional, and important, feature that the countries discussed in detail in this volume share. Although treated separately in the book, the "postcolonial" and "postcommunist" cases (especially in the cases of the Eurasian states of the former Soviet Union) are, in my view, *all* postcolonial states. While scholars continue to debate whether the USSR was an empire and, if it was, what kind of empire, the justification of dominance from a metropolitan center in the Soviet case was not that different from the imperial rationalizations of the great European powers. Where race distinguished between the superior and the inferior and thereby served to legitimize white rule over native peoples in Africa and Asia, an ostensibly egalitarian ideology in the Soviet Union made distinctions between superior and inferior classes, levels of development, and degrees of proletarianization and peasant backwardness that supported Moscow's dominion over peoples who required a helping hand. The Soviet system, like the great European empires, formalized boundaries, defined ethnicities and nationalities, and in its educational projects provided the basic elements to future nation-building.

The Postcolonial Cases of Malaysia, Rwanda, and Somalia

Diane Mauzy's chapter on Malaya stimulates an interesting question: why does nationalism seek independence? In a variety of nationalisms, certainly in those of imperial Russia and the late Soviet Union, there was a steady rise in political assertions—from cultural rights to autonomy to sovereignty to independence. There should be no mystery here. In the best-run empires, at least in their own vision, the greater good of the whole state, its interests and security, took precedence over any particular ethnicity or nation's interests. In actuality, this often meant the good of a particular dynasty or ruler, or the interest of a dominant, ruling nation. With nationalism came the conviction not only that sovereignty and the right to rule reside in the people constituted as the nation but that the people know best and can best realize their own interest.

Despite all the advantages that accrue with empire—such as greater security in the international arena and larger markets—nationalists make compelling arguments that as representatives of the nation they best reflect the mentalities and aspirations of the people. It may be that such rhetoric is self-serving and legitimizes a new national elite in power, rather than the now-delegitimized imperial rulers, but at least the leaders of the nation must be approved in some form by the people. Nation-states need not be truly democratic, but they are in some sense the expression of populism. Given the logic of the discourse of the nation, it is extremely difficult to stop the slide from cultural or linguistic demands to greater political participation and eventual self-rule and independence. The coincidence of nationalist rhetoric with the more mundane personal and political interests of leaders makes the drive to independence almost irresistible if the right thresholds and opportunities arise.

Yet for all the power of rhetoric and the logic of the discourse, national communities must also have the capacity to know themselves and act in their own name. Here the various communication theories of the nation are particularly suggestive in giving us a prehistory of the nation.[2] The communities that could imagine themselves as nations were only in part the creatures of patriotic scholars and poets; they were also compelled by soldiers and government leaders to live under single sovereigns in given state boundaries. They were prodded by teachers and linguistic reformers, commercially minded printers and journalists, to learn a language that could be reproduced on paper and understood widely. And, finally, they were brought together physically in unanticipated ways by the growth of towns; the building of roads, railroads, and telegraphs; and the expansion of markets and new industries. The rise of nations and nationalism has a social as well as a discursive history, and the two must be told together.

A principal political problem in the twentieth century, and now in the twenty-first, is how to fit nation and state together, how to make the cultural community and the territorial political unit congruent. In Rwanda, as John Clark convincingly demonstrates, there was no "national" identification that bound Hutu and Tutsi together in a single Banyarwanda nation. Rather, two exclusivist, antagonistic nationalisms—Rawandan Tutsi and Rawandan Hutu—faced each other in a bloody contest for state power. The very formation of these "national" identities in colonial times had been part of a Belgian project of segregation and dominance of Tutsi minority over Hutu majority. Class and cultural distinctions, along with the ambitions of politicians, fed into perpetuating mutually exclusive identities. Without the imperial power to mediate, state power in the hands of one group created anxiety and insecurity, indeed the threat of annihilation, in the other. Once a small group of militants determined on a murderous course of extermination of its enemies and found an opportunity (with the death of President Habyarimana), difference, antagonism, and conflict degenerated into genocide.

The Somalian case presents a fascinating contrast with Rwanda. Peter Schraeder's chapter underscores how difficult nation making is even in a country marked by ethnic, linguistic, and religious homogeneity, where elites elaborated a pan-Somalian nationalism to bind Somalians in various countries—Ethiopia, Kenya, Djibouti, British Somaliland, and Italian Somaliland—together in an inclusive Somalian ethnonational state. That ambitious irredentist project foundered when confronted by the resistance of Ethiopia, backed by the Soviets and Cubans, and the deep structure of clan loyalties and politics within Somalia. Here ethnic solidarity was overwhelmed by regionalism and clan allegiances, and identification with a Somali nation proved less powerful than other loyalties. The unrecognized secession of the northern Somaliland Republic, the independence of Djibouti, and the collapse of Somalia into clan warfare seem to argue that this is a case less of a nation in search of a state than a nationalism in search of a nation.

What does Somalia tell us about constructivist versus primordialist and instrumentalist theories about identity? Primordialism assumes that identities are fixed, constant, and closely bound to "natural" ties like family and bloodlines. Schraeder argues that the enduring affective ties of all Somalis led them "regardless of clan groupings—[to] recognize their common identity and belonging to some overarching Somali ethnic group." He identifies this pan-Somali identity, rather than the clan identity, as primordialist. Yet a constructivist would emphasize the ways in which identifications are mutable and multiple and how even the most "natural" of identities, like gender, tribe, or clan, are embedded in cultural understandings. The pan-Somali identification competes with the seemingly most primordial local or clan identity but is unable, except in some elite formulations, to become more salient than the allegiance to clan. Instrumentalism derives from constructivism and locates the construction in elites' strategic calculations about their own interests. In Somalia the constructed nationalism of the elites, despite authoritarian and quite brutal impositions by governments, failed to take hold and overwhelm the more local and clan loyalties. Rather than being an argument for primordialism, the Somali story is an invitation to investigate precisely how clan identifications occur and are maintained, reinforced, and, perhaps, in some cases, overcome. The very process of clan identification itself may be an instrumentalist imposition by men with guns. Rupert Emerson's perceptive reading of Africa as a continent "rich in nationalisms but poor in nations" may be supplemented with the observation that Somalia is a country rich in ambitious politicians but poor in effective nation-builders.

Malaya/Malaysia is an interesting example of how an ethnic nationalism might evolve into a more civic nationalism. The transition to independence was founded on a "bargain" that gave ethnic Malays dominance in the state but with specific rights for non-ethnic Malays. When that dominance was challenged, the very shape of the state was changed (the expulsion in 1965 of Singapore) and the democratic system suspended (after the 1969 elections). But with the growing demographic and economic weight of ethnic

Malays, with the Malay language solidly secured, and with the sense of threat to Malayness diminished, the more civic sense of *Bangsa Malaysia,* though fragile and contested, gained ground. The inimical Other was no longer the local non-Malay but the globalizing West. Mauzy's story illustrates the malleability of nationalism, within limits, and the strategic uses to which skilled leaders can employ alternatively primordial notions of identity and top-down constructions of civic identity.

The Postcolonial Cases of Eurasia

Taras Kuzio's provocative chapter expands the definition of civic nationalism to include what a number of scholars would call varieties of ethnic nationalism. By juggling categories, however, he forces analysts to think more carefully about how to distinguish—or whether it is worth distinguishing—between these two ideal types. He argues that the preindependence ethnic nationalism was marginalized after the achievement of statehood and that in Ukraine today there is simply a competition between varieties of civic nationalism. Ukrainian nationalism today is a pragmatic, even necessary, response to the large number of ethnic Russians and Russophone "Ukrainians" in the country. Ukrainian civic nationalists defend the idea of an independent Ukrainian state and its territorial integrity; its idea of belonging to the nation, reflected in its discourse and laws about citizenship, is inclusive. Ethnic nationalists, on the other hand, can be found among the Eastern Slavic and Russophilic parties who favor the merger of Ukraine with Russia or other Eastern Slavic peoples, and among Ukrainians who propose a pan-Ukrainian expansion to match state borders with ethnographic ones.

Kuzio buttresses his positive evaluation of Ukraine's civic nationalism by showing that most of the political parties in Ukraine favor the government's program of gradual Ukrainization while preserving polyethnic rights. A number of scholars, like Arel and Laitin, however, have taken a different tack and propose that the nationalizing policy of the Ukrainian state, promoting Ukrainian language, education, and culture, contradicts the stated civic ends of Ukraine's nationality policies.[3] Kuzio does not examine, at least in this chapter, the baleful effects of Ukrainization on Russians and Russophones. Instead, he introduces a normative argument that this is a program of affirmative action "for righting some of the wrongs committed against the Ukrainian language and culture during tsarist and

Soviet rule." By stretching some of the conventional uses of civic nationalism, as well as some other terms, he opens up a hornets' nest of definitions. If, one may ask, the defense of a multinational state or empire by Russians in the past can be labeled (as Kuzio does) *imperialist* rather than *nationalist,* why should Ukrainian leaders not be considered imperialists for holding together a multinational state, pushing through a policy of (moderate) cultural homogenization, and favoring one ethnic nation over another?

Ukraine gives us an excellent example of the dilemma of the modern nation-state in formation. Just as early modern dynastic states carried out projects of cultural and administrative homogenization that eventually allowed them to be considered nations, so postcolonial states of the late twentieth century may find themselves acting like little empires, promoting the ruling nation, discriminating against minorities, or even, if the opportunity arises, expanding into neighboring territories to make the ethnic and state boundaries conform. Happily for the post-Soviet space, Ukraine and most of the other newly independent states have generally been satisfied with their Soviet borders, and pragmatic former Communists, now transformed into leaders of the nation, have been more interested in stability and material well-being (often for themselves and their cronies) than in grand irredentist adventures. Indeed, several of the most destabilizing cases in the post-Soviet world occurred where nationalists, rather than Communists, came to power (for example, Georgia and Armenia).

Lithuania is another country where the Communist Party contributed to ethnic peace. A republic in which a mass nationalist movement (*Sąjūdis*) threatened the very foundations of the Soviet state, Lithuania was the first union republic to declare itself independent of the Soviet Union. The Communists under Algirdas Brazauskas, who had already in the years of perestroika withdrawn from the all–Soviet Union party, won the first postindependence election, in part through the support of the non-Lithuanian minorities. A kind of tacit pact existed between the Communists and the nationalists, as the Communists adopted a more nationalist stance. Given the demographic hegemony in the country of the ethnic Lithuanians, there was little to be feared from adopting the "zero option" and granting citizenship to all who lived in the country. Terry Clark notes the problems with ethnic Poles in particular, but the picture drawn is one of relative tolerance and lack of tension in a setting where civic nationalism in the law coexists quite easily with ethnic nationalism among the dominant population. The very myth of the nation shared by Lithuanians—as innocent sufferers with little to gain from outsiders—serves to consolidate Lithuanians within their own ethnic community and leave non-Lithuanians to make their own way.

One might have expected the Armenian story to have paralleled that of Lithuania. The most ethnically homogeneous of Soviet union republics, Armenia had no significant problems with internal minorities (though the 160,000 Azerbaijanis were expelled once the Karabakh conflict erupted). The Communist Party attempted, after some hesitation, to collaborate with the Armenian National Movement but was overwhelmed by the mass support for the claims to Karabakh and, later, the turn toward independence. Yet instead of developing a civic nationalism, Armenians articulated a primordialist ethnonationalism with irredentist claims to "Armenian lands" in neighboring countries. The country was well served, however, by a pragmatic moderate leadership under Levon Ter-Petrosian (1990–98), who curtailed the more excessive demands of militant nationalists until he fell from power after proposing a compromise solution to the Karabakh problem. Razmik Panossian argues that the original nationalism of the early independence period gave way to a "postnationalist politics" steadily from 1994 to 1995. Instead of politicians and ordinary people unified in seeking common national goals, intraelite rivalries over power and wealth at the top and the mundane problems of survival at the bottom divided the country and turned people toward political apathy, despair about their future, and emigration to Russia and Los Angeles.

Panossian's concept of postnationalist politics is both revealing and problematic. Clearly, something was different in Armenia (and Lithuania, for that matter) in the ways in which political issues mobilized the population in the years just before and after independence. With sights set on founding a new state, or winning a war, the country could temporarily put aside quotidian difficulties of light and heat, food and water. But with the achievements of independence and victory also came consolidation of a new political and social order that fell far short of the anticipated democratic polity and prosperous market economy.

Yet one wonders whether, as Panossian claims, politics really became "postnationalist" in Armenia. Politics became "normal" or "ordinary," yes, but as Panossian points out, political events and policies continued to be framed in the language of a particular nationalism. Karabakh remained the most salient political issue: it precipitated the fall of a government, it prevented the opening of borders and freer regional trade and development, and it aligned a powerful neighbor, Turkey, with Armenia's local enemy. And it was nationalism, in a militant incarnation, that limited the country's options. A discourse in which language about exclusion from the nation, betrayal of national interests, and dehumanization of opponents became normal made compromise and collaboration both among Armenians and in international bargaining almost impossible. Rhetorical violence can turn quickly into physical violence not only in marriages but in domestic politics, and on October 27, 1999, two of the three leading politicians in Armenia were assassinated by extreme nationalists who saw themselves as defenders of Armenia against the "bloodsuckers" of the nation.

As instrumentalist, strategic, and calculated as the use of nationalist language may be at times by elites, it is extremely important that theorists and analysts of nationalism take seriously two propositions: (1) that nationalists are very often "sincere" and passionate about their cause and (2) that the receptivity in populations of nationalist appeals depends as much (or even more) on emotions as it does on rational calculation. In his chapter on Georgia, Stephen Jones emphasizes how the overwhelming support among ethnic Georgians for Zviad Gamsakhurdia in 1990–91 was predicated on a widely felt sense of anxiety—the threat of Georgia's disintegration, fear of Russian military power, perceived neglect of Georgian interests by the Soviet state, and a deep sense of victimization in their own country. The demonstrations by Abkhazians and Ossetians, the killings by Soviet troops of Georgians on April 9, 1989, and a more generalized and long-experienced feeling that Georgians were losing their demographic hold on their own republic all fed into a toxic emotional commitment to a radically exclusivist Georgian nationalism. Enemies were everywhere; Georgians had to stand alone, united, against their internal foes. Gamsakhurdia's rhetoric belittling the one-third of the population that was not ethnically Georgian created a sense of threat among the non-Georgians, who sought protection from Russia, thus confirming the Georgian notion of betrayal of and danger to the nation.

Jones shows that Eduard Shevardnadze's arrival initiated a move from a self-destructive ethnonationalism toward a more tolerant and inclusive idea of the Georgian state. While not fully civic, since it preserved a privileged place for ethnic Georgians, the evolving ideology of Shevardnadze's government at least made pragmatic gestures toward greater respect for non-Georgians and even opened a discussion on federalism. The citizenship law of March 1993, like that of Lithuania, recognized all residents regardless of ethnicity or language proficiency as citizens. While militants can still be heard, and minorities still experience discrimination, Georgians are less hyperbolic in their rhetoric than they were at the beginning of the 1990s. *Postnationalism* would be too strong a characterization of the situation in Georgia (as I believe it is in Armenia as well), but the atmosphere is certainly postchauvinist.[4]

Reconsidering Types of Nationalism & Their Transformations

Nationalism is an even more difficult phenomenon to define than the *nation,* a word as contested as any you are likely to find in social science. *Nationalism* is used to mean everything from loving folk culture and motifs in opera to state patriotism or racist imperialism. Although I believe that too many disparate phenomena have been labeled *nationalism,* I think it valuable to think of nationalism as an ideology or political movement that pursues (and here I borrow and revise Barrington's words) "*through argument or other activity . . . a set of rights and privileges for the self-defined members of the nation . . .* [which may include] *territorial autonomy or independence.*" Here I have left the door open to cultural nationalism, which in several cases, for example, the Estonians in the nineteenth century, preceded and for a long time seemed to be an adequate substitute for a political territorial nationalism. In other words, there are historical instances when nationalism exists even before and in the absence of the nation itself.

Taking into account the specifics of nationalism after independence in the cases discussed in this volume, I would like to review and expand upon Barrington's five variants of nationalism. The authors of the chapters in this volume have provided us with examples of the five variants, but they have also demonstrated the importance of considering the development of nationalism prior to independence and the way in which this development shapes the causes, trajectories, goals, and effects of nationalism after independence. At least two forms of nationalism exist before the full formation of independent nation-states.

State-seeking nationalisms involve movements or parties that accept or assume the reality of the nation and work to realize it in a polity. They can be in some contexts the same as anti-imperial, anticolonial nationalisms. Such nationalisms presuppose some shared features—such as language, earlier historic polities identified with a people, an ethnonym, or belief in a common origin—that are then employed by nationalists to justify political claims. *Ethnic (or civic) identity-creating nationalisms* involve the activities of scholars, patriots, and politicians to construct a knowledge of the "nation"—to select its past, to invent its traditions, and "to recover" its folklore—all in service to an idea of continuity with a long, even ancient, past. This priority of primordiality and antiquity gives, in the global discourse of the nation, legitimacy to the claim to territory and statehood, or at least autonomy, and protection of cultural or linguistic rights. Ethnic (or civic) identity-creating nationalisms may exist prior to the actual existence of the nation.

Out of these two types of nationalism, and the often-revolutionary efforts of nationalists, come modern national states. With their arrival, as Barrington has detailed, a number of other specific forms of nationalism may appear, which we can broadly place into two categories related to the two forms of preindependence nationalism mentioned in the preceding. The first set of these variants focuses on the boundaries and sovereignty of the state. The *sovereignty-protecting* variant of nationalism justifies discrimination against minorities pursuing secession or irredentism. A subset of this nationalism is "mobilizing nationalism," an effort to tap national or patriotic themes to move the population to undertake great efforts (defense, industrialization, etc.). Mobilizing nationalism is the nationalism that concerns Posen in his well-known article about the mass army.[5] The other variant focused on state boundaries is an imperialist "hypernationalism." This *external-territory-claiming nationalism* is the aggressive assertion of a state's or nation's superiority over others or other territories and willingness to use force to achieve subjugation of others.

The second set of nationalism variants flows from the identity-creating variant of preindependence nationalism. *Civic nation-building nationalism* is related to state patriotism. It involves developing loyalty and identification with a polity based on civic principles that supercede (or at least are not reducible to) ethnicity and religion, race, or other cultural, biological, or ideological differences. The *ethnic nation-protecting* variant of nationalism, on the other hand, involves the effort by the majority or dominant or titular ethnicity to consolidate and broaden its influence, culture, language, and power within a state that it seeks to establish as an ethnically national state. *Co-national-protecting nationalism* (Brubaker's "homeland" nationalism) occurs when states look beyond their own borders for membership in the nation, seeking to represent or include members of its "nation" who live in another state.

Related to this last variant is a form of nationalism that Barrington does not address: *diasporic nationalism.* Nationalisms seeking to connect co-nationals need not develop only within an existing territory considered to be the "national homeland." Fragments of the nation outside the homeland boundaries may seek unity with or protection from the homeland state. This disconnected minority, or "diaspora," while not necessarily being disloyal to its state of residence, maintains its primary attachment to the national homeland. Some diaspora communities, geographically far from their homeland, like Armenians in America, may be involved in ethnic identity-creating nationalism prior to independence as well as efforts to protect the nation and its territory after independence.

The final amendment I will add to Barrington's discussion of postindependence variants of nationalism is a brief comment on their fluidity. As the authors in this volume have highlighted, it is not only likely that two or more of these variants will exist in the same case at the same time. It is also likely that the postindependence nationalism will progress from one form to another. Again, several sequential combinations or "paths" are possible.

I will highlight one such path here that is particularly relevant to the postcommunist states, where ethnic understandings of the nation prior to independence were popular. Some governments continued this emphasis after independence, adopting policies to protect the ethnic nation. Estonia and Latvia are the most conspicuous examples on the territory of the former Soviet Union but not the only ones by any means. In these two Baltic states, ethnically driven policies regarding citizenship, language use, and education in the early and mid-1990s began to give way in the late 1990s and early years of the twenty-first century. Efforts at "integrating" the minority populations from 2000 to 2005 hint that ideas of a more civic national identity—though still centered around knowledge of the titular group language—may be taking hold. This evolution from ethnic "nation-protecting" to civic "nation-building" has been encouraged by European international organizations. But it is also consistent with a decreasing perception among Estonians and Latvians that the minorities in their countries pose a threat to their national cultures and to the states they now control.[6] Such decreases in perceived threat over time are not unusual following the establishment of independence.

Conclusion

Two questions have been posed throughout this volume: Why after the nation has achieved statehood is there still nationalism? And what does it do? As Barrington puts it in his introduction, "If the national membership boundaries are well-established and accepted . . . *and* correspond to the borders of the new state, . . . nationalism after independence would be difficult to sustain." But these are conditions that do not prevail in most of the countries under review in this book, nor should we expect them in postcolonial cases.

While they are immensely important moments of transition, independence and sovereignty are only way stations in the history of the nation. Nations are never fully made. Like other humanly conceived communities, they are always in process. As some nation-states in this volume are entering the international community of states and taking on new attributes of sovereignty, other, older states are cautiously negotiating away aspects of their sovereignty, surrendering what had earlier been so difficult to win to supranational entities like the European Union. Particularly in newer states, nationalism continues to function as a mobilizer of loyalty to the contested authority of the national state, the definer of boundaries and rules of inclusion and exclusion.

The very content of what a particular nation is, what it ought to mean to its citizens, can never be taken for granted or permanently fixed. Thus, returning to my "radical middle" propositions about the nation, national identity is more rigid than most constructivists acknowledge, but at the same time the nation must be constantly reinscribed in the consciousness of its members. As I write elsewhere:

> Like other discourses, talk about and everyday embodiments of the nation both constitute the felt presence of the national and hide the fractures, divisions, and relations of power within the nation. But, then, that is why intellectuals and politicians, military bands and postage stamps, have so much work to do. Ultimately more fragile than it would admit, the nation must constantly be reproduced in thousands of ways until it becomes as ordinary and quotidian as the water in which fish swim. Ultimately, ordinary people must join in that daily plebiscite of which Ernest Renan spoke, or what at times seemed so evident and permanent can give way to more tangible concerns.[7]

This effort at constant reproduction highlights the other elements of my "radical middle" position. Postindependence nations are modern and constructed, *but* the reconstruction is built on existing foundations; the remodeling project is the task of elites, *but* it is a task that requires them to employ themes, traditions, and symbols that resonate more broadly. Elites must take account of what has gone before, what is thought to be primordial, even as they attempt to lead the nation in a more civic direction.

In the post-Soviet nation-states, identification with ethnicity (*natsional'nost'* in Russian) has remained very strong; in many cases much stronger than with the state in which people find themselves living. Citizenship might be granted by law or earned by learning the language of the titular nationality, but that legal identity often competes at a disadvantage with a deep, primordial sense of ethnic belonging. The chapters in this volume point out that many post-Soviet states have incorporated civic nationalist approaches in the early years of independence. As Ian Bremmer argues in his chapter, much of this has to do with pressure from the outside (from Russia and/or Europe). But the leaders of these states have also, for both strategic and emotional reasons, returned at times to the "existing foundation"—the ethnic symbols familiar to the masses and the ethnic lines of "us" and "them"—and promoted the primordialism that marked Soviet thinking on nationality.[8]

This balancing act that the "radical middle" approach seeks to capture is the task that postindependence elites faced (and continue to face). The comparisons between states generated in the British, French, and Italian empires and those formalized and developed in the Soviet Union (which increasingly in the literature is treated as an empire) present us with a range of postcolonial situations. The intentions and methods of different empires led to different outcomes. Divide and rule strategies, promoting one ethnicity over another, privileging a ruling metropolitan nation over peripheral peoples—all within a powerful racialized discourse of development—had powerful but different effects on the colonized peoples.

Yet there are also important similarities. In all of these cases a great "dialectic of empire" made it necessary for the peoples of the peripheries ultimately to take their liberation in their own hands. Empires justified themselves by proclaiming their civilizing mission (or the building of a higher form of human existence, capitalism, or socialism). But every step they took toward successfully building a more mobile, better-educated, more modern society undermined their very reason for maintaining their dominance. Who needs European sahibs if native peoples have become educated and "civilized" enough to run their own affairs? Who needs Communist Party bosses from the center if the peoples of the non-Russian republics (and Russia itself!) have acquired the skills and consciousness to represent and govern themselves? The empire, by its very achievements (*dostizheniia,* a favorite Soviet word), provides the shovels with which its subjects dig its grave.

Nationalism remains a slippery term, difficult to define and to measure. In its place many analysts have concentrated instead on national identity or identification and sought to elucidate the intensity or salience of ethnic and civic identities.[9] Identity, for all its changeability, forces us to look at where understandings of self, group, and place have come from. The chapters in this book demonstrate that postindependence states do not start from scratch with new national identities.

I have chosen to have the post-Soviet cases studied in this volume share the "postcolonial" label with Malaysia, Rwanda, and Somalia to highlight how elites must build their sense of nation, their nationalism, on the identities that have come from the (colonial) experience prior to independence. As fresh a start as independence must seem to those actually experiencing it, the specter of past generations weighs heavily on the new states. Analysts, as many in this volume have shown, can only begin to explore the present and future of postindependence nationalism with a serious look back into the past. The past takes its revenge . . . if we choose to ignore it.

NOTES

My thanks also to Lowell Barrington as well as Henry E. Brady for suggestions on how to improve this chapter.

1. William H. Sewell, Jr., "The Concept(s) of Culture," in *Beyond the Cultural Turn: New Directions in the Study of Society and Culture,* ed. Victoria E. Bonnell and Lynn Hunt (Berkeley: University of California Press, 1999), 52.

2. See, for example, Karl Deutsch, *Nationalism and Social Communication: An Inquiry into the Foundations of Nationality* (New York: Wiley, 1953); Ernest Gellner, *Nations and Nationalism* (Ithaca: Cornell University Press, 1983); and Benedict Anderson, *Imagined Communities: Reflections on the Origin and Spread of Nationalism* (London: Verso, 1983).

3. David L. Laitin, *Identity in Formation: The Russian-Speaking Populations in the Near Abroad* (Ithaca: Cornell University Press, 1998); and Dominique Arel, "Language Policies in Independent Ukraine: Towards One or Two State Languages?" *Nationalities Papers* 23, no. 3 (1995): 597–622.

4. The Georgian political analyst Ghia Nodia once suggested to me that the progressive moderation of nationalism among Georgians is the result of their defeat in the

wars of the first years of independence, and I speculated that the intense (and often intolerant) commitment to ethnonationalism, particularly among the Armenian intelligentsia, may be related to the Armenian victory in the wars with Azerbaijan.

5. Barry R. Posen, "Nationalism, the Mass Army, and Military Power," *International Security* 18, no. 2 (autumn 1993): 80–124.

6. For more on this topic, see Lowell Barrington, "Integration Policies in Estonia and Latvia: Can They Serve as Models for Other Multiethnic States?" (paper presented at the annual meeting of the Association for the Study of Nationalities, New York, April 2003).

7. Ronald Grigor Suny, "Constructing Primordialism: Old Histories for New Nations," *Journal of Modern History* 73, no. 4 (December 2001): 871.

8. For a discussion of post-Soviet thinking on nationality in Armenia and Kazakhstan, see ibid., 862–96.

9. See, for example, Laitin, *Identity in Formation;* the discussion of this book and others by Lowell Barrington, "Russian-Speakers in the Ukraine and Kazakhstan: 'Nationality,' 'Population,' or Neither?" *Post-Soviet Affairs* 27, no. 2 (April–June 2001): 129–58, and comments by Laitin and Barrington, 159–66; as well as the very suggestive papers forthcoming by Henry E. Brady and Cynthia S. Kaplan, "Categorically Wrong? Nominal versus Graded Measures of Ethnic Identity," *Studies in Comparative International Development* 35, no. 3 (fall 2000): 56–91; "Ethnicity and Context: Mass Mobilization during Transitions" (unpublished); and "Frames, Groups, and Events in Estonia" (unpublished).

Contributors

Lowell W. Barrington is associate professor of political science at Marquette University. He received his Ph.D. from the University of Michigan. His specializations include postcommunist politics, citizenship, ethnicity and nationalism, and comparative democratization. His publications include articles on postcommunist citizenship and ethnicity issues in *World Politics, Post-Soviet Affairs, Europe-Asia Studies,* the *European Journal of Political Research, Nationalities Papers,* the *Review of Central and East European Law, Post-Soviet Geography and Economics,* and *PS: Political Science and Politics.* He is also the author of book chapters in *From Migrants to Citizens: Membership in a Changing World* (2000) and *Dilemmas of State-Led Nation Building in Ukraine* (2002). He is currently working on a book manuscript titled *Comparative Politics: Structures and Choices.*

Ian Bremmer is president of Eurasia Group and Senior Fellow at the World Policy Institute. He received his Ph.D. in political science from Stanford University and has held positions at the Harriman Institute, Hoover Institution, the EastWest Institute, and Lawrence Livermore National Laboratory. He is a columnist for the *Financial Times* and commentator on *CNN, FOXNews,* and *CNBC.* An expert on U.S. foreign policy, Eurasian states in transition, and global political risk, he has published widely on nation- and state-building and international relations in global emerging markets. His publications include *New States, New Politics: Building the Post Soviet Nations* (1997) and articles and essays in *International Affairs, National Interest,* the *World Policy Journal,* the *Journal of Democracy, New Republic,* the *Los Angeles Times,* the *Wall Street Journal,* the *International Herald Tribune,* and the *New York Times.*

John F. Clark is associate professor of international relations at Florida International University in Miami. He received his Ph.D. from the University of Virginia. He has carried out research in Congo-Brazzaville (1990, 1997) and Congo-Kinshasa (1994). In 1999–2000, he was a Fulbright scholar at Makerere University, Kampala (Uganda). He is coeditor of *Political Reform in Francophone Africa* and has published in the *Journal of Democracy, Studies in Comparative International Development*, the *Journal of Modern African Studies, Africa Today,* and *Current History.*

Terry D. Clark is professor of political science and director of the graduate program in international relations at Creighton University. He received his Ph.D. from the University of Illinois at Urbana-Champaign. He has published widely on democratic institutional development in the postcommunist states. His work has appeared in *Comparative Political Studies, Slavic Studies, East European Politics and Societies,* and *Nationalities Papers.* He has authored two books, including *Beyond Post-Communist Studies: Political Science and the New Democracies of Europe* (2002).

Joshua B. Forrest is the Director of the Kerr Institute of African History, Politics and Culture at La Roche College, Pittsburgh. He received his Ph.D. from the University of Wisconsin–Madison. His latest books are *Subnationalism in Africa: Ethnicity, Alliances, and Politics* (2004) and *Lineages of State Fragility: Rural Civil Society in Guinea-Bissau* (2003). He has also published a number of book chapters and articles concerning ethnic politics, democracy building, the African "inverted" state, and comparisons with medieval European states. His work has appeared in the *Journal of Commonwealth and Comparative Politics*, the *Journal of Democracy*, the *World Policy Journal, Comparative Politics, Studies in International Comparative Development,* and the *Journal of Modern African Studies.*

Stephen Jones is professor of Russian and Eurasian studies at Mount Holyoke College. He received his Ph.D. from the London School of Economics and Political Science. He has taught at the University of California, University of London, and Oxford University. In 2001, he conducted research in Georgia under an IREX grant and was a member of the Institute for Advanced Study in Princeton. He has written over fifty articles and chapters on current events in the former Soviet republic of Georgia and is currently completing the second volume of his *Georgian Social Democracy: In Opposition and Power.* The first volume is *Socialism in Georgian Colors: The European Road to Social Democracy, 1883–1917* (2005).

Taras Kuzio is a visiting professor at the Elliott School of International Affairs, George Washington University. He is a former Resident Fellow, Centre for Russian and East European Studies, University of Toronto; director of the NATO Information Office in Kyiv; and Senior Research Fellow at the Centre for Russian and East European Studies of the University of Birmingham. He has published widely in political science and area studies journals on nationalism, transition and democratization, and Ukrainian and postcommunist affairs. His books include *Ukraine: Perestroika to Independence* (2000), *Ukraine: State and Nation Building* (1998), *Ukraine under Kuchma* (1997), *Ukrainian Security Policy* (1995), and the edited collection *Contemporary Ukraine* (1998). He has also jointly authored *Politics and Society in Ukraine* (1999) and jointly edited *Dilemmas of State-Led Nation Building in Ukraine* (2002), *Ukrainian Foreign and Security Policy: Theoretical and Comparative Perspectives* (2002), and *State and Institution Building in Ukraine* (1999).

Diane K. Mauzy is professor of political science at the University of British Columbia (Vancouver), where she also received her Ph.D. She specializes in the politics of Southeast Asia, particularly Malaysia, Singapore, and Indonesia. She is the author of about forty books and articles. Her latest books (coauthored) are *Malaysian Politics under Mahathir* (1999) and *Singapore Politics under the People's Action Party* (2002), and her recent articles have appeared in *Pacific Review* and *Round Table.*

Razmik Panossian is the Director of Programmes at Rights and Democracy. He taught nationalism and post-Soviet transition/democratization at the Department of Government, London School of Economics and Political Science (LSE), where he received his Ph.D. His dissertation on Armenian nationalism and diaspora won the Lord Bryce Prize for Best Dissertation in Comparative and International Politics in the UK. He has published numerous articles and book chapters on contemporary Armenian politics and the South Caucasus. His new book is *The Armenians: From Kings and Priests to Merchants and Commissars.*

Peter J. Schraeder is professor of political science at Loyola University, Chicago, where he is a specialist of African politics and international relations. He was recently a Fulbright scholar in Tunisia (2002–3), spent 2003–5 teaching in Rome, and is the author or editor of nine books, including *African Politics and Society: A Mosaic in Transformation* (2004) and *Exporting Democracy: Rhetoric versus Reality* (2002). He is currently working on a book, *Beyond the 'Big Man": Democratization and Its Impacts on the Formulation and Implementation of African Foreign Policies.*

Ronald Grigor Suny is professor of history at the University of Michigan. He received his Ph.D. from Columbia University. His work integrates comparative politics and Russian history, with special attention to the non-Russian peoples. He is the author of hundreds of articles, as well as *The Making of the Georgian Nation* (1988), *The Revenge of the Past: Nationalism, Revolution, and the Collapse of the Soviet Union* (1993); *Looking toward Ararat: The Armenians in Modern History* (1993), and *The Soviet Experiment: Russia, the USSR, and the Successor States* (1998).

Index